Insight Into Value

Insight

Into Value

An Exploration of the Premises of a Phenomenological
Psychology

Andrew R. Fuller

STATE UNIVERSITY OF NEW YORK PRESS

Published by
State University of New York Press, Albany

Printed in the United States of America

For information, address State University of New York
Press, State University Plaza, Albany, N.Y., 12246

Library of Congress Cataloging-in-Publication Data

Fuller, Andrew Reid.
  Insight into value: an exploration of the premises of a
phenomenological psychology / Andrew R. Fuller.
     p.   cm.
  Includes bibliographical references.
  ISBN 0-7914-0329-7. — ISBN 0-7914-0330-0 (pbk.)
  1. Phenomenological psychology.   I. Title.
BF204.5.F85   1990
150.19′2—dc20   89-39369
                                                                        CIP

10 9 8 7 6 5 4 3 2 1

For My Mother and Father

The rose is without why; it blooms because it blooms.
It cares not for itself; asks not if it's seen.

—Angelus Silesius

Contents

Preface

This book attempts to sketch out the possibilities of a psychology very different in character from the standard textbook one. It grew out of a sense, hardly unique to this investigator, of a pressing need for a "science of behavior" such as would do justice to the fullness of human life. More precisely, it grew out of a sense of need for a method that, rather than reducing human behavior to some lowest common denominator, would approach it on its own level of occurrence—a method that even now by and large remains unavailable and whose essentials remain to be worked out. The basic outlines sketched here form a phenomenological psychology. With phenomenology a method for disclosing "the things themselves" (in Husserl's words), phenomenological psychology is a method for disclosing "the psyche itself," human behavior in all its richness and variety, just as it shows itself to be on its own terms.

The present examination of the premises of a phenomenological psychology, then, is the working out of a method. The application of this method consists in clarifying psychological concepts at their source in experience. Just such a clarification, it is believed, is what mainstream psychology sorely lacks—the lack of conceptual clarity is no light matter, for it holds the danger of literally not knowing what one is talking about. By thus defining itself as a method for gaining clarified psychological concepts, a phenomenological psychology is a philosophical return to psychology's foundations, a reopening of questions regarded by many as closed once and for all.

A characteristic of the foundational phenomenological psychology undertaken in these pages, then, is its theoretical or philosophical status as a conceptual enterprise. Another characteristic is the systematic way in which it strives to embrace—in a preliminary manner, to be sure—the full range of human behavior, from perception to thinking, imagining, learning, remembering, feeling, interpreting, disposition, motivation, the unconscious. To the extent this book's systematic efforts attain a measure of clarity on basic issues, it is hoped that it may serve as a point of departure for further work, not excluding experimental research. The present study, the outcome of an eleven-year effort, is exactly a beginning—phenomenology always is.

This investigation places itself in efforts in the direction of a human-scientific psychology by drawing heavily on both classical Gestalt theory, in particular the work of Wolfgang Köhler and Aron Gurwitsch, and on existential phenomenology, in particular the writings of Martin Heidegger and Maurice Merleau-Ponty. The book is an attempt at an interdisciplinary synthesis of these two major twentieth century traditions. Although existential phenomenology has much to gain from Gestalt psychology's notions of organization and Gestalt lawfulness, Gestalt psychology stands to gain perhaps even more from the nonobjectivistic philosophical orientation made available to it by existential thought. These two approaches thus complement and mutually enrich one another as they are brought to bear on one another on the topic that has gradually come to form the natural center of the present phenomenological psychology—"insight into value." Although certain portions of the work can be read as an introduction to existential phenomenology (especially Chapters 2 through 4), and others as an introduction to Gestalt psychology (especially Chapters 5 through 8), the most important thing is that it be read as the dialogue between the two traditions, in view of the service such a dialogue can render to the understanding of human behavior.

I would like to take this opportunity to thank Professors Calvin Schrag, whose 1978 NEH Summer Seminar played a decisive role in setting me on the path leading directly to the present work, and Joseph Catalano for their generous help and encouragement. I would also like to thank Bill Portilla and Gene Rasmussen for their technical assistance in preparing the manuscript. Tina Luciano, my secretary at the College of Staten Island, has been of invaluable assistance to me over the years, and for this I thank her. Finally, I can never adequately convey my thanks to my wife Barbara for always being there for me.

1 The Objective Space of Meaning

The crises of psychology result from
reasons of principle and not from
some delay of the research in this or
that particular domain.

—*Merleau-Ponty*, 1968, p. 23

Meaning

This book on insight into value, as its subtitle indicates, is an exploration of the premises of a phenomenological psychology. Such a psychology is one that focuses on meaning or, more precisely, on the human preoccupation with meaning. Given this centrality of meaning, a considerable part of the inquiry is devoted to a clarification of the term. A first indication of its usage here is given in what immediately follows. A discussion of the traditional approach to meaning is then undertaken, which forms the bulk of the present chapter. The phenomenological approach to meaning is first considered in Chapter 2.

We turn off the ignition, lock the car door, and pocket the keys. We check to see how much cash we have with us. We come across a crumpled piece of paper in our pocket and discard it. We notice the pretty red tulips just over there. We enter the shopping mall and make our way to its central court. We see our friend and, looking at our watch, note that we are a few minutes late. This is a very routine description of the sorts of things that occupy us in everyday life. We are always preoccupied with something: tasks, things we are using or that get in our way, other people. These "somethings" that are all around us and with which we are constantly becoming engaged are meanings. The term *meaning* refers, then, to the things we deal with in daily life. It refers to people, too. The meaning of our keys is something we just took out of the ignition and put in our pocket. The meaning of tulips is those familiar flowers over there. The meaning of our friend is the very person that we know so well and are presently going to meet. Meanings are our others, then: the things and people we are always becoming involved with in our everyday life, things and people "as what" they are.

Meanings—car, keys, tulips, piece of paper, mall, friend, stores,

1

pavement, food, watch, house, books, trees—also are commonly called *perceptions*. The very term implies an activity of interpreting. Conventional psychology refers to perceptions this way, as will be seen, and phenomenological psychology similarly believes that all perceptions, all meanings, are interpretations. But the manner in which these psychologies interpret meanings as interpretations differs strikingly. A crucial difference between conventional psychology and its phenomenological counterpart turns on the question of the status of meanings as interpretations and, more specifically, on the question of meaning's location relative to human behavior.

The question, Where is meaning located? is the question, What is the space of meaning? And, given the constancy of human preoccupation with meaning, to seek the space of meaning is at the same time to seek the space of human behavior. Although it will be found that conventional psychology locates meaning and behavior in an objective space, phenomenological psychology will be seen to locate them in an existential one. This chapter explores the *objective space of meaning* conventionally presupposed by psychology. Chapter 2 considers phenomenology, and Chapter 3 the topic of human life as existence. Chapter 4 then turns to the existential space of meaning presupposed by phenomenologically oriented psychology. This book makes frequent reference to the contrast that will be drawn in these early chapters between the objective and the existential spaces of meaning.

Conventional Psychology's Approach to Meaning

Contemporary psychology is many different things. Every conceivable view of what it means to be human seems to have found its expression in the form of one psychology or another. The resulting psychologies conflict and compete with one another, forming anything but an integrated discipline. And yet, standard introductory psychology texts are remarkably similar to one another in their underlying philosophy: in their view of what it means to be human and in what light human behavior is to be considered for its proper scientific understanding. This is so in spite of the fact that all such introductions guide the reader through a variety of research traditions and theoretical viewpoints. Thirty-five recent (1984–1989) introductory psychology textbooks were surveyed in preparing this chapter. All were found to adopt the viewpoint of modern philosophy—a viewpoint that owes its origins to René Descartes and that will be considered later in this chapter—and, more particularly, all were found to share a basic theoretical viewpoint on the place and status of meaning. In view of this uniformity of outlook, it seems justified to speak of a *conventional psychology*. The next paragraphs explore this unified vision.

One introductory psychology textbook reads, *"It is apparent that the world as we know it is created from sensory impressions*" (Coon, 1985, p. 71). "The world as we know it," which is to say, the world of perceptual meanings, is said to be "created from" what are referred to as "sensory impressions," from the results of influences brought to bear upon the human organism's sense organs by the external environment. Even as he asserts the derivation of everyday perceptions from sensory impressions, the textbook author sharply distinguishes between the two realms, separated as they are said to be by an act of creation. All the introductory psychology textbooks make what essentially is the same distinction. In one case, the distinction is drawn between "sensing and perceiving"; in another between "sensory experience and complex perceptual processes"; in yet another between "sensory processes and perception"; but most commonly it is between "sensation and perception." With the textbooks assuming such a clear-cut distinction between sensory impressions, on the one hand, and perception-meaning, on the other, questions naturally arise concerning the manner in which the latter is said to derive from the former. What precisely is the relationship between sensory and perceptual processes? Moreover, how do sensory processes stand in relation to the external world? The latter question is considered first. Introductory psychology texts constitute the source of the citations in the next two subsections.

External Stimuli and Sensory Impressions

Conventional psychology proposes that the story of perceptual meaning begins with the external world and its stimuli. Sensation is the name for "the pickup of stimuli from the world by means of the senses" (Santrock, 1986, p. 109). Stimuli, viewed as physical energies belonging to the *real* physical world outside, bombard the organism, communicating messages to it about that world. Stimuli are thought to act as causes, and sensory impressions to be their effects: stimuli and sensations stand in "a *cause-and-effect* relationship" (Wortman, Loftus, and Marshall, 1988, p. 86). "A stimulus is any form of energy (sound waves, light waves, heat, pressure) to which an organism is capable of responding. A sensation is a response to that energy by a sensory system" (ibid.). Stimuli trigger "chemical, electrical, and mechanical activity in sense receptors" (Scarr and Vander Zanden, 1984, p. 152). The sensory impressions thus instituted are said to be the organism's sole source of information about the real world outside. "Sensation is essentially the process whereby stimulation of receptor cells in various parts of the body (the eyes, ears, nose, mouth, and surface of the skin) sends nerve impulses to the brain, where these impulses register as a touch, a sound, a taste, a splash of color, and so forth" (Wortman et al., 1988, p. 85). "Your knowledge of the external world . . . comes entirely from chemical and electrical processes occurring in the nervous system, particularly in the brain" (Scarr and Vander Zanden, 1984, p. 152). Standing to physical stimulation as effect to cause, then, sensory impressions in the brain are said to provide the organism with its only knowledge of the external world.

Virtually all the textbooks surveyed make a further assumption about sensory impressions. They equate sensory impressions with *sensations*, and sensations are considered to be essentially " 'raw' " and "disconnected" (Ornstein, 1985, p. 215), "raw information" about the environment (Smith, Sarason, and Sarason, 1986, p. 146). Standing alone, sensations have no order among themselves, no internal connection with one another whatever.

Sensory Impressions and Perception

"Raw" sensations without an inner articulation of their own, sensory impressions do not convey perceptual meanings, do not convey cars, trees, and people—thus the sharp distinction between sensory impressions and perception already alluded to. Sensory impressions convey information only as provided by stimuli, the fragmented physical energies bombarding the organism from without. Corresponding to fragmented stimuli, then, are fragmented sensory impressions, disconnected sensations with no more organization, no more meaning about them, than the stimuli whose effects they are. At the level of stimuli and raw sensory impressions, no answer is given, or indeed can be given, to the question of the origin of meaning. And yet, conventional textbook psychology's very treatment of sensory impressions as raw and disconnected fatefully predetermines the sort of answer that the texts must furnish to this question, for the question of meaning has now been narrowed down to the manner in which perceptual meaning arises out of essentially fragmented, hence meaning-less, sensory impressions. It thus comes as no surprise that the textbooks universally propose perception to be a process by which sensory impressions are interpreted, organized, and integrated. "Raw visual sensations are like the unassembled parts of a washing machine; they must be put together in an organized way before they are useful to us" (Lahey, 1989, p. 114). "Perception is the process by which an organism interprets sensory input so that it *acquires* meaning" (Lefton, 1985, p. 169; emphasis mine). "Active synthesizing processes *construct* perceptions out of sensory and memory information" (Worchel and Shebilske, 1986, p. 120; emphasis mine). "*Sensation* is the process of responding to a simple physical stimulus, such as a spot of light or a musical note. *Perception* is the more complex process of actively interpreting a pattern of stimuli as an organized mental image" (Hassett and White, 1989, p. 140).

Conventional psychology further specifies that what accomplishes this interpreting of the sensory impressions instigated inside us by the real physical world is another part of that world: the brain. The brain is said to order and interpret raw sense data, thus furnishing them with organization and arriving at meaning (Scarr and Vander Zanden, 1984, p. 152), to organize and interpret the information it receives from the senses into meaningful experiences (ibid., p. 170); to organize sensory input into stable and orderly percepts of meaningful—personally relevant—objects (Zimbardo, 1988, p. 185); to assemble sensations into a usable representation of the world (Coon, 1985, p. 101); to give order and meaning to the sensations it receives, to automatically interpret or perceive sensations as soon as the brain receives them (Wortman et al., 1988, p. 85).

The final outcome of "sensation and perception" is a model or "mental image," a representation inside the organism of the physical world outside, "the world out there" duplicated "in here." Perception is said to take sensory data and process them "in your brain to build a meaningful model of the Frisbee [you just tossed to your friend]" (Bootzin, Bower, Zajonc, and Hall, 1986, p. 135); "Perception . . . refers to the processes by which our brains arrive at meaningful interpretations of basic sensations. . . . What happens in the brain is obviously crucial to our ability to understand what is 'out there': the brain organizes and gives meaning to the limited information gathered by our senses" (ibid., p. 138). "*Perception,* in its narrow usage, refers to the . . . stage in which an internal representation of an object is formed, and an experienced percept of the external stimulation is developed" (Zimbardo, 1988, p. 185). Such an inner model, moreover, is said to represent what is considered to be the real physical world outside fairly well, well enough in any case for successful practical commerce with it. "Your sensory and perceptual systems . . . give you windows to the world" that allow you to detect and discriminate among stimuli (Wortman et al., 1988, p. 85); "Information is initially provided by our sensory and perceptual processes, which serve as our 'windows' to the world" (Lindzey, Thompson, and Spring, 1988, p. 123). "Most perception is a reasonably accurate replica of stimuli as they exist in the real world" (Benjamin, Hopkins, and Nation, 1987, p. 100).

Textbook psychology considers physical processes to be the essential occurrence at each stage along the line, from stimuli, through sensory impressions, to the brain's work of interpreting. The final result of all this physical activity is perceptual meaning, the everyday "world as we know it"; through chemical and electrical processes in the nervous system, "the world out there gets in." Such everyday meaning, although a "reasonably accurate" likeness inside the organism of "what's there" in the real world outside, nevertheless bears no *direct* resemblance to what, in the view of conventional psychology, is really going on; that is, to the basic physical processes that, underlying meaning, bring it about. The inner likeness (perception-meaning) remains forever different in kind from the real physical world outside, for these are envisioned as two different orders of being. For conventional psychology the world of meanings is not the real physical world. The Frisbee is not really "out there"—which, in keeping with the philosophy upon which conventional psychology rests, is physical in character and entirely devoid of meaning. "The perceptual world is a representation . . . of the physical world" (Krebs and Blackman, 1988, p. 146). "People's perceptions are *not* exact and literal representations of what is 'out there' in the environment" (Wortman et al., 1988, p. 86). "*What we see, hear, and otherwise sense is not what is really there in the outside world*" (Kalat, 1986, p. 86). "The perceived world differs from the real world" (ibid., p. 102)—color perceived, for example, differs from the real world of the wavelengths of light reflected by surfaces. The inner replica (meaning), separated as it is from the real world outside by the brain's activity of interpreting, at best furnishes indirect indices of the true status of that world.

In brief, conventional psychology holds that sensory impressions—whether explictly termed *sensations* or not—are converted into meanings through an activity of constructing. The brain turns what is meaningless into a meaningful pattern through a process of interpreting. Such an interpreting of sensory impressions is termed a *synthesizing*, a *constructing*, an *organizing*, an *integrating*, an *active transforming*, an *ordering*, a *making sense*, an *assembling,* a *creating*. The product of the brain's interpreting is a perception-meaning, which, although not what's "out there" in the "real world" of stimuli and not directly revealing the actual character or workings of that "real world," for all practical purposes stands in for that "world" reasonably well.

Descartes and the Rise of Modern Philosophy

The Splitting Apart of the Subjective and the Objective

The previous section considered conventional psychology's view of the origin of meaning in the brain's activity of interpreting the sensory impressions instituted inside the organism by stimuli from the "real world" outside. This section considers certain aspects of modern philosophy. Succeeding sections proceed to make the case that conventional psychology's basic orientation, and its portrayal of meaning in particular, originate in modern philosophy and in such a way that conventional psychology must itself be classed as a branch of that philosophy, the branch whose task is to bring to fulfillment one of the philosophy's basic intentions.

Descartes (1596–1650), who has been called the father of modern philosophy, makes a sharp distinction between the realm of the objective and that of the subjective. The subjective realm is the inner domain of mind or thought (*res cogitans*). The objective realm is the outer domain of nature considered as pure spatial extension (*res extensa*). These two realms are viewed as closed off the one from the other. Each domain is simply itself, self-contained and self-defined, neither one needing the other to be what it essentially is. Each, in other words, is absolute and in-itself. Mind is purely and simply mind; the subjective is purely subjective, with nothing at all of the objective (the extended) about it. Extension is purely and simply extension; the objective is purely objective, with nothing at all of the subjective (the mental) about it. The *mind* is defined as that which is not spatial, a realm without extension. *Extension* is defined as that which is not mental, a realm devoid of meaning. These two self-sufficient realms are defined, then, in their having nothing at all in common with one another, in their heterogeneity.

The Inner Realm of the Subjective

The realm of the subjective is the realm of consciousness, a realm of inner thought closed in upon itself, a domain of interiority set apart from everything that is not itself, from the realm of pure spatial extension.

In his *Meditations on First Philosophy*, Descartes tells us what he means by inner thought. "I am a thing that thinks, that is to say, that doubts, affirms, denies, that knows a few things, that is ignorant of many, (that loves, that hates), that wills, that desires, that also imagines and perceives; . . . although the things which I perceive and imagine are perhaps nothing at all apart from me and in themselves, I am nevertheless assured that these modes of thought that I call perceptions and imaginations, inasmuch only as they are modes of thought, certainly reside (and are met with) in me" (1969, p. 179). Thoughts—feelings, decisions, judgments, fantasies, perceptions— for Descartes are all modifications of the mind, the mind's meanings. These modifications, these "modes of thought," are appearances populating an inner, subjective domain of mind: mental occurrences.

The Outer Realm of the Objective

Whereas the realm of the subjective in Descartes's philosophy is inner thought, the realm of the objective is outer nature. Such outer nature is not nature as we know it in everyday life, however, not nature as constituted by such everyday meanings as flowers, lakes, and animals. External nature is projected rather in a particular way in Cartesian thought.

It is important to realize that the rise of modern philosophy with Descartes was also the time of the emergence of modern science. Phenomenological philosopher Aron Gurwitsch, writing on *The Crisis of European Sciences and Transcendental Phenomenology*, the last work of the founder of phenomenology Edmund Husserl, points out that Husserl refers to the new science getting underway at the beginning of the modern era as *Galilean* in style, as *Galilean physics*. In the work of Galileo, Gurwitsch elaborates, reality comes to be taken as a "thoroughly rational universe accessible to a totally rational (i.e., mathematical) science" (1966, p. 406). This Galilean "mathematization of nature" (Husserl's words) has decisively shaped the whole of the modern period, even defining what qualifies as scientific knowledge (ibid., p. 412), and indeed is not without its consequences today. The mathematization of nature is accomplished by an *abstraction* through which only the corporeal aspects of things are taken into account, the only topics of study being "spatial configurations and spatiotemporal events" (ibid., p. 408). This mathematization is further accomplished by a process of *idealization*, a mental operation through which a realm of geometrical figures—ideal forms such as triangles, circles, and straight lines—is constituted (ibid., p. 407). Through abstraction and idealization, Galileo, geometrizing nature, is thus seen to conceive it "as a closed and self-contained corporeal world within which all events are determined in advance" (ibid., p. 412). With this, Gurwitsch goes on to point out, the stage was set for the later Cartesian dualism.

The kinship between Galilean physics and modern philosophy is anything but coincidental. What Descartes wanted to accomplish in his philosophy of nature was precisely the justification of Galilean science, the establishment of the validity of such a science as the sole provider of true knowledge about external nature. "Descartes's main intention," in Gurwitsch's words, "was the validation of the incipient new science of physics, the justification of a tenet whose boldness we, the heirs to a scientific tradition, can appreciate only with considerable difficulty. This is the tenet that an external, extramental, and extraconscious world exists, but that this external world is in reality not as it appears in everyday perceptual experience but as it is conceived and constructed in mathematical terms in the new science" (1974, p. 214). Nature for Descartes, and this includes the bodies of humans and animals, is not meaningful nature as it appears all around us, but nature as the purely objective—geometrized—nature projected by the new science of physics: nature as pure corporeal extension. As existential phenomenologist Martin Heidegger puts it, nature had to be "the self-contained system of motion of units of mass related spatiotemporally," and nature's events had to be measurable changes in place in the course of time (1977, p. 119). Nature and its events, by Heidegger's account of Descartes's view, now are understood in advance as pure spatial extension, *so that the new science can be*. To arrive at "true nature," nature as the object of investigation of the new Galilean science, the philosopher Descartes *had* to abstract everyday meaning from it. For both Husserl-Gurwitsch and Heidegger, then, Descartes's notion of the world outside the mind was in the service of the new science getting underway in his time. For a philosophy that sets out to validate Galilean science, external nature cannot be the way it looks, but rather must be "as it is conceived and constructed in mathematical terms in the new science" (Gurwitsch, 1974, p. 214). There is simply no room in such a nature for everyday meaning.

At the beginning of the modern age, then, nature is set up as having a certain kind of being. It is now man—the term is used advisedly—who says what nature can be. Striving to get beyond the conflicting "truths" of everyday life, and in this way arrive at a certainty that he himself guarantees in advance, man defines the character of the real. Nature's reality is now specified solely in terms of the new Galilean science, purely geometrically. Nature is set up in such a way that quantitatively determinable items, such as force, location, and time, can become the guiding notions in the investigation of nature. This "prior mathematical projection of nature" (in Heidegger's words) stipulates in advance what must be nature. "Things now show themselves only in the relations of places and time points and in the measures of mass and working forces" (Heidegger, 1967, p. 93). Only that qualifies as nature which can be encompassed by Euclidean geometry. The spatial is nature—because man says so.

In the service of the new Galilean science, then, the philosopher Descartes sets nature up as an absolute—self-contained, self-sufficient, self-defined—objective realm in-itself, a realm of pure extension. To be more explicit about this, extension is extension in the familiar three dimensions of geometry. Extension in length, width, and depth constitutes for Descartes the "world's" true character (Heidegger, 1962a, p. 123). What makes nature be nature, what nature is, is extension; and everything that, in the course of time, happens in nature, in order to be at all, must be an event of three-dimensional extension. Whatever does not take its place in the space-time continuum as a modification of extension, the mind and its meanings, for Descartes is simply not nature. All events in nature occur, then, as temporally developing modes of extension. As "applied geometry" (in Gurwitsch's words), the new Galilean science is able to get at just such events of extension mathematically. What happens in three-dimensional space lends itself, in what is its essential, to measurement. Change in such a space of pure extension becomes calculable extent of change. "Becoming is seen as change of place, . . . transposition. All becoming is regarded as motion" (Heidegger, 1959, p. 163). Because the processes of nature, moreover, are "but the space-time determinations of the motion of points of mass" (Heidegger, 1967, p. 91), there is only one blueprint for all bodies, all bodies are alike. "No motion or direction of motion is superior to any other" (Heidegger, 1977, p. 119). Every place, every moment is equal to every other place or moment. No place has any claim to preference over any other, all are the same (ibid.). Modern philosophy and science define nature not in its sensible quality, then, but in its mathematically quantifiable extension.

The units of pure extension that constitute true nature for the new Galilean science are units of mass in-themselves and outside of one another.

When such units change place, spatial effects ensue. In accordance with certain laws, units of mass "move" or are "moved" by other units that happen to stand in their way. Units of mass have effects on one another. But such an application of force can be only external in character. One unit can displace another unit only by influencing it from outside. Each unit, after all, is in-itself and without internal connection with any other unit of mass. In the space-time continuum, something at a distance can causally affect something else, moreover, only if there is a mathematically determinable process of getting through. An action must locally and linearly make its way, in its effects, through space and all its divisions, interval by interval, point of application by point of application, to whatever it is that comes to be affected. No intervening space can have been skipped over in any nonlocal, nonlinear fashion. If there are gaps that have not been bridged, the process collapses, at least to that extent. Wherever an effect occurs, actual local physical contact already has been made; an objective event that science can in principle detect (measure) has occurred. Local physical effects spread far beyond the original action—locally and externally, by reason of linear, "end-to-end causality" (Merleau-Ponty, 1968, p. 232)—through intermediary actions. Consider, for example, the following illustration of the manner in which science in the Galilean style proceeds. When someone hits a certain key on a piano, a string of a certain tenseness and length is struck. Because of this string's mathematical properties, the air surrounding it is moved, and moved in a precise way. Sound waves are instituted that travel at various cycles per second (CPS). When molecules of air move, the molecules of air in front of them are pushed together. These collide with other molecules, which in turn are pushed together. In this way, the sound wave is transmitted through the medium. Such sound waves are the basic energy received and processed by the ear and brain. The ear picks up the vibrations from the air—is externally "moved" by vibrating air molecules. All this is one locally continuous process in the space-time continuum. For the tone (meaning) to be heard, after processing in the brain, no segment of space can have been bypassed. There rather must have been a linearly continuous transition from piano to ear and brain, a single unbroken cause-and-effect chain. And for a particular tone to be heard this time, and once again some time later, the objective causal relations must remain constant, beginning with the piano string itself; and these a Galilean science can measure. It is these mathematically calculable causal relations temporally unfolding in three-dimensional space that are real, that constitute nature's true reality, for a thinking that sets out to justify Galilean science. There are no tones, no sounds in nature—sound waves are not sounds—as conceived by Galilean science, any more than there are Frisbees.

    Modern philosophy (a la Descartes), thus taking its lead from Galilean physics, spatializes nature, turning it into measurable relations in three-dimensional space, *res extensa*. What now makes a body be a body is its pure spreadoutness (pure extension) in three-dimensional space. The word *objective* is used in this essay to refer to the realm of nature conceived as such pure spreadoutness in the space-time continuum; the terms *objective* and *physical* are used more or less interchangeably. The objective world, with the objective modifications that constitute it—modifications such as electrical and chemical processes occurring inside the objective organism—is nature set up in advance as purely physical, nature as mathematically constructed by Galilean science. Nature thus considered as the in-itself of three-dimensional extension is the way nature really is for Descartes. It takes modern physics to "pierce the veil of appearances" (Gurwitsch's words)—to overcome that everyday ignorance wherein we take things to be the way they look—and get to the real being of nature, to units of mass, to the objective capability of surfaces to variably reflect light, to the objectively measurable wavelength of light that makes the tulips appear to be red when in actuality they are not. Mathematics—"the mathematization of nature" (a la Husserl), "the prior mathematical projection of nature" (a la Heidegger)—it is supposed, as the ideal of knowledge of external reality, alone gets to things as they really and truly are.

Descartes and the Status of Everyday Meaning

Descartes, in justifying Galilean science, thus views objective modifications alone as constituting the true reality of nature. No room is allowed in objective nature, in the realm of pure extension, for everyday meaning. Extension, pure spreadoutness, to the contrary is defined in advance as meaning's very exclusion, the very exclusion of quality and differences in quality, of this and that, of the right and the wrong, of the better and the worse. In objective space, all bodies, following a single blueprint, are the same; all equal, with none to be preferred over any other. Everyday meaning (sensible quality) for Descartes is a subjective modification of the mind, not an objective modification of nature: a mode of thought rather than a mode of extension.

Where, then, does Descartes suppose everyday meanings—lakes, animals, and trees—come from? How does he conceive their ultimate status as inner thoughts? Heidegger points out that objective nature for Descartes is the basic layer upon which everything else within the world is built (1962a, p. 131). Having stripped the external world (outer nature) of everyday meaning—having lodged everyday meaning subjectively in the mind—the resulting purely extended nature is then taken to be the original real world, "the genuine substructure of all things" (Heidegger, 1967, p. 51). Descartes thus is seen to hold that everyday environmental qualities *derive from* nature as conceived by the new Galilean science. Qualitative meanings are taken to be ultimately quantitative modifications of extension (Heidegger, 1962a, p. 131). Everyday qualities, such modifications of the mind as originate through the senses, are said to be ultimately quantities, then, modifications of objective nature. Our everyday perceptions have no standing of their own for Descartes. The sun overhead, for example, is held to be an idea subjectively effected inside our minds by objective nature. The real sun, in objective space, institutes causal processes that, affecting our objective bodies, finally give rise to the everyday meaning, "sun overhead." The real objective sun, of whose mathematically determinable properties a science in the Galilean style gains true knowledge, thus is said to be the final causal determinant of the merely subjective sun, its origin. The idea of the sun, Descartes writes, that "derives its origin from the senses," our everyday perception of the sun, belongs "in the category of adventitious ideas" (1969, p. 183). The mathematical idea of the sun alone represents the sun as it really is in nature. But that sun is not the sun overhead, not the sun whose light we see and warmth we feel.

Everyday perceptions, no less than the objective forces that bring them about, come down in Descartes's view to events in an objective space of pure extension. An *objective space of everyday meaning* is asserted. Qualitative meaning, deprived of any cognitive merit of its own, is reduced to quantitative changes in pure extension, to changes in location over time of units of mass. A qualitative tone heard, for example, for Galilean science is nothing but the product of quantitative modifications of extension (vibrations, electrochemical processes instituted within the organism). Although there are no sounds in nature considered objectively, objective nature is such that it gives rise to the subjective appearances of sounds, which appearances, regularly correlated with variations in physical nature, are like a veil that, while concealing the true being of nature, can be pierced by modern science (a la Gurwitsch). Modern science, to its satisfaction, can account fully for sounds, and indeed for the full range of sensible qualities, objectively in three-dimensional space, without granting them a validity of their own.

As for human values, those meanings at the heart of everyday actuality, Descartes is left considering the likes of the beautiful, the useful, and the good as value predicates that get "stamped" onto merely objective things (Heidegger, 1962a, p. 132). "The implement and the tool are considered as material things, only subsequently prepared, so that a special value adheres to them" (Heidegger, 1967, p. 51). Value qualities for Descartes, then, are predicates residing only in the mind, subjective judgments secondarily added to a founding stratum of pure extension, properties superimposed on an objective nature in which no values are to be found. "A thing is approached as an object of observation and perception, and perception is then, as it is typically put, complemented by value judgment" (Heidegger, 1985, p. 183).

As the modern era unfolded and the notion of a mind in-itself (*res cogitans* or mental substance or soul) lost its power to convince, the mind in its entirety came to be viewed as the workings of nature projected as pure extension, the doing of an objective body objectively stimulated. Everything real came to be defined as essentially objective in character, capable of being subjected to measurement—"everything real exists in some quantity"—and in this way of being brought under the control of natural-scientific calculation and control. No occurrence now belongs to anything other than an all-embracing objective space. All things real, the self and all its meanings included, are now viewed as modifications in time of three-dimensional extension. It came to be thought, as French existential phenomenologist Maurice Merleau-Ponty puts it, that "the 'subjective' and the 'objective' . . . are finally two orders of objects" (1968, p. 20). Descartes remains a dualist. It was left to his successors to make the move to a simple monism of objective processes, to *objectivism*.

Objectivistic Psychology

As we now return to psychology, it is to psychology in view of Cartesian philosophy and the new Galilean science this philosophy sets out to validate. The natural science of psychology originated a century ago as an attempt to round out Galilean science. If, in accordance with the widespread objectivism of the second half of the nineteenth century—a presupposition not without its influence today—all reality unfolds in a single objective space and nowhere else, then not only the planets and the stars, not only physical bodies, are to be accounted for in objective terms, but the mind-behavior and its meanings as well. For objectivism, the objective *is* the real, without qualification.

It is not so much that, in the late nineteenth century, psychology chose to become a science in the Galilean manner, but that Galilean science chose to become psychology. Natural-scientific psychology is the branch of Galilean science that sets out to give a complete account of all meanings, and of human behavior in their regard, as events in and of objective space. Psychology as a natural science sets out to be a physics of the mind and behavior. The science of behavior bases itself on physics in such a way, in Gurwitsch's words, "that it finally appears as an extension of physics" (1966, p. 4). Accounting for perception, Gurwitsch points out, the psychologist thus presupposes the universe as constructed in physics, taking "the human organism as a physical system acted upon by physical events" (ibid., p. 99). Objectivistic thought, Merleau-Ponty remarks, views all possible events in the universe as objective in character, with perception as but one more such event (1962, p. 207). Psychology—"psychology as a natural science"—begins historically as an objectivism, as a science in the

Galilean style boldly setting out to bring the mind and its meanings into its grasp. Nothing is thought to escape nature and its laws, not even the psyche, which now is to be brought under a set of natural-scientific laws in its entirety (ibid., p. 94). The self and meaning now are conceived solely in terms of their objective circumstances. The human organism thus came to be considered a network of objective processes, related to exterior nature as "function to variable" (Merleau-Ponty, 1968, p. 26).

Now, as a hundred years ago, traditional mainstream psychology remains in its essentials a Cartesianism that makes its own the strict separation between the world as physics constructs it—"objective nature"— and the "qualitative, perceptual, and therefore 'subjective' " way in which it appears (Gurwitsch, 1966, p. 3). As the psychology textbooks of the 1980s have been heard to assert, *"What we see, hear, and otherwise sense is not what is really there in the outside world"* (Kalat, 1986, p. 86). "The perceived world differs from the real world" (ibid., p. 102). *"It is apparent that the world as we know it is created from sensory impressions"* (Coon, 1985, p. 71). "Your knowledge of the external world . . . comes entirely from chemical and electrical processes occurring in the nervous system" (Scarr and Vander Zanden, 1984, p. 152)—and that's how "the world out there gets in." Everyday perceptual meanings thus still clearly are distinguished, exactly as they were for Descartes, from what is really and truly going on in nature; that is, in nature projected objectively. Now as then, objective events are considered the really determinative events in perception: physical energies propagated in an objective medium and reaching the objective organism, stimulated receptor organs, processing by the brain.

Now as then, conventionally Galilean-Cartesian psychology considers sensory data in terms of the relation these hold to the physical energies that surround and bombard the organism. Fragmented environmental stimuli, "with the dignity of a cause" (Merleau-Ponty, 1963, p. 9), are seen to institute sensory events inside the organism (Gurwitsch, 1966, p. 3). In the words of the introductory text of Wortman et al., "A stimulus is any form of energy . . . to which an organism is capable of responding. . . Stimuli and sensations . . . have a *cause-and-effect* relationship" (1988, p. 86). Or, as the text by Scarr and Vander Zanden puts it, "Physical change in the external or internal environment triggers chemical, electrical, and mechanical activity in sense receptors" (1984, p. 152).

Natural-scientific psychology continues to consider sensory data initiated by external stimuli the most basic and elementary facts of perception. As phenomenological philosophers have pointed out, raw sensory impressions (sensations) are the constant for traditional psychology, "an elementary stratum of psychical data depending only on objective stimuli" (Gurwitsch, 1966, p. 24), an "unorganized mass," a "mosaic" (Merleau-Ponty, 1963, p. 166), basic raw materials in need of organization

(Gurwitsch, 1966, p. 24). The textbooks, remarkably faithful to the tradition, refer to sensory impressions as lacking organization and standing in need of integration, as "raw and disconnected" (Ornstein, 1985, p. 215), "raw information" about the environment (Smith et al., 1986, 146); "Raw visual sensations are like the unassembled parts of a washing machine" (Lahey, 1989, p. 114).

Now, exactly as a hundred years ago, mainstream psychology asserts that perceptions develop out of "mere sense-data" through the intervention of extraneous factors that interpret sensations and bestow meaning on them (Gurwitsch, 1964, p. 88). As the introductory psychology text of Rubin and McNeil phrases it, "In the brain, information from the senses is organized so that it has some meaning for us" (1987, p. 101). Or, as we find in the text of Lefton, "Perception is the process by which an organism interprets sensory input so that it acquires meaning" (1985, p. 169).

It was thought then and is thought now, as Merleau-Ponty has put it, that one can follow, from the first impressions external stimuli make on the organism to the consequent processing of sensations in the brain, "the projection of the external world in the living body" (1962, p. 55). Now as then, conventional psychology holds to "a universe which would produce in us representations which are distinct from it by means of a causal action" (Merleau-Ponty, 1963, p. 188); believes in a universe that, as the textbooks have it, would produce in us "meaningful models" of itself (Bootzin et al., 1986, p. 135), "replicas" of things as they exist in the external world (Benjamin, Hopkins, and Nation, 1987, p. 100).

Behavior is considered today, as it was in the nineteenth century, to unfold causally in objective space in accordance with natural-scientific lawfulness. In textbook terms, "Psychology as a science must be based on the assumption that behavior is strictly subject to physical laws just like any other natural phenomenon" (Carlson, 1984, p. 5). "The *determinist* point of view holds that events are caused by other events. . . . Psychologists assume that if the causal laws underlying human behavior can be understood, it is possible, in principle at least, to predict all human behavior" (Spear, Penrod, and Baker, 1988, p. 16). "Physical change . . . triggers . . . activity in sense receptors. After complex processing in the nervous system, a pattern of activity is produced in certain areas of the brain" (Scarr and Vander Zanden, 1984, p. 152).

By attaching meaning to it, the objective brain rounds out the objective stimulation initiated by the objective external world; and Galilean science rounds itself out by accounting for the occurrence of meaning in an essentially meaningless nature. This, we are told, is how we end up with a world, not "as the world really is," but with the "world as we know it." Thus it is that subjective meanings, interpretations generated by the objective brain, pop up in the causal chain specified by objectivistic philosophy. And someday, it is thought, neurophysiology will be able to specify any meaning's exact physical location and conditions and then once and for all will have given a complete account of what people naively take to be a surrounding world of meaning.

The radicalized Cartesianism that conventional psychology represents, having set out to bring Galilean science to its completion, not only treats perception as a causal outcome in objective space, but other basic psychological processes as well. These processes likewise are considered to be at root but modes of extension. This paragraph samples the views of textbook psychology on such other processes. Stimuli, for example, are said to "trigger" emotions (Smith et al., 1986, p. 309; Rubin and McNeil, 1987, p. 264); emotion is a "response to a stimulus" (Pettijohn, 1989, p. 232). And motivation "can be thought of as *the forces* acting on or within an organism that initiate and direct behavior as well as governing its intensity" (McGee and Wilson, 1984, p. 245; emphasis mine). Motivation "can be thought as *the forces* that initiate and control behavior, and the variables that determine the intensity and persistence of that behavior" (Pettijohn, 1989, p. 210; emphasis mine). Adopting such a causal approach to the wellsprings of behavior, it is then eminently reasonable to inquire, "What internal and external forces stimulate passive organisms to become *actors*?" (Zimbardo, 1988, p. 375). Learning is said to refer to "relatively longlasting changes in an individual's behavior that are *produced by* environmental events" (Carlson, 1984, pp. 116–117; emphasis mine). Memories are said to be objectively stored in the brain, physically represented in objective space (ibid., p. 447), electrically or chemically contained within brain tissue (Dworetsky, 1985, p. 210). Once something is encoded in memory and thus *put into* storage in the brain, once put away in the memory bank, a memory is an objective in-itself on deposit and on call, "mental savings" that "we can *pull out* again if we have the right cue or entry key" (Smith et al., 1986, p. 251). Forgetting, by such an account, is a failure to retrieve objectively stored memories. Perhaps some other objective memory blocks the path objectively leading to the desired material, gets in the way, and thus interferes with its retrieval (see, for example, McGee and Wilson, 1984, p. 178), or perhaps the appropriate retrieval cue is unavailable, in which case the memory nonetheless is objectively there, somewhere in the brain's objective space, it just won't turn up: "forgetting is much like being unable to find a misplaced book in a library. The book (or memory) is there but not retrievable at the moment" (ibid., p. 180). And, having compared memory to the workings of a camera and a projector, Scarr and Vander Zanden liken thinking to the workings of a computer: "If storage and retrieval were the only processes to handle information, people would be little more than glorified cameras and projectors. But in fact, human beings are capable of doing things with information that make the most complex computer seem simple by comparison" (1984, p. 237). The repeated comparison of behavioral processes in these references to objects manifests the pervasiveness of conventional psychology's objectivism.

Inside and Outside in Modern Thought

If an objective body is defined as self-contained and in-itself, a link in a causal chain that can be affected by other bodies only locally and externally, by reason of linear, "end-to-end causality" (Merleau-Ponty, 1968, p. 232), then the human body considered objectively likewise is such a link. This already was the view of Descartes for whom the human body is a machine governed by rigid objective constraints, and it is the view of conventional psychology. Given such a viewpoint, it is natural, moreover, and even necessary, for conventional psychology to divide objective reality into an internal psychological world and an external environmental world, to posit a dividing line, itself objectively specifiable, between internal and external worlds. This objective boundary is the skin and other sense organs.

The objective human body (human being) thus always is objectively somewhere (on this side of the skin), and all other objective realities, other human bodies included, are located somewhere else (outside the skin). The external world is a world of physical energies. The internal world also essentially is a realm of physical occurrences. Its particularity lies in its location on the inside of the skin. The objective human body is inside the skin, outside the external world of stimuli; in-itself, outside all those objective bodies that are not itself. Outside, the objective causal influence is called a *stimulus*. Inside, the influencing stimulus issues in further influences, in sensory impressions, and later in perceptions, memories, thoughts, emotions, and motivating forces, but also in behavior directed back out to the external world. All of these further influences are viewed by conventional textbook psychology as having a setting of their own in objective organismic processes.

Any external influence that comes to bear upon the human organism thus viewed as closed in upon itself—objectively defined in its extension by the skin boundary—must be regarded as *either* here *or* there in the space-time continuum. Such an influence must be locally somewhere rather than somewhere else, either on this side or that of the skin boundary, or perhaps just now crossing over it. For any objective influence to hold sway, it must accomplish its work in accordance with the essential character of the objective space of pure extension already alluded to. For a stimulus in the external world to have an effect on the internal world of the organism, then, in the course of time, it must physically traverse three-dimensional space, locally take certain physical paths, and in the process objectively cross the boundary that marks an essentially self-contained organism from its environment. The influence, moreover, must infringe upon and physically overtake the space of what is to be influenced; the retina, for example. This is accomplished through objective effects linearly radiating out, in keeping with certain laws, in continuous objective space from source to whatever happens to be overtaken. An influence, at least in principle, always can be traced from one specific location in objective space to the newly attained specific location where it is presently having an effect. Affecting the organism, then, an objective influence passes locally and linearly through objective space, effect by effect, from the source of stimulation, through the environment, to sense organs, to the brain, to meaning and its vicissitudes (memory, thought). And "the world out there gets in."

In accordance with the objectivism of conventional psychology, everyday meaning exists as a link in a causal chain, the product of a series of objective events. The chain that leads to meaning begins with physical energies (stimuli) in the environment and ends with a synthetic activity on the part of the brain. This latter activity constructs meaning, attaching it to that which, essentially fragmented, is without meaning. One answer thus is given to the question raised at the beginning of this chapter regarding the status and place of meaning. Conventional psychology, following in Descartes's footsteps, furnishes us with the answer that the status of everyday meaning—the sun overhead, for example—is not an original one; that meanings or perceptions and their vicissitudes do not belong to the real surrounding world, a realm defined by its pure extension in the space-time continuum. Meaning is seen to take place only inside the organism, where the self likewise is said to be found, and only after an objective processing of stimuli and sensations has taken its course. Outside the organism exist only the physical energies of nature viewed as three-dimensional extension. Given that in an objectivistic scheme of things meaning, like every occurrence in objective space, must be calculably either here or there, and, given that the organism is measurably (objectively) inside itself, as are all those influences set in motion by external forces, where else could the subjective domain of meanings be but inside the organism—strange as it sounds, objectively inside it—as the localized output of objective organismic processes? An objective account thus grants everyday perceptual meanings neither the status nor the location that we are accustomed to attribute to them. Meaning, the "world as we know it," in the eyes of conventionally objectivistic psychology, has but the status of an *epiphenomenon*, a secondary result produced by more basic (objective) processes, a secondary outcome with no standing of its own in reality.

Malls, our friend, the pretty tulips, every last value, and even our self itself are all said to occur inside the organism, then: epiphenomena first arising in an inner sphere of consciousness. It is inside that modern psychology presupposes that we have contact with all our meanings. The study of *sensation*, as one psychology text puts it, is seeing "how information from the outside world gets inside the body," whereas the study of *perception* is seeing "what happens to that sensory information once it gets to the brain" (Landy, 1987, p. 93). With the external world and its processes supposed as having a purely physical character, there is no way that a subject, who moves in the realm of qualitative meaning and not in the realm of quantitatively determinable physical energies, could conceivably have any direct contact with external reality.[1] "The world as we know it" is not the world as it "really" is outside; and this, as already seen, the textbooks explicitly assert. The subject thus is judged to be ultimately confined to its subjective states, to modifications of the mind, to the subjective meanings that an objective brain has somehow managed to generate.

Conventional modern psychology, then, rather than locating meanings all around us—the way they seem to be—places them in the realm of the mental, in an inner, closed, and private realm, a realm whose nonobjective properties can appear only as truly mysterious to objectivistic thought. Consciousness, as described by introductory psychology textbooks, is "all the internal mental events and responses to external stimuli of which a person is aware" (Hassett and White, 1989, p. 106); "an awareness of the thoughts, images, sensations, and emotions that flow through the mind at any given moment" (Bootzin et al., 1986, p. 729); "an active awareness of the many thoughts, images, perceptions, and emotions that occupy one's mind at any given time" (Wortman et al., 1988, p. 536); "the subjective awareness that you have at a given time of your inner sensations, images, thoughts, and feelings of the world about you. . . . You cannot touch, see, hear, taste, or smell consciousness. Nor can you directly count, weigh, or measure it. And, except as you may inform others about it, this internal mental world is quite private, something closed to other people" (Scarr and Vander Zanden, 1984, p. 78).

According to conventional textbook psychology, we are confined to an internal world that is closed off and private, to our internal states. Gurwitsch has termed this doctrine *the theory of ideas,* which, stated more precisely, affirms that all mental states are modes of a consciousness that is a closed sphere of subjective interiority, of a consciousness completely cut off from everything belonging to the objective world external to it. The mind, in Gurwitsch's words, is forever "confined to its own states. Only its own experiences, its modes and modifications, are directly and immediately given to the conscious ego" (1974, p. 217). The theory of ideas, which according to Gurwitsch has dominated the whole of modern philosophy up to the founding of phenomenology with Husserl, holds that all we ever deal with directly are our own ideas, internal representations.

Conventional psychology thus joins the total thrust of modern philosophy in affirming the subjective and private character of the human subject's, the mind's, meanings. Meanings, the "world as we know it," are subjective ideas inside us, psychological occurrences, modifications of the mind. With these alone are we said to have commerce. Conventional psychology, springing directly from the modern tradition, is a traditional theory of ideas, which in textbook terms goes something like this: "*Sensations* are private or subjective events" (Darley, Glucksberg, and Kinchla, 1988, p. 81); "The process of receiving information from the outside world, translating it and transmitting it to the brain is called *sensation*. The process of interpreting that information and forming ideas about the world is called *perception*" (Lahey, 1989, p. 85); "How do you know that this book exists? You may answer that you can feel it and touch it, but the sight and feel of this book are aspects of your *perceptual* world. Your answer is a report of the events that are occurring in your mind" (Krebs and Blackman, 1988, p. 146). Conventional psychology, in adopting the theory of ideas and in propagating it even to the present day, is quintessentially modern, a true heir of Descartes.

Psychology as Philosophy

Every science is a philosophy, resting on basic presuppositions. A scientific field is first laid open when a certain region of things is projected in advance a certain way, with this or that manner of being. Objective facts are not simply there for the discovery, but rather have to be set up in their very objectivity. An open space has to be cleared for them, where they can show up and be ascertained. Facts, as Heidegger has pointed out, only come into view *after* nature has been "mathematically projected in advance," only *after* nature has been set up as possessing a purely objective character; the very possibility of modern science lies in its founders' realization that there are no such things as "bare facts" (1962a, p. 414). Science is a highly creative human endeavor, not the uncovering of determinate facts, of things as they always were. Explanation, in Merleau-Ponty's words, "is not discovered but created" (1962, p. 115).

Every psychology is a philosophy, its life breathed into it by its founding presuppositions, and necessarily so. "For us there is no difference between psychology and philosophy. Psychology is always an implicit and budding philosophy, and philosophy has never given up its contact with facts" (Merleau-Ponty, 1973a, p. 10). Conventional psychology is a point of view born of philosophy and nurtured by collaborative human effort. This psychology projects human behavior a certain way in order to gain mastery over it. It has its historically determined presuppositions, even when these have gone underground to function as if they didn't exist at all. The aim of this chapter has been to indicate the basic philosophical motive underlying conventional psychology. Its aim, moreover, is to suggest that such a motive is but one of a number of possible motives underlying a variety of possible philosophies of psychology. It has been found that conventional psychology is an objectivism, a Cartesianism radicalized in one of that philosophy's basic possibilities. Conventional psychology is born of modern philosophy as that branch whose goal is to bring the mathematical project of nature to completion, to push Galilean science to its limits by explaining human behavior in its entirety as a function of events in objective space. Conventional psychology is an integral part of modern philosophy. One may reasonably consider it a necessity of the age. All in all, then, conventional psychology's philosophical status consists in its objectivistic preconceiving of human being and its meanings.

This chapter's inquiry into the philosophical status of conventional psychology admittedly has ulterior motives. It aims to prepare for the presentation of a philosophy of psychology fundamentally different in motive from the conventional philosophy of psychology. Such an alternative phenomenological philosophy of psychology—phenomenological psychology, for short—maintaining that objectivistic approaches in psychology, rather than doing justice to the human world, in fact do it violence, objects to the way conventional psychology ever so casually levels the self and its meanings to the objective common denominator supposed in advance. Rather than beginning with a construction that reduces everyday meanings to mere epiphenomenal status, phenomenological psychology makes such qualitative meanings, and human behavior in their regard, its very point of departure. Phenomenological psychology believes that everyday meaning and meaning-oriented behavior, to be understood, must be taken seriously just as they present themselves, in terms of their own requirements and not in terms of their prior projection in objective space. Phenomenological psychology is not opposed in principle to *objective* approaches in psychology or to a philosophy of psychology that makes room for such approaches. What it opposes is an all-leveling *objectivism*. It objects only to the philosophy of psychology that insists that objective approaches *alone* have scientific validity; that is, only to the philosophy of psychology unaware that objective behavioral facts do not exist, as it were, in-themselves outside of the objectivizing project that first sets them up, that such facts are not *the* facts; only to the philosophy of psychology unaware that other legitimate projects of human behavior are not only possible but desirable.

Phenomenological psychology, as an attempt to reopen basic questions about human behavior and the meanings with which behavior is preoccupied, is explicitly philosophical in character. And so what follows in this study will sound at least as philosophical as it does psychological, and for the most part undoubtedly more so. This investigation takes a long second look at meaning, at its status and location. Given the necessary task of coming to grips with meaning on its own terms rather than as an inner psychological event, such a prolonged consideration of meaning is unavoidable. In the final analysis, however, it is not that phenomenological psychology is philosophy and that conventional psychology is science. Both psychologies are philosophies and both are in pursuit of rigorous and systematic understanding of the patterns characteristic of human behavior. However, whereas human-scientific phenomenological psychology is at an early and explicit stage of its philosophizing, the philosophy of natural-scientific psychology is at a late phase of its development, its presupposing barely recognizable as a presupposing at all and hence by and large implicit. The very implicitness of conventional psychology's underlying philosophy makes it seem so obvious, as if it were simply presenting things as they really and truly are, as though it were not a philosophy at all.

2 *Phenomenology*

All proof is always only a subsequent
undertaking on the basis of
presuppositions. Anything at all can
be proved, depending only on what
presuppositions are made.

—*Heidegger*, 1971b, p. 222

Choices

Conventional psychology, in what is essential to its treatment of everyday meaning, is an objectivism. Meaning-perception and its vicissitudes, such as remembering and thinking, spring forth for this philosophy as effects from a realm defined by nonmeaning, an objective realm of ready-made entities. An objective brain is viewed as operating on the objective aftereffects in the organism of causal actions instigated by objective environmental stimuli. Conventional psychology presupposes that stimuli, sense organs, the brain, the meanings generated by the brain, and more yet, constitute a single causal chain in one and the same continuum of three-dimensional objective space, a single chain in an objective space of meaning and meaning-oriented behavior. Holding to the preferred *idea* of pure extension, objectivistic psychology is a Cartesian philosophy-Galilean science. This guiding idea determines that meanings can be only subjective occurrences in an inner, private domain; that meanings must be the outcome of certain objective operations.

Objectivism is *reductionism*, a metaphysical position that postulates, in Gurwitsch's words, that "all phenomena . . . are to be reduced to, i.e., resolved into, facts and occurrences investigated in the science of physics" (1974, p. 136). Reductionism is an attempt to account, in advance and in principle, for all the processes of the universe in physical terms, for all natural phenomena as "vast complications of physical phenomena combining and interacting with one another" (ibid.). Reductionistic metaphysics thus traces all events back to working units of mass that are always determinable causally in the space-time continuum. "Physics passes for the fundamental and even the only science" (ibid.). Reductionism dominates vast stretches of conventional textbook psychology, being virtually equivalent to "scientific"

23

psychology. Meaning, the self, the human body all are reduced to objective occurrences, the lawfulness of whose changes this psychology has set as its task to specify.

The objectivistic reductionism of conventional psychology is only one way of looking at things, "a preference" (Merleau-Ponty, 1968, p. 17). A phenomenologically oriented psychology for its part, refusing to consider the domain of meaning as a subjective aftereffect of physical processes, rejects an "objective space of meaning." Excluding the prior exclusion of meaning from a proper status of its own, indeed viewing this prior exclusion as a typically modern power play (prediction, control), phenomenological psychology prefers to be party to a psychological science in which everyday meanings figure centrally for what they themselves are, which is what human beings live for. Not even the objectivist philosopher of science lives for anything other than meanings—objectivistic doctrine is precisely one of those qualitative meanings. It is argued that what is needed to do justice to everyday meanings, and to human behavior in their regard, is a psychology governed by a presupposing that, rather than taking these meanings as mere subjective end products, seizes upon them as its starting point. Such a presupposing is to be found in the philosophy of phenomenology, which, broadly defined, is the rigorous and systematic investigation of everyday meaning on its own ground. This philosophy, and especially its status as a method for disclosing everyday meaning, is considered in the following sections. A discussion of phenomenological psychology proper is then undertaken. The chapter's final sections turn to a consideration of phenomenology's theory of intentionality.

The Lifeworld

Phenomenology requires that meanings, rather than being reduced to another order of things, be taken just as they present themselves in everyday life. Toward this end, phenomenology concerns itself with the *lifeworld*, Husserl's term for the world as we encounter it in everyday experience, the world in which we pursue our goals and objectives, the scene of all our activities (Gurwitsch, 1966, pp. 120–121; 1974, p. 3). The lifeworld, in Gurwitsch's words, consists of "all items and objects which present themselves in prescientific experience and as they present themselves prior to their scientific interpretation in the specific modern sense" (1974, p. 17). The lifeworld consists of "objects of value, e.g., works of art, buildings which serve specific purposes, like abodes, places for work, schools, libraries, churches, and so on. Objects pertaining to the lifeworld present themselves as tools, instruments, and utensils related to human needs and desires" (ibid., p. 143). The lifeworld, in other words, is the world of everyday meanings, the world of malls, tulips, and lakes.

What happened with the rise of modern science, according to Husserl, was this. A method that objectifies nature to make better (that is, more scientific) predictions about it, such a method or, more precisely, the nature this method thus objectified, came to be taken for nature's "true being" (1970, pp. 51–52). At the same time, as Gurwitsch remarks in this connection, the lifeworld, "which for us is the only truly real world," was turned into a "merely subjective phenomenon" (1974, p. 17). Phenomenology finds such a procedure unacceptable. To account for "orders of existence other than the lifeworld," there is after all nowhere else to start but the lifeworld (Gurwitsch, 1966, p. 121). Modern science simply has no other source for its materials than the lifeworld of ordinary experience. Upon the lifeworld, and the lifeworld alone, the typically modern abstraction is performed by means of which nature is constructed as pure spatial extension. What is built by abstraction from the lifeworld, phenomenology maintains— although clearly not without its merits—cannot be turned into the ultimate origin of one and the same lifeworld. No, Gurwitsch asserts, "Reality is, and always remains, the lifeworld" (1974, p. 56). Herein lies a fundamental justification for a lifeworld science of everyday meaning. The lifeworld holds a privileged position—has a definitive priority—and along with it perception (meaning). Scientific observation itself occurs in the lifeworld and in the lifeworld alone—to undermine the status of such lifeworld observation is to undermine science itself. The lifeworld, all in all, is the place of all human endeavors, *our first, last, and only world*, "the only truly real world" (in Gurwitsch's words). Reversing a previously cited textbook formulation, phenomenology may be said to hold that "the world as we know it *is* the way it looks"—at least in a general way.

Lifeworld meanings retain forever a priority, then, over every idealizing abstraction performed on them. This priority of "the things themselves" (Husserl) over the will to predict and control is a basic presupposition of phenomenology, opening up its field of investigation. To thus grant a priority to lifeworld meaning is at once to grant a priority to phenomenology as that discipline whose explicit intention it is to investigate meaning on its own lifeworld ground. Phenomenology has a claim to priority as the science of meaning—phenomenological psychology shares in this claim in its own special way as the science of meaning-oriented behavior. A phenomenological science, to be sure, although no less rigorous or systematic than Galilean science, will look very different from such a science—the sense of the term *science* undergoes a pronounced transformation when modified by the adjective *phenomenological*.

Objectivism, the conventional preference for the ultimate priority of the objective, for an objective origin of the lifeworld and its meanings, is challenged head-on by the phenomenological assertion of a definitive priority of the lifeworld. Phenomenology abandons once and for all the notion that underlying everyday meanings is a physical stratum with more reality than the meanings to which it gives rise; rejects the reductionistic notion that a physical approach to meaning is the only properly "scientific" one. "'Objective nature,' 'nature as it really is in itself,' " Gurwitsch points out, is not to be taken as "true reality" beneath the "merely subjective" appearances of the lifeworld, the true state of affairs to which the appropriate methods alone have access (1966, p. 422).

These considerations are not meant to be taken as an attempt to *prove* the phenomenological presupposition of a science of lifeworld meaning. Proof only follows presupposing, "as a subsequent undertaking on the basis of presuppositions" (Heidegger, 1971b, p. 222). Proof is only consequent to commitment. The phenomenological starting point can no more be proved than the Galilean one. These reflections are meant rather to give a first indication of the plausibility of the phenomenological presupposition.

Considerations of Method

Phenomenology is the science of the lifeworld and its events of meaning. Phenomenology, it was suggested earlier, is the demand that the lifeworld and its meanings be taken just as these present themselves, without the prior imposition of constructions of any sort, including, and especially, those of modern Galilean science. Adoption of the phenomenological method means a refusal to conceive everyday meanings in advance, to preconceive them, as objectively generated by the brain and subjectively lodged in an inner realm of mind. The brownness of the chair then is found to belong to the chair itself and not taken as a "subjective sensation" provoked by processes impinging upon our sense organs, and which are to be described in mathematico-physical terms (Gurwitsch, 1974, p. 19). The chair is not limited to its various sensible qualities, moreover, but is *perceived* from the first as something to sit on, as a chair. Things present themselves in their original sensory givenness as serving certain ends (ibid.). "Chairness" is not something added on to "raw" sensations inside the organism. "The perception of a thing," in Gurwitsch's words, "is not to be understood as though a sense or meaning were superveniently bestowed or imposed on a mere corporeal object which, prior to that imposition, was devoid of all sense" (ibid., p. 20). Essential to our perception of the everyday meaning chair, then, is precisely its being a chair. Phenomenology takes the chair to be just what it is and just the way it looks and finds it to be located where it stands in the lifeworld, on the floor next to the table.

Phenomenological method, then, deals with things "just as they appear" in the lifeworld (Gurwitsch, 1966, p. 109). The perceived, as perceived, is "described solely on its own grounds and merits, without any reference to an extra-phenomenal reality" (ibid., p. 105). Or, in Heidegger's classic formulation, "*Phenomenon* signifies *that which shows itself in itself*, the *manifest*," that which "lies in the light of day or can be brought to the light" (1962a, p. 51). Phenomenology, then, is letting "that which shows itself be seen from itself in the very way in which it shows itself from itself" (ibid., p. 58). Phenomenon is the event of self-showing meaning, and phenomenology is the rigorous investigation of such events. The rallying call of phenomenology has been Husserl's phrase, "to the things themselves"; that is, to the phenomena themselves, to lifeworld meanings themselves in their total event character. This is a call to the highest rigor, to the most strenuous efforts. In pursuit of "the things themselves," Heidegger points out, phenomenology is in fundamental opposition to all mere constructions, accidental findings, and seeming proofs (ibid., p. 50). To thus engage in phenomenology requires ridding "ourselves of the habit of always hearing only what we already understand" (Heidegger, 1971a, p. 58).

Employing the phenomenological method means taking a step back from our usual everyday involvement in things, from our normal fascination with things and projects—with beings in their sheer obviousness—and in particular from what has become the commonsense commitment to a "scientific" view of the universe. One steps back to gain the distance necessary for a fresh look at things on their lifeworld ground as self-presenting phenomena. As French phenomenological philosopher Paul Ricoeur remarks, "Initially I am lost and forgotten in the world, lost in the things, lost in the ideas, lost in the plants and animals, lost in mathematics" (1967, p. 20). Phenomenology attempts to overcome this initial state of alienation through a bracketing, a setting aside, of what Husserl calls the *natural attitude*, which is to say, of our everyday tendency to treat things as absolute and in-themselves, ready-made "out there," and the same for everybody; "out there" just waiting to be seized hold of by a science in the Galilean manner and rendered fully explicit in the truth of their objectivity. Phenomenology is a bracketing of things as though they existed in-themselves, be it for scientific or for prescientific understanding—this setting to one side of the natural attitude is what Husserl calls the *phenomenological reduction*. Positively, phenomenology means taking our world as a human world of meaning, and the facts and theories of science as themselves meanings. It means taking our world as a world in which things, rather than being objectively ready-made, have a history of becoming that properly belongs to them, in which history human becoming is profoundly implicated.

Method of Phenomenological Description

Phenomenology is another name for the enterprise of describing phenomena. Phenomenological description—which is, as Heidegger points out, a tautology—is a portrayal of phenomena, the attempt to bring to a self-display the complete structure of events of meaning. Description is an attempt to bring the phenomena to rigorous and systematic expression as they themselves, "the things themselves," show themselves to be, without the blinding intervention of conventional presuppositions. Phenomenologists are concerned most generally with coming to grips with what in fact is going on, rather than with what everybody "knows" to be so; with gaining conceptual clarity in what regards meaning events in their actuality. To describe phenomenologically is to bring the phenomenon under consideration—our experience of a chair, for example, or of the pretty red tulips—to definition just as it presents itself from itself. To describe is to indicate what a phenomenon is and is not, and also what is not it. To describe is to attempt to bring to a self-showing whatever enters into and contributes to a meaning event in its totality; psychological processes, for example, and lifeworld laws governing meaning formation. To describe is to render meaning events manifest in their variety; as events of perceiving things, for example, or of remembering them, or of moving them around. To describe is to pursue the character of the relationships obtaining among the various sorts of phenomena. To describe is to specify the location of meaning in its lifeworld context; of a screwdriver in its context of other tools, for example. To describe is to point out the ubiquity and centrality of events of meaning in human life.

Phenomenological description, to be understood, must not remain abstract and at a distance. The student of phenomenology rather must become personally engaged in the phenomenon being described, must indeed become a student of the phenomena, of "the things themselves." There needs to occur a sense of realization of what is being described, a sense of personal identification with the description being offered. The phenomenon must come to be felt in its living immediacy—for it is precisely this immediacy of life, this living flux, that phenomenology is after—or the description has not yet been entered into in what is its essential. Phenomenology is an approach to meaning events, then, that requires interested parties to become personally involved in the work undertaken, checking out every description proposed, every claim that a phenomenon has been brought to a self-display, against firsthand experiences of their own. If the description is found to match what one already implicitly knows to be the case, the description has been confirmed. Only life experience is adequate to the description of life experience. No authority, no mathematical constructions of meaning events in their calculability are of any assistance here. The only thing that counts is letting the phenomenon have an impact on its own ground; the descriptions phenomenologists bring to expression are meant to serve no other end than this. This often is a slow and difficult process, one that insists on taking its own course.

Phenomenological description has but one original avenue to its understanding of events of lifeworld meaning; namely, the meaning events themselves. Example is of the first order of importance for phenomenology. Only in instances of meaning, only in the occurrences of everyday life, can the essential structure of meaning events be discerned and clarity attained.

Phenomenological Interpreting

To describe the full structure of an event of meaning—all that a meaning is, the complete phenomenon—involves displaying the manner in which the meaning takes place, the qualitative "how" of its occurrence. *How* something happens in its lifeworld setting is essential to *what* it is. Describing a meaning's "how," then, is not above and beyond describing its "what." A meaning never exists in isolation but always in a lifeworld context of other meanings and always for someone who has some interest in the matter; the chair in its context of other furniture, for example, and as something to sit on. To bring this how of the chair to expression is what it means to describe the chair's concrete givenness as the something it is, its complete lifeworld situation or quality as a meaning. All that a chair is, its complete description as a phenomenon, is determined only by determining its place in the world of someone's everyday preoccupation.

In attempting to display the complete how of a meaning's lifeworld occurrence, the meaning's full event structure, phenomenological description has already become phenomenological interpreting. Not content with what for the most part does show itself, meanings as we are straightforwardly involved with them in our daily rounds, phenomenology attempts to render explicit any meaning's largely hidden event character, its *being*. *The* phenomenon of phenomenology, behind which there is nothing else, is the *being of beings* (Heidegger, 1962a, pp. 59–61). The method of phenomenological description is interpreting the being of meanings. Phenomenology, in Heidegger's words, is "a *hermeneutic* in the primordial signification of this word, where it designates this business of interpreting" (ibid., p. 62). The phenomenon of phenomenology is not fullness of conscious presence, the sheer luminosity of this or that everyday meaning and of our intentions in its regard, but the entirety of the as-much-hidden as self-presenting event of meaning presencing. Meaning's event structure is given to us phenomenally, according to phenomenology, but implicitly, *en*folded in such a way that, routinely absorbed in the particularity of things (natural attitude), it is all too easy for us to overlook it. Meaning's complete structure, all that is involved in the structuring of any meaning, it was remarked earlier, is not *behind* or *beneath* the totality of what presents itself, but hidden *within* it. An effort of phenomenological understanding, interpreting, is necessary to render the structure explicit, to *un*fold what is already implicitly available to us in meaning events but which tends to escape our notice. Phenomenology is engaged in the project of bringing into the open (interpreting) and of faithfully portraying (describing) the total lifeworld structure of meaning events—whatever makes a meaning be a meaning—in the very way that this structure presents itself to us when given careful phenomenological consideration. Phenomenology has nothing to say about anything that it does not already know something about; that is, about anything that doesn't somehow already present itself phenomenally, at least as implicitly wrapped up in the total meaning event being reflected upon.

It was suggested in Chapter 1 that psychological interpretations differ as to what is involved in events of meaning, as to just what is holding itself back in such events. Both conventional psychology and phenomenological psychology agree that our meanings—lifeworld things or other people who share the lifeworld with us, the tulips, our friend, a magazine—taken of and by themselves, are not the final word for a psychological science; that something indeed is concealing itself in every event of meaning; that an effort of interpreting is required to bring into the open all that is involved in the giving of meaning and yet is holding itself back. Both psychologies want more. Conventional psychology constructs its interpretation of meaning through projecting meaning's objective circumstances; namely, environmental stimuli, sense organs, neurons, cortical interpretation, storage, and so on. Conventional psychology determines a meaning's how not on the basis of its lifeworld context, but on that of an altogether different order. Conventional psychology determines *what* a chair is through projecting its objective *how*. Conventional psychology *explains* subjective meaning as the inner output of objective processes. Phenomenology, it has been noted, brackets things in their lived obviousness, in the spell they cast over us in everyday life, a spell that convinces us that they exist "out there" ready-made and in-themselves. Phenomenology likewise brackets their obvious objectiveness as preconceived by Galilean science, which amounts to nothing less than their ready-madeness, their in-itselfness, on a presumably more fundamental level. Phenomenological interpreting suspends all objectivizing interpreting. Phenomenology interprets meaning as structured within, and not behind or beneath, the lifeworld; meaning's event structure is considered to be of the same order as meaning itself. Phenomenology strives to bring the concealed processes of meaning to as complete an expression as possible and thereby to liberate us from our lostness in the particularities of meanings, in their "obvious" ready-madeness.

Implicated in every event of meaning presencing, as suggested earlier in this chapter, is an interested someone to whom the meaning is what it is. This role of a someone, ubiquitous as it is in meaning events, is precisely one of the features of meaning's total structuring that tends to remain enfolded, and thus to pass unnoticed in everyday life. It is just such a role—a role that conventional psychology, relegating the production of meaning to the objective brain, seems to deny altogether—that phenomenology has a special interest in explicating. Coming to terms with meaning events without prejudice on their own terms demands a break with the sort of objectivizing realism (natural attitude) incapable of extricating itself from its immersion in the ready-madeness of things. Unaware of their role as codeterminants of the very meanings that confront them, people tend to fall under the suggestive influence of purportedly autonomous beings, to fall prey to their domination. Meanings ready-made in-themselves take over, assuming at times even immensity of power—in which case people turn their lives over to authoritarian gods, material possessions, charismatic public figures, a science able to calculate and improve all things. Even when they do not go so far as to worship the very meanings they have a role in bringing to presence, there is still a tendency for people to believe that meanings are powers they run up against, like the proverbial sound in the forest, that meanings are simply "there," ready-made and authoritative in-themselves, something that happens whether anyone is on the scene or not, something no one can do anything about. Phenomenology is the requirement that the natural attitude issuing in beliefs such as these be set aside and that an involved someone be recognized as making an essential contribution to every meaning event whatsoever—to the sound that, as a meaning, is something heard by someone (no someone, no sound!). A recognition of this sort, it is believed, deprives meanings of the ready-madeness of power they have usurped for themselves and come to wield over our life. Putting an end to our projecting of powers onto meanings (compare, e.g., Feuerbach, Marx, Fromm, Jung), to our having to answer to them in turn, helps restore ourselves to ourselves, helps us overcome the alienation of the natural attitude by which, lost in things, we have yet to come home to ourselves. Phenomenology pursues just such a recovery.

Phenomenological Concern with the Structural Invariants of Meaning Events

To describe phenomenologically is to portray lifeworld meanings. But lifeworld meanings involve a total structure—the meaning's how, the phenomenon in its totality—all of which does not explicitly present itself in the course of straightforward commerce with the lifeworld. Phenomenological description becomes, upon this realization, phenomenological interpreting. The phenomenon phenomenology seeks to bring out of its hiddenness is whatever makes a meaning be itself. Interested and admiring eyes, appropriate light, arrangement, and background, in part, make tulips the pretty flowers they show themselves to be. Without these, the tulips simply would not be the meaning they are. In the pursuit of the understanding of the full event of meaning, phenomenology is concerned with displaying whatever is *structurally invariant* in the given event of meaning, the phenomenon's unvarying constitution. Phenomenology is the attempt, then, to interpretively bring to light those structural constants, such as lifeworld context and the involvement of a someone, which enable meaning to be itself and without which it would not be what it is; those "relationships and structures" that one cannot "suppress or change without the thing ceasing to be itself" (Merleau-Ponty, 1968, p. 111). Husserl calls the search for such constants the *eidetic reduction*.

Phenomenological description-interpreting is a search, then, for the unvarying structural patterns that run through meaning events. Phenomenology seeks to understand everyday meanings by projecting them on those invariants properly their own, on the full structure that makes them just what they are when taken with the seriousness they merit on their own lifeworld ground, rather than on the necessities of nature considered objectively.

Taking the invariant structure of a perceptual event as an illustration, we soon find that it is possible to accommodate only one side of a perceived lifeworld meaning at a time. We have to walk around a table, for example, to see in its full givenness what we already recognize from one of its sides. For the table—for anything—to come to presence as itself in perception, it is essential that it first turn one side to us, and only then show its other sides. Perceived things necessarily come to integration gradually, in a progressive self-display of their constituent moments. To understand the story being told, we have to wait for it to unfold in its various turns. To see what a museum has to offer, we have to explore it floor by floor, room by room, work by work, this aspect of a work and then that one. If we want to examine a coat or a chair, if we are trying to get a feel for the music, it has to be done one step at a time. At a certain point we have to turn the coat over, or move on to the next room, or turn our head, or remain on the alert for what is about to occur. It is a structural invariant of perception, then, without which there would be no perceiving and no perceived, that it proceed perspectivally in a onesided manner, that it take time. These and other invariants of meaning events will be explored in the various chapters of this book.

Combining the discussions of these sections on phenomenological method, it may be said that the phenomenon phenomenological description seeks to portray on its own ground through interpretive explication is the total unvarying structure of the process by which everyday meaning comes to be given. *Phenomenological description interprets the invariant structure exhibited by the lifeworld and its events of meaning.*

Phenomenological Psychology

The intention of this book is to explore the premises of a phenomenological psychology and not to serve as an introduction to the more general philosophy of phenomenology. Phenomenological psychology, like any psychology, concerns itself with human behavior. What distinguishes phenomenological psychology from other psychologies is its concern with human behavior as implicated in meaning's total lifeworld event structure. Given phenomenology as the science of lifeworld events of meaning, a definition of phenomenological psychology might be the hermeneutic science of human immersion in and preoccupation with lifeworld events of meaning. Whereas the total phenomenon phenomenology pursues is an interweaving of behavior and contextualized lifeworld meaning, phenomenological psychology, for its part, is out to uncover, without prior mathematical construction, the behavioral side of the total unvarying structure of phenomena, meaning-oriented behavior's complete "*how.*" Phenomenological psychology is a science that is dedicated to *understanding* behavior in its total everyday context rather than to *explaining* it in terms of its objective conditions; precisely therein lies its hermeneutic character (compare Wilhelm Dilthey).

Cartesian thinking, conventional psychology included, has turned everyday meaning into a real part of the mind, an inner representation of what is presumed to be an external physical world. This has resulted, it is believed, in substantial confusion in our day and is one of the reasons for the book's attempt to clarify meaning first and only then meaning's behavioral complement. Chapters 3 and 4 of this study are a consideration of the existential character taken on by phenomenology since the 1920s. Chapters 5 through 7 focus on meaning, from a Gestalt theoretical perspective in particular, and Chapters 8 through 11 on meaning-oriented behavior. Chapters 12 through 14 round out the present study's consideration of the relationship between meaning and meaning-oriented behavior.

Natural-Scientific Psychology and Human-Scientific Psychology

A certain portrait of human behavior emerges from a natural-scientific (objectivizing) approach to behavior's role in meaning events. A different one altogether emerges from a human-scientific (phenomenological) approach. In both cases the portrait has to be executed, through construction (abstraction and idealization) in the objectivistic attempt, through hermeneutic description in the phenomenological one. The objectivistic presupposition, the projection of human behavior and everyday meaning on an objective space, is invoked in the name of a "scientific" psychology, in the interest of explaining and controlling behavior. The phenomenological presupposition, the locating of human behavior and everyday meaning in a space of their own, is invoked in the name of a scientific approach appropriate to human life and its meanings, in the interest of adequacy. The ideal guiding the development of modern psychology, Gurwitsch remarks, is one of a "universal objectivistic science" after the style of geometry (1966,

p. 437). In accordance with this ideal, the same kind of causal relations that hold between physical events are held to prevail between psychological occurrences. And yet, although modern psychology has striven for natural-scientific exactness throughout its existence, Gurwitsch goes on to comment, rather than even coming close to attaining its ideal, "its history has been a sequence of crises. The reason for its failure is the absurdity of the ideal itself" (ibid.). The essential character of the psychological realm, Gurwitsch then points out, simply does not lend itself to mathematization (abstraction and idealization). It consequently makes no sense to search for "exact psychological laws and theories," for exactness after the model of physics (ibid.). In fact, "just the pursuit of this chimerical aim," Gurwitsch believes, "has prevented the development of a genuine and pure psychology" (ibid., p. 445). Concerned with the lived structure of behavior and its meanings, with the actuality of human life, phenomenological psychology offers itself as a viable alternative to the attempts of objectivistic psychology at an "exact theoretization of the psychological domain."

The Clarification of Psychological Concepts

Phenomenological psychology maintains that the psyche itself and its everyday meanings need to become the standard from which psychological concepts destined to form the foundation of a truly scientific—"genuine and pure" (Gurwitsch's words)—psychology are to be developed. To be sure, if one insists that psychology, to be a science at all, has no alternative but to conceptualize the psyche exclusively in objective terms, then a plea for a clarification of psychological concepts on phenomenological grounds can fall only on deaf ears. But a call for the development of psychological concepts directly from human involvement in lifeworld events of meaning presencing perhaps will seem reasonable to those who look upon the objectivistic presupposition as far too limiting.

On the necessity of a phenomenological basis for psychological concepts, Gestalt psychologist Wolfgang Köhler asserts that we will never "solve any problems of ultimate principle until we go back to the source of our concepts—in other words, until we use the phenomenological method, the qualitative analysis of experience" (1938, p. x). Phenomenology, he points out, "is the field in which all concepts find their final justification" (ibid., p. 88). Psychological givenness, the descriptively oriented psychologist insists, needs to become the ultimate presupposition of psychological theory, so that we can know what we are talking about. "In so far as we have not given a coherent and adequate sense to [notions like image and perception] by reflecting on our experiences and perceptions," writes Merleau-Ponty, "we will not know what they mean and what the facts concerning image and perception really show" (1964a, p. 59). And again,

"It is a question . . . of replacing habitual concepts . . . by concepts which are consciously clarified and are therefore far less likely to remove us from experience as it is lived" (ibid., p. 61). And finally, "Our present concept of [the human being] is not at all scientific. It is vague, confused, and in need of psychological clarification. Phenomenological analysis is a clarifying effort of this kind" (ibid., p. 63). All in all, then, phenomenological psychology is a hermeneutic method for clarifying the invariant structure of human behavior in terms of the meanings with which that behavior is preoccupied from the first.

A basic task phenomenological psychology sets for itself, then, is the clarification of basic psychological concepts: phenomenological psychology is essentially a conceptual enterprise. Given what conventionally objectivistic psychology stands for, the conceptual content of present psychology texts has to be approached with some caution. It cannot be presumed that basic notions of human behavior as the textbooks present them have achieved an appropriate state of conceptual clarity. Is emotion truly a response "triggered" by stimuli? Are affectivity and perception-cognition really distinct human capacities, two different compartments within the organism with only external relations to one another? Are humans actually passive robots, and is motivation in fact being propelled into action by forces? Is it really the brain that thinks? And is the brain in fact a "truly wonderful computer"? Is perception indeed the interpreting of "raw" sensations? Is meaning no more than a subjective outcome objectively generated? Is learning really under unmitigated environmental control? Is memory in actuality stored stuff? Is forgetting in fact like being unable to find a misplaced book? In Chapter 1 introductory psychology texts were shown to make assertions essentially like these about basic behavioral processes. Do such affirmations adequately express the essentials of the behaviors in question? Are they sufficiently clarifying for psychology to know what it is talking about? Or do they proceed from an ontology (theory of reality) that is no match for concrete day-to-day behavior? Phenomenological psychology, as projected in the chapters to follow, sets out to clarify the very behaviors conventional textbook psychology also considers: behaviors of perceiving, learning, remembering, imagining, feeling, and so on.[1] Phenomenological psychology pursues its aim, however, in view of the total context of such behaviors in everyday life; in view of them, that is, as activities of a someone who lives for the meanings with which that someone forms a single interwovenness (a la Merleau-Ponty).

The Place of Everyday Meanings and Our Relation to Them

Meanings, as always for phenomenology, are our everyday others just as these present themselves to us in everyday life: the chair as something to sit on; our friend as the friend we are seeing the movie with; Main Street as the street on which the post office and bank are located; and the like. Lifeworld things, along with the people with whom we encounter them, are perceived meanings of ours. But perceived others are not the only meanings with which we become implicated in our daily lifeworld rounds. Meanings are anything whatsoever we encounter, anything that crosses our path. All those things that make their appearance in our dreams are meanings. What we remember are meanings. Our thoughts and ideas are meanings. Scientific theories are meanings. Facts are meanings, and so are values. Stories, including religious stories and teachings about divine intervention in human affairs—our very ideas and images of God—are meanings. The things we feel are meanings, as are the goals we pursue. All these are meanings. The meanings on this list differ from one another in their mode of presencing, it is true—a meaning dreamt, for example, presents itself to us in a manner that is fundamentally different from that of a meaning perceived—but all are other to us, our others. Phenomenologically, none of these meanings is a part of our mind. None has a psychological character.

A word of explanation is in order regarding the usage of the term *meaning* as extended in the preceding paragraph. Chapter 1 identified meanings with perceptions. But now the term *meaning* is said to encompass all our others, whatever their mode of presencing. The resolution of this discrepancy lies in phenomenology's conviction that perception is the fundamental mode of all meaning, that nonperceptual meanings of whatever sort take their origin in and refer back to perceptual ones (see, for example, Chapter 4, "The Primacy of Perception"). Nonperceptual meanings, in their own way, to be sure, and with a great deal of latitude, follow in every case, in the train of perceptual ones, as after their source. We perceive something. Later on we remember it or wish for it. We may even tell a story about it, or it may find its way into our dreams. At root, however, no matter how it comes to be varied, the meaning retains its original ties to perception. Perceptual meanings further expressed in other modes, nonperceptual meanings remain forever variations of the perceived lifeworld. All in all, then, all meaning has something of a perceptual character about it. It is in the perceptual lifeworld alone that we are involved first, last, and always. Even Galilean science, as pointed out earlier in this chapter, derives through abstraction from the concreteness of the perceived lifeworld.

Phenomenology discovers our meanings to be universally nonmental lifeworld others. Such a position is contrary to the modern tradition in its entirety, conventional psychology included, which holds that all our meanings belong to an inner realm of consciousness. This belief, "the theory of ideas" (a la Gurwitsch), was considered in Chapter 1 ("Inside and Outside in Modern Thought"). Since Descartes, Heidegger remarks, as everyone "knows," we "actually only apprehend 'contents of consciousness'" (1985,

p. 30). Outside the organism and its objective boundaries, in the view of conventional textbook psychology, are physical energies. Inside, by contrast, exist meanings. And the question then fatefully becomes, How does what's out there get in here?

Describing our everyday meanings hermeneutically as they present themselves in their natural lifeworld context, meanings turn out to be anything but subjective features of an internal mental landscape. Things show themselves rather the only place they could show themselves, which is in the place from which they confront us. Things and people, as things and people, do not encounter us inside at all. Meanings haven't "gotten in," but, to the contrary, are rather all around us—where objective thought locates only physical energies. Descriptively, the universal setting for all our meanings is the lifeworld. Meanings are *lifeworld* events. In Gurwitsch's words, "We do not, so to speak, move within a self-contained domain of interiority" (1974, p. 243). On the contrary, "It is the thing itself that presents itself . . . and with which we are in contact" (ibid., p. 236). "Our direct and immediate objects are the very things, persons, states of affairs . . . with which we are dealing" (Gurwitsch, 1970, p. 366). We do not, Merleau-Ponty remarks, grasp ourselves "as a microcosm into which messages of external events would make their way mediately. . . . [Our] gaze extends over the things themselves" (1963, p. 189).

Phenomenology's Theory of Intentionality

"Because of the intentionality of consciousness," Gurwitsch remarks, "we are in direct contact with the world. Living our conscious life, we are 'at' the world, 'at' the things encountered in that world" (1974, p. 236). *Intentionality* is phenomenology's name for that invariant structure of events of meaning by which human behavior is related to nonmental lifeworld meanings, to what is not behavior, to behavior's others. Behavior, structured intentionally, always is aiming at and attaining meanings. When we perceive something, for example, we are not dealing with a subjective modification of the mind, but with the very lifeworld meaning itself. In Heidegger's words, "That toward which perception is directed in conformity with its sense is the perceived itself" (1982, p. 63). "Perceiving is a *release* of extant things which *lets them be encountered*" (ibid., p. 70). "When I look, I am not intent upon seeing a representation of something, but the chair. . . . I simply see *it*—it itself" (Heidegger, 1985, pp. 35–37). Perception concerns itself with whatever is being perceived and by no means with some presumed content of consciousness. Merleau-Ponty insists that we "take literally what vision teaches us: namely, that through it we come in contact with the sun and the stars" (1964a, p. 187).

"Every comportment," Heidegger writes, "is a comporting-toward"

(1982, p. 58). Thus, in accordance with the usual formulation of the intentionality of behavior, perceiving is always perceiving *of* something, wishing is always wishing *for* something, dreaming is dreaming *of* something, remembering is in every case remembering *of* something, lifting is a lifting *of* something, conceptualizing is a conceptualizing *of* something, hating is always hating *of* something, and so forth. Neither what is perceived, wished for, remembered, dreamt of, conceptualized, lifted, hated is a mental modification, an inner part of ourselves. All are others rather, lifeworld others to which intentional behavior is directed. All in all, then, by the theory of intentionality, we are directly involved with meanings, and by no means with inner mental states. Consciousness, by this theory, is simply not, as one introductory psychology textbook puts it, a "state in which a person is aware of sensations, thoughts, and feelings" (Pettijohn, 1989, p. 401).

What we perceive, by the theory of intentionality, is no inner representation, but then neither is what we "only" think about or "just" remember. Meanings thought about or meanings remembered share with meanings perceived (from which they originate) a place beyond behavior, beyond thinking and remembering and perceiving, in the lifeworld. Thus, Heidegger remarks that, even when we are "merely thinking of something, what is represented is not a representation, not a content of consciousness, but the matter itself" (1985, p. 35). When we recall a sailboat trip, he goes on to say, what is remembered is the sailboat and the trip itself and not some representation of them in consciousness. And he points out in another context that even in the perceptual illusion of a tree appearing as a man, what is given is not a representation of the man in consciousness but the man himself, the meaning the man is (1982, p. 63). We encounter, moreover, as Gurwitsch points out, "numbers and geometrical systems, which are not mental states or psychological occurrences" (1974, p. 235)—they are no more inner psychic occurrences than the chair I'm sitting on. Our meanings, then, are in every case other to ourselves. Meanings do not populate the mind. The only reason for continuing to hold otherwise is the objectivistic presupposition by whose logic meanings simply must be located on this side of the skin border, in an inner realm of mind. Not bound by the ideology of objectivism—human behavior is neither inside nor outside *objectively*, and neither are its meanings—phenomenology is free to portray meanings where it finds them; namely, beyond behavior as that toward which behavior aims, beyond behavior in their sheer otherness to behavior, beyond behavior with a life and hold of their own. Phenomenology takes quite seriously experiences in which ideas hit people, for example, like the experiences of an Einstein, who is said to have had to use care shaving lest he cut himself when taken by surprise by new ideas.

With Husserl's theory of intentionality—with the insight, that is, that the mind is not a self-contained domain of interiority—the Cartesian dualism that proclaimed such a realm breaks down (Gurwitsch, 1974, p. 235), as does the radicalized Cartesianism that is objectivistic monism.

Intentionality and Psychologism

Lifeworld meanings, in phenomenology's theory of intentionality, are by no means contents of the mind. Nor are they reducible to the psychological events that sponsor them, to activities of the brain or the mind. Essential to Husserl's launching of phenomenology was his rejection of just this viewpoint, a doctrine called *psychologism*. Meanings are not reducible to psychological processes and structures—not even when these processes are abnormal in character, hallucinations, for example, or belong to an individual judged to be disturbed, a Van Gogh, for example. Meanings instead have a structure, a logic, and a dynamics of their own. A theoretical formulation in physics, for example, belongs to the network of formulations that is physics and not to the psyche. A work of art is just that, a *work*, beyond the psyche, with requirements all its own, demands that weigh upon artist and audience alike. A story has a life and dynamics of its own that are not reducible to the psychological processes of the person who first told it. And when a myth—or a dream—is alive, its nonpsychological dynamics has us in its grips. Myths motivate us, at times to selfless behavior, at times to violence. The dream terrifies us sometimes, uplifts us at other times, has something peculiar about it most of the time. We sometimes get more worked up at the recall of an incident than when it first happened, becoming angry at the lifeworld someone himself who did wrong by us, and by no means at that "someone" as the inner outcome of the brain's creative activities. Nor does the Gestalt manner in which meanings exist, their organizational constants (their "dynamic self-distribution" and the laws that govern it; see Chapters 5 and 6), come down to workings of the psyche. Conventional psychology, reducing meanings to their objective conditions, is a psychologism. To psychologistic reductionism, phenomenological psychology opposes the definitive priority of the lifeworld and its nonpsychological logic.

Intentionality and Sensations

"In opposition to the subjectivistic misinterpretations that perception is directed in the first instance only to something subjective, that is, to sensations, it was necessary to show that perception is directed toward the extant itself" (Heidegger, 1982, p. 71). Phenomenology's descriptive aspirations, and in particular its theory of intentionality, amount to a definitive abandoning of the notion of sensation, of "sensation and perception." By the phenomenological account of meaning events, we are in direct contact with things that are "meaningful patterns" (a la Merleau-Ponty), with things that have an organization of their own, and not with fragmented sensory impressions. Once the "prejudice of sensation" has been set aside, what is given immediately is not the sensory impression, the external world making its way into the organism, "but the meaning, the structure, the spontaneous arrangement of parts" (Merleau-Ponty, 1962, p. 58). It is simply not the case that we construct things out of meaningless—"raw and disconnected"—sensations (ibid., p. 37). When we look at something, say, a tree, that to which we are directed, that with which we are involved, is the perceived tree itself: seeing the tree as the lifeworld meaning it is is the very essence of the perception, its total thrust. To affirm that, in Heidegger's words, we are "in the first place oriented toward sensations is all just pure theory" (1982, p. 63). Or, as Heidegger puts it elsewhere, "In our very being in the world we are first always already involved with the world itself, and not with 'sensations' first and then, on the basis of a kind of theater, finally involved with the things" (1985, p. 266).

If one indeed supposes, as conventional psychology tends to, that a sensation can be isolated—"a touch, a sound, a taste, a splash of color, and so on" (Wortman et al., 1988, p. 85)—what in fact is being indicated is a perception, not a sensation. "What is called sensation," in the words of Merleau-Ponty, "is only the most rudimentary of perceptions" (1962, p. 241). Even the simplest something always is situated somewhere, with an assigned lifeworld place, a meaning against its ground. The single tone that breaks the silence is never an isolated sound. The very lifeworld silence it breaks, standing within the tone's essential event structure as the tone's ground, is constitutive of the tone as it comes to be heard. A dot is only a dot against the whiteness of the paper on which it appears. The dot is a lifeworld something and not a sensation. From a descriptive point of view, then, we never come across a sensation, nor could we. We never encounter an isolated anything—anything whatsoever is always what it is against something else. What is called *sensation*, then, is simply not, as one textbook has it, "the process of responding to a simple physical stimulus, such as a spot of light or a musical note" (Hassett and White, 1989, p. 140). One is always two, and indeed three, four, and so on. Sensations do not exist.

Intentionality and Introspection

Phenomenology's theory of intentionality, properly understood, puts to rest once and for all the notion that phenomenology is any sort of introspectionism. Phenomenology in fact explicitly denies that human beings ever deal with mental contents: with sensations, images, and meanings in an inner and private sphere of consciousness. Phenomenology, taking things for what they integrally show themselves to be rather than breaking them down into the elements of consciousness conventionally said to constitute them, unabashedly commits what psychological introspectionism has called the *stimulus error*. Phenomenology is the science of meaning events and not of inner consciousness. In point of fact, conventional psychology, and the currently popular information processing model of cognition in particular, resemble certain basic traits of introspectionism (cf. Neisser, 1976, p. 7) in a way that phenomenology never could.

By insisting on the intentionality of human behavior, then, phenomenology has left behind any sort of subjective approach to things. Given this rejection and given the amount of attention phenomenology has directed to the exploration of the nonpsychological lifeworld, it is ironic indeed that conventional psychology, when it pays any attention to the phenomenology being discussed here, describes it as an essentially subjective approach to behavior. However, in view of conventional psychology's tenacity in maintaining itself as a radicalized version of Cartesian philosophy, which is to say, as an objectivism, it is understandable that this psychology can consider subjective only a psychology that is preoccupied above all with the self's involvement in meaning. Conventional psychology moves within the subject-object dichotomy, in terms of which ontology the self and its meanings are termed subjective by prior definition, by reason of the prior "mathematization of nature."

The Tree in Bloom in the Meadow

This chapter on phenomenology draws to its conclusion with a telling passage in which Heidegger challenges the notion that meanings exist inside us, that "the world is our idea":

> We stand before a tree in bloom . . . and the tree stands before us. The tree faces us. The tree and we meet one another, as the tree stands there and we stand face with it. As we are in this relation of one to the other and before the other, the tree and we *are*. This face-to-face meeting is not, then, one of these "ideas" buzzing about in our heads. . . . While science records the brain currents, what becomes of the tree in bloom? What becomes of the meadow? . . . What becomes of the face-to-face, the meeting, . . . in which the tree presents itself and [someone] comes to stand face-to-face with the tree? . . . Does the tree stand "in our consciousness," or does it stand in the meadow? Does the meadow lie in the soul, as experience, or is it spread out there on earth? Is the earth in our head? Or do we stand on the earth? . . . It will not do to admit . . . that, naturally, we are standing face to face with a tree in bloom, only to affirm the very next moment as equally obvious that this view, naturally, typifies only the naive, because pre-scientific, comprehen-

sion of things. . . . In truth, we are today rather inclined to favor a supposedly superior physical and physiological knowledge, and to drop the blooming tree. . . . The thing that matters first and foremost, and finally, is not to drop the tree in bloom, but for once let it stand where it stands. Why do we say "finally"? Because to this day, thought has never let the tree stand where it stands. (1968, pp. 41–44)

3 Existence

Things recede into relations.

—*Heidegger*, 1985, p. 187

Existential Phenomenology

Phenomenology is the plea for a confrontation with "the things themselves," phenomena on their own lifeworld ground. And phenomenology at the same time is a method for understanding these "things," these everyday events of meaning: an *interpretive describing* of the *invariant structure* of meaning events. One such lifeworld structure is intentionality (Chapter 2). Martin Heidegger has given intentionality in particular and phenomenology in general a concrete and historical, possibility-oriented, *existential* orientation. This chapter surveys Heidegger's and, to a lesser extent, Merleau-Ponty's, *existential phenomenological* approach to meaning events, attempting in the process to further elucidate the invariant structure of such events. The chapter concerns itself with the relation between meaning and world, and with the openness of human beings, alongside one another, to lifeworld events of meaning presencing. Chapter 4 continues this exploration by considering the *existential space of meaning*.

Meaning, Involvement, World

The preceding chapter on phenomenology has insisted that, rather than populating an inner realm of the mind, everyday meanings stand in every case in the lifeworld as the others of someone's concern (theory of intentionality). Meanings indeed stand where they stand, but it is an invariant of events of meaning that meanings do not stand alone. No meaning is ready-made in-itself, self-defined, able to be itself without the cooperation of anything else. The project of an existential phenomenology proposes instead a field theory of meaning presencing. Meanings exist in a network of references to one another. This network in its totality, it will be seen, is what Heidegger calls *world*. This chapter begins by considering meanings other than our fellow human beings, meanings such as chairs, trees, tulips, malls, cars, and lawn mowers and their relations to one another within the referential totality of the world. How Galilean science rids itself of such lifeworld meanings then once again is considered, this time in view of meaning's relationship to world. Attention next is given to those who share the world with us, to the role of other people in our lives. Finally considered is the character of human existence itself, the being of that being which constitutes the openness necessary for the presencing of any meaning whatsoever.

Ready-to-Hand Meanings within the World

What makes a thing be a thing for Heidegger (that is, be the everyday meaning it is) is its place in a context of things, its function or involvement in a network of other everyday things. A lawn mower, for example, is geared for the service it can render in cutting the lawn. A hammer is "in order to hammer"; a door is "'in order to make leaving, entering, and closing possible.' Equipment is 'in order to'" (Heidegger, 1982, p. 292). The everyday thing that we employ to accomplish something—*equipment*—is what it is, then, in terms of its use. A lawn mower is never more a lawn mower, never more fulfilled in its meaning, than when it is cutting the lawn, the hammer when it is hammering. Precisely when it is put into service does the tool presence as what it is, not when it is merely being looked at (Heidegger, 1962a, p. 98). Its lifeworld involvement in writing on the blackboard first makes a piece of chalk be this "chalk-thing." Chalk is what it is in its place in the lifeworld. "The child's question, 'What is this thing?', is thus answered by stating what it is used for, defining what one finds in terms of what one does with it" (Heidegger, 1985, pp. 260–261). Things *are* what they are used for.

Meaning and environmental thing are inseparable from the first. Nothing is before or behind the meaning; no objective substratum, such as presupposed by traditional modern thought, is more basic than the meaning, to which the meaning would become attached only secondarily. A property of usefulness, the quality of "chalkness" or "chairness," is not something that the mind subjectively and constructively tacks onto the inner effects (sensations) of objective stuff (environmental stimuli) to bring about the everyday meaning chalk or chair. Rather such meanings are given all around us in their involvement with and reference to one another, which is at the same time the possibility of our entering into relation with them. The lawn mower is involved in a network of other things: gasoline to fuel it, oil for lubrication, fertilizer, hose and sprinkler, a garage for storage. And the lawn mower takes its place in the garage with other yard equipment. The garage is part of the house, the house part of the neighborhood, the neighborhood part of the town, and so on. The lawn mower belongs to a broad equipmental context or milieu. Precisely in occupying a place in such a lifeworld context does the lawn mower first truly become itself. Likewise, when we hammer, "we let the hammer function *with* something" (Heidegger, 1982, p. 293): with nails, to hang this picture, and thus decorate our home. There is always a "totality of equipment" in which the single everyday thing takes its place to become the meaning it is. Equipment always belongs to other equipment: the pad on which we write to the pen with which we write, to the desk at which we sit, to the lamp that provides the light we need, to the chair on which we sit (Heidegger, 1962a, p. 97). Everyday things like tables and chairs are not bits of extension in objective space, which added up somehow, only later come to constitute the room in which they are located. Rather what is closest to us is the room as a place in which to reside (ibid., p. 98). All in all, then, individual everyday things take their place in every case in an everyday context. It is precisely the contextual involvement of a piece of furniture in a room that makes it the meaning it is.

Heidegger calls everyday equipment—the "in order to" with its multiple references of something to something—the *ready-to-hand*. A ready-to-hand thing—a hammer, a lawn mower, a piece of chalk—is an everyday lifeworld meaning with an everyday use. The reference of an everyday meaning to a totality of involvements, its place in this totality and the service it can render, makes up a meaning's *readiness-to-hand* (ibid.). The readiness-to-hand of a hammer, for example, consists in its place relative to nails, saw, and other equipment, *in order to* make something secure, and in this way ensure ourselves of shelter when the weather turns bad: hammering is "for the sake of" protection against bad weather (ibid., p. 116).

Not only equipment in the narrower sense, however, gives itself in one and the same totality of involvements. Other everyday meanings, meanings found in nature, are equally ready-to-hand. A lawn mower is unthinkable, for example, without lawns, without grass with its capacity to grow. And there is the sun, which shines on the grass and makes it grow. And there are clouds and lakes which provide the lawn—and us—with water. Moreover, we find in a single web a great variety of life forms: animals, insects, fish, plants, trees—sources of annoyance at times, but also of clothing, food, lumber, leather. And we find minerals that we employ, for example, in manufacturing cars. And there is the quarry of rock we use in constructing our buildings. The lawn, the grass, the sun, food, animals, minerals, trees, quarries, all such meanings are ready-to-hand. They make up, together with such things as hammers and lawn mowers, a single totality of references to one another.

As already noted, *world* is Heidegger's technical name for this *referential totality* of the ready-to-hand, this totality of involvements of things with one another. World is the total context of relationships with which we find ourselves concernfully preoccupied in daily life; all our ready-to-hand meanings in their presencing, the all-embracing horizon of all events of ready-to-hand meaning. World, as world, has the character of the "totality of relations of the in-order-to, for-the-sake-of, for-that-purpose, to-that-end" (Heidegger, 1982, p. 262).

Heidegger speaks of "the referential whole of the world" as "a whole of *significant* connections," and he names this whole of significant connections *significance.* The "for-the-sake-of-which," the "in-order-to," the "towards-this," the "in-which" (that *in which* something is involved), the "with-which" (that *with which* something is involved), these relationships form a "primordial totality"; "the relational totality of this signifying we call '*significance*' " (1962a, p. 120). Significance, Heidegger goes on to say, is what constitutes the structure of the world. Everyday ready-to-hand meanings *signify* one another (as "in-order-to," "towards-this," "in-which," "with-which") at the same time as they *signify* some human purpose (some "for-the-sake-of-which"): chair signifies desk signifies computer; these signify work; work signifies paycheck; paycheck signifies the purchase of food; food signifies nourishment. This signifying is the fundamental structural invariant or constant in the referential connectedness of things to one another, as well as in their assignment to human life. The term *significance* frequently is used in what follows to indicate the world in its essential structure as a "referential totality" of the ready-to-hand. The verb *signify* also will come to be frequently used, beginning especially with the next chapter, to indicate the way lifeworld meanings reach out to and signal one another.

In everyday life we never come across things in isolation from one another, fragments. "Things constantly step back into the referential totality, or, more properly stated, in the immediacy of everyday occupation they never even first step out of it. . . . Things recede into relations" (Heidegger, 1985, p. 187). Everyday things give rise to and define each other—become what they are, a chair, a table, a lamp, a pen—as has been noted, in terms of their "contextual involvement" with one another. Ready-to-hand meanings, internally related to, and thus "in," one another, from the first, have an essentially relative character. Confronted with any ready-to-hand thing, world as the totality of references or involvements already is projected. "World is understood beforehand when objects encounter us" (Heidegger, 1982, p. 299). "The world is that in terms of which the ready-to-hand is ready-to-hand" (Heidegger, 1962a, p. 114). Something is something, then—meaning, what it is—as part to whole. The totality of relations, the whole, precedes the part; the network or context of items has priority over the single item. Any part is first encountered as a member of some whole. Even when we wonder what some piece of equipment is, it encounters us in terms of the significance of the world as "something for we don't know what." Ready-to-hand things, rather than being *in*-themselves, are invariantly *beyond* themselves to their context of other ready-to-hand meanings. Any everyday meaning whatsoever takes its place, then, within some *context of significance* that is determinative of it as the ready-to-hand meaning it is. Reworking an earlier formulation, it may be said that something is what it is—*"something as something"* (Heidegger, 1985, p. 261)—by reason of the place it comes to hold within a larger context of significance. Significance makes any particular ready-to-hand thing possible, allowing it to presence precisely as what it is (Heidegger, 1962a, pp. 135–138). Everyday ready-to-hand meanings *are* within the world.

The Present-at-Hand and Its Origin in the Ready-to-Hand

Ready-to-hand meanings, referred to one another and to us in what is their essential, belong to world. The world in its significance is anything but a mere *sum* of its parts, a mere aggregate of meanings. "The world does not 'consist' of the ready-to-hand" (ibid., p. 106). To suppose that our first reality is that of isolated objects, which we would then have to piece together to make up a world, would be to seriously misunderstand the world's significance. It is rather the case, as suggested in the preceding section, that the world is prior to every single individual ready-to-hand meaning. The whole of references—ready-to-hand meanings signifying one another, referentiality, significance—is prior. Things are relations, not beings in-themselves. "In a workshop . . . the totality of involvements which is constitutive for the ready-to-hand in its readiness-to-hand is 'earlier' than any single item of equipment" (ibid., p. 116). There are, in Heidegger's existential field theory of the presencing of meanings, no absolute beings, nothing self-defined and existing objectively in-itself as a bit of pure extension, nothing objective—or subjective, for that matter. We can, of course, *take* things as absolute and then proceed to merely look at them in their sheer *presence* in-themselves, for example, in their sheer spatial extension (objectivity). Conventional psychology does just that. Galilean science, in its movement of abstracting and idealizing, turns away from the broader context of significance in which things "around the corner" from each other give rise to one another as ready-to-hand meanings. The realm of what Heidegger calls the *present-at-hand* makes its appearance in just this turning away. Heidegger defines *presence-at-hand* as a relationship that objective entities, entities defined by their prior projection as ready-made units of pure extension, have to each other in terms of their objectivity. Objectively present-at-hand entities are projected in such a way as to be simply available in their full presence in-themselves, without any reference beyond themselves to significance. And the objective properties these beings are then made to manifest, along with the objective effects they are then seen to exact on one another in three-dimensional space, can be calculated with a great deal of accuracy.

The Cartesian project of nature as pure extension (Chapter 1) for Heidegger is "a project of thingness which, as it were, skips over the things" (1967, p. 92). This prior projection is concerned with the world that surrounds us, "it is a project of thingness." But this world is projected in such a way that everyday ready-to-hand meanings are bypassed altogether, everyday things are "skipped over." When an everyday piece of equipment, a hammer, for instance, is set up in its objectivity, it undergoes a change. The tool's relations of significance having been neutralized, the world takes its leave. The hammer stops being an everyday meaning with an everyday use. No longer taken as something used to fasten things, the "hammer" becomes this present-at-hand object with, for example, a certain calculable property of heaviness. It turns into an object that, governed by gravitation, exerts a measurable pressure on what lies beneath it. A ready-to-hand everyday meaning has been converted into a present-at-hand unit of mass lacking significance that, when set in motion, causally affects ("moves") other units of mass. This manner of talking is based on what is suitable for nature considered as pure three-dimensional extension. We are encountering an everyday meaning, but in a new way. A ready-to-hand thing of use has been converted into a present-at-hand something merely there to be *looked at* (Heidegger, 1962a, p. 412). An everyday meaning has been transformed into an objectively calculable something, an in-itself whose "place" has become "a spatiotemporal position, a 'world-point' " no different from any other; no longer occupying an environmental place, the "hammer" is now in one of "a pure multiplicity of positions" (ibid., p. 413). All in all, then, for Cartesian thought, the thing is not your everyday ready-to-hand meaning. It is "material" instead, "a point of mass in the pure space-time order" (Heidegger, 1967, p. 51). Meaning has been stripped from a nature that has now come to be projected in advance as pure three-dimensional extension.

What is important for the purposes of this book is to realize that one first gets to the realm of presence-at-hand, the objectively present-at-hand first comes into view, only by going through the ready-to-hand and only by means of a deliberate divesting of the ready-to-hand of its significance, of its readiness-to-hand. Or, as was pointed out in Chapter 2 ("The Lifeworld"), one gets to nature objectively conceived only by a lifeworld-grounded process of abstraction and idealization (Husserl's "mathematization of nature"). Presence-at-hand arises precisely in the shifting of one's manner of presupposing things. Readiness-to-hand being the original state of our surrounding meanings, to arrive at what is there for a mere being looked at (the present-at-hand), "cognition must first penetrate *beyond*" the referentially involved meanings of our everyday concern (Heidegger, 1962a, p. 101). The world of everyday meanings, the lifeworld, as has been duly noted, is "our first, last, and only world," "the only truly real world" (Gurwitsch, 1974, p. 17), the ultimate site of even the most abstract of endeavors. The lifeworld holds a definitive priority. The present-at-hand in the final analysis is *relative*, too: relative to the ready-to-hand that is its origin; relative as well to the objectivizing abstraction that, projecting it in advance, first sets it up as *absolute* and in-itself.

Phenomenology rejects the view that nature at its most basic is the way it shows itself when subjected to the objectifying abstraction of Galilean science-Cartesian philosophy, rejects the view that nature's true being is objective presence-at-hand. Phenomenology, as remarked earlier, aims at a recovery from just such a lostness in what after all is only one way of looking at things. Its readiness-to-hand disregarded, "nature" is rendered merely present-at-hand. But then "the nature which 'stirs and strives,' which assails us and enthralls us as landscape, remains hidden" (Heidegger, 1962a, p. 100). The plants the botanist studies are not the flowers in our garden (ibid.). Having stripped readiness-to-hand away from the world, having in this way ordered objects to come forward and show themselves in-themselves and in essential isolation from one another, moreover, having proclaimed the resulting objective "world" to be the ultimate founding reality—the "real world" as opposed to the "world as we know it"—there is no way back to the significance of the world. The presupposition that perception is but the interpretive tacking on of epiphenomenal meaning to presumably ultimate units of mass leaves the everyday world with barely phantom status. The only way "back" to the significance of the world is never to leave it in the first place; is not to explain the realm of the ready-to-hand through what is derived abstractly from it only late in the game.

Conventionally objectivistic psychology attempts to explain human behavior and its everyday meanings in terms of abstract, present-at-hand (objective) processes dominated by linear, "end-to-end causality" (Merleau-Ponty, 1968, p. 232). Phenomenological psychology, a term that now indicates a psychology that draws its inspiration from phenomenological thought as given an existential orientation, by contrast, views meaning as something other than a stage in a present-at-hand chain. Ready-to-hand meanings, within the world rather than inside our heads, are seen as ahead of human beings. Human life in this way comes to be viewed as moved not by a mechanical, external causality, not by present-at-hand motivational forces in objective space, but by situated lifeworld meanings, with a force and weight of their own.

The World and Other People

In our preoccupation with the world, this totality of references of everyday things to one another, we are constantly coming across a special kind of meaning: other human beings. Other people are special meanings of ours because they have the same preoccupation with the world that we do. Human beings are invariantly preoccupied with the world together, open communally to lifeworld meaning events. To be *someone* is necessarily to be *with other someones*. The ready-to-hand thing being manufactured, Heidegger points out, is designed in view of the person who is to use or wear it. Encountering such a thing, we thus come across other people as well (1962a, p. 100). The picture being hung, the lawn being cut, the chalk being used, the contract being drafted, the cow being milked—all these are done with other people in mind. Human beings are determined from the first and always by *being-with* other human beings (Heidegger, 1982, p. 296). We share events of meaning presencing, then, the very world in which ready-to-hand meanings are encountered, with one another. "'Thou' means 'you who are with me in a world' " (ibid., p. 298). People are "at" the world together. *We* form, with the referential totality of the ready-to-hand, a single field or system (Chapter 14).

"Things are things," Merleau-Ponty remarks, "accessible to other perceiving subjects" (1963, p. 189). In the world together, we coperceive the world, cosponsor nonpsychological meaning. We share meanings with one another in their very coming to formation in their place of involvement within the world. Meanings, beyond any one of us and standing where they stand in the lifeworld, are invariantly comeanings, coperceptions. We do not each of us process information instigated by an external world, sensations, inside ourselves, only then, on the foundation of such an internal processing, to get the lifeworld and its meanings out as mental end products. People "process" the world itself, not effects impressed on them by external stimuli; and people "process" the world together. We and our friend, to use Merleau-Ponty's illustration, point out to each other the features of the town we are visiting (1962, pp. 405–406). When our friend gestures toward the church, it is the gesture itself that shows the building to us, the building itself. Our friend is not producing visions inside us that are merely similar to the ones she is having inside herself. It is rather that her gestures "invade" our world and guide our gaze. Each of us does not have an inner flow of sensations only indirectly related to a similar flow inside the other; we are never aware of being confined to a realm of inner sensations, nor do we think other people are either (ibid.). We are present in and explore the town together, the town itself. The town is "the same for both of us, . . . down to its very thisness" (ibid., p. 406). People, giving their experiences of things to one another, have these experiences together. Our experience of one another consists in just such a sharing, in having experiences of meaning in common, in giving meanings to one another. Individuals are in communication with one another through the world in which they both have a stake from the first.

Shared preoccupation with world and, on that basis, coexistence, are fundamental facts of human life, then, invariants of its structure. People are not objectively outside one another, private spheres of subjectivity tucked away inside their skin. To know what another person is up to, we do not consult an inner replica (interpreted sensory impressions) representative of that someone, and then proceed to infer what's on their mind inside our mind, as the conventional psychology of basic human processes would require. Engaged with other people in the world of our everyday concern—implicated in one another's destinies in our communal preoccupation with the world—from the first and always, we directly perceive rather what others are up to, hear their hopes and frustrations from their very lips. We always and already are beyond ourselves to one another, interwoven at once into the world's significance and into one another's lives. We are "at" meanings within the world together. We explore the town together, together enjoy the concert, talk to one another about our common meanings, share the joke. We are by no means encapsulated subjects, who only later must make the move to get out of ourselves and achieve contact with one another. We are a *being-with* one another, a being someone together. Our communal existence in the world is discussed further in Chapter Fourteen, "The Bodily Self–Other Selves–World System."

Dasein: Openness to the World

Dasein: Being in the World

Da in German means *there* and *Sein* means *to be*. The title *Dasein* taken literally, therefore, means *to be there, there being*. It is the term Heidegger gives to human being as "*the* site which being requires in order to disclose itself" (1959, p. 171). The human being, Heidegger says, "is the site of openness, the there [Da]" (ibid.). "The Dasein is its Da, its here-there" (Heidegger, 1982, p. 300), the openness of events of meaning, the openness that meanings, not subsisting ready-made in-themselves, need in order to come to pass.

Because meaning invariantly occurs as part to whole, the openness of Dasein to events of meaning is from the first a preoccupation with the referential totality of the world, with significance—always, as pointed out in the preceding section, in structural unity (functional interdependence) with other Daseins. Dasein, the "there" of being, is openness to the world; that is, to the final context or network that enables the presencing of any meaning whatever. Heidegger calls this essential openness of Dasein to the world *being-in-the-world*. Dasein as being-in-the-world is a "dwelling in familiarity with" the world, a "being involved with" it, a "competence" in its regard. "Self and world belong together" (ibid., p. 298), and in such a way that for Dasein to be familiar with world is what makes Dasein be Dasein (Heidegger, 1962a, p. 119). Dasein is *"always already 'outside'* in the world"—outside not in the sense of on the other side of the objective boundary of the skin—but "'outside' as . . . dwelling with the world" (Heidegger, 1985, p. 164), always and already involved with a world, preoccupied from the first with a network of everyday ready-to-hand meanings.

Things become what they are within the world—the chair becomes a chair; the chalk, chalk; the hammer, a hammer; the sun, the sun overhead—precisely for Dasein, for that being whose being it is to be outside with them in their involvement with one another, for that being whose being it is to deal in competent familiarity with the world (see the subsection "Dasein: Existence" for further comments on this competence of being-in-the-world). Dasein's openness to the world consists in letting meanings be, in letting ready-to-hand things become involved with one another within the world, in letting them function, in using them for some purpose or another. Dasein is implicated in every event of meaning whatsoever: whenever something shows itself as itself, Dasein is already on the scene. Without the openness of Dasein, things would not have the opportunity they need to assume their function within a context of significance, which means they would not appear as themselves: they would not be meanings.

Dasein is openness to world, then, the "there" of being (meaning presencing), being-in-the-world. The following sections consider some other ways in which Heidegger has characterized Dasein: as *submitted to world*, as *existence*, as *surpassing to world*. These characterizations all aim at the same essential openness of Dasein to the referential totality of the world.

Dasein: Submitted to World

Dasein is itself only in being preoccupied with a context of the ready-to-hand. Dasein is *submitted* to world from the first. The world and its meanings, and not some inner self and its cultivation, are Dasein's possibility, that to which Dasein always and already is given over. Dasein has been *thrown* into the world, surrendered to it. "The Dasein must be *with* things" (Heidegger, 1982, p. 161). Dwelling with things, it is Dasein's destiny to be concerned with them, to enjoy them at times, to become distressed by them at others. Dasein is by no means preoccupied with ideas inside its head, then, is not limited to commerce with modifications of the mind, a la Descartes and conventional psychology, but has been handed over in its deepest interiority to the world of everyday ready-to-hand meanings. About this, its essential finiteness (finitude), human beings have no choice. As Merleau-Ponty puts it, we are "condemned to meaning." The intentionality of behavior (Chapter 2) is a basic expression of this submission of Dasein to the world. Dasein, not merely passing through this earthly domain, has been delivered over first, last, and always to the world of its concern. So completely has Dasein been given over in openness to the world that even when Dasein turns away from the world, as in sleep, the world stalks it, as in dreams, insisting on a renewed hearing. Dasein simply cannot slough off meaning and still be Dasein. So thorough is this submission to the world and the things that constitute it that Dasein, losing sight of the fact that its being lies in its openness, can find itself, as in our day, believing that it, too, is one of these things, things that it all too readily mistakes as ready-made and in-themselves (natural attitude); that it can forget that it is the "there" of being and instead take itself as one more objective thing, an objective body propelled into action by objective forces (conventional psychology), "a truly marvelous computer."

Dasein: Existence

Dasein, surrendered to the referential totality of the ready-to-hand from the first and always, "operates" within that totality. Dasein as being-in-the-world is a being absorbed in the references that constitute the readiness-to-hand of an equipmental complex (Heidegger, 1962a, p. 107). Dasein is familiarity with and competence toward everyday meanings within their network of significance, an "I am able to" with regard to the relational totality of world. Dasein, having the know-how of the world (Heidegger, 1982, p. 276) and "capable of" things, "is nothing but *being possible*. The Dasein which I myself am in each instance is defined in its being by my being able to say of it, *I am, that is, I can*" (Heidegger, 1985, p. 298). In what follows, I take the liberty of using the phrase *being possible* as an equivalent name for Dasein's being-in-the-world.

Heidegger calls the being of the being that is a match for the world (1962a, pp. 182–188) *existence* (1982, p. 28); adjectival form: *existential*. To say that Dasein exists is to say that "it is for the sake of its own capacity-to-be-in-the-world" (ibid., p. 170), "for the sake of [its] being and its capacity-for-being" (Heidegger, 1984, p. 186). Dasein exists "for its own sake." This does not mean that Dasein is destined to live selfishly or even to make its first priority the pursuit of its own fulfillment or actualization. Dasein's existence "for its own sake" means rather that Dasein is *someone*, is characterized by its *someoneness*, a someoneness it has to be. Dasein is the concrete being we human beings are, an entity in whose being we have a stake, an entity that we have *to be* in each instance in our own way (Heidegger, 1985, pp. 152–153). Existing, we are a task we have coming to ourselves. The term *existence* points to the fact that Dasein *is* as an ability to be in the world (Heidegger, 1962a, p. 274). "The being of Dasein is to be sought in its possible ways to be itself" (Heidegger, 1985, p. 248). Dasein, "for its own sake," is defined as being what it can be: defined, if you will, as having no definition.

To call Dasein's mode of being *existence* is to say that Dasein does not have a thing's manner of being. "'The Dasein exists' means, among other things, that the Dasein is in such a way that in being it comports itself toward what is extant but not toward it as toward something subjective" (Heidegger, 1982, p. 64). A window or chair does not exist because it cannot direct itself toward entities, cannot comport toward them intentionally. Existence—someone—in comporting toward lifeworld meanings, is a capacity to touch and be touched by them; and is at stake in how it lives this capacity for touching and being touched. Dasein has an interest in its own being. Dasein is immersed in itself as a possibility, the way no thing is. Dasein is its being and has this being to be and so, when we ask about Dasein, "we must at least ask, *Who* is this entity? and not, *What* is this entity?" (Heidegger, 1985, pp. 236–237). Not finished the way ready-to-hand things are—not having the mode of being of readiness-to-hand, much less that of presence-at-hand—Dasein's being is an issue for itself. Dasein cares and has no choice but to care.

Being able to touch and be touched, being a "who," an existing and caring someone, means being open to oneself as a self. Dasein, feeling itself, awakens to itself, awakens as itself, comes to be as a person. Thus, feeling its presence to itself as someone, Dasein immediately feels the presence of meanings. Feeling itself as an "I can," Dasein at once is confronted feelingly by the meanings to which it is submitted from the first. Dasein is what it can be, and what it can be is the "there" of meaning events: openness to "something as something," openness to something "as what" it can be. Meaning is precisely *for someone*, for that being that, feeling itself, feels things on their own ground of possibility within the world. All in all, then, Dasein—existence—is the event of someone and, with that, of the world. The "I can" of Dasein: someone being someone, openness to the "can-be" of meanings, things gaining "world-entry" (Heidegger). Things—not having it in them to discover themselves, not open to themselves or to anything else—cannot touch or be touched. Things do not have it in them to care.

Dasein is not encapsulated in itself; but so far as it *is*, in being its "to be," in being someone, it is preoccupied with nonpsychological lifeworld meanings. Dasein as existence has itself to achieve, and this task can be executed only in the world to which it is submitted from the first. To be a self is to have its selfhood, its being possible, to be. "It has been given to There-being [Dasein] *to be*" (Richardson, 1974, p. 64); and for Dasein "to be" is to live itself as a being delivered over to world. Dasein has its openness, in which its selfhood consists, to be.

Dasein: Surpassing to World

Dasein is characterized by a *not* at every turn: *not* its own maker, submitted to meanings and a world *not* of its own choice, *not* going to live forever, *not* able to get things into focus all at once, *not* closed off in itself, *not* guaranteed success in any of its projects (in fact guaranteed a measure of failure in them all), *not* fixed and finished in its actuality, a gamble never completely won. And yet essentially finite Dasein, existence, someone, can be itself, which can mean only that it can be its own possibility, its own "I can." *Not* a ready-made or finished thing, *not* closed off in-itself, Dasein is open, openness itself. Dasein is "possibility being" itself, beyond itself as a being, beyond itself to world. Dasein is not a subject, not inside itself, not confined to its own mental states. Dasein needs the world to be what it is; that is, what it can be—itself. Dasein surpasses all beings, including itself as a self-enclosed and self-sufficient subject, "and its surpassing is surpassing to world . . . . This surpassing makes it possible that Dasein can be something like itself" (Heidegger, 1984, p. 182). Existence "means to step beyond, or, better, having stepped beyond" (Heidegger, 1982, p. 300). It is this "over-and-out-beyond" of Dasein that enables it to comport to beings as the beings they are, makes it possible for Dasein to comport to "something as something."

Dasein is beyond itself—beyond all beings in their isolation from one another—to the network of references that is prior to and defines any individual meaning. Dasein, in encountering individual meanings, is already beyond them to world (significance): outside, outside existentially, outside to the world. "World, as the totality of the essential possibilities of Dasein as transcending, *surpasses* all actual beings" (Heidegger, 1984, p. 192).

Dasein as existence is the occurrence of a being that is beyond all beings, that is "over and out beyond" to the world. Dasein, the site where things have the very room they need to become involved with one another and thus to first manifest themselves for what they are—that is, to presence in their meaning—is an "overstepping" (surpassing) to the world. The various titles Heidegger attributes to Dasein all can be seen to converge here, in the characterization of Dasein as existential surpassing to the world. Cleared in itself and not through any other being, Dasein as being-in-the-world *is* itself the clearing, *is* itself the "there" (Heidegger, 1962a, p. 171). What is at issue for existence is to be the opening that it already is, the site beyond all beings that has been cleared for beings to show themselves, the site beyond all beings that first lets beings be what they are—the site that it takes someone to be, the site that someone has to be. Dasein's being is openness to the world, and the world, neither a being nor a collection of beings, is the horizon of meanings, the network that has been thrown open with the advent of Dasein, the open expanse in which beings can first signify one another and, taking their place as meanings, become themselves. "With the existence of [human life] there occurs an irruption into the totality of the essent such that, by this event, the essent becomes manifest in itself, i.e., manifest as essent" (Heidegger, 1962b, p. 235).

The intentional directedness of behavior to particular meanings (Chapter 2) is to be understood in the context of Dasein's existential surpassing to the world. Intentionality is not the getting out of itself of a subject, who then manages somehow to meet up with objects that are ready-made and present-at-hand in-themselves. "The Dasein does not 'transport' itself to the things by leaping out of a presumably subjective sphere over into a sphere of objects" (Heidegger, 1982, p. 161). Dasein rather has its origin in that very overstepping of every being by which beings gain "world-entry" (in Heidegger's words) as meanings. Dasein is outside to the world from the first, alongside the entities it is perceiving, remembering, imagining, wishing for, and so forth. Perception is not a subject going out and grasping things, only then to return, in Heidegger's words, "with one's booty to the 'cabinet' of consciousness" (1962a, p. 89). In perceiving, but also in remembering, it is rather the essential character of Dasein to remain forever outside (ibid.). Human existence was never inside its skin to begin with, as objectivism must suppose, and hence, as already has been suggested, for Dasein to be outside cannot mean that it crosses an objective skin boundary that closes it in on every side. "Outside" in its existential context, as also suggested, means rather always and already beyond all beings to world. It means never having to cross the boundary of the skin in the first place. It means that for Dasein the skin is no barrier at all, that Dasein always and already is ahead of itself. A self "for its own sake," Dasein overshoots itself and becomes an "upswing toward the possible"; as such, becomes "the occasion . . . for beings to emerge as beings" (Heidegger, 1984, p. 193), the occasion for the presencing of meanings within their context of significance. "World-entry" happens when transcendence (existential surpassing) happens. Everyday meanings, with the existence of Dasein, take their place on their own ground of significance within the world. Dasein lets things become manifest as "what and how they are" (ibid., p. 216), which is not to say that things are the way Dasein might have preferred them to be: "On the basis of [the upswing into possibility], Dasein is, in each case, beyond beings, as we say, but it is beyond in such a way that it, first of all, experiences beings in their resistance, against which transcending Dasein is powerless" (ibid., p. 215).

All in all, then, Dasein is the being that, beyond all beings, exists as a competence delivered over to meanings in their significance, a competence it has to be. Intentionality is not the directedness of a subject toward beings, not the activity of a consciousness "at" present-at-hand beings (objects in their sheer presence). Intentionality is to be understood rather in terms of the original surpassing of Dasein to world, as an occurrence within that surpassing. "With an adequate interpretation of intentionality, the traditional concept of subject and of subjectivity becomes questionable" (Heidegger, 1982, p. 65). It is not that Dasein does not relate to individual everyday meanings, but that such relations as Dasein does have to particular things take their origin in every case in Dasein's surpassing to the referential totality of the world.

Dasein: No Inner Realm

It is evident by now that existential phenomenology understands human life as consisting of anything but an inner mind. There is no such mind, no subjective realm to which we are confined and within which alone we encounter our meanings (the theory of ideas), no *consciousness* in that sense of the term. Dasein is not inside itself. "The thing does not relate to a cognitive faculty interior to the subject. . . . For the Dasein there is no outside, for which reason it is also absurd to talk about an inside" (ibid., p. 66). Dasein has no objective inside or outside, no subjective inside in sheer isolation from a split-off objective realm. Rather, Dasein constitutes, with things and other people, a single interwovenness (a la Merleau-Ponty). Dasein as existence thus always and already is ahead of itself to its possibilities as being-in-the-world, beyond every subjective or objective in-itself. Dasein is through and through a surpassing, "being-outside" (Heidegger, 1962a, p. 205). As Merleau-Ponty puts it, a human being is "nothing but a project of the world" (1962, p. 430), "nothing but a view of the world" (ibid., p. 406). And again, the self's comportments outstrip themselves so thoroughly that "no interiority of consciousness" is left at all (ibid., p. 376). And finally, "there is no inner man, man is in the world, and only in the world does he know himself" (ibid., p. xi).

4 The Existential Space of Meaning

Dasein brings its "there" along with it.

—*Heidegger*, 1962a, p. 171

Meaning and Existence

The early chapters of this book have objected to the notions of the *subjective* and the *objective* as dichotomized in modern thought: subjective as an inner and private realm of the mind and its meanings, a self-contained realm to which we alone have immediate and direct access; objective as a realm of physical processes spread out outside one another in the space-time continuum, a realm self-contained in-itself and utterly devoid of meaning. Particularly objected to has been the monistic doctrine of objectivism, the metaphysical belief to the effect that everything in the universe has an ultimately objective character, that reality and objectivity are synonymous terms. Objectivism is the reduction of all meanings to the status of epiphenomena, mere appearances in an inner and private realm of the subjective, inner models differing in kind from the "real" world "out there," something like that world at best, which "world" only a science in the Galilean style is judged capable of representing as it "truly" is. The objectivistic presupposition as adopted by conventional psychology is based on the will to predict and change behavior, on modern science as technology (compare Heidegger), on the ideology of control rather than on the desire to come to grips with meaning events on their own lifeworld ground. This presupposition, it is believed, has kept psychology from attaining its potential as a science adequate to human behavior and its meanings, and it will keep psychology from doing so as long as it remains in force. "The crises of psychology," writes Merleau-Ponty, "result from reasons of principle and not from some delay of the research in this or that particular domain" (1968, p. 23). To bring the underlying reasons for conventional psychology's continuing state of crisis to light, it will not do to remain at the level of the theories espoused as a matter of course in psychology, with an eye perhaps to their revision and improvement. The presuppositions underlying psychology's concepts, as well as the inherent limits of these presuppositions, rather have to be brought under careful scrutiny. What is called for is a critical philosophical approach to psychology.

Phenomenological psychology's hermeneutically oriented descriptions of the "things themselves" in the fullness of their event structure lead away from the objectivistic presupposition of an all-encompassing purely extended space, and at once away from its corollary, the merely subjective status of the self and its meanings. The "real" objective and the "mere" subjective appear increasingly to be but prejudices of modern thought. Chapters 2 and 3 of this book have proposed a philosophy alternative to that version of modern philosophy that founds conventional psychology. The self has been found not to reside inside a private and subjective realm, but instead always and already to be outside alongside the world and its meanings—outside in the existential and not in the objective sense. The brain, in the view of existential phenomenology, does not put the tree together inside the mind. Rather, the tree is found to be together over there where it stands, and we can walk over to it and feel its bark, grab hold of its branches, walk around it, climb it. And the tree is a whole of meaning in the midst of other trees, on the other side of the path, and a stone's throw from the park bench where we eat lunch. We are outside, and so is the tree, in an event of meaning presencing. We are outside together in the *open expanse of the "there,"* beyond beings in their sheer isolation from one another and into a network of references and assignments. Being possible (Dasein) spells the breaking open of a cleared site where meanings can signify each other as the relational totality of world: "There is world only insofar as Dasein exists" (Heidegger, 1984, p. 195). In the clearing is expressed the totality of concernful preoccupation (Dasein) and significance (world), the total interpenetration of a network of everyday meanings and of a community of human beings in a single field of relations or system (Chapter 14). Dasein's existential surpassing—its being "over and out beyond," its transcendence—is not, in Heidegger's words,

> a relation between interior and exterior realms such that a barrier belonging to the subject would be crossed over, a barrier that would separate the subject from the outer realm. . . . Transcendence lies in the fact that . . . beings, among which Dasein is and to which Dasein belongs, are surpassed by Dasein. . . . We characterize the basic phenomenon of Dasein's transcendence with the expression *being-in-the-world*. Insofar as Dasein exists, . . . beings have . . . already been overleapt, and beings thus possess the possibility of manifesting themselves in themselves. (Ibid., pp. 165–166)

Things can show themselves as themselves, as what they can be as meanings, because they are beyond themselves to one another in the referential totality of world, because they are beyond themselves at the same time to that being whose being consists precisely in its openness to this totality, to that being beyond itself to world. Viewing meanings in their essential relationship to the clearing (the "there," the "upswing into possibility") by no means diminishes the otherness of meaning, then, meaning's proper nonpsychological integrity within the lifeworld. Such a move in fact first allows a tree to stand where it stands, true to itself, in the meadow. A tree now comes into its own as the tree it is, not as an aggregate of "molecules in motion" in a realm of pure three-dimensional extension, not as a collection of billiard-ball-like particles set in motion by the forces of an objective nature, and not as a subjective meaning conferred upon meaningless sensations inside the organism, but as itself, as "that tree over there." The system of relations constitutive of worldhood, Heidegger remarks, provides just the basis everyday things need to manifest themselves as themselves, for what they are "'substantially,' 'in themselves'" (1962a, p. 122). In coming to terms with something in its place within a context of significance, Dasein—being possible—lets that something "*be* so-and-so *as* it is already" (ibid., p. 117).

By reason of significance, then, things come into their own as they are " 'substantially,' 'in-themselves' "; that is, as they are from themselves, as everyday things in the truth of their proper suchness. Outside, beyond themselves to one another within the referential totality of the world—outside, become meanings—things manifest themselves in their proper integrity as what they can be. A tree becomes what it is as a meaning, a tree manifesting itself as a tree, at that very moment when someone comes upon it in its place in the meadow. A chair is never more itself than when functioning within its context of other furniture. A word is truly itself only in signifying and being signified by other words. The tree, the chair, and the word first come into their own, into their truth, within a whole of significant connections. Something is what it is—a ready-to-hand meaning—within its context of significance for someone who is a competent familiarity in its regard. Everyday meanings are in the "there"; not objectively *in* it, but *in* it in terms of the existential space of meaning to be explicitly discussed in this chapter. Meanings, the self, and other people are *in* the existential space of possibility, where there is neither objective inside nor objective outside, in the existential space of being possible open to the possibilities of meaning.

The Primacy of Perception

Chapter 2 pointed to a fundamental priority of the lifeworld. It was also suggested there ("The Place of Everyday Meanings and Our Relation to Them") that the privileged lifeworld is first and foremost a perceptual realm, a realm of manifest sensible qualities. Individual lifeworld things, along with the lifeworld as a whole, show themselves in their concrete givenness as such sensible qualities, a network of interwoven colors, tastes, sounds, smells, tactile qualities, which lifeworld qualities are anything but isolated sensations. The sensible qualities that, signifying one another, constitute our everyday others come in a variety of sorts and gradations. Perceiving, our one avenue to the endlessly variable unities of sensible meaning that form our world, is communing with such unities, communing with the meanings themselves (Merleau-Ponty, 1962, p. 320). It is the perceived lifeworld, this language of sensible qualities, that first comes to expression in the openness of the "there." This perceptual lifeworld is basic to all our endeavors, the point of departure forever underlying even our most abstract notions and wildly idealistic undertakings. Dreams, memories, ideas all originate one way or another, and however distantly, in the directly perceived lifeworld. It is to this world that we find ourselves always and of necessity returning. The perceived lifeworld is the world of bright red tulips, smiling children, cheerful tunes, tall buildings, green grass, noisy lawn mowers, juicy apples. There is no way to prove something as fundamental as *the primacy of perception* (Merleau-Ponty, 1964a)—and who would want or need to? The primacy of perceived meanings such as the ones just cited, and indeed of the referential network of the perceived which embraces them all, is a given of our life, reality in the first place, the last word. The perceived world is the horizon within which all things presence and all human activities take place. In the words of Merleau-Ponty, "All consciousness is perceptual. . . . The perceived world is the always presupposed foundation of all rationality, all value and all existence" (ibid., p. 13). *Consciousness,* if indeed the word is to be retained, rather than an inner subjective realm, is first and foremost a perceiving of the referential network of sensible qualities (world) to which human life is submitted from the first and always. Consciousness is "turned primarily toward the world, turned toward things; it is above all a relation to the world" (ibid., pp. 116–117).

It is from the world of sensible qualities as these converse with one another as communicating wholes of meaning—the real world for phenomenology—that conventional textbook psychology abstracts. As has already been noted, there indeed is nowhere else on earth for anyone to begin. When conventional textbook psychology talks about stimuli, sensations, and brain processes and about internal meanings as outcomes, it has already left the concretely perceived lifeworld far behind. The abstract space of objective thought—the objective space of meaning projected by conventional psychology—is one from which any claim to originality on the part of directly perceived sensible meaning is excluded by prior definition. The concrete space of the lifeworld, by contrast, is a space defined by the prior givenness of sensible meaning. Just as insistently as natural-scientific psychology constructively locates meaning and the self in objective space, phenomenological psychology descriptively locates them in the perceptual space of the lifeworld. Just as insistently as the one excludes perceived meaning—sensible quality—from its fundamental space, the other includes it. In the objective space of meaning, the abstraction having been turned into the real, essentially mental meaning is made to derive from space constructed objectively. In the perceptual space of lifeworld significance, by contrast, nonmental meaning is taken as the basic and original, irreducible fact. As already noted, the perceptual space of the lifeworld here is termed *existential space,* the *existential space of meaning.*

The Existential Space of Meaning

Dasein is the upsurge of the "there," the advent of the open expanse where it is possible for things to presence from themselves in the fullness of their sensible concreteness. Existential space, cleared space, opens up with the "upswing into possibility" of Dasein and the world, of being-in-the-world.

The Space of the Existential Surpassing to the World

Existential space is the space thrown open with Dasein's surpassing to significance, the space where Dasein surpasses itself and every conceivable in-itself so as to be outside existentially with a network of sensible qualities expressing one another as lifeworld wholes of meaning. Existential space is first and foremost the way the "there" is concretely structured as an open expanse in which meanings and Dasein reach beyond themselves and commune with one another. The existential space of the perceived is a concrete growing together of Dasein and everyday meaning, the always and already accomplished surpassing of a community of Daseins to the concrete spatial interweaving of a network of the perceived.

Objective space is the three-dimensional space of units of mass. The existential space of surpassing, by contrast, is the space of internally related sensible qualities, of meaning growing into meaning; the space of qualities stretching back and forth to one another, reciprocally intending and qualifying one another, sharing a life. The continuousness of objective space, which can allow of no gaps, is the essential separation of units of mass (in-themselves) from one another. The clearedness of the existential space of significance, on the other hand, is one of gaps, openings, distances that unite rather than keep apart, a space where unity always and already is achieved in a thoroughly reciprocal signifying of one another of sensible qualities. Objective space is a space of local events, of "end-to-end causality" (Merleau-Ponty, 1968, p. 232); objective influences, as noted in Chapter 1, have to make their way through the continuum of objective space linearly, measure by measure, establishing actual physical contact as they go. Existential space, for its part, is translocal in character—in the sense that, with any perceived meaning whatsoever, what only later is called *objective space* and its measurably equal intervals always and already have been jumped. Translocal signifying rules existential space: every sensible thing awakens to its life through activities of signifying that already have transported it beyond its mere location. In existential space Dasein and sensible meanings are relative to one another in always and already being overleapt as beings, in the manner in which they are destined the one to the other in view of some context of significance.

Lived Dimensionality

The dimensionality of objective space (the three dimensions of pure extension) is space as constructed by conventional modern thought. The dimensionality proper to existential space is concretely lived, a *lived dimensionality* of spread out sensible qualities spreading out to one another, of stretched sensible qualities stretching to and interweaving with one another. Lived dimensionality is the radically qualitative, phenomenal spreadoutness of the existential surpassing to significance.

The lived dimensionality of existential space is the concrete stretch (tension), then, of sensible meanings spreading to one another in the lifeworld. A dimensionally expressed whole of sensible meaning is sensible moments dimensionally expressing one another. Existential space, anything but an abstraction, is a rich and promiscuous sensible significance spreading out around us as far as the eye can see, the ear can hear. Sensible qualities reach everywhere, back and forth in all directions, in the lived dimensionality of significance (existential space). The sturdy brown chair is linked to the nicely set table. Both belong to the thickly carpeted dining room with its off-white walls and ceiling. The house in its sensible givenness stretches to neighboring houses in their concrete givenness. The neighborhood stretches to other neighborhoods. The bustling town stretches to the verdant country; and the country, to the immense blue ocean. The ocean stretches to the verdant country, and the verdant country to the bustling town. The verdant country stretches both to the immense blue ocean and to the bustling town. The apple pie baking in the oven has an inherently wonderful smell to it, is hot to the touch, is turning golden brown, is sure to taste as good as it looks. The melody runs throughout the sensible sounds that constitute it. The juiciness of the orange stretches every which way inside its peel. The interest the novel holds for us lies in the actual unfolding of its narrative, in the sensible wholes of meaning called *words, sentences, paragraphs, chapters.* The loveliness of the face lies in the expressive qualities that dimensionally constitute it, from mouth to ears to eyes to nose to chin to cheeks. Real things go from here to there, have a top, a middle and a bottom, a left and a right, an inside and an outside, a front and a back, are rounded or are squared off, are this color or that, this color and that, have a high sound or a low sound, are smooth or rough, hard or yielding, smell this way or that, and so on. We perceive these real things in, indeed as, the sensible qualities that, tense with and harmonizing with one another within their context of significance, make up their lived dimensionality, and so can anyone else.

The coffee mug is hollowed out in such a way that coffee is contained within it, on its inside. Its outside, colored blue in its stretch all the way around, faces us and other things as well. Its bottom is flat both inside and out. Not only do we see the cup's stretches, we also feel them with our hands, for which it has the same stretched shape as it has for our eyes. We smell the richness of the coffee's aroma as it reaches our nostrils. The cup's characteristic sound stretches to our ears, and indeed to other ears, when set down on the table. The cup, sitting on the table, stretches across a certain area of the table's surface, temporarily hiding that area from view. When we lift the cup to take a sip of coffee, the cup's stretch comes to stretch, in the existential space of significance, from the table to our lips. The coffee warms the tongue it is now stretching across. The material the cup is made of has a certain character to it, is of such and such a thickness. Tapped by a spoon, the cup makes a characteristic sound. Dropped, the cup shatters, the coffee spilling and spreading across the floor. All this, and more, is what the cup of coffee *is,* this unity of concretely stretched qualities signifying one another, this whole of sensible meaning. Dasein is beyond itself and alongside spatial qualities such as these, alongside the lived dimensional suchness of the perceived as it constitutes a certain context of significance. Sensible meaning is not psychologically tacked on inside the organism to the inner aftereffects of external "molecules in motion." The organism does not confer upon fragmented sensations the status, first, of mere things, then, of values. Lifeworld meanings exist for us from the first rather in their sheer sensible givenness. "The question arises as to what more truly is," Heidegger invites us to ponder, "that crude chair with the tobacco pipe depicted in the painting by Van Gogh, or the waves which correspond to the color used in the painting, or the states which we have 'in us' while looking at the picture? . . . The color of the thing belongs to the thing. . . . The thing's color itself, the yellow, for instance, is simply this yellow as belonging to the field of grain" (1967, p. 210). Stretched sensible qualities, then, spreading to and signifying one another in and from their place within a broader environmental context, are just what make the pie a pie, the chair a chair, the tree a tree, the face a face, the painting a painting. Qualities (meanings) are the lifeworld itself. Our "first, last, and only world" is laden with juiciness, brightness, usefulness, crunchiness, lusciousness, warmth, beauty, softness, luster, sweetness, angularity, wetness, thickness, sharpness—and with their opposites. The existential space of meaning is a space of qualities such as these stretching to one another, tense (stretched) with one another, signifying one another in all the richness of their lived dimensionality.

The Bodily Self

The wholes of sensible meanings that constitute lifeworld reality exist precisely as grafted on to the life of a someone who is a match for them. The lived dimensionality of everyday meaning has its counterpart in the concrete bodily dimensionality of a self, in a bodily self perfectly adjusted to it. "Dasein is thrown, factical, thoroughly amidst nature in its bodiliness" (Heidegger, 1984, p. 166). This section takes up the topic of the concrete dimensionality of Dasein: Dasein's bodiliness. The notion of Dasein as a bodily self serves as a crucial link between the lived dimensionality of the existential space of meaning, considered in preceding sections, and Dasein's ability to manage that space, considered in the section immediately following this. The bodily self, itself sensible to itself and to other bodily selves, is itself Dasein, is itself openness to the sensible manifold of the lifeworld, the itself dimensionally stretched "there" of this manifold. Bodily self and sensible world, partaking of one and the same lived dimensionality of existential space, are intimate with one another.

Descartes viewed the body as *res extensa*, as an unfeeling bit of extension that, objectively in-itself, does not have it within itself to embody sensible meaning. The self and its meanings, in the view of conventional psychology, although essentially foreign to such a Cartesian object-body, are somehow created by that body. Merleau-Ponty, in particular, has criticized this dichotomy of self and meaning, on the one hand, and objective body, on the other—of subjective and objective spheres—and to replace it has introduced an altogether new conception of the body as a *center of meaning* in the world, the notion of the bodily self just referred to. Rather than just one more object moved by other objects, this lived body is itself a self, a bodily self at once thoroughly pervaded by meaning and giving rise to it; a bodily self at once dimensionally immersed in things and the very possibility of these same things. The body as sketched by Merleau-Ponty is the unity of characteristics that, torn apart, give rise, only later, to artificially separated subject and object. Such a lived body no longer is just one more objective event in a universe composed exclusively of objective events, the very exclusion of subjectivity, but "forms between the pure subject and object a third genus of being" (Merleau-Ponty, 1962, p. 350), "a 'perceiving thing,' a 'subject-object'" (Merleau-Ponty, 1964c, p. 166). The self is bodily, the body is a self. Our body is somebody, "our expression in the world, the visible form of our intentions" (Merleau-Ponty, 1964a, p. 5).

The lived body always and already has surpassed itself as a being, as a collection of anatomical organs, of causally linked, objective in-themselves. Our eye moving to catch a glimpse of something in motion, in Merleau-Ponty's words, "is not the displacement of an object in relation to another object, but progress toward reality" (1962, p. 279). The bodily self, this center of meaning, is our very possibility of reaching out to and becoming implicated in sensible meaning, our thrust to the world, being possible itself as concretely submitted to and already in the process of attaining the reality that surrounds it on every side. The bodily self is a dimensional spreadoutness that, sensing its own sensible qualities, also senses those of the world; a lived spreadoutness that, immersed in things even to the point of sharing one and the same bodiliness with them, echoes them in its own dimensionality; a stretched sensitivity that, feeling its own dimensions, feels those of meaning, is "there" for them (for a further consideration of the bodily self as affective openness, see Chapter 11, "Feeling and the Bodily Self"). The body, ourselves, surpasses to the world. The bodily self is our "potentiality of a certain world" (ibid., p. 106), "a system of behavior that aims at the world" (Merleau-Ponty, 1964a, p. 118), "a knowing-body" (Merleau-Ponty, 1962, p. 408), "a body made to explore the world" (Merleau-Ponty, 1973b, p. 123), "the field of perception and action" (Merleau-Ponty, 1964a, p. 16). We are "a body which rises towards the world" (Merleau-Ponty, 1962, p. 75). "I become involved in things with my body, they co-exist with me as an incarnate subject" (ibid., p. 185).

Interwoven with the "flesh" of the world, our body is "flesh," too, able to see and touch, yet itself visible and tangible: "the sensible sentient" (Merleau-Ponty, 1968, p. 136). We are "a flesh that suffers when it is wounded, hands that touch. . . . If [the body] touches [things] and sees them, this is only because, being of their family, itself visible and tangible, it uses its own being as a means to participate in theirs, because each of the two beings is an archetype for the other, because the body belongs to the order of things as the world is universal flesh" (ibid., p. 137).

The Body-Mind "Problem"

The body-mind problem comes to be seen, in the context of the notion of the bodily self, to be a pseudoproblem created by the splitting of human life into heterogeneous subjective and objective aspects. Merleau-Ponty's existential philosophy, catching sight of the profound unity of body and mind, of the self as embodied openness to sensible wholes of meaning—body *and* mind, before they were pried apart as object and subject—and thus thinking beyond the subject-object dichotomy, bids farewell to the body-mind "problem." The vexing problem of the relation of two domains with absolutely nothing in common with one another, and indeed of the conceivable character of such a relation, simply no longer is a problem.

Conventional modern thought locates lifeworld meanings, the very lifeworld itself, in an inner subjective realm of the mind. Meanings by such an account are simply ours or, to be more exact, the brain's. Existential phenomenology puts meanings back where they belong, in the nonmental lifeworld. And the body, rather than an object in-itself (objective body) that mysteriously projects a subject in-itself (subjective mind: the self and its meanings), now comes to be viewed as the self itself, our total openness to lifeworld meanings. With the realization that the body is not enclosed within its skin, that rather it is existentially beyond itself to its possibilities, possibilities that it affectively echoes in its deepest recesses, the *body-mind problem* is transformed into a *body-world relation*. The Cartesian dualism of inner subject and outer object thus yields to the body-world duality.

The brain is in functional harmony with the rest of the body, a crucial part indeed of the bodily self as a single differentiated whole given over in openness to the referential whole of the world. The totality of our bodily life, instead of being "at" pieces or bits of information entering into it, is "at" the world. Properly understood as part to whole, the brain is "at" the world, sponsoring lifeworld meaning. The brain—the body, ourselves—*exists*.

The Bodily Self's Familiarity with Lived Space

Dasein, bodily being in the world, is competent familiarity with significance; a dwelling, alongside other selves, in intimate commerce with a context of ready-to-hand meanings. For the self to have the know-how of lived space is for it to belong to this space in such a way as to be able to move through and commune with the world's stretches ably and with confidence. For Dasein to be familiar with everyday space means for Dasein, the very openness of the presencing of meaning, itself to be spatial through and through, to be the lived dimensionality of a bodily self that can touch and be touched by the lived bodily dimensionality of the world. A match for the stretched and spreading sensible qualities of lived space, bodily Dasein, by being itself—by being the someone it has to be—enacts existential spatiality, enacts the open expanse of the "there" where meanings presence.

When one reaches for and bites into the unity of sensible qualities that is an apple, existential spatiality is enacted. One's hand is not traversing equally spaced objective intervals, being master instead of the lived spatiality of the situation. In reaching for the apple, the hand has the know-how of the space of significance, is capable of existential space and, with that, is a dimensional match for the lived dimensionality of the apple. One's hand, possessed of a feel for the apple, is outside encircling it. And the sensible apple—mostly red, approximately round, smooth and shiny, firm to the touch, so big—is simultaneously with one's hand. One's hand surpasses each and every element of itself considered objectively as an organ. One's hand reaching to the apple is not bone and cartilage. No more than one's body is a collection of anatomical organs is one's hand such an organ. One's hand, indeed one's total differentiated body, is someone. Bones and cartilage always and already have been surpassed as elements to be the felt stretch that is one's hand reaching for and closing in on the unity of stretching sensible qualities that is the apple. One's sensible hand, one's body, is oneself, being-possible. One's hand *exists,* it has itself to be. One's hand is an "I can," and no "it." One's hand's space, that of oneself as a bodily self, is an existential space of possibility, of significance.

As a dimensionally stretched bodily self, then, one is a match for the bodily dimensionality of everyday ready-to-hand meanings. Things have an inside, an other side. One can, indeed must, view sensible meanings from many perspectives; that is an invariant or constant of perceptual events (Chapter 2 subsection "Phenomenological Concern with the Structural Invariants of Meaning Events"). To gain familiarity with things, one has to approach them, or move away from them, or turn them over. And that is just what a self constituted by its corporeal immersion in and sensitivity to things is capable of doing: "it is through the body that I go to the world" (Merleau-Ponty, 1962, p. 316). Because, as Gurwitsch points out, one and the same thing has various sides and aspects under which it presents itself, it becomes necessary for one, to become acquainted with it perceptually, to "pass from perception to perception," and in this way allow the thing to "progressively reveal its attributes and properties" (1966, p. 429). The spatial competency of bodily Dasein is an ability to approach something in its various sensible sides and let them signify one another as such and such a whole of meaning, with its place within the world. When the stretch of one's body dimensionally stretches in the direction of the differentiated stretch that is the apple, one stretches in anticipation to the apple's presently hidden inside. One stretches to the taste that awaits there and that stretches inward from the stretch of the apple's shiny red skin. One stretches to the apple's density, a density that stretches as far as the apple does, a nonobjective density that, consumed, will hold one over until dinner. Biting into the apple, one finds that its sensible qualities of juiciness, tastiness, and firmness go all the way through. But then one also finds that the apple has a core that one would rather not eat. One finds in all this that the various moments or sides of the apple are one, that its sensible sides are spatially beyond themselves to one another to form one and the same apple, that they are precisely what the apple is (see Chapter 5), a single whole of sensible meaning, signifying and signified by other wholes of sensible meaning within a given context of significance. When one looks at the apple as it presents one of its sides to us, in one of its stretches, it is the apple itself that one sees. What presents itself in each of our various perceptions is the same apple, the thing itself (ibid.).

The very lived dimensionality that pulses through perceived lifeworld meanings, it is being suggested, pulses through our body, ourselves. Others perceive us and indeed we perceive our own sensible dimensionality, up to a point. Bodily self and world partake of the same bodiliness. Our bodily dimensionality is a lived, felt dimensionality surpassing to the lived body of the world. Like the world's body, our lived body is differentiated into various bodily moments. These sensible, and indeed sentient, moments of our body are outside one another, but not in objective space, where the beginning of one bodily segment merely marks the end of the other and its causal influence. Our body's personally felt and interpersonally perceived sensible moments are outside one another rather in their differences from one another, in the very differences that allow them to work together synergistically as a single differentiated someone capably feeling its way around in the world and managing things. Bodily members are in active communication with one another to form one whole, our body, our self: one someone conspiring to attain lifeworld meanings in their living context of significance. Reaching for the apple is the hand of someone, a bodily someone whose whole posture is engaged in this activity. That someone's total bodily dimensionality is *in* the hand, the whole in the part, the whole at that part, the part bringing with it the whole (see Chapter 5 subsection "The Functional Significance of Parts in Wholes").

When one reaches for the apple, one is after the meaning apple and not a bit of pure extension. An abstracted unit of mass cannot be eaten. Apples are not apples in objective space. There are no backsides in objective space, no first bite, no second bite, no variations in texture, no pleasant tastes, no colors. It is a necessity of space projected objectively that things be leveled down to measurable units of mass devoid of lifeworld quality. One's hand surpasses itself to be a hand reaching for an apple. In this surpassing of Dasein to apple, the apple likewise is surpassed, to be an apple. Hand and apple, each in that lived dimensionality that is properly its own, are beyond themselves to one another in the "there" of existential space, in the existential space of meaning, in the realm of shared, lived dimensionality.

Our bodily dimensionality and the dimensionality of other selves, as well as that of everyday meanings in general, are givens of our reality. And yet, this existential dimensionality, this stretched spreadoutness, this multidirectional, polymorphous tenseness, is something that unfolds only as bodily Dasein makes its way through the lifeworld. Existential space is something enacted. The lived dimensionality of stretched sensible qualities comes to be given precisely in the giving of it by an engaged bodily someone. Our body comes alive in the fullness of its felt dimensionality when we take up some task, as we pull ourselves together and gear into it, and so do our meanings. Dasein releases lived dimensionality, its own and that of meaning's stretching sensible qualities, as Dasein goes. Bodily Dasein, knowing its way around and seeing its way clear, opens up space as it confidently moves through it. The "around the corner" becomes around the corner as Dasein nears the corner and rounds it. The backside is backside to the frontside that Dasein only now is considering, a backside that will first show itself to Dasein as Dasein turns the meaning over in its hand or walks around it. The lived dimensionality of the tree looms larger and larger the closer we draw to it. The juiciness stretches through the apple as one takes bite after bite. The door presents itself as the door it would be best to go through as we get ready to enter the building. The symphony's movements stretch to one another as a single whole of meaning as we give our ear to it. Regarding our participation in the lived unfolding of things, Gurwitsch points out that the various ways in which a perceived thing comes to present itself—front, back, top, bottom, beginning, end, middle, this sensible quality, then that—depend on movements of our body (ibid., p. 430). Our body, with its sensory and motor capacities, plays a crucial role in all perception. To see a particular feature or aspect of something, we have to turn our head or redirect our eyes, approach it or move away from it, pick it up and examine it more carefully, run our fingers over it, squeeze it, bring it to our nose and smell it, thump it (ibid.). Dasein, in its role as openness to the spatiality of significance, as bodily being-in-the-world, opens the lived dimensional space of sensible meaning as it moves through it, as it competently stretches along the world's stretches and familiarizes itself with them. Dasein, by reason of its preoccupation with its destiny, the sensible lifeworld meanings themselves to which it is submitted from the first, is the occasion for the openness of existential space.

Objective space clearly is not, in phenomenology's view, the one underlying space on the basis of which all other spaces are consequently built up. That prerogative belongs rather to lived spatiality. Before existential spatiality, there simply was no spatiality at all to speak of. Except as constructed (Husserl's "mathematization of nature"; Heidegger's "prior mathematical projection of nature"), except as an idea, there is no such thing as objective nature, and even as constructed, objectivity only exists as a meaning projected within the all-embracing context of existential spatiality. Real space is not in-itself nor is it between objects. Space, "before being a relation between objects, is based on my relation to things" (Merleau-Ponty, 1962, p. 286). Lived space is an original given of bodily Dasein's being always and already submitted to a referential network of sensible meaning, irreducible to anything else. There is nothing behind or beneath it to explain it.

Closeness and Bringing Close

The next sections take a closer look at two important aspects of lived spatiality as interpreted by Heidegger, Dasein's activity of *bringing close* and the *closeness* of meanings, and the *place* of Dasein and of meanings in existential space. The former is considered in this section, the latter in the one to follow.

Bodily Dasein, as competence in what regards significance—as being-in-the-world, as existence—is its "there" and has this "there"—this openness to world and its events of meaning—to be. The "there" that Dasein is, no subjective in-itself, is the openness of Dasein for itself and, with that, the openness for it of the world, as well as of other Daseins. This "there" is an opening up or bursting forth of meaning events in all the stretches of their concrete sensible qualitativeness. Dasein enacts itself as openness, releasing lived dimensionality, its own as a bodily self included, in the feel it has for the lived space of significance, in the confident manner in which it makes its way through this space. Dasein as "there" is a disclosing (dis-closing: opening up) of spatiality, the laying open of the "here" of an "I-here" and the "yonder" of ready-to-hand meanings. The "there" (opening) that Dasein essentially is and has to be is a "here" in essential relationship to a "yonder" ready-to-hand, an "I-here" toward a "yonder" (Heidegger, 1962a, p. 171). The existential spatiality of Dasein is grounded in being-in-the-world: "'here' and 'yonder' are possible only in a 'there'. . . . Dasein brings its 'there' along with it" (ibid.). Dasein is the itself situated openness of a referential totality of ready-to-hand entities. Dasein is delivered over to such entities in its very being, "there" bodily to enact their concrete spatiality, and its own. Dasein cannot do otherwise and still be "there," and still be Dasein. Its very being as "there" is a making room for the ready-to-hand.

Dasein is a movement toward "yonder" ready-to-hand meanings, then, is "over there" with them. Everyday meanings have the spatial character of *closeness* to Dasein in terms of Dasein's handling and using them (ibid., p. 135). Corporeally immersed in things and a match for them, being-in-the-world frees things for their mattering to it as the things they are (ibid., p. 139). Dasein *brings* those things *close* with which it is concernfully preoccupied, makes no room for such things as are of no matter to it. "Whatever . . . concern dwells alongside beforehand is what is closest" (ibid., p. 142). We bring close what we care about, things in which we have a stake, whether in their positive or negative character. The immediately preceding section's descriptions of Dasein's able handling of lived space in fact already were descriptions of the behavior of bringing close now under explicit consideration: hungry and reaching for an apple, the apple is brought close.

Lifeworld remoteness and closeness are not a matter of objectively measurable distances. A measurably long path can be short by comparison to a measurably short one filled with obstacles: "the objective distances of things present-at-hand do not coincide with the remoteness and closeness of what is ready-to-hand within the world" (ibid., pp. 140–141). Exact knowledge of distances, as a matter of fact, typically is blind to the ready-to-hand. Nor is what is closest to us in the existential space of significance at the smallest objectively measurable distance. The painting we look at is closer to us at the moment than our glasses. Should we lose our glasses, however, they, precisely in their absence, in all likelihood will be brought close as the object of our concern. So far as our preoccupations in existential space are concerned, the sidewalk we walk on is farther away from us than the friend we have just spotted across the street. If we consider the following objectively straight line, we find that A is "closer" to B than to C: −A−B−C−. But this is the case only under the presupposition of objective space, where "closeness" is taken as a property of entities in-themselves, as a self-given fact in the space of pure extension. A is "closer" to B in objective space than it is to C, but such objective "closeness" does not rule human life and its meaning-oriented behavior. If the preceding diagram, for example, were to represent two friends sitting on the subway at locations A and C with a stranger at location B, then it is clear that in personal (existential) space A would be closer to C than to B. What is close to people is what matters to them, what they are bringing close in the existential space of the dimensional possibilities of everyday meaning. Existential space, in what is close or remote, varies with the direction of our preoccupations of the moment, as well as with our proficiencies for enacting meaning as these have developed in the course of a lifetime.

Because people "pervade" and "persist through" spaces "by virtue of their very nature," according to Heidegger, because they have the know-how of space, because, translocally "over there" with things, they are spatial through and through, they are able to go through spaces. "When I go toward the door of the lecture hall, I am already there, and I could not go to it at all if I were not such that I am there. I am never here only, as this encapsulated body; rather, I am there, that is, I already pervade the room, and only thus can I go through it. . . . Man's relation to locations, and through locations to spaces, inheres in his dwelling" (Heidegger, 1971b, p. 157). Objects in-themselves populating an objective space always and already having been overleapt in bodily Dasein's surpassing to the world, Dasein does not have to go through space interval by interval to bring meanings close and be with them. In having been given its "there" to be, Dasein is ahead of itself rather, already through space and letting meanings matter dimensionally. One already is existentially with the apple, bringing it close, the sensible apple itself, when one first thinks of it, before ever touching or taking a bite out of it. In fact, only by first bringing it close as a meaning within its context of significance can one touch and eat the apple at all.

Such is the character of the existential space of the lifeworld, then, that we get through to and are near to what matters to us even when we are "only" thinking or daydreaming about it (see Chapter 2, "Phenomenology's Theory of Intentionality"). We always and already are outside with what we are now "only" envisioning, outside transacting with a lifeworld network of meanings, rather than inside contemplating copies of a supposed external physical reality. In Heidegger's words, "We do not represent distant things merely in our mind—as the textbooks have it—so that only mental representations of distant things run through our minds and heads as substitutes for the things. If all of us now think, from where we are right here, of the old bridge in Heidelberg, this thinking toward that location is not a mere experience inside the persons present here; rather, it belongs to the very nature of our thinking *of* that bridge that *in itself* thinking gets through, persists through, the distance to that location. From this spot right here, we are there at the bridge—we are by no means at some representational content in our consciousness" (ibid., pp. 156–157). What is close to us at the moment might well be our misplaced glasses. They may be the only thing we can possibly think about. Looking for them here and there in the lifeworld space of significance, no one will ever convince us that we are looking for a mere representation—even though it's our glasses in their very absence that's at issue. We are looking for the missing glasses themselves, and that's that. And we look for them where they might be, that is, in the lifeworld.

As we bring the ready-to-hand close, so also do we, pervading and persisting through spaces, bring another bodily someone close. In neither case is this spatial enacting a matter of measured distance or mere visible presence. Viennese psychiatrist Viktor Frankl's account of his experience in a concentration camp in World War II makes the point very well:

> My mind clung to my wife's image, imagining it with an uncanny acuteness. I hear her answering me, saw her smile, her frank and encouraging look. Real or not, her look was more luminous than the sun which was beginning to rise. . . . I understood how a man who has nothing left in this world still may know bliss, be it only for a brief moment, in the contemplation of his beloved. . . . My mind still clung to the image of my wife. A thought crossed my mind: I didn't even know if she were still alive. I knew only one thing—which I have learned well by now: Love goes very far beyond the physical person of the beloved. It finds its deepest meaning in his spiritual being, his inner self. Whether or not he is actually present, whether or not he is still alive at all, ceases somehow to be of importance. (1959, pp. 58–60)

Dasein is concernfully preoccupied with the world that matters to it at the moment, which is where bodily Dasein dwells. Bringing things close, Heidegger writes, "perhaps uncovers the 'reality' of the world at its most real; it has nothing to do with 'subjective' arbitrariness or subjectivistic 'ways of taking' an entity which 'in itself' is otherwise" (1962a, p. 141). Bringing-close reveals the "true world" in all the qualitative richness of its lived dimensionality.

Place

The Place of Ready-to-Hand Meanings

The existential space of meaning is one of possibility, the space of corporeally dimensional being possible (bodily Dasein) open at once to itself and to sensible meaning, the space of the possibility of meaning presencing from itself on its own lifeworld ground. The event of Dasein is the breaking open of an existential space of possibility, the event of a bodily someone capable of bringing meanings close and letting them matter in all the concreteness of their lived dimensional qualitativeness. Ready-to-hand meanings, as noted (see Chapter 3 subsection "Ready-to-Hand Meanings within the World"), never occur alone, but always in a context of other meanings, always as cogiven within significance. Bringing a meaning close in its possibility, bringing something close in its quality as something, means bringing it close in its *place,* with whatever *directionality* is proper to it in its context of other meanings. Directionality is the manner in which a meaning points beyond itself and signifies other meanings; the way a lawn mower signals lawn and neighborhood, for example. Meaning, in and from its place, signifies and is signified by other meanings in and from their place, defines and is defined by these others. Thus signified and defined, thus located with a directionality all its own—thus involved—meaning takes its place as itself in the existential space of possibility.

Bringing a ready-to-hand meaning close is letting it take its place directionally, in the fullness and richness of its sensible dimensionality; releasing it to its possibilities of involvement within a context of significance. "Equipment has its *place*" (Heidegger, 1962a, p. 136); "environmental things are all placed" (Heidegger, 1985, p. 226). All in all, what matters first and foremost when a ready-to-hand something is brought close is the network of meanings with which Dasein is preoccupied and in terms of which ready-to-hand things take their place as dimensionally directed to one another: the chair to the table to the food, to the plate, knife, fork, and napkin, "for the sake of" eating. Existential space is "split up into places" (Heidegger, 1962a, p. 138). Itself dimensionally stretched with sensible qualities of its own, bodily Dasein is tuned in advance as Dasein to the lived dimensionality of sensible ready-to-handy meanings stretching to one another. Everyday meaning always has some direction of involvement, some place, in existential space. Something is what it is as directionally placed in existential space.

The oriented space of everyday meaning, the existential space of its lived dimensionality, is never indifferent the way objective space is. In objective space, all locations are equivalent, all intervals equal, becoming the mere change of place. In existential space, by contrast, in Heidegger's words, "the 'above' is what is 'on the ceiling'; the 'below' is what is 'on the floor'; the 'behind' is what is 'at the door'" (ibid., pp. 136–137); the location of an everyday meaning is discovered not by the calculation of its coordinates in objective space but in our everyday familiarity and preoccupation with it. Meaning literally has no place to call its own in a space of pure extension. What objectivistic psychology brings close, the meanings that matter to it, are not everyday meanings in a space of possibility that is properly their own, but a set of idealized abstractions that reduce such meanings to calculable determinations in objective space.

The Place of Dasein

Everyday meaning has its place in existential spatiality, and so does Dasein. Dasein's place in the lived dimensionality of existential space, however, is not the involvement of ready-to-hand meanings with one another. Much less is it a present-at-hand determination in a realm of pure extension, where place is excluded in advance. Dasein's place rather, Dasein's very definition, is its concrete possibilities for disclosing meanings, its ability to help meanings gain a place of their own in the open (Chapter 3, "Dasein: Openness to World"). The place of Dasein is its openness to events of meaning presencing, its being the "there" of meaning events. Bodily Dasein's place is that of an "I here" that is "yonder" with things (ibid., p. 171). Its place, its "here," is a being dimensionally alongside ready-to-hand meanings "over there," a competent being alongside meanings that brings them close in view of their place within significance. All in all, then, bodily Dasein's mode of being is one that is spatially proper to it, concernful preoccupation with meanings: being possible.

The Place of Other People

Dasein pervades and persists through space. A spatial complex opens with Dasein. Not only does Dasein discover ready-to-hand meanings in and through this "pervading," this "persisting through," Dasein also discovers other people in their proper meaning and spatiality (see Chapter 3, "The World and Other People"). Another human being as our meaning is a self "for the sake of itself," a person. The other as our meaning is not a ready-to-hand meaning, is not an "in-order-to"; another someone does not belong to a totality of involvements within the world, any more than we do. The other's place in existential spatiality rather is being-in-the-world, a self, being possible, an "I can," like ourselves. The other is a bodily "I here" dimensionally open, in the felt sense it has of itself, at once to itself, to other bodily selves, and to world.

We come across another person as possessing the existential spatiality of Dasein, then, as just described. Our fellow Dasein is located, as are we. The place of other people is our place, the place of being-in-the-world. The place of other persons is the place of a someone who brings things close, the place of a someone to whom things, showing themselves as what they are, come to count for something. The place of another Dasein is that of a self that is oriented with regard to the network of the ready-to-hand, competently finding its way about in it, discovering the way its places directionally tie in with one another. The place of another is a making room for itself and for a network of the ready-to-hand, a letting things function in their place. Other people are, like ourselves, a dimensionally stretched bodily "here" that always and already is stretching "yonder" to dimensionally stretched sensible meanings. The place of the other person is that of a clearing for the presencing of meaning, an open space for beings to enter world and become themselves. The other person is "there," "over and out beyond" to meaning events. And this is indeed how we discover another someone in existential space: tending a garden, selling tickets, swimming in the pool, walking down the street, intending, alongside ourselves—alongside others—the same lifeworld, with the same lived dimensionality, that we are, that others are. Another person presencing as our meaning is a bodily someone who, like ourselves, is preoccupied in familiarity with the sensible world of meaning. "Over there" is someone. We *place* the other as another someone, who, in having their someoneness (openness) to be, makes their way through space and makes room for things.

Just as our hand is existentially the hand of someone, and not mere bones and cartilage, so too is the hand of another Dasein the hand of someone. Our hand is ourselves. Their hand is themselves. When we shake hands with another someone, we are two bodily selves stretching to one another in the lived dimensionality of existential space. Shaking hands is not the mere proximity of two in-themselves, two organs, but the meeting of two selves in the lived space of possibility, two someones beyond themselves to one another, together opening up a common space. Shaking hands, the skin, rather than acting as a barrier enclosing two objective organs, serves as an opening of two dimensionally stretched gestures stretching to one another, two someones seeing, hearing, touching one another, and thus participating in one another's lives, in a single lived spatiality. The other is not a bag of bones, an aggregate of anatomical organs, chemicals with a determinable scrap value. We meet the other rather precisely as someone, a bodily existence in the world alongside ourselves.

The Existential and the Objective Spaces of Meaning

The first chapters of this essay have explored two logics, the phenomenological and the objectivistic, by means of which attempts are made to understand human behavior and its world. Objectivistic logic begins explicitly with a certain conception of bodily things as spatial extension and ends by reducing all things human to space objectivity projected. Consider, for example, the following late words of Freud, "We assume that mental life is the function of an apparatus to which we ascribe the characteristics of being extended in space and of being made up of several portions" (1949, p. 14). Phenomenological logic finds its center in a network of everyday meanings with a spatiality all its own, an existential spatiality. Objectivistic logic, by contrast, declares the external world to possess an objective character, to be a domain of pure extension entirely devoid of meaning.

Phenomenology finds the external world to be in the first instance a perceptual world of self-giving wholes of sensible meaning, with a dimensionally stretched bodiliness and integrity of their own, a lifeworld. The existential phenomenologist asserts that human beings are outside with the sensible lifeworld from the first and always, outside surpassing to meaning events, to the dimensional coming into its truth of meaning in its place—not that we were ever *inside* in an objectively determinable subjective manner in the first place; we were always outside, existentially. We are outside with "that tree over there," outside with sensible qualities that are properly the tree's own and that run throughout its stretches; outside with the tree in the meadow itself, even when we are recalling it or planning to convert it into firewood. Objectivistic philosophy, for its part, holds that, when we perceive a tree, both the perceiving (self) and the perceived (tree) are on the interior of the objective organism, on this side of the skin that bounds the organism in; that physical energies (stimuli), objective events external to one another, are the exclusive constituents of the organism's "true" external "world"; that the inner perception of the "tree" is the ultimate outcome of a linear causal chain first instituted by just such physical energies; that the organism and its milieu are equally exponents of a single all-embracing objective space of pure extension.

How can intelligent people make statements that stand in such thorough opposition to one another? Because they operate from different standpoints. Because these standpoints are philosophies that proceed on the basis of opposing presuppositions. And because the "same" terms as used by the two philosophies of psychology are defined by their respective logics, the "same" parts within different wholes. "Outside" for objectivism, for example, means "on the other side of some spatiotemporal barrier," whereas "outside" for existential phenomenology, as in "Dasein is outside with the tree," is the "over and out beyond itself" of the "upswing into possibility," the "outside" of the surpassing to world and its events of meaning presencing. There is no room, no cleared existential space, for any "surpassing to world" in objective thinking, just as there is no room for a "this or that side of a strictly physical boundary" in existential phenomenology. Some individuals, when they hear the phenomenologist claim, for example, that Dasein is outside with the tree, tend to hear a contradiction because they understand "outside" to mean "outside the skin"—and it is indeed absurd to imagine an organism turning itself inside out to be objectively next to the objective "tree." But, what the phenomenologist is actually saying is that Dasein, in existential space, surpasses itself and every last absolutely self-sufficient being to arrive at the tree as a tree in the meadow, the tree in the fullness of its relativity as a meaning, in all its lived dimensional suchness.

This chapter has attempted to present a rough sketch of the concrete existential spatiality of everyday meaning and Dasein. Not physically located in objective space, ready-to-hand meaning—referred to other meanings, assigned to Dasein—takes its place dimensionally within a living context of significance. The individual Dasein is a conspiring of an articulated and self-regulating personal system of sensible and sentient bodily stretches—hands, head, chest, legs, and so on—with other personal systems like itself, other individual Daseins, to form an articulated and self-regulating system of Daseins interwoven with the significance of the world. This total context—this field or system (Chapter 14), this all-embracing bodiliness, this cobodiliness—arises with Dasein's existential surpassing to world. Everyday meaning is Dasein's nonmental other, actualized in its "can-be," spatially stretched and brought close. The spatiality of meaning is its being beyond itself in openness to other meanings within a lived spatiality of significance, and not its location in objective space, not its being on one side or the other of an objective skin border. Phenomenological psychology begins with the premise that lifeworld meaning, which conventional psychology is simply unable to calculate, comes into its truth, with an integrity of its own, in existential space.

5 The Gestalt Logic of Meaning

The given is itself in varying degrees
"structured" ("gestaltet").

—*Wertheimer*, 1967a, p. 14

The Notion of Gestalt

It has been asserted any number of times in previous chapters that meaning is not the inner subjective product of objective forces; that, possessing a nonpsychological character of its own, meaning belongs instead, in all its sensible qualitativeness, to the surrounding lifeworld. Meaning is something or someone with which Dasein has become preoccupied, about which Dasein cares in some way, precisely as that something or someone is brought close in its lived dimensionality. It was pointed out in Chapter 4 that the various sides of an apple—inside, outside, otherside—are one; that the sides the apple shows us, forming a single sensible meaning, are precisely what the apple is. Through a consideration of key aspects of Gestalt theory, the present chapter elaborates upon meaning as such a dimensional unity of sides. Explicitly to be taken up, then, is the organization internal to lifeworld meanings, their "Gestalt logic." Chapters 6 and 7 continue this exploration of the structural character, both internal and external, of lifeworld meaning. In Chapter 8 the discussion shifts away from meaning and its organization and toward Dasein's insightful preoccupation with meaning. This chapter, along with the next two, although deeply rooted in the descriptions that the Gestalt psychologists furnished us, is already at work revising certain basic assumptions of Gestalt theory from an existential phenomenological point of view, in particular as regards signifying and significance; Chapters 8 and 12 thematize this reworking of Gestalt theory.

The founders of Gestalt psychology—Max Wertheimer, Wolfgang Köhler and Kurt Koffka—began their work phenomenologically by describing psychological events that did not fit into the mold of prevailing psychological accounts. The word *Gestalt* (a German noun; plural, *Gestalten*) summarizes this work, standing in effect for the principle of this school. Due to the impossibility of adequately translating the word, *gestalt* is used here as an English, and thus uncapitalized, term (plural, gestalts).

Anticipating the results to be achieved later in this chapter, a gestalt may be said to be *a unity that, rather than being either the sum of its parts or more than their sum, is their very organization, their system.* Wertheimer expresses the fundamental formula of Gestalt theory this way: "There are wholes, the behavior of which is not determined by that of their individual elements, but where the part-processes are themselves determined by the intrinsic nature of the whole" (1967b, p. 2). Gestalt psychology, as Gurwitsch points out, essentially is a theory of organization.

Köhler has remarked that phenomenology, "the qualitative analysis of experience," is "the field in which all concepts find their final justification" (1938, p. 88). He accordingly insists that psychology, if it is to solve any problems of ultimate principle, must engage in a phenomenological return to the source of its concepts in experience (ibid., p. x; see Chapter 2 subsection "The Clarification of Psychological Concepts"). Classical Gestalt psychology begins in just this way, as a description of things psychological, without the traditional biases, atomism, in particular (see "The Absolute and the Relative," a subsection later in this chapter), that perennially have plagued psychology. Many of conventional psychology's concepts, having to do with such basic processes as learning, remembering, thinking, feeling, motivation, and perceiving, to which processes whole chapters of introductory textbooks are devoted, remain even to this day as uninformed phenomenologically, and consequently as inadequate as they ever were (Chapter 1). Such concepts, lacking fundamental clarity, are vague and confused to the point that they are more likely than not "to remove us from experience as it is lived" (Merleau-Ponty, 1964a, p. 61). Phenomenological psychology and Gestalt psychology are of one mind in this regard, that psychology, if indeed it is to know what it is talking about, stands in urgent need of a return to the experiential source of its concepts. Gestalt psychology, moreover, is an exploration of certain structural invariants in the formation of our meanings, principles of organization in terms of which gestalts first come to formation. But such structural necessities characteristic of events of meaning presencing are precisely what phenomenology is also out to formulate (see Chapter 2 subsection "Phenomenological Concern with the Structural Invariants of Meaning Events"). Precisely in view of all that existential phenomenological thought stands to gain from classical Gestalt psychology as a systematically developed theory of organization does Gestalt psychology occupy a place of prominence in the present essay, not only in this chapter but in the ones to follow as well.

Gestalt: Segregated Unity

Köhler briefly characterizes a gestalt as a *segregated unity*. A gestalt has boundaries that delimit it, setting it off from everything that is not itself.

It is a self-limiting togetherness, a relatively self-standing unity, a "functional whole" (in Koffka's words).

Constitutive of a gestalt is whatever belongs to it as the self-bounding unity that it is at the moment. The tree we are looking at, or the child playing, or the symphony being listened to is such a segregated unity. The child is perceived in his or her total bodily dimensionality, head to limbs to torso. The tree spreads out in its unity from trunk to branches to bark and leaves to partially exposed roots. The symphony is a unity that stands off in its concrete stretch from first note to last. A melody within a symphony can itself be a relatively segregated unity. A pair of x's or a group of children playing, always from a perceiver's point of view, always as a meaning, similarly is a segregated unity. The ball the children are playing with likewise is part of the perceived whole of meaning the children form at the moment. A segregated unity thus can be a single gestalt, a child, or a field of gestalts (gestalt of gestalts), a group of children playing with a ball. Gestalts form a field of gestalts precisely insofar as they form a segregated unity; to the very extent that the gestalts involved, dimensionally stretching to one another, concretely signify each other at the moment as a single bounded whole of meaning.

A gestalt is an action, not even a stationary figure is without its tensions (stretches). A circular, at once backwards and forwards, activity of stretching and signifying always and already is in process among any of a gestalt's moments. This activity renders the gestalt a system of roles (functional significances) standing off from everything that does not figure in the system. "Segregation follows the lines of organizational structure" (Gurwitsch, 1964, p. 138). The constituents together form the segregated unit "in their interdependence and interdetermination, in their demanding, supporting, complementing, and qualifying each other" (ibid.). A gestalt's members forever are dynamically achieving their organization as a gestalt, forever forming and reforming ("gestalting" and "regestalting") as the segregated whole of meaning they represent for someone. We never encounter absolutes in-themselves. Unformed elements, sensations, exist only in theory. Because no unformed materials exist, because we can never encounter anything that is not already organized and indeed perpetually in the process of achieving that organization, what most truly exists is the formative process itself, lifeworld moments actively configuring as this meaning or that. All in all, any lifeworld meaning comes to exist for us in the signifying of one another of its constitutive moments, in a dynamic signifying in and through which sensible lifeworld moments attain the status of a bounded form (gestalt). Meanings, always and already dynamically achieving form, always and already are formed, set off in one form or another. *Form,* it may be noted, is one of the more common attempts to translate the German word *Gestalt:* Köhler translates Gestalt as *form* and as *shape*.

Segregated Unity and Figure-Ground Structure

" 'To have shape," ' Köhler writes, "is a peculiarity which distinguishes certain areas of the visual field from others which have no shape in this sense. In our example [of a map of the Mediterranean coast], so long as the Mediterranean has shape, the area corresponding to Italy has no shape, and vice versa" (1947, p. 107). A segregated unity is in every case something that stands off from a background of what is not itself. With what stands back and outlines a gestalt functioning as *ground,* a gestalt is segregated *figure.* Figure is what stands forth as a whole of meaning, the unity of a gestalt's moments as these signify and express one another in their roles in the whole. What presents itself as figure is "slightly raised; it is located *in front* of the environment" (Köhler, 1969, p. 55). Ground is what recedes, whatever does not come forward and become segregated as figure. Figure is formed, ground is relatively formless. Consider, for example, the demonstration of Gestalt theory in Figure 5–1. When the propeller blades stand forth as figure, Köhler points out, "this region becomes compact and more substantial; the 'mere ground' is loose and empty by comparison" (1967, p. 59).

Figure is total meaning at the moment, then, the totality of what stands forth as segregated form: gestalt, field of gestalts, field of fields. Ground is all that outlines the figure and bounds it off, all that provides the figure with definition from beyond. In Koffka's words, "The figure depends for its characteristics upon the ground on which it appears. The ground serves as a *framework* in which the figure is suspended and thereby determines the figure" (1935, p. 184). Ground bounds and gives shape. It contributes essentially to the forming of segregated unities, to the "gestalting" of meaning. There thus is a thoroughly reciprocal signifying in play, not only among a gestalt's moments but also between a gestalt (figure) and its ground.

Figure 5–1

A gestalt owes its concrete qualitative dimensionality as a segregated meaning to both these signifyings, to both actions. A gestalt's external context conditions its internal signifying, then, determining even what becomes a gestalt in the first place. In Köhler's words,

> Relatively segregated units which stand apart in the visual field have been called Gestalten. The characters of local events depend upon their place in the Gestalt in which they occur, but this is also true of the segregation of Gestalten themselves as regards the entire visual field. It is not enough that a certain region should be homogeneously colored in order for it to constitute an independent Gestalt, but the environment also must be appropriately colored. This is especially clear in the distinction between "figure" and "ground." (1967, pp. 59–60)

Köhler proceeds to say that the visual field in its entirety determines the way in which its parts are segregated. Figure and ground stand to each other, then, in a structural relationship of functional interdepending. The particular horizon opened releases this figure; the figure released at once relegates certain materials surrounding it to background status. Background and figure reciprocally express and structure one another. "Dynamic interaction in the field decides what becomes a unit, what is excluded from it, what is figure, and what falls back as mere ground" (Köhler, 1971, p. 50). What is always being structured, and sometimes restructured, then, is never the segregated figure in-itself, but the gestalt-background relationship. Self-standing meaning is never the final word. Meaning is always meaning in its place (compare Chapter 3, "Meaning, Involvement, World"; Chapter 4 subsection "The Place of Ready-to-Hand Meanings"). Meaning always depends on a broader context that provides it with definition, the broader network of relations that is its framework. The effective background of any meaning in the final analysis is the relational totality of *world*. One can distinguish, then, between any meaning's immediate (present, presently given) ground and its place within a broader context of significance.

The figure-ground structure is everywhere in evidence in perception. Even a simple spot against a homogeneous background possesses all the features of a figure. In like manner, a sudden noise that breaks the silence presents itself as a figure emerging from its ground. Stillness is "the experience of an auditory background *par excellence* out of which sounds emerge and into which they relapse" (Gurwitsch, 1964, p. 112). The figure-ground structure is an invariant in the presencing of any meaning whatsoever, be it in the perceptual or in some other mode. Even the simplest of segregated lifeworld moments is already a gestalt, a figure formed in part by its structural relationship with its ground (see Chapter 2 subsection "Intentionality and Sensations").

Field of Gestalts

A gestalt is composed of its moments or parts. Nevertheless, as already suggested, a gestalt frequently comes to serve as a moment of a larger segregated whole of meaning, as part of a *field of gestalts* standing forth as lifeworld figure.

Parts signify one another as a gestalt. Themselves serving as parts in a larger whole, gestalts signify and express one another as a field of gestalts. A field of gestalts, like any gestalt, is an action, a meaning forever in the process of achieving its organization. What counts as a member of a field of gestalts varies, sometimes from moment to moment. Looking here, three people form a single field, but, before we know it, someone joins them and they become a foursome. The game of cards or football game is now this field of events, now that. We see a group of paintings on the wall (field of paintings). Taking a closer look at one of them, a particular field of figures comes to actualize itself for our inspection. A word is a field of letters, a sentence a field of words, an essay a field of sentences. Groceries are a field of items in our cart, a bouquet a field of flowers, an outfit a field of garments. What counts as the segregated unity (figure) of the moment depends on the total articulation prevailing at the moment; on the observer and the observed, and on their interaction in accordance with Gestalt lawfulness (Chapter 6).

Gestalt Qualities

The following observation marked the historical beginning of Gestalt theory in the nineteenth century: Gestalts have distinctive characters that are not found in their constituent parts when these constituents are considered in isolation, but that properly belong to gestalts only as wholes. These whole properties of gestalts have been termed *gestalt qualities*. A gestalt's gestalt quality may be characterized briefly as the particular sensible suchness of a gestalt, the meaning a gestalt has, a meaning nowhere to be found in the gestalt's parts considered as pieces.

Our everyday world, Gurwitsch comments, abounds with such qualities as the useful and the useless, the agreeable and the disagreeable, the attractive and the repulsive, the beautiful and the ugly (1966, p. 290). Gestalt qualities, in Köhler's words, "occur everywhere in perception. Even a whole visual field, for instance, may look 'clear,' and another almost 'chaotic'; and even more important: the movements of one person are seen as 'steady,' those of another as 'erratic'; the faces of some individuals impress us as relaxed, those of others as tense or keen or empty or soft, and so forth" (1969, p. 46). And again, "When things are called 'tall' or 'bulky,' persons 'slender' or 'stout,' movements 'clumsy' or 'graceful,' reference is made to definite [gestalt qualities]. When we describe events as 'sudden' or 'smooth,' 'jerky' or 'continuous,' we refer to the same class" (1971, p. 382). And finally, "The Gestalt qualities which the musicians call 'major' and 'minor' are characteristics of musical phrases rather than of individual tones" (1969, pp. 53–54).

Gestalt qualities are not locatable as such, as qualities, in objective space. The space-time continuum being the prior exclusion of meaning, qualities have simply no place to call their own in the in-itself of objective units of mass; in an external realm of physical stimuli, for example. There can be no gestalt qualities in the "world" projected objectively. No more than gestalt qualities can be derived from an objective realm, moreover, can they be derived from a gestalt's constitutive parts taken in sheer isolation from one another, from fragmented, hence meaning-less, sensations, which formulation is but a restatement of the very definition of gestalt qualities (see also "A Gestalt Is Not the Sum of Its Parts"). Finally, the Gestalt theoretical position being adopted here, contrary to the theoretical position of conventional textbook psychology, holds that gestalt qualities are not meanings that the brain adds on to fragmented sensory impressions to turn them into perceptions (see "A Gestalt Is Not More than the Sum of Its Parts"). Positively, this Gestalt position locates gestalt quality in the gestalt itself, as the very way a gestalt is presently attaining its organization in the reciprocal signifying of one another of its sensible moments, as the meaning any gestalt is (see the later section "A Gestalt as the Organization of Its Constituents").

A Gestalt Is Not the Sum of Its Parts

A gestalt is not the sum of its parts (moments, members). This classical Gestalt theoretical formulation may also be rendered by: $G \neq A + B$, where G stands for gestalt; A and B for any and all of the members of a particular gestalt (only two characters are used for purposes of simplification; for completeness as many characters would be needed as the gestalt has members: $A + B + C + D + E + F + \ldots$); $\neq$ for the negation of equivalence; and $+$ for the operation of adding or collecting the members. A gestalt does not issue, in other words, from a sum of A and B; that is, from assembling what might be supposed to be a gestalt's isolated parts, parts ready-made and in-themselves, pieces without internal communication with one another. Neither a gestalt nor its properties (whole properties or gestalt qualities) derive from a sum of the properties the separate parts might possess. Gestalts are "total processes," Merleau-Ponty says, "whose properties are not the sum of those which the isolated parts would possess" (1963, p. 47).

A gestalt's sensible characteristics, rather than following strictly from its parts viewed in isolation, have an emergent character. A hot dog, a bun, and mustard taste surprisingly good together. Something happens with the whole that is neither to be found in its parts taken individually nor to be predicted from them. That colors will clash or go well together is first determined by their actual dialogue. Four lines stretching to and expressing one another a certain way give rise to a rectangle (with, for example, its four interior right angles), a suchness nowhere to be found in the lines taken separately in-themselves. The meaning of a sentence springs from the concrete course its words take as they enter into reciprocal relations with one another. All in all, a gestalt's interacting moments (colors, flavors, textures, words, sounds, etc.), rather than adding up, *develop* into a certain whole of meaning.

A meaning does not arise, then, from a mere external combining of elements, the whole is not the aggregate of its parts. Stretching to one another in a multidirectional signifying, a gestalt's sensible moments belong to one another intrinsically rather as the whole of meaning they are in the process of giving rise to at the moment. A gestalt is constituted by *sensible* qualities tense with and *signifying* one another, then, and not *fragmented sensations*.

A Gestalt as the Organization of Its Constituents

What makes these four x's unite as two pairs, $x\,x \quad x\,x$, is the definite way they relate to and define—determine, decide, change, modify, signify, qualify— one another. This thoroughgoing relativity to one another of these moments, this definition of one by the other, is not something that the x's considered separately could conceivably ever accomplish. A gestalt, by Gurwitsch's definition, "is an ensemble of items which mutually support and determine one another" (1966, p. 25). Each constituent of a gestalt "is qualified and made to be what it is by relation to, and significance for, the other constituents" (Gurwitsch, 1965, pp. 21–22). A gestalt is the thoroughly reciprocal action of lifeworld moments as these enter into internal relations with and express one another as a certain whole of meaning. A gestalt, briefly, is the very organization of its members. The x on the right intends (stretches towards, aims at) the x on the left and makes it be the x on the left, at the same time as the x on the left intends the x on the right and makes it be this specific x on the right. The x on the left and the x on the right, internally relating to and signifying each other in their possibility of forming a pair of x's, give each other their meaning as this gestalt. The pair of x's on the right and the pair of x's on the left, circularly determining one another, make each other be this particular group of two pairs of x's; give to one another their specific character as pair on the left or pair on the right. "Up" dynamically makes "down" be "down," and "down" dynamically makes "up" be "up"—and by no means incidentally, for, if, liking "up" so much, we tried to eliminate "down," we would, in succeeding, eliminate not only "down" but "up" as well. Something's "top" signifies its "bottom," and its "bottom" signifies its "top," and in such a way that "top" and "bottom," concretely stretching to one another, make each other into what they are as a particular whole of meaning; "top" makes "bottom" be "bottom" even as it is made to be "top" by "bottom"—one moment of a gestalt circularly influences another of its moments in its very being influenced by that other moment. When there was no evil, neither was there any good to speak of. Her eyes signify her nose signify her mouth signify her cheeks signify her ears signify her hair; her dimensionally sensible features expressing one another in a thoroughgoing reciprocity, she comes to presence with just these looks, with now this expression, now that one. What makes a joke funny—*be* a joke—is the humorous way its constituent moments take one another by surprise. The beginning and early moments of the symphony give what is to follow its possibilities of further development; but the further turns of the music reciprocally and retroactively transform the character of the onset and earlier development of the music. The symphony's various moments, in stretching to and modifying one another circularly, in an unfolding backwards and forwards movement, are just what the symphony is. The coffee mug is its sensible qualities: blue outside and white inside, empty interior space, light and manageable, round all the way around and flat on the bottom, with a handle for easy grasping, and so forth.

Particular sensible qualities reaching to and changing one another, then, are just what constitute the whole of meaning that any gestalt is. A rose is unthinkable in its place as an everyday meaning except in the lived dimensionality of its smell, color, shape, moistness, smoothness, its unfolding opening-up, and so on. That is what a real rose in fact *is*. Its essence is not found in an analytical probing that lays its component parts out on the table, but precisely in the live way its rich red petals embrace one another as this relativity of just these sensible qualities (see the subsection "Gestalt: 'Characteristics in Relation' ").

"A whole is meaningful," Wertheimer says, "when concrete mutual dependency obtains among its parts" (1967a, p. 16). Gestalt psychologists have referred to this interdepending at the origin of a gestalt, this reciprocal action of a gestalt's members on one another as sketched in this section, this present self-governing activity, as a *dynamic self-distribution* (see Chapter 12 subsection "Dynamic Self-Distribution"). Such dynamic self-distribution is a basic tenet of gestalt theory. "To say that a phenomenon is one of 'form' (*Gestalt*)," writes Merleau-Ponty, "is . . . to say that it develops according to a law of *internal* equilibrium, as if by *auto-organization*" (1964a, p. 121). And again, "It is this auto-distribution which is expressed by the notion of form. . . . The notion of form does nothing other than express the descriptive properties of certain natural wholes" (1963, p. 51).

If an arrow, →, is allowed to stand for the intrinsic determination of any one member of a gestalt by any other of its members, such an influence or signifying of *B* by *A* (*x* on left making *x* on right be *x* on right, for example) can then be represented in this way: *A* → *B*. We can similarly represent the determination of *A* by *B* (*x* on right making *x* on left be *x* on left) this way: *A* ← *B*. We can, moreover, represent the overall reciprocal and self-regulating interaction formative of a gestalt in this way: *A* ↔ *B* (*x* on right making *x* on left be *x* on left making *x* on right be *x* on right making *x*'s be a pair with one *x* on right and the other on the left; *x* on left ↔ *x* on right). *A* ↔ *B* is a symbol, then, for the circularly reciprocal intending or signifying that characterizes the lived dimensionality of any gestalt in existential space, its "auto-organization." *A* ↔ *B* symbolizes the occurrence of a natural whole of meaning, the music in its total unfolding, the human face as someone, the rectangle as a rectangle.

When we say, "Hit the ball!," *Hit* takes its concrete meaning from *the ball,* from the way *the ball* stretches backward as a stretch to the stretch *Hit* (*Hit* ← *the ball*) and concretely modifies it. *Hit* has another meaning altogether when we say, "Hit the road" or "He hit the ceiling" (*Hit* ← *the road; He hit* ← *the ceiling*). But, likewise, *the ball* takes its meaning from *Hit* (*Hit* → *the ball*); *Hit* and *the ball* take their meanings from each other (*Hit* ↔ *the ball*). *The ball* is something else entirely when we say, "We went to the ball" (*We went to* → *the ball*). Each of these utterances has a meaning of its own that presently arises in the self-governing organization of its constituent members, *A* ↔ *B*. Reciprocal determination, dynamic self-distribution, is everywhere in operation in language, as it is in the everyday meanings of our lives quite in general.

In brief, on the one hand, a gestalt is not the sum of its parts, $G \neq A + B$; whereas, on the other, a gestalt properly may be characterized as the dynamically self-regulating, thoroughly reciprocal determination of its constituents by one another, $G = A \leftrightarrow B$. A gestalt, Köhler remarks, is "the *whole having* a form" (1971, p. 164). Gestalt psychology, he goes on to say, is preoccupied with this tendency to organization and the formation of segregated unities, with the dynamics of organization (ibid.). A gestalt is a system, an integral organization, with, in Gurwitsch's words, "*internal unification of the functional significances of its constituents, . . . the balanced and equilibrated belonging and functioning together of the parts, the functional tissue which the parts form*" (1964, p. 139).

Return to the Organization of the Immediately Given

By emphasizing the emergence of gestalts directly and immediately from the moments that constitute them, as the very organizing of one another of such moments, Gestalt theory turns away from the conventional two-stage theory of meaning, from "sensation and perception." Gestalt theory, with existential phenomenology, rejects the notion that there are "raw" sensory data with an absolute existence in-themselves. Rather, perceived meanings are given immediately, always and already organized. As Gurwitsch says, *"All features displayed by perception must be treated on the same footing"* (ibid., p. 91). There is no substratum of unformed, unchanging, meaningless fragments. Meaning instead is original. This dismissal of the pure psychological element (the "atom"), the "raw" sensation, comes with the introduction of a descriptive (phenomenological) orientation in psychology.

   "The given," Wertheimer writes, *"is itself in varying degrees 'structured' ('gestaltet')"* (1967a, p. 14). Organization is evidenced at every level in experience. Gestalt psychology finds, as Gurwitsch puts it, that what "presents itself in direct and immediate experience is structured and organized to a greater or lesser extent" (1964, p. 115). It is precisely herein that lies Gestalt psychology's landmark discovery. A gestalt is never not meaningful: lifeworld moment always signifies lifeworld moment *as something*. A gestalt is an organization on the level of meaning, which is to say that meaning occurs on its own phenomenal level. What is given in experience is not isolated elements, but "totals and total processes with characteristic properties, tendencies, organizational forms and structures of their own" (ibid.). Returning to "the things themselves," it turns out that basic to experience are wholes that have an irreducible meaning from the first. What we have are "not sensations with gaps between them, into which memories may be supposed to slip" (Merleau-Ponty, 1962, pp. 21–22), but presently unfolding lifeworld events (the town we are exploring, the book we are reading, the friend we are visiting). Members *A, B, C,* and so on indeed are the materials entering into a gestalt, but these materials always and already are self-forming: the immediately self-distributing moments dimensionally constitutive of a gestalt, always and already formed, bounded, with shape, figure against its background, always and already a meaning. A gestalt not only always and already *has* meaning, it always and already *is* meaning, immediately what it is as the organization of its sensible members. A gestalt, Gurwitsch writes, is a whole that, "by virtue of its intrinsic articulation and structure, possesses coherence and consolidation and, thus, detaches itself as an organized and closed unit from the surrounding field" (1964, p. 115). All in all, what is original in our reality is an interweaving of sensible lifeworld moments, organization in and through significance. *Meaning is original with a gestalt.* Stimuli and sensations, and not organization, in fact are the true latecomers, late constructions of modern sentiment, and not original founding givens; as Koffka puts it, "Sensations and their attributes appear as products of a particular kind of organization achieved by human beings in highly developed civilizations, but no longer as the raw material out of which all consciousness is built" (1935, p. 360).

l

The Absolute and the Relative

By its return to the organization of the immediately given, Gestalt theory amounts to a rejection of the principle of *atomism*. Atomism is the conventional doctrine that holds that reality can be broken down into ultimate fragments entirely extrinsic to one another, into "atoms" or pieces. Such self-defined and self-contained determinate elements, stimuli and their corresponding sensations, for example, are viewed as existing in-themselves in the space-time continuum. Thus taken as *absolute*, these elements, *absolved* of all significance, and hence of all internal change due to significance, enter intact into a variety of combinations. "The method of elementary analysis," writes Merleau-Ponty, "decomposes the whole into a sum of real parts" (1963, p. 75).

By emphasizing the origin of the gestalt in the self-regulating and reciprocal interacting of its members, by contrast, Gestalt theory espouses the *relative*; that is, that which is decided and defined not only by itself, but also by something else, and in fact by many other things. Gestalt theory holds to the relatedness of all meaning. The relativity of a lifeworld moment lies in its being *referred* to something else for its very determination as the moment it is, its being referred beyond itself to other moments that signify and are signified by it. In the formulation $A \leftarrow B$, A is represented as determined by, and hence as mixed up, in the destiny of B from the first. A, in other words, is relative to B. In the formulation $A \leftrightarrow B$, A and B are represented in their thoroughly circular relativity to one another, a gestalt's relative moments, relativities. A and B complete, complement, one another. Conventional atomistic logic prescribes, without qualification, that reality is reducible to its basic units, which units are forever what they are in-themselves: $A = A = A = A = A$, and so on; $B = B = B = B = B$, and so on. This defines the *atom* or element. Gestalt logic describes A as signified by B in what A is as a meaning (and vice versa). A is not simply self-defined, is not simply itself. This lack of simple identity with itself, this absence of total presence in-itself (presence-at-hand), may be represented by $A \neq A$. $A \leftrightarrow B$: A and B reciprocally and circularly signify and express one another as a whole of meaning; A influences B as it is influenced by B, B influences A as it is influenced by A.

Because no member of a gestalt exists in an absolute manner in-itself for Gestalt theory and because in forming a gestalt the members reciprocally and dynamically define the reality of one another at every moment, real change occurs in our world. When lifeworld moments first signify one another for someone, they come to change each other in novel and unpredictable ways. Things are not once and for all what they always were in-themselves, influencing one another only externally by reason of linear, "end-to-end causality" (Merleau-Ponty, 1968, p. 232). Meanings instead forever are being decided. Meaning, as already suggested, is emergent. *Becoming*, real development in the existential space of possibility—and not mere change of objective location in an objective space of the ready-made—is intrinsic to meaning at every level of its integration.

Gestalt: "Characteristics in Relation"

Lifeworld moment A is determined, limited, by lifeworld moment B: $A \leftarrow B$. A is not simply itself, not simply self-defined: $A \neq A$. This coming to be dynamically decided before our very eyes of a gestalt's moments represents a major challenge to conventional Western thought.

There, of course, is not only change initiated from beyond ($A \neq A$, $B \neq B$, and so on). There also is a certain self-givenness about moment A and moment B, a certain way for moment A to be A, and for B to be B ($A = A$, $B = B$). The term x on left became x on left because of x on right, but x on left is x on left also because of characteristics and a location that properly are its own. There even is a certain way in which A or B can change and be changed; a certain way, moreover, in which each cannot change without being turned into something else again. Gestalt logic moves most fundamentally, then, in the following paradox: $A = A$, $A \neq A$; $B = B$, $B \neq B$. Both formulations, A is A, A is not A, are to be held at once. Moments A, B, C, D, and so forth both are and are not themselves. This in fact is what it means to be a lifeworld moment. To both be and not be itself is structurally invariant for any of a gestalt's constituents, any lifeworld moment. Such a Gestalt logic of meaning is summarized aptly by Köhler's formulation of a gestalt as "characteristics in relation." On the one hand, the members of a gestalt or of a field of gestalts have characteristics of their own. A rectangle, for example, is made up of four lines. Each line is itself, exercising a suchness of its own ($A = A$). But each line is concretely defined, on the other hand, by its actual place in the rectangle it coconstitutes with the other lines ($A \leftarrow B$, C, D; $A \neq A$). $A = A$ and $A \neq A$: characteristics ($A = A$) in relation ($A \neq A$). The notes that form a melody constitute it for what they are, for how each sounds ($A = A$). But, how each sounds depends concretely on the other notes that signify it, on the way it is changed from beyond ($A \neq A$). In this melody such and such a note is cheerful, in that one it is sad. The word *take* has a certain characteristic meaning in itself ($A = A$). But this dictionary meaning is vague and the word, to come into its own as a word, needs concrete specification by a context of other words ($A \neq A$). *Take* can be decided in a variety of ways: "She took over," "He was taken," "He is taking a break," "Take his coat," "They took the pledge," "We took in $6,000." The one *take* is differentially changed in the various sentences: *take* $\leftarrow B$, C, D, E, F, or G. The paradox $A = A$ and $A \neq A$ is enacted in these phrases; indeed, in its own way, in any gestalt. The Gestalt logic of the lifeworld is enacted. And in the coming to formation of a gestalt, a meaning first arises in the concreteness of its lived dimensionality as a unity of sensible qualities. The give-and-take that defines the role of any part in its whole is further explored in the immediately following section.

The Functional Significance of Parts in Wholes

Functional significance expresses something of the innermost essence, and hence logic, of gestalts: Gestalt logic. Functional significance is the role a part plays in the whole, a part's place in a whole of meaning.

A gestalt's members reciprocally give one another their roles in the gestalt they form. It is this functional significance which, in Gurwitsch's words, "gives to each [member] its qualification in a concrete case" (1964, p. 135). Each of the gestalt's constituents "is qualified and made to be what it is by its relation to, and significance for, the other constituents" (Gurwitch, 1965, pp. 21–22). It thus can be said that the members of a gestalt are contained in one another (Gurwitsch, 1974, p. 252), existing through, depending upon, determining, demanding, and mutually supporting one another (Gurwitsch, 1964, p. 145). The structure of the gestalt of which it is a part determines what a part is (Gurwitsch, 1966, p. 189); *structure,* by Köhler's definition, refers to "a functional aspect of processes," to the distribution processes assume "as a consequence of the dynamic interrelations or interactions among their parts" (1969, p. 92). A constituent exists only within a *"system of functional significances"* that determine each other. All constituents require and carry one another (Gurwitsch, 1966, p. 210).

On the one hand, the functional significance of each member of a gestalt stems from the gestalt's total structure and organization, whereas, on the other, each member, by reason of its functional significance, makes its proper contribution to this total structure (Gurwitsch, 1964, pp. 115–116). Both formulations express the same state of affairs. In Merleau-Ponty's words,

> Groups rather than juxtaposed elements are principal and primary in our perception. . . . The melody is not a sum of notes, since each note only counts by virtue of the function it serves in the whole, which is why the melody does not perceptibly change when transposed, that is, when all its notes are changed while their interrelationships and the structure of the whole remain the same. On the other hand, just one single change in these interrelationships will be enough to modify the entire make-up of the melody. Such a perception of the whole is more natural and more primary than the perception of isolated elements. (1964b, pp. 48–49)

Functional Significance of a Part as Determined by the Whole

The part's "quality, its existence, its raison d'être," Gurwitsch points out, are determined by its functional significance within a whole, are derived from what is assigned to it by the inner articulation of the gestalt of which it is a part (1966, pp. 25–26). A part's functional significance defines its dimensional existence within the larger meaning. "What I really have," Wertheimer writes, "what I hear of each individual note, what I experience at each place in the melody is a *part* which is itself determined by the character of the whole. . . . It belongs to the flesh and blood of the things given in experience, how, in what role, in what function they are in their whole" (1967b, p. 5). The part is the whole at its place. Because the part thus realizes the whole where it stands among the whole's other coconstituents, it can be said that the whole exists in each part (Gurwitsch, 1964, p. 145). The part expresses the whole; the whole is expressed in each part. As moment succeeds moment in a melody, the melody presences in its entirety: "In each of its notes the melody is present as a whole" (Gurwitsch, 1965, p. 22); the melody is a single unfolding gestalt quality that is always changing. In that the part assumes its identity by realizing the whole in its place, whole and part are anything but extrinsic to one another.

Köhler points out that, "when we look at the molar unit which is called a square, four points in the boundary of this figure have the character of being 'corners'" (1969, p. 54), but that the very "same" points in the very "same" spots would no longer be *corners* if these were points of the circumference of a circle. "Being a corner is, therefore, not a property which these points have as such; rather, it is a property which they acquire within a particular larger context" (ibid.). The "same" constituent playing a different role in another system of functional significances—the word *take* placed in a different sentence or the "same" note in a different song (see "Characteristics in Relation") or a corner taken from a rectangle and made to serve as part of an *H*—is now dimensionally different, with a different sensible quality about it, because of the codetermining effect of that system on it ($A \neq A$). A part's position in the whole determines its properties, its *dependent properties* (Köhler, 1938, p. 75). All in all, then, the properties qualifying any given member of a gestalt, its *dependent part quality,* are one with its functional significance, its place within a gestalt's structural articulation (Gurwitsch, 1964, pp. 132–136). In psychology, Köhler writes, "we have wholes which, instead of being the sum of parts existing independently, give their parts specific functions or properties that can only be defined in relation to the whole in question" (1971, p. 145). In its dependent part quality within a gestalt a part can itself be called a meaning, the part for what, "as what," it is, the part that it shows itself as being within its whole.

Functional Significance as Determination of the Whole

The characteristics of a part are determined, then, by the part's functional significance in the whole, in the total system of functional significances. Assuming its role in a whole, a part enters into relationship with the whole's other parts and becomes, with them, "characteristics in relation." But, as already suggested, the part is not only determined by the whole, but makes its own particular contribution ($A = A$), in what is dimensionally most characteristic of it, to the organization of the whole. As Gurwitsch puts it, "As each note of the melody has its functional significance with regard to the other notes, and may in this sense be said to derive it from them, so it confers, in turn, their functional significances on the other notes" (1965, p. 22).

A constituent's removal from a given system is rarely restricted to the member itself; other members are changed. The gestalt loses its original character and a new one arises. Gurwitsch, commenting on Koffka's assertion that in a gestalt "every part has its place and its property as part of the whole," remarks that in a gestalt all the parts reciprocally support one another and that the change of any one part is bound to affect all the others; that is, the gestalt in its entirety (1966, p. 239). A different note in a certain place in a melody makes the melody different, and perhaps wrong. A rounded "corner" ruins the "rectangle."

The way a part determines the whole, its weight in the whole, is determined by its role in the whole; that is, is codetermined by the other members with which it interdepends to form a whole. Neither of these determinations (determining, being determined) comes first. Thoroughgoing reciprocal (circular) determination prevails. Gestalt theory thus replaces the traditional conception of parts and wholes, in terms of isolated elements, with a functionalistic conception. Parts are now defined as whole-parts, with dependent part qualities, essentially determined in their meaning by their functional significance in the whole. "Parts and wholes are defined with reference to, and prove correlative of, each other" (Gurwitsch, 1964, p. 149). Neither the part nor the whole is actualized before the other.

Gestalt Quality as the Gestalt Itself

Gestalt qualities, it has been pointed out, were important historically in the launching of Gestalt psychology. It therefore is critical to understand how gestalt qualities stand with regard to the gestalts they qualify. The Gestalt theory presented in this chapter, and indeed the very definition of a gestalt given, in point of fact already determine the direction in which closure is to be found on this issue. A gestalt quality (whole property) has been said to be the "particular sensible suchness of a gestalt, the meaning a gestalt has" (see

"Gestalt Qualities"), and a gestalt has been characterized as the very signifying of one another of its members, self-organizing expression, immediately given meaning (see "Gestalt as the Organization of Its Constituents"). Taken together, these assertions amount to saying that gestalt quality and gestalt are the same immediately given meaning, that a gestalt quality is nothing other than the meaning original with a gestalt (dynamic self-distribution) from the first. "The Gestalt-quality is the Gestalt itself with its intrinsic structure" (Gurwitsch, 1966, p. 27). Gestalt quality is nothing but the *way* sensible lifeworld moments signify one another as a whole of meaning.

A gestalt's suchness is not something added on to it, then, but exactly what it is as the dynamic self-distribution of its moments. Gestalt quality is not *something more* tacked on to disconnected atoms to give them the meaning they lack (see "A Gestalt Is Not More than the Sum of Its Parts," the next section). As always and already organized, as not a mere sum of disconnected atoms, an already qualitatively meaningful gestalt does not stand in need such a *more*. No aggregate of pieces, a whole is not to be distinguished from its quality in the first place. No, gestalt quality is simply the gestalt (form) itself as characteristically itself. Although gestalt quality is nowhere to be found in the members of a whole taken separately, gestalt quality is precisely their self-forming as this or that gestalt, lifeworld moments signifying each other from the first *as something*. Niagara Falls is the very beauty, majesty, and expressive power we find it to be upon becoming witness to it. The essence of Niagara Falls, the gestalt quality of Niagara Falls, is just the *way* its sensible constituents dynamically stretch to and signify one another, just the meaning it is as a gestalt. The gestalt quality of the music is precisely the way its moments structurally play into and signify one another, their gestalt. A story is the characteristic way certain narrated events lead into one another as an immediately given whole of meaning. A right angle is just the way two lines meet as a meaning. The dancer's grace is nothing but the graceful way her movements form a segregated unity. The character of a sentence is exactly the meaning that develops in the expressing of one another of its words.

The lifeworld is from the first a network of expressive unities, of gestalt qualities. Discussing "Scheler's Theory of Milieu," Gurwitsch writes, "The threatening, the uncanny, dread-inspiring, enchanting, ingratiating, friendly, and the like, are the primary 'data' of the milieu; they are that which first of all 'obtrude' from the milieu and give the respective surroundings their characteristic imprint. . . . These unities of expression are themselves given" (1979, p. 61). The lifeworld always and already is meaningful.

With a gestalt the action of its parts—"Seeing is the perception of action," in the words of gestalt psychologist Rudolf Arnheim (1974, p.

16)—gestalt quality is simply the gestalt in the act of playing itself, the rose as a rose. Meaning no more preexists in-itself, as a form stored among other forms in memory, than do a meaning's constituents, as sensations. Meaning rather is the dynamically self-organizing *event* of its sensible qualities. Take away the present organizing, this particular reciprocal relating (signifying) of these members, this gestalt, and you take away this gestalt quality, this meaning. A new organizing, a new gestalt, a new gestalt quality, immediately takes its place.

A Gestalt Is Not More Than the Sum of Its Parts

A gestalt is the event of its members in the fullness of their lived dimensional quality. Gestalt is meaning, the very way an organization of sensible qualities plays itself. Meaning or gestalt quality is not something, "a new element," added on to disconnected elements; a gestalt was never such a sum to begin with. Meaning is not a contribution of any sort above and beyond the complex of parts forming the gestalt, but original rather to the organization any gestalt is. And yet Chapter 1 found that a dualism of parts (sensations) and their whole properties (meaning or perception) remains the philosophy governing the understanding of basic behavioral processes in conventional psychology. Conventional thought holds that not only are there parts, *A* and *B* in the present notation, in every "whole," but that there also is something in the works that binds them together and makes them into something *more* than what they might be as a mere sum of splashes of color, single sounds, touches, tastes, and so on (see, for example, Wortman, Loftus, and Marshall, 1988, p. 85). What is contributed, in the belief of orthodox textbook psychology, as a kind of additional element, is the gestalt quality or meaning, the form or gestalt itself. The objective brain is said to interpret "raw" sense data, the disjointed parts supposedly entering into the "whole," and to confer meaning on them, to turn them into inner perceptions (meanings). According to this widespread viewpoint, the "whole" is *more* than the sum of its parts. Now there are not only the parts but, above and beyond them, the meaning, the "more" that the brain, performing on extrinsic "raw materials" *A* and *B,* creates by an activity of interpreting or synthesizing. An extraneous intervention on the part of the objective brain takes unorganized elements and turns them into organized perceptions. And this occurs, it is traditionally presupposed, on the basis of a consultation with memory, through an importation from objective storage of materials (forms) deposited in the brain in the course of past experience. Psychological theorists who do not allow of a *present* interplay of a gestalt's moments, of a current dynamic self-distribution of the processes in play in gestalt formation, thus are seen to be thrown back on an account of "gestalts" in terms of controlling mechanisms or constraints instituted in the *past.* Past tense thus is made to account for present perception. This would mean that we are not really seeing the tree we supposed we were. Present alone in the environment by this account are stimuli. Present inside the organism are sensations instituted by environmental stimuli; also present inside is the brain's activity of interpreting these sensations, with the help of presently stored memories of previously experienced "trees." What is not present by this account is the tree in the meadow, the tree we thought we had just come upon. The tree's form rather is being conjured up by the brain from objectively stored memories, from the past, from the effects of the past presently inside us in the objective space of the brain, and imposed on the necessarily incomplete information presently reaching the organism from the environment. Meaning (form) is being given to sensations. So far as meaning is concerned, therefore, this theory leaves us only ever experiencing the past. What is present for conventional psychology, in truth a realm of sheer presence (presence-at-hand), is the "real world" of stimuli and other objective occurrences. Meaning or perception, by contrast, is viewed as a subjective re-creation on the basis of what was. For traditional psychological theory, then, the past brings about "organization," the past organizes our present. Meaning has no present of its own, much less a future, and neither have we. The present phenomenological approach finds this account of meaning formation lacking in that plausibility, that legitimacy even, that a clarification of concepts on the basis of "the things themselves" alone can provide. It is difficult, if not impossible, moreover, to understand how this theory could account for the first occurrence of any meaning or perception whatsoever, when the sensations presently reaching the brain would have no prior "organization," no prior form, to fall back on.

All in all, then, for conventional psychology an objective intervention subjectivizes, creating a realm of meanings internal to the psychological constitution of the organism, generating meanings as "modifications of the mind." A "whole" is said to be composed of its elements *and* the meaning conferred upon them by an extraneous synthesizing activity of the brain. Gurwitsch points out that all traditional theories are of the opinion that perceptions thus develop out of "mere sense-data" through the intervention of extraneous factors that interpret sensations and bestow meaning on them (1964, p. 88).

Gestalt theory, affirming the immediacy of perception's organization, the immediacy of meaning of a gestalt, denies the extrinsic unifying activity (bestowal of meaning) demanded by conventional thought. In Gurwitsch's words, "*There is no unifying principle or agency over and above the parts or constituents*" (ibid., p. 139). Mutually signifying and demanding one another from the first rather, the parts (the gestalt) do not need such an extraneous unifier. The melody is not added on as a new element to the complex of notes (Gurwitsch, 1966, p. 256). Higher functions do not give form to unstructured sensory data. "What is immediately given, the phenomenological primal material, is given only as articulated and structured" (ibid.). "The Gestalt springs from the organization of the parts themselves," remarks Arnheim, "not from a quality added to the parts. *We do not say: the whole is 'more' than the sum of its parts;* we prefer to assert that the whole is 'something else' than the sum of its parts" (1961, p. 91; emphasis mine). The average student being exposed to Gestalt psychology nevertheless learns to identify it with the slogan, "The whole is more than the sum of the parts," a formulation that is incorrect and thus unacceptable to Gestalt psychologists (Arnheim, 1986b, p. 820; see also this section). A gestalt is not *more than* a sum, rather it is *qualitatively different from* a sum. In Köhler's words, "A specific sensory whole is *qualitatively* different from the complex that one might predict by considering only its parts in isolation" (1971, p. 161). The difference between parts and whole for Gestalt psychology is not quantitative in character, then, not the addition of one more in-itself (imported from objective storage in memory). The whole is seen to be different in character from a sum ($G \neq A + B; G = A \leftrightarrow B$). "Is it really true that when I hear a melody I have a *sum* of individual tones (pieces) which constitute the primary foundation of my experience?" Wertheimer asks. And he responds that the reverse is indeed the case, "What I really have, what I hear of each individual note, what I experience at each place in the melody is a *part* which is itself determined by the character of the whole" (1967b, p. 5). The melody does not originate from the sum of its parts through the intervention of some extraneous factor; the melody is no secondary process. The character of each of the melody's parts, to the contrary, depends from the first on its place in the whole. "The flesh and blood of a tone depends from the start upon its role in the melody. . . . It belongs to the flesh and blood of the things given in experience, how, in what role, in what function they are in their whole" (ibid.). We never first hear, Heidegger says, a "pure noise"—to accomplish that takes "a very artificial and complicated frame of mind"—but the passing car, the marching band, the menace of the wind, the bird's call, the water falling; not having to do first with sensations, we do not find ourselves giving shape to a "swirl of sensations to provide the springboard from which the subject leaps off and finally arrives at a 'world' " (1962a, p. 207).

In the Gestalt formula, $G = A \leftrightarrow B$, $\leftrightarrow$ does not represent something extra, an extra piece, some-thing more. All there is to a gestalt rather is the moments involved and their activity. What makes the x's be the pair, $x\,x$, are the nonmental lifeworld x's themselves. The perceived is just what it is in its lifeworld constitution. The sign $\leftrightarrow$ is really not anything at all: not any thing, no thing, no-thing, nothing. It simply indicates the present relating of a gestalt's members to one another in and from their place within a context of significance, which is all any gestalt is. For A and B to dynamically regulate one another means that no extra anything is needed to produce the whole of which they are parts. The gestalt notion of organization represented by $\leftrightarrow$ eliminates a necessary recourse to an extrinsic constructive operation, such as the one proposed by conventional thought, to account for gestalt qualities. In brief, saying that a gestalt is something *other than* the mere extrinsic summing of its parts means that a gestalt in its qualitative suchness (gestalt quality, meaning) simply is the self-regulating and reciprocal interacting of its lifeworld members. The other side of $G \neq A + B$ is $G = A \leftrightarrow B$. Saying, by contrast, that the "whole" originates in its parts considered as "raw" sensations ("G" $= A + B$) requires, because meaning is nowhere to be found in the parts taken as elements and because experienced wholes are clearly not *merely* the sum of their parts, that one also affirm that the "whole" is more than the sum of its parts. The other side of "G" $= A + B$ ("gestalt" as mere aggregate) can be only "G" $> A + B$. With M standing for interpretively bestowed meaning or form, "G" $= A + B$ has to become "G" $= A + B + M$ (aggregate of pieces plus meaning), that is, has to become "G" $> A + B$. Saying that the "whole" is constructed on the basis of sensations requires that something be added to the sensations to account for meaning as actually experienced.

In view of this, it is ironic indeed that introductory psychology textbooks not infrequently characterize Gestalt theory as the position that holds that the whole is more than the sum of it parts. The slogan of the Gestalt psychologist is said to have been: "The whole is more than the sum of its parts" (Kalat, 1986, p. 108; Gerow, 1989, p. 11; Krebs and Blackman, 1988, p. 13). "These scientists emphasized that perception involved more than the mere addition of sensations impinging on the sensory systems. In other words, the whole (perception) is more than the sum of its parts (sensations)" (Wallace, Goldstein, and Nathan, 1987, p. 135). The Gestalt theorists "insisted that the psychological experience is greater than the sum of its parts" (Price, Glickstein, Horton, Sherman, and Fazio, 1987, p. 12), that "the whole is *greater* than the sum of its parts" (McMahon and McMahon, 1986, p. 128; see also Crider, Goethals, Kavanaugh, and Solomon, 1989, p. 110; Landy, 1987, p. 130). The proponents of Gestalt psychology "believed it is impossible to understand form perception simply by analyzing each of the many sensations registered in the brain when we see, hear, smell, taste, or touch something. Often, they argued, our perceptions are *more* than the sensations that give rise to them. That 'more' is a meaningful pattern or whole, which in German is called a *Gestalt*" (Wortman et al., 1988, 106). Because Gestalt theory is the explicit denial of "the many sensations registered in the brain" "giving rise" to our perceptions, the way this last quotation thoroughly reverses Gestalt theoretical thinking is extraordinary. The suspicion mounts that conventional psychology is so thoroughly imbued with the objectivist requirement of "raw" elements, with atomism, that, confronted with a denial of the whole as the sum of its parts, it can imagine only that something *more* must be involved. Conventional psychology, failing to grasp even the problem of organization, ends up turning Gestalt psychology into its own traditional two-stage theory of perception.

Organization and Variability

From an existential point of view, the advent of Dasein spells the breaking open of a space of possibility between lifeworld meanings where they can signify one another in any number of ways. There is in this openness room for the moments of a gestalt to first become, and then remain, themselves as they express and change one another. Subject and object having been decentered, the signifying of moments by one another is now seen to be the veritable center where lifeworld moments gather. Signifying is the freedom of lifeworld moments, a freedom that lets moments surpass themselves and meet this way, then that, as this gestalt and then as that one. Significance, the *way* the world is, allows the multiple moments of the lifeworld to interdepend for someone in their own possibilities of meaning in countless variations, to come to expression as countless gestalts. A few thousand words, for example, *become* thousands and thousands of books, in a rich variety of literary forms. A limited number of available lifeworld moments relate in the open expanse of the "there" to form an endless variety of gestalts, meanings: trees, lakes, faces, songs, speeches. Because lifeworld moments can meet for what they themselves characteristically are, and change one another in the process; because no objective something is binding the moments together and extraneously conferring form (meaning) upon them; because *something more* is not slipped in between lifeworld moments; because an open space of signifying is between them—because of all this, virtually anything is possible in the way of figures that can *presently* arise for us as lifeworld meanings (see Chapter 13 for a further discussion of the variability and decidability of meaning). All sorts of things can be decided out of lifeworld givens in the existential space of possibility. Because of the openness between sensible qualities, they can converse with one another, commune, and in the process differentially leap into concrete dimensional unity as one bounded figure or another. Because of the clearing opened with Dasein, sensible lifeworld moments can express themselves and one another, can change one another, and in the process first truly become themselves. As has been suggested once before in this chapter, *there is becoming*. Reality, with its circular lifeworld signifying, is more like a conversation for existential phenomenology, a saying, than it is like a game of billiards. It is more linguistic than mechanistic.

Thus, in the configuration,

$$x\,x \quad x\,x \quad x\,x \quad x\,x \quad x\,x$$

x's signify and express each other in their quality as five pairs of x's. The openness at issue among the x's is not the empty space on the paper. This openness instead is the circular signifying in process among the x's. The breaking open being pointed at is the very possibility of such a signifying. No higher-order contribution by the objective brain makes unformed materials into the expressive unity under consideration. The signifying presently in operation among the x's is nothing but the x's themselves as they reciprocally express one another in their possibility as five pairs of x's: the signifying is no thing. But, in the following figure, the "same" x's are available in such a way as to be able to signify each other in their possibility as a triangle:

$$x$$
$$x \quad x$$
$$x \qquad x$$
$$x \quad x \quad x \quad x$$

Here the moments, entering into a different signifying of one another, regulate one another as a different gestalt. Existential openness, the always and already having been surpassed of beings in-themselves, allows first one signifying and then the other. Gestalt lawfulness (Chapter 6), on the other hand, determines how the materials as they are available will concretely signify one another for a competent someone; that is, how they will actually look.

The Complementarity of Gestalt Theory and Existential Thought

As a theory of organization, and in particular as a theory of Gestalt lawfulness and of the role of such lawfulness in meaning's dynamic self-distribution, Gestalt psychology has a valuable contribution to make to existential phenomenology. The next chapter considers the topic of Gestalt lawfulness. The chapter after that then turns to the important theory of value implicit in this notion of lawfulness. Whereas existential phenomenology has much to learn from Gestalt theory on such topics as dynamic self-distribution, Gestalt laws, and value, Gestalt theory has much to gain, and on even more fundamental issues, from existential phenomenology. The benefits these complementary traditions stand to reap from one another will become increasingly evident in the course of the following chapters.

6 Requiredness

Nor are "Gestalten" the sums of
aggregated contents erected
subjectively upon primarily given
pieces: contingent, subjectively
determined, adventitious structures.
. . . We are dealing here with wholes
and whole-processes possessed of
specific inner, intrinsic laws; we are
considering structures with their
concrete structural principles.

—*Wertheimer*, 1967a, p. 15

The Nonarbitrary Character of Meaning Formation

Stretching to and signifying one another, lifeworld moments first come to
formation as segregated figures. Qualities interdepend and give rise to new
and emergent qualities. Meaning grows into meaning. This development of
meaning in the reciprocal signifying of one another of sensible qualities
proceeds in a dynamically self-regulating manner. Not bound together by an
external intervention, a gestalt's moments presently enter into communication with and define one another as a living whole of meaning. But the
question then arises as to why currently available lifeworld moments come to
organize themselves as this gestalt rather than as that one. Granted that the
formation of gestalts is not a matter of the automatic kicking in of constraints
instituted sometime in the past, is the dynamic self-distribution now allowed
them a matter of chance, of mere probabilities? Or, are there, perhaps,
nonarbitrary reasons for gestalt formation? Are there principles, laws of
structure, governing events of meaning presencing? Gestalt theory holds to
just such "concrete structural principles" (Wertheimer, 1967a, p. 15) and has
attempted to formulate them. Conventional psychology, for its part, bound
fast to its atomistic presupposition, has never gotten far enough to take these
most important laws with the seriousness they merit as the starting point for
a psychological science adequate to lifeworld meaning and meaning-oriented
behavior. This chapter explores the notion of Gestalt lawfulness, and does so
finally in terms of *requiredness,* a preferred term in Köhler's writings (see in

105

particular, 1938, Chapter 3). A Gestalt law of requiredness is proposed as a general structural principle guiding the signifying of one another of lifeworld moments.

The Law of Good Gestalt

Gestalt Lawfulness

Our world is perceived in an orderly manner, as an orderly world. The past does not, for Gestalt psychology, mechanically impose this orderliness on raw, fundamentally fragmentary and disconnected, elements. Dynamics in organization rather presently determines present outcome, present order. On the one hand, meaning is a self-determining action (gestalt). In Köhler's words, "The order of facts in a visual field is to a high degree the outcome of a [dynamic] self-distribution of processes" (1947, p. 78). And again, "Dynamic distributions are functional wholes" (ibid., p. 80). On the other hand, such dynamic processes tend toward order rather than chaos, toward goodness of organization, a notion that, Köhler points out, apparently never occurred to Descartes, who insisted on the necessary role of mechanical constraints for the maintenance of order in nature (1969, p. 78). Köhler finds this tendency of dynamic self-distribution toward orderly and useful events to be a truly remarkable state of affairs, one indicative of the operation of certain Gestalt laws.

Traditional psychology locates the constants governing perception in data; namely, in pure sensations. But with Gestalt psychology, Gurwitsch points out, because no room is left for "an elementary stratum of psychical data depending only on objective stimuli," the perceptual constants no longer can be located "in *facts* or *data* but reside only in *laws*" (Gurwitsch, 1966, p. 24). Gestalt psychology thus finds in the laws governing perceptual transformations the constants or invariants of perception and sets itself the task of establishing these laws (ibid.). Gestalt theory, rejecting a higher mediation through which elementary data are synthesized into percepts (meanings), maintains that a whole's members are always and already organized, that organization is an immediate given of our reality (Chapter 5). Governing this organizing that has always been going on are principles intrinsic to gestalt formation, constant factors that are nothing less than *structural invariants* of events of meaning formation. "Formal factors"— such as those of similarity, proximity, common fate, and closure—are seen to be dynamically at work in the formation of gestalts from the first, generally regulating the internal structuring of given phenomena (ibid., p. 30).

Gestalt Laws of Similarity, Proximity, and Good Continuation

Gestalt psychology holds that certain structural invariants or laws, constants, are in play in the dynamics of meaning formation. It was Wertheimer especially who, in Köhler's words, formulated "simple descriptive principles which govern the *grouping* of segregated objects" (1969, p. 56). Lifeworld moments and figures that are close to or resemble one another, for example, tend to be seen together as a single meaning. We spontaneously see alternating rows of *X*'s and *O*'s in the following.

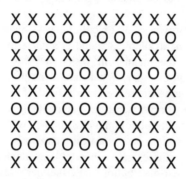

But now we see, just as naturally, alternating columns of *X*'s and *O*'s.

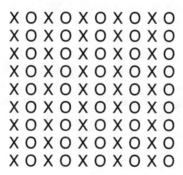

Our first reaction might be to suppose that we see rows in the first case, and columns in the second, because that is what is there. No problem of organization is seen to exist because organization is taken for granted. There is a natural tendency (the natural attitude, Chapter 2) to suppose that the rows or the columns are themselves objectively given on the page; that they are simply there, stimuli in-themselves standing in no need of *attaining* organization. Such an attitude in fact presumes upon the organization already achieved, and so thoroughly that "organization" becomes an objective given of the stimuli before us rather than an event, rather than a dynamic process.

Köhler remarks in this connection, "Once I tried to convince a Behaviorist that when, in speaking of a male bird, he referred to a female as 'a stimulus' he ignored the problems and facts of organization" (1947, p. 97). Köhler's efforts, perhaps not surprisingly, were to no avail. Meaningful patterns, Köhler insists in another context, are outcomes of perceptual organization, and such outcomes should never be called *stimuli* (1971, p. 105). All in all, for Gestalt psychology organization is not a given of stimuli, which are fragmented physical energies altogether devoid of order, but rather something that comes to be attained, presently, in accordance with certain Gestalt principles.[1]

The quality of rowness or of columnness in the earlier illustrations stems from the way the available X's and O's *come* to signify each other in the two cases; from the manner in which the two displays *attain* their respective organization or order. What makes the lifeworld material as it is available in the first case interdepend as a field of rows (gestalt quality of rowness), and the lifeworld material as it is available in the second as a field of columns (gestalt quality of columnness), is the law or factor of similarity. Gestalt laws such as this one constitute *demands* as to how lifeworld materials, always as these are concretely available, can self-form in perception (dynamic self-distribution). Wertheimer's law of similarity states that similar figures, other things being equal, tend to form a single larger segregated figure.

The X's and O's in the given illustrations form a larger field of alternating columns or of rows:

1. because similar materials (X's or O's) are lined up next to one another on the page either horizontally or vertically, because lifeworld materials are available thus, and *because of the law of similarity;* hence because horizontal or vertical lines, relatively segregated figures consisting of eight X's or eight O's, naturally arise in perception;

2. and because, in the first case, every other line is available as a horizontal line consisting of either X's or O's, every other line thus being available as alike, and *because of the law of similarity;* hence because alternating horizontal lines (rows) of X's and O's arise spontaneously; because, in the second case, every other line is available as a vertical line consisting of either X's or O's, every other line thus being available as alike, and *because of the law of similarity*; hence because alternating vertical lines (columns) of X's and O's naturally come to formation.

It may seem obvious that X's (or O's) will be seen together when they form a certain "pattern of stimuli," but the law of similarity specifies a reason, a perceptual constant, for such an "obvious" occurrence. The issue for Gestalt theory is accounting for the constitution of patterns, for the constitution of so-called patterns of stimuli in the first place.[2] It may be instructive to consider what would become of our X's and O's if governing perception were a purely fictitious law of *dissimilarity*, one that would require that dissimilar items be seen together. Alternating X's and O's, in the case of such a law, presumably would group themselves together as lines, and we would find ourselves seeing rows where we presently see columns and columns where we presently see rows. Perhaps even more interesting are the likely results (in contexts such as the present one where it is not reasonable to invoke an all-determining role of past experience) were no law at all in operation governing meaning formation. Is it not then to be expected either that no lines at all would form, that pure homogeneity would rule, or that "*all* possible forms"—zigzags, crosses, triangles, rectangles, letters, numbers, etc.—in fact would be given (Köhler, 1971, p. 162)? But homogeneity does not rule, and every possible gestalt does not come to formation, nor do lines composed of alternating X's and O's present themselves for our view. The *fact* of the matter, one that no empirically minded psychologist should want to overlook, is that similar items are seen together. Similarity rules as a matter of fact. The phenomenological demand is that we abide by facts just such as these.

The materials (X's, O's) as they are available in the two illustrations (as situated on the page in the two cases) set one limit on the gestalts that self-form. Gestalt lawfulness (factor of similarity) sets another. The proficiencies and preoccupations of the perceiver, not of immediate interest in the present readily perceivable illustrations, set another yet (Chapter 10, "Insight as Interpreting"). The organization any gestalt actually attains is a function of the interplay of these three conditioning factors. Organization is in every case co-organization. With Gestalt lawfulness a constant in gestalt formation, the proficiencies and preoccupations of the observer, on the one hand, and lifeworld materials as these are currently available, on the other, are circumstantial factors. Invariant Gestalt laws, in conjunction with varying circumstantial factors, are responsible for the meaning that in fact attains self-expression.

Available materials never account, then, of and by themselves, for the gestalts in fact actualized in events of meaning presencing. Rather, important processes of organization always and already are in process. Though what we encounter always and already is immediately organized, its organization always and already is in the process of being achieved. The available materials first reach us in their concrete actualization in a current signifying as this or that meaning—which is to say, as perceived, in accordance with Gestalt lawfulness, by a competent and interested someone—and never in the sheer givenness of their mere availability. Available materials are not stimuli. The only way we actually ever know anything at all about what is available in the lifeworld is from lifeworld materials as other than merely available, from lifeworld materials as always and already *co-organized* by both of the other limiting factors (Gestalt lawfulness, observer capabilities).

The materials as they are available in the present illustrations come to formation perceptually as X's and O's signifying one another as rows (as rows signifying one another), or as X's and O's signifying one another as columns (as columns signifying one another), because items that are similar to one another tend to cluster together in perception. The factor of similarity codetermines how available lifeworld moments are assigned their roles (functional significance) in the whole, and thus how, with what quality, these moments in fact stretch to one another to form a whole of sensible meaning in existential space. What is immediately perceived is being organized, is coming to formation, in its very being perceived. As Arnheim has remarked, "Seeing is the perception of action" (1974, p. 16). And again, "*Visual experience is dynamic. . . .* What a person or animal perceives . . . is, perhaps first of all, an interplay of directed tensions. . . . These tensions are as inherent in any percept as size, shape, location, or color" (ibid., p. 11). Perception is the actualization by someone, in accordance with Gestalt lawfulness, of a potential lifeworld *signifying*. The materials of the earlier illustrations spring into action upon inspection; becoming tense with (stretched to) one another at the moment, sensible lifeworld moments come to signify each other in the immediacy of their lived dimensionality. And alternating rows or columns are seen. It is as if nothing at all were taking place, and yet both patterns are dynamically alive with lawfully governed tensions (stretchings). These directed tensions are the core of the action that is the array of alternating rows or alternating columns. In more demanding situations, such as that of an incomplete context or of difficult materials, these tensions are more clearly in evidence, in their troubling character, as is the determining role of the observer.

Gestalt laws are not discovered in advance by their prior mathematical projection, but rather descriptively in the lifeworld meanings themselves, in the necessary manner in which such meanings are found in fact to come to formation. Gestalt laws do nothing but formulate certain constancies in what is going on around us all the time. These laws belong to the phenomena themselves, then, and are not accounts constructed in terms of a presumed transphenomenal "reality." The laws express the experienced play of directed (law-governed) structural tensions, *demands* made on perception that available materials come to formation in certain ways and not in others, *structural demands*.

It is difficult to disrupt the organization readily attained, for example, in the illustration of an array of rows and to see, let us say, an array of columns, anything but a law of *dis*similarity is in play.

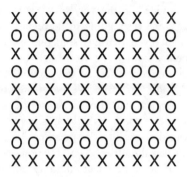

As soon as we begin to succeed in the attempt to see columns, we find our eyes spontaneously reverting to the original organization of rows. This figure is *balanced* to a high degree as an array of alternating rows and, trying to see anything else, tensions immediately mount in its direction and reinstate it. The interaction between the materials as available and the Gestalt law of similarity, as issuing in this figure, is a stable, insistent one. Such an interaction does not offer the co-organizing observer the ready option of entertaining other patterns. Structural demands are in operation rather, requiring that the pattern be one of alternating rows. But consider the following illustration.

When *X*'s and *O*'s become available in this altered manner, a loosening of organizational stability is in evidence. Various configurations now lend themselves to view. One sees an array of rows with relative ease, but also an array of columns, and not necessarily in that order. Other patterns likewise can be discerned without great effort: three pairs of columns, for example, or the four quadrants of the total pattern as four rectangles. This illustration, with its several potential signifyings, reveals more directly than the illustration of alternating rows (or columns) that lifeworld materials are not available simply in-themselves; that an organizing indeed already is in process. The illustration demonstrates in particular that the observer is a determining factor in the meaning being perceived at the moment. What the available materials "provide" in the way of a "stimulus" is a "stimulus" only *for someone,* for some responding in its regard, for the attention (the stretching toward) an involved (caring) someone is able to give it. "One cannot assign a moment in which the world acts on the organism," writes Merleau-Ponty, "since the very effect of this 'action' expresses the internal law of the organism" (1963, p. 161). We never are confronted by stimuli; that is, by physical energies that affect a sensory system in a linear and constant fashion (constancy hypothesis). What is in play, rather, is a circular relating between lifeworld possibilities of meaning, on the one hand, and the attitude of an observer, on the other: "The relations between the organism and its milieu are not relations of linear causality but of circular causality" (ibid., p. 15). *Nothing is ever seen simply because it is there* (the natural attitude). There always is an observer, and the observer always makes a difference. "The contact between the observer and the observed enters into the definition of the 'real' " (Merleau-Ponty, 1968, p. 16). No more than there are sensations (Chapter 5), are there any such things as stimuli.

In the last illustration, moreover, several different arrangements are seen, but not all possible ones. We see the ones that are more balanced in their patterning. This indicates the operation of Gestalt lawfulness, of the law of similarity, but also of a law of proximity. Wertheimer's law of proximity states that, other things being equal, figures that are close to one another tend to form a single larger figure. In the illustration under consideration, alternating X's and O's can, by reason of their vertical closeness to one another, form a temporarily stable pattern of columns, in which eventuality the factor of proximity comes to outweigh that of similarity. Stimuli do not walk into one's life. An observer invariably plays a role. But neither does subjective inclination or whim create the organization of the lifeworld, so to speak, out of its own substance. *Gestalt lawfulness governs in every case the circular transactions of observer and observed.* Gestalt laws, "concrete structural principles" (in Wertheimer's words), introduce a measure of necessity, of demand, into the perceived.

Besides the operation of laws of similarity and proximity in meaning formation, *a law of good continuation* likewise is in play. Gurwitsch points out, for example, that a melody that has been broken off is perceived as incomplete, as requiring that it be continued, and that it be continued in conformity with the direction already formed up to the moment. Those parts that already have made their appearance require completion in accordance with their functional significance. The incomplete system demands a certain completion; parts still to be integrated must meet definite conditions. "Under favorable circumstances, the incomplete system develops strong tendencies of its own towards completing itself. There arise movements of closure along the lines of good continuation" (Gurwitsch, 1964, p. 151). A musical theme, once established, may continue in a number of different ways, but not every turn is musically possible; that is, is in accordance with musical demands. If what comes later does not *fit* with what has already unfolded, "there occur the characteristic phenomena of 'out of tune,' 'surprise,' and eventually 'explosion' of the musical contexture" (ibid., p. 153). Demands circulate in the signifying of one another of lifeworld moments, then, in the direction of a completion with certain *good* characteristics. An incomplete sentence stretches to the words yet to come. Structural demands are instituted as to both form (grammar) and meaning. The sentence, "The children sings," is an example of bad continuation as to form. The sentence, "The gardenias expostulated angularly at their generous misfortune," is an example of bad continuation as to meaning. A direction established in an array of letters or numbers similarly demands its own good continuation. What is needed for the good continuation of *o o x x o o x x o,* other things being equal, is another *o.* The sequence 1–3–5–7 calls for 9 in the next place.

The Law of Good Gestalt

Given the circumstances, certain Gestalt laws—similarity, proximity, good continuation, closure—guide the formation of meanings, determining even what can become a meaning in the first place. But the Gestalt law of special interest here, the single law of which the other laws are "particular expressions," particular factors that may or may not be in play, is what has been called the *law of good gestalt* (also known as the *law of pregnance* [*Praegnanz*]). "The most general law underlying all change is The Law of *Praegnanz* according to which every gestalt becomes as 'good' as possible" (Wulf, 1967, p. 148). Having pointed out that Wertheimer first formulated the rules that the formation of thing-percepts obey with an understanding of their full import, Köhler proceeds to state that Wertheimer also formulated "a more general principle of which these rules seem to be more particular expressions"; namely, that a field's organization will be as clear and simple as the circumstances allow (1938, p. 195). A development, for example, in the direction of good—simple, balanced, clear—continuation makes for good organization, for a good gestalt, and a good gestalt is the structural state that every gestalt invariantly seeks to attain. Wertheimer remarks that we know how the members of a pattern we are designing ought to succeed one another. "One knows what a 'good' continuation is, how 'inner coherence' is to be achieved, etc.; one recognizes a resultant 'good gestalt' simply by its own 'inner necessity' " (1967c, p. 83). Wertheimer explicitly remarks, moreover, that the "Factor of similarity" is a "special instance of the *Factor of the Good Gestalt*" (ibid., p. 84n). In the first illustrations cited earlier, the good gestalt is one either of rows or of columns, because it is a necessity of any gestalt that it come to formation *as best it can,* and because similar items *look best together.* It is a structural necessity of the materials as they are available that they immediately display themselves in the one case as an array of alternating rows, and in the other as an array of alternating columns.[3] The word *necessity* here and elsewhere in this book indicates the urgency with which a meaning presses for its balanced fulfillment, in accordance with intrinsic structural demands. Necessity is an invariant in the coming to formation of all meaning. All meaning strives for its own perfection as a good gestalt. The law of good gestalt may be considered a law of the actualization of meaning in its necessity, the unrelenting demand that meaning be as good as it can be.

A gestalt's tendency toward the ideal status of a "good gestalt" is a structural constant or invariant governing gestalt formation, co-organizing any meaning whatsoever. A gestalt is an action (process) in which tensions are at play in the direction of the best meaning (outcome) possible. "[The] strictly descriptive concept of Gestalt," Gurwitsch writes, "entails functional concepts and laws, the most important of which is the law of pregnance, or the law of good Gestalt" (1966, p. 27), a tendency to "the best possible shape," "to the best possible Gestalt" under the circumstances (ibid., p. 37). Or, as Köhler puts it, "The products of perceptual organization tend to be most clearly structured" (1971, p. 409), to be balanced, incisive, clear-cut, strong; the tendency is to maximal regularity and simplicity (1938, pp. 195–198). "['Good'] embraces such properties as regularity, symmetry, simplicity" (Koffka, 1935, p. 110), "a maximum of stability, clarity, and good arrangement" (Gurwitsch, 1966, pp. 27–28), integrity, the "pure embodiment of essence" (Rausch cited in Arnheim, 1986b, p. 821).

Maestro Leonard Bernstein, in commenting on Beethoven's fifth symphony, speaks of the "rightness" of each last note and decision entering into its composition—choices that Beethoven's notebook show were labored and agonized over—a sense of inexorability as if no other choices could have been as appropriate. The fifth symphony, as Wertheimer would say, has an "inner necessity" (1967c, p. 83) about it as a work, as though it could not possibly be improved upon, so clearly and incisively is the meaning expressed, so good and right is it. It is an excellent example of the "good gestalt."

The "Not Good Enough" Gestalt

The purity, clarity, and incisiveness characteristic of the good gestalt, a gestalt's "inner necessity" (a la Wertheimer), certainly are not always attained. The materials as they are available, as has already been noted, place limits on the goodness that can be achieved through the operation of Gestalt laws, as do the competencies and interests of a participating observer. The available materials structure themselves (dynamic self-distribution) the best they can, given the particularities of an engaged someone. The resulting organization may or may not be "good enough." If it is not, the emergent gestalt is found to be in a state of unrest, a play of troubling tensions to be in process. Such lifeworld tensions find their psychological complement in the observer's sense of dissatisfaction with the meaning as presently constituted. This dissatisfaction may motivate the observer to make efforts at improving the meaning, or perhaps to reject it outright. Improvement is attainable at times with the rearrangement of the meaning's moments, at times with the addition of a new moment. $x\ x\quad x\ x\quad x\ x\quad xx$ can be improved by moving the x on the far right over one space: $x\ x\quad x\ x\quad x\ x\quad x\ x$. A dish may be greatly improved by the addition of a certain seasoning. Some concoctions, on the other hand, are better thrown away and the whole thing started over from scratch. Some acts of depravity, moreover, are simply "to be condemned."

We are confronted, then, with gestalts that are "not good enough." *Praegnant,* Arnheim points out, is a technical term Wertheimer used to distinguish "the clear-cut versions of shapes and shape relations from mere approximations and intermediate stages," to characterize "most perfect structural states" (1986b, p. 823). Wertheimer singles out the right angle, as well as the typically acute or obtuse angles, as instances of "primary percepts," and shapes in-between as "not quite right," "unpleasantly off key." "Max Wertheimer has pointed out that an angle of ninety-three degrees is seen not as what it is, but as a somehow inadequate right angle. When the angle is presented tachistoscopically, i.e., at short exposure, observers frequently report seeing a right angle, afflicted perhaps with some undefinable imperfection" (Arnheim, 1974, p. 15): perception spontaneously improves the "not quite good enough" ninety-three degree angle, to the extent it can. Some arrangements, being stronger than others, "seem to 'triumph' "; "intermediate arrangements," on the other hand, "are less distinctive, more equivocal" (Wertheimer, 1967c, pp. 82–83).

The operation of the law of good gestalt is most readily discerned, on the one hand, in those gestalts that are truly outstanding—truly remarkable ones, ones in which a participating observer takes real satisfaction—and, on the other, in gestalts that are clearly wanting—decidedly unfulfilled and distressing gestalts. A single ideal is discovered in both types of experience (namely, the ideal of a law of goodness), an ideal clearly attained in the "good gestalt," an ideal decidedly not attained in the "not good enough" gestalt.

Force and Counterforce in the Dynamics of the Good Gestalt

The law of good gestalt, as usually formulated, sometimes is taken as a tendency only to the greatest uniformity, the greatest evened-out and balanced status; the preceding introduction to this law may have created that very impression. Arnheim (1986b) attempts to correct such a possible misinterpretation. The law of good gestalt formulates a structural tendency to the best form possible, and best does indeed embrace such characteristics as most regular, simplest, clearest. But the ideal sought in the dynamic self-distribution of our perceptions is not merely one of balance and regularity. Goodness is not simply the lowest possible degree of structural tension. Rather, two forces are at work in a gestalt's striving for goodness. The complex dynamics of organization in field situations, Arnheim remarks, "is not fully described by the tendency toward simple, regular, symmetrical structure but requires acknowledgment of a countertendency that meets tension reduction with tension enhancement" (ibid., p. 823). And indeed, if the tendency to the simplest, most balanced structure were the only tendency in play, all that would ever result would be "a homogeneous field like lumps of sugar dissolved in water" (ibid., p. 821). Arnheim argues, to the contrary, that "Gestalt theory must provide for a countertendency, equal in rank to the one promoting simplest structure, a tendency that articulates shapes" (ibid.). Perceived shapes can be accounted for, in Arnheim's view, only in terms of the continual complementing of one another of both these tendencies. It might be said that, although the expressing of a meaning is to be as simple and as regular as possible (force), the meaning being expressed is to be as fully itself, as fulfilled as a meaning, as possible (counterforce). The tendency to articulation, to a gestalt's coming to term in all that it properly can be as a self-expressive meaning, and the countertendency to balance and simplicity, then, interact in form perception. The esthetic aspect entering into the formation of all gestalts, Arnheim remarks, is due to the dynamic interplay of both tendencies, to the interaction in each case of a "tendency toward tension-increasing articulation" and of a "countertendency toward equilibration" (ibid., p. 822).

Essential to perceptual organization, then, is the operation of opposed tendencies. Optimal form, Arnheim points out, often requires an enhancement of certain structural features, and the introduction at times into the structure of new and disturbing features, the introduction of disorder and of a loss of balance. An unsettling problem may come to insinuate itself, for example, into a structure that we may have been quite comfortable with. The paper may have been finished to our satisfaction when it suddenly occurs to us that we have failed to address a most important issue. We may resent such intrusions, but it is just such problems that hold the promise of a meaning's movement beyond its present less than ideal status. Meaning, striving to attain completeness, allows itself a measure of instability. There is a loss of balance and an enhancement of tension, the manifestation of a tendency to articulation, in the interest of the meaning's becoming most truly itself, the best meaning it can be in accordance with the law of good gestalt. A tendency to simplicity and balance is all the while also in play, pressing for the balanced and regular integration of the required innovations. The two complementary tendencies constituting the Gestalt process make the stimulus more clear-cut and more unambiguously itself, and together account for the transformations meaning undergoes. "One of them increases symmetry and regularity and cleanses the stimulus of distracting, unessential detail; the other intensifies its characteristic features" (ibid., p. 823). Speaking of the ideally good gestalt, Arnheim remarks, "The very term *Gestalt* indicates in German a sublimated or exalted shape or form. Works of art and music were frequently cited in the gestalt literature as outstanding examples of gestalten, not only because they depend so obviously on perfect structural organization but also because they purified perceptual form to obtain the clearest and most incisive expression of the work's meaning" (ibid., p. 821). A well-executed caricature, moreover, leaving to one side the meaning's more normal features (tension reduction) and exaggerating just those tensions most essential to it (tension enhancement), is a good illustration of the twofold process in question.

Whereas the tendency to the simplest, most regular, and balanced form (tension reduction) is a formal tendency inherent in the coming to formation of all meaning—one and the same ideal for all meaning—the tendency to articulation (tension enhancement) is a tendency inherent in meaning formation for meaning to attain an individuated state, its fulfillment as an individual. All in all, the law of good gestalt, as evidenced in the two tendencies constitutive of its operation, is a law governing the fulfillment of individual meanings along ideal organizational lines.

Requiredness

In this section and in the ones to follow the notion of requiredness is introduced and its immediate connections to the law of good gestalt are pointed out. In view of the lifeworld context of any meaning whatsoever, the law of good gestalt eventually is reformulated as a law of requiredness.

Direction of Requiredness

Objective units of mass, in-themselves and indifferent to one another, engage one another only externally, by reason of linear causality (Chapter 1). Units of mass, lacking place, do not structurally signify one another in their dimensional differences from, and links to, one another. A lifeworld that always and already is organized, by contrast, is a realm of sensible qualities tense with and in immediate internal communication with one another; a realm of meanings stretching to and signifying one another with a certain *direction of requiredness* from the first, in terms of their place. Place has not yet been neutralized in lifeworld space, the way it must be in objective space. The lifeworld of our everyday concern is not a mosaic of neutral objects merely pieced together. Table, chairs, napkins, knife, food, fork, all these stretch and point to one another and to many other things. Each has a direction of requiredness of its own by reference to the others, its directional place within the overall context. Each has its particular ready-to-hand involvement. Gasoline is *right* for fueling the lawn mower, which in turn is right for cutting the lawn. And when we are done cutting the lawn and are left with clumps of grass, plastic bags and a rake are structurally right for the job of cleaning up. They, or their functional equivalent, are what *ought* to be used to finish up the job. A pair of scissors is right for cutting a piece of string, whereas a newspaper is not; the newspaper is *wrong* in this context. The lifeworld is simply not a sum of indifferent objects, onto which we impose value qualities. We find our way about the lifeworld in terms of its given significance rather, in terms of directionally interwoven places. Things stretch to and signal one another in and from their place, with tensions commensurate to the task at hand, and a rake or a pair of scissors or whatever turns up as just right for meeting the context's structural requirements. The lifeworld is tense with directionality.

The term *requiredness* refers here to the *rightness* of direction of a meaning. More precisely, requiredness specifies a meaning whose direction is structurally either positive or negative, *right* or *wrong,* given its context. Positive requiredness, positively required meaning, indicates a good gestalt, one that structurally ought to be, a gestalt that is directionally right in its place. A positive requiredness is a meaning fulfilled both in the way it articulates just those features that are most characteristically its own and in the balance, clarity, and simplicity—goodness of form—with which it incarnates just these features. A positively required meaning is a gestalt that is successful within its context both materially and formally. Negative requiredness, negatively required meaning, on the other hand, indicates a "not good enough" or bad gestalt, one that is directionally wrong in its place, one that structurally "ought not be," one that is deficient formally, materially, or both.

The long grass points at, signals, wants, the lawn mower and not the scissors. A smoothly running lawn mower is a positive requiredness in this context; it is the most clear-cut meaning for the task. A broken-down mower or a pair of scissors, given one and the same context, has a negative direction of requiredness about it. The context itself typically indicates to us, often by a resounding lack of success on our part, that we must modify our approach to it, that this is not the place for such and such a piece of equipment. The lawn signifies the scissors with which we are trying to cut it as wrong in this place. The lawn rejects the pair of scissors for its negative direction of requiredness. The law of good gestalt is in evidence here, in its negative manifestation. What this context of nonpsychological meanings wants, what it demands in order to enter into its fulfillment as a context, is an exchange of tools. Only in this way can the ideal of a good gestalt be realized. A context is right if its parts fit one another, if, say, the tool we have chosen is the right one for the job: meanings dimensionally stretching to one another are, after all, what constitute any context. A context is wrong, on the other hand, if its parts do not fit one another, if one of the context's parts is out of place, for example (Köhler, 1938, p. 255). For a ready-to-hand meaning to become articulated in what is most characteristically its own, then, is for it to attain a positive direction of requiredness relative to its context (compare Chapter 3 subsection "Ready-to-Hand Meanings within the World"). Everyday meanings, not good or "not good enough" in-themselves (see the following subsection), are right or wrong in their place, in accordance with contextual necessities.

Requiredness, the directional rightness or wrongness of a meaning, is by no means only a matter of ready-to-hand equipment. Meanings of all sorts show themselves as anything but indifferent to the variety of contexts in which they are emergent. Meanings, universally governed by a law of good gestalt—universally striving to be as balanced, clear, and fulfilled as circumstances permit—are qualified as right or wrong in their place in ethical, logical, grammatical, esthetic, political, religious, culinary, or any contexts. An action may be right or wrong morally; the food great or spoiled; a performance beautiful or flawed; the argument valid or specious. When we speak, Köhler points out, "one word is now 'wrong,' the other 'right,' " the plural is what is required in this place and not the singular (ibid., p. 212). A tie can be just right in its context of shirt and jacket. Sexual intercourse is wrong when forced upon someone. The moon is sometimes hauntingly beautiful in its setting of sky and clouds. Clowning around is inappropriate at a burial service.

Requiredness within and beyond a Gestalt

A required meaning has the structural characteristic of being a dependent part of a context, and of taking its requiredness, in part, from that context. "A datum, an entity or an act," in Köhler's words, "is required *within a context* of other data, entities or acts. This holds both for negative and for positive requiredness" (ibid., p. 255). And again, "All requiredness *transcends* from certain parts of a context to others of the same context" (ibid., p. 256). Requiredness is a *dependent* characteristic of its context, a translocal trait without an independent existence of its own. Requiredness is a matter of place. Requiredness, it might be said, *is* place. All in all, a meaning, deriving its functional significance from the whole to which it stands as part, takes on positive requiredness when it is appropriate to its context, negative requiredness when it is not.

In introducing the notion of a meaning's direction of requiredness in the immediately preceding section, the emphasis was on the situatedness of a meaning within the *external* context defining its direction of requiredness, on a meaning's structural necessity as determined by its broader context of significance. Yet, in introducing the notion of Gestalt laws earlier in this chapter, examples such as an incomplete melody and arrays of columns and rows were considered, examples in which a gestalt's *internal* structural necessity was at issue. This tension is resolved in the following considerations. A meaning's requiredness within its external context of significance is in every case necessarily a matter of the signifying internal to it. It is the ready-to-hand meaning itself, after all, its sensible moments dimensionally beyond themselves and signifying one another, that has a positive or negative direction of requiredness about it in its place. It is the meaning itself as the organization of its sides that is or is not a fitting member of the larger whole to which it stands as part. Still, a gestalt is existentially the required meaning it is only in its functional significance within such a larger context, in terms of the other meanings to which it transcends, to which it is dimensionally beyond as a whole of meaning, and with which it forms a larger whole at the moment. The positive or negative quality of a gestalt's internal organization—that is, of the gestalt itself in its meaning—is codetermined in every case by the referential totality within which it is situated. A broader context codetermines, in part, what is good internal signifying, good internal requiredness of a gestalt's moments vis-a-vis one another; the whole as always, has a certain priority over part. The task something is to fulfill (the place it is to occupy) determines, within limits, what a good piece of equipment should look like, which is to say, how its moments ought to attain balanced fulfillment as a meaning.

The law of good gestalt is reformulated in the next section as a law of requiredness. The requiredness of a whole of meaning is nothing in itself but in every case requiredness within a context (a la Köhler) or place (a la Heidegger). The coming terminological shift is intended as a continuing reminder of this fact, a constant taking note of the fact that a required meaning, even as its parts yield its formation (Chapter 5), in every case is relative to a broader context of significance that codefines it as the meaning it is (Chapter 3 and 4). Gestalt lawfulness is never restricted to a segregated figure's internal goodness alone, as though a gestalt were simply self-standing and present-at-hand in-itself, as a law of *good gestalt* might suggest (and as some interpreters have taken it to be). A law of requiredness indeed does guide a meaning's internal structuring in the direction of its balanced self-fulfillment. But what thus is pursued always is the internal requiredness of a meaning that is what it is only by reason of its place within an unfolding lifeworld context (external requiredness). The rightness of a symphony, a book, or a scientific theory is in terms only of its place in a history of composing, writing, or scientific theorizing. The rightness of a piece of equipment is in view only of a certain equipmental context. All in all, then, a law of requiredness signals that lifeworld meanings not only have an internal requiredness about them, but an external one as well; that a meaning's external requiredness, granting it "world-entry" (Heidegger's words), has a certain priority over its internal requiredness; that these two requiredness, these two signifyings in the direction of an ideal state of affairs, reciprocally condition one another at every turn (compare the reciprocal determination of figure and ground cited in Chapter 5 subsection "Segregated Unity and Figure-Ground Structure").

Reformulation of the Law of Good Gestalt in Terms of Requiredness

There is a general tendency for meaning to develop in the direction of positive requiredness in its place and for an imperfect meaning to distance itself from its state of negative requiredness in its place. For a meaning, segregated whole of meaning (gestalt) or dependent part of such a whole, to be good is for it to come to its balanced fulfillment within the larger whole of which it is a part: positive requiredness in its place. For a meaning, segregated whole of meaning or dependent part of such a whole, to be "not good enough" is for it to fail to attain a state of balanced fulfillment within the larger whole of which it is part: negative requiredness in its place. The law of good gestalt thus is formulated as a law of requiredness, as a lawfulness of place. Gestalt lawfulness is now approached in view of a meaning's role as a part in the necessity of its whole, in terms of any part's requiring and being required by the whole's other parts, whatever the dimensional extent of the whole in question: a single gestalt, a field of gestalts, a field of fields. A law of requiredness formulates the tendency universally in evidence in meaning formation, then, for meaning to achieve a positive state of requiredness not only in its internal signifying (requiredness of the single gestalt's parts vis-a-vis one another) but in its external signifying as well (requiredness of a single gestalt's internal signifying vis-a-vis its broader referential context). A law of requiredness thus is a statement of meaning's tendency to achieve a state where it is just right, just what it ought to be, both as to its inner constitution and as to its broader relations of significance; to attain as balanced and clear a fulfillment as any meaning can in its place. Within the limits set by given human capacity and preoccupations, as well as by what is potentially available in the lifeworld, there is a tendency toward optimal rightness in what concerns the formation of meanings within the world. In the remainder of this book, the phrases *law of requiredness, law of a meaning's structure, law of good gestalt* will be used more or less interchangeably.

Further Reflections on Negative Requiredness

Köhler points out that, when a context only approximates an ideal state, "requiredness tends to assume a perfectionist or correctionist character," the direction in which perfection is to be attained being directly given in the situation itself (ibid., p. 256). Thus, when we are hungry, we find that the restaurant that is still some distance away "ought to be closer." In a similar way, a certain part of a visual pattern may appear as being "just a little too low" or "too far to the right." Requiredness thus "tends to *improve* given situations by pointing to changes which would result in such improvement" (ibid., p. 257). A context sometimes is found to reject one of its parts altogether, moreover, in which case improvement is "to be attained" by the removal of the offending part.

Negative requiredness is found in meanings that bother and disturb us. The tendency inherent in a negatively required gestalt to move away from its negative state expresses the law of good gestalt at least as effectively as the tendency of a positively required gestalt to rest in its positive state, and indeed often more strikingly so. Negative requiredness is negative against the standard set by the ideal of the good gestalt. Troubling tensions away from a meaning's present negative requiredness and toward a more ideal state in fact are the very import of experiencing a negative requiredness. A negative meaning consists of just such tensions, the way a positive meaning consists of its positive tensions. A negative meaning (segregated whole of meaning or part of such a whole) is one rejected by other meanings, a meaning that is wrong in its place—the way a positive meaning is one accepted, one that is right in its place.

Negative requiredness, constituted by restless tensions, is a meaning that is not at peace. A crooked picture, for example, draws our attention away from its possible esthetic character and toward its troublesome relation to the wall behind it. What is required here is by no means at the whim of the observer. In play rather are structural necessities belonging to the lifeworld itself. The picture protests its existing status and begs to be set straight, and some people simply can't resist this demand. A spot on a dress mars its elegance. It is the spot itself, relative to the dress, that we find disturbingly wrong; wrongness here is no subjective judgment that *we* impose on the garment. In Arnheim's example, a disk off-center relative to a square that surrounds it displays a certain restlessness. "It looks as though it had been at the center and wished to return, or as though it wants to move away even farther" (1974, p. 11).

Meaning's Origin in the Excitement of Its Requiredness

Any number of meanings could be actualized in our immediately surrounding lifeworld. Most potential signifyings (potential meanings) never come to be realized, however, and this is for any of a number of reasons. For one thing, we may not have the requisite proficiencies; to correctly distinguish among various types of insects, for example. For another, we simply may not have any interest in the matter; we may not care to know, for example, where a certain dark alley leads or what a complex technical report has to say. Some lifeworld meanings, on the other hand, presence for us in their sheer overfamiliarity, as a matter of habit. Even though the law of requiredness is in play in the occurrence of all meaning, in their habitual reoccurrence as well, this law finally is about meanings that are presently alive and only now reaching for their rightness, the birth and further transformation of meaning in its necessity. The interests of the present book lie with just such meanings, and very little with merely habitual meanings, and even less with meanings that have never mattered in the first place.

The law of requiredness, it is being suggested, is first and foremost a structural principle governing meaning (signifying) in the *originality* of its formation. An original meaning is one coming to formation in a necessity being exacted of it by the law of good gestalt only now, a meaning presently coming to be a meaning in the requiredness of its place, a meaning first arising in the phenomenal freshness of structural possibilities and demands all its own. Original meaning is meaning *in its genesis*, meaning *in its origin* as a pursuit for goodness or rightness. An original meaning, in brief, is a meaning arising in the event of a *structural necessity* properly its own, *a meaning in process in the necessity of its requiredness*, a meaning being born of such an excitement.

Even meanings that fail to presence in their structural originality at the moment—misunderstood or misperceived meanings, for example—presence as though they were indeed in process in the structural necessity of possibilities or demands properly their own, as though they were in fact the structurally required meanings they pretend to be. Nonoriginal meanings presence, then, no less than authentically original ones, in view of an ideal of original (structurally necessary) requiredness, in view of the original excitement any such requiredness spells for someone's life. A telos of originality is nothing less than any meaning's raison d'être, the very phenomenon of phenomenology, even when its originality, rather than truly attained, is only apparent. A law of requiredness governs the functional interdepending (dynamic self-distribution) giving rise to any meaning or network of meanings whatsoever. Requiredness (goodness or lack of goodness of place) first makes any meaning the meaning it is, regulates the formation all meaning. Any meaning is the meaning it is as the meaning it *can be*, the best meaning possible under the circumstances.

Merely conventional meanings of all sorts, secondhand beliefs without the corresponding structural experiences to back them up, are instances of meanings that, along with misunderstood and misperceived meanings, are lacking in originality. Such conventional beliefs, the former conviction that tomatoes are poisonous, for example, function precisely as though they were original requirednesses, as though true beliefs. Conventional beliefs, like misunderstood and misperceived meanings, arise as if with originality, as if in the structural necessity of their law. They could not be the meanings they are otherwise. Habitual meanings, by contrast, very well may have come to formation some time ago in an original experience of the necessity of their requiredness. Now, however, their aliveness by and large behind them, these meanings simply repeat themselves, frequently to *good* end, it might be added.

Original meanings are meanings whose directed tensions are having it out only now. And this having it out is always *for someone*. Requiredness always arises for the being that, dimensionally beyond itself to the world, can be touched by meanings, who can be bothered by them, who can take satisfaction in them. Meaning's origin in the nonpsychological requiredness of its lifeworld place is at once its origin in the positive or negative psychological excitement—interest—it holds for a bodily someone. A meaning's originally exciting aliveness is fully coordinated to an excited someone: dimensionally spread out, exciting lifeworld meaning and dimensionally spread out, excited bodily someone interwoven in the existential space of the possible. There is a certain live requiredness about a cool drink on a stiflingly hot afternoon, about pleasant surroundings, a Mozart piano concerto, a heroic action on someone's part. We live our lives for requirednesses such as these, meanings presently in process in the necessity of their requiredness. The very coming to formation of originally required meanings depends on their being on the cutting edge of someone's life; for then and only then, first coming to matter in their place, do they gain "world-entry" (Heidegger's words); only then does the excitement that is their origin stir to life.

Even if such exciting meanings have happened for us before, on one or a number of occasions, there is still a certain firstness to meanings currently unfolding in the originality of their structural necessity, a freshness about the signifying structurally at their core. This aliveness of the moment excites us; this excitement inherent in its law-governed tensions is the reason for our excitement. The work of art, even though well-known to us, enthralls us, because once again it comes alive in the positive possibilities of self-expression intrinsic to its signifying. We may be fascinated by certain meanings—certain persons, for example, or certain hobbies or certain scientific puzzles—for decades. In such cases, meanings unfold anew—are reborn, sometimes are even transfigured—on occasion after occasion, time and again in their structurally original requiredness. The event is experienced each time as a new arising of the meaning in question. The meaning forms anew each time in the play of dynamically self-distributing tensions in pursuit of the ideal of the good gestalt, forms anew in the truth of its necessity. What excites are currently mounting tensions, lifeworld tensions originally constitutive of the meaning at the moment. What returns each time is the manner in which available sensible moments come to signify each other in the freshness of their lived dimensionality, as if for the first time ever.

No meaning originates in its sheer neutrality: "The most general law underlying all change is The Law of *Praegnanz*, according to which every Gestalt becomes as 'good' as possible" (Wulf, 1967, p. 148). Change is initiated, meaning self-forms—meaning first forms, meaning transforms—in a striving for an ideal outcome. Rightness and wrongness always are making their appearance in the formation of meaning, which is the same as saying that in every case someone already has a stake in the matter. No indifferent fact was ever indifferent to begin with. An interested someone, precisely as excited by the meaning in question, played in every case a co-organizing role in its regard (see Chapter 8, "A Phenomenological Theory of Insight"). We now can casually pass such a fact by only because it once arose as something of some interest to us, because once it made a directional difference in our concernful preoccupations with the lifeworld. We may have never really noticed the phone booth we pass every day. But, should we have to make an emergency call, the lifeworld reconstitutes itself before our very eyes, and the booth that was always there comes to be seen, in the exciting freshness of a meaning originally come to life only now. Although a law of requiredness is indeed the law governing the self-actualization of meaning, an interested someone nevertheless in every case is on the scene coactualizing meaning. Requiredness indeed makes a meaning be a meaning, but requiredness can be only for someone who cares, who can touch and be touched by the rightness or wrongness of a meaning in its place.

Intrinsic Requiredness

A meaning coming to formation in the excitement of its requiredness can be viewed as both process and outcome. A meaning structurally in *process* in the necessity of its requiredness, in possibilities or demands inherently its own, is precisely what has been termed an *original meaning* in this chapter. Necessity of process of an original meaning is nothing other than the law of good gestalt or requiredness itself and, as such, regulates meaning in the total course of its development. Meaning originates and unfolds, forms and transforms, in the necessity of law-governed inner and outer tensions, in the pursuit of its "can-be." Structural demands thus are at work in every stage of the process of an original meaning's self-forming;

being discovered, for example, in the necessity of its good continuation or closure. As to the inner law of a Beethoven symphony, for example, Wertheimer writes, "It would be possible for one to select one part of the whole and work from that towards an idea of the structural principle motivating and determining the whole" (1967b, p. 11). The law of requiredness permeates the formative process of an original meaning. Requiredness as process of original meaning is structurally intrinsic to it: *intrinsic requiredness* (a la Köhler). An original meaning is a meaning in process in its intrinsic requiredness, in the necessity of possibilities properly its own, its "inner necessity" (in Wertheimer's words).

Requiredness is both process (law-governed action) and outcome (lifeworld dimensional quality). The conclusion was reached in Chapter 5 that gestalt and gestalt quality are one and the same meaning; that a gestalt as the very organization of its moments not only *has* meaning, not only *has* gestalt quality, but *is* meaning, *is* gestalt quality. Gestalt quality is the something "as which" moments signifying one another (gestalt) *are,* outcome at one with the process (law-governed tensions) yielding it, the *way* the process is. What the law-governed process (gestalt as action) has been in pursuit of all along, moreover, is nothing else than any meaning's balanced fulfillment, nothing else than a certain excellence of quality. What has been lawfully in *process* from the first, in other words, is a certain fitting *outcome*. All in all, then, requiredness of outcome—gestalt quality at one with the process yielding it, required meaning lawfully in process all along—is fully intrinsic to a gestalt: an intrinsic belongingness, intrinsically required meaning, *intrinsic requiredness*.

Requiredness as original process, lifeworld moment lawfully signifying lifeworld moment, is meaning in search of its fulfillment as an outcome. As intrinsic to meaning as the process that has governed it throughout, as what the process of requiredness has been about from the first, requiredness of outcome is not something "more" the brain or mind extrinsically adds on only later to more basic "stuff," "stuff" of an essentially different character from its overlay. Process and outcome, not the separated objectivity of process and subjectivity of outcome proposed by conventional psychology, (at least in the first instance) are one and the same intrinsic requiredness, two ways of talking about the same original event of meaning.

Whereas meaning in the intrinsic requiredness (structural necessity) of its process, by the terminology of this chapter, is an *original* meaning, Chapter 13 will come to call a meaning in the intrinsic requiredness of its outcome a *valid* meaning. A valid meaning is intrinsically the requiredness it shows itself as being, a meaning that is presencing in the "can-be" of structural demands all its own.

Insight

Although the Gestalt logic of wholes (Chapter 5) and their requiredness (Chapter 6) is a logic of the lifeworld, this logic could not unfold without a co-organizing participation on the part of someone. Requiredness, at the origin of any gestalt or meaning, in every case is of some interest to someone who, in bringing it close, lets it matter in the excitement of its structural law. Such personal involvement in the coming to formation of original meanings, such partaking of a meaning's excitement, this psychological co-organizing of meaning in the structural necessity of its requiredness, is *insight*. The psychological behavior of insight is explored in Chapters 8 through 11. Insight, anything but the behavior of a subject in-itself, is the very openness of being possible to the necessities of lifeworld meaning, the essence of human rationality.

Required Meaning as the Expression of Being

Originally required meanings, in accordance with their law of structure, present themselves as themselves. Required meaning, the expressing of one another of its constitutive moments, is self-expression, and it encounters us as such, in its own weight and from its own ground. But no required meaning is simply itself. It is signified, changed, by other lifeworld meanings with which it is in relation. Required meaning is not only self-expression but expression of the broader lifeworld as well. Required meaning only expresses itself within the world for someone, moreover, as the other of concernful human preoccupation. Required meaning is *self-expression, expression of world, expression of Dasein*. Requiredness is not the expression of any being—requiredness surpasses all beings, subjective and objective—but of being itself.

A Rose Is a Rose

The constant in meaning formation for all modern philosophical and psychological systems, according to Gurwitsch, has been the sensation. But now, he remarks, with Gestalt psychology, the constant has become the law, laws of gestalt formation. The major Gestalt law, the one that encompasses all the others, is that of good gestalt. This law formulates a basic experience of the Gestalt psychologists, that gestalts will be as good as possible, as positively required in their meaning as possible, under the circumstances. Things that are similar or near each other, for example, looking best that way, tend to cluster together as meanings—and it not infrequently takes a real effort to disrupt the organization thus achieved.

If we look at what presents itself to us as a gorgeous rose, conventional psychology would say that what is "really" there are stimuli, light of a certain wavelength, for example. The rose's color, its beauty, all its lived dimensional qualities, do not belong, for this ontology, to the "real world" outside the organism. Perceptions or meanings, the rose in its qualities, are considered rather subjective interpretations residing inside us. The present approach, informed at once by existential phenomenology and Gestalt theory, insists, to the contrary, that what is *there* first and foremost in the world is precisely the rose itself, in all the richness of its sensible qualities, exactly as these are in direct communication with one another and with those of the broader world; that, in accordance with the law of requiredness, this rose is showing itself to us to its best advantage, attaining the best form it dimensionally can as a rose; in a word, that the rose, attaining its "inner necessity" (Wertheimer's words), in truth is gorgeous, and nothing more basic or true can be said of it. All in all, then, what is said here is that the rose's intrinsically required gestalt quality of roseness (requiredness as outcome) is just the way the rose self-forms in the originality of its excitement for someone (requiredness as process). The postmodern (i.e., post-Cartesian) position that a rose *is* a rose—that its beauty is intrinsic to what it essentially and originally is in its lifeworld place, that beauty (positively required gestalt quality or outcome) is intrinsically what the rose (gestalt or process) is *all* about, that beauty is the rose—will undoubtedly offend many a modern ear, thrusting as it does at the heart of a widely and highly cherished subjectivism.

Dynamics: Within the World

Someone's personal involvement is an invariant in the coming to formation of any meaning whatsoever. Such involvement co-organizes self-forming meaning, at once placing limits on meaning and releasing it to its possibilities. The law of good gestalt nevertheless is not a psychological law. The dynamics of the formation and transformation of meaning belongs to nonpsychological meaning and not to psychological structure. The Gestalt laws governing the formation and transformation of meaning are laws of meaning, and not of the brain or of the mind, as conventional psychology nevertheless continues to suppose.

It was shown in Chapter 5 that the true character of a gestalt is missed if it is described as more than the sum of its parts. It was pointed out there that a gestalt's whole properties are not extrinsically imposed supplements, but, to the contrary, that meaning, original to a gestalt, is itself immediately given within the lifeworld, that self-organizing gestalt is always and already self-giving lifeworld meaning. This position entails the further belief that the law-governed stresses and strains—tensions (stretches) in the direction of positive requiredness, tensions away from negative requiredness—at the heart of the formation and further reformation or transformation of a gestalt likewise are immediately given; that these, too, have their location in the existential spatiality of the world, in the "there." Gestalt laws, along with the tensions that evidence them, do not come down to laws of association, internal information processing, or what have you. The directed tensions governing the formation of meaning, rather than being inside us psychologistically (Chapter 2), unfold before us and indeed all around us; being clearly in evidence, for example, in the necessity with which a meaning strives for its own good continuation. These tensions are the way the lifeworld becomes the lifeworld and, rather than physical forces, are the key to an understanding of human feeling and motivation. An original whole emerges from its parts in its place *in the lifeworld*, in the necessity of a *lifeworld* signifying. The law of requiredness is a lifeworld law. Dynamic processes unfold in things, and that's where our life unfolds, too, in the world to which we are submitted from the first.

Nonpsychological meaning, born of the tensions circulating in the law-governed dynamic self-distribution of its moments, insists on coming to formation on its own terms, with a weight of its own. Meanings address us in just this insistence and this weight. Meaning leads and has its ways. Meanings are sometimes amazing and fascinating, sometimes recalcitrant or scolding. Meanings startle us at times. Sometimes they become too much for us. The noted conductor Erich Leinsdorf remarks in the May 15, 1988, edition of *The New York Times Book Review,* "We cannot find out what genius is as long as we insist the term applies to a person. We ought to apply it only to works of genius and forget the effort to coordinate our judgments of a person. In one letter Wagner says of one of his own operas, 'I find it more and more difficult to understand how I could have done such a thing.' " We often find ourselves struggling with meaning. We are occasionally overtaken by meanings and led down paths of meaning we never intended.

The Tenseness of the Good Gestalt

Structural dynamics renders a bad gestalt restless, as wishing to be otherwise. "Not good enough" gestalts are in motion *as* "not good enough" gestalts. But good gestalts, meanings at rest in their goodness, are not simply in a tension-free state. The dynamics of action does not come to be set aside when the law of good gestalt attains a measure of success. Noticeably good gestalts are in motion, too. They, too, remain in process. Structural tensions, and the corresponding demands made upon us, are actively in play in any lifeworld meaning whatsoever. However, the tensions constituting a good gestalt, at least for the time being, have achieved a measure of balance; such tensions are not in pursuit of a state other than the one in which they find themselves. Tensions, operating in varying directions, prevail, but as tensions in balance, tensions in harmony with one another. Arnheim points out that a disk placed exactly at the center of a square that surrounds it is at rest, but that the balance achieved is "alive with tension" (1974, p. 16). Good gestalts are "loaded with energy," with balanced energy (ibid.); hence, in part, their goodness (see Chapter 7 subsection "Beauty Values"). "Restfulness does not signify the absence of active forces. 'Dead center' is not dead. . . . Seeing is the perception of action" (ibid.). Meaning, reality, is process, directed tension, meaning stretched to and signifying meaning in view of an ideal of meaning. The lifeworld is a network of actions, tense with requirednesses of a great many sorts.

Hierarchy of Requirednesses

Attempts have been made to devise a universally binding hierarchy of requirednesses, most notably in psychology by Abraham Maslow, for whom the next higher requiredness presupposes, rests, and builds upon the requiredness(es) actualized before it. Without passing judgment on this scheme, it can be said that, descriptively, individuals in fact do have their own preferred requirednesses, and that these mostly informally ranked requirednesses vary from individual to individual, as well as from culture to culture. Some people place the acquisition of wealth as the ultimate requiredness (the highest good) and make everything else secondary to it. Others prefer the maintenance of personal integrity and order their undertakings around this center. Still others prefer the pursuit of beauty. And so on. People subordinate what they consider lower requirednesses to those they find superior. Requirednesses are found to be arranged in various orders as a matter of fact. But factually this order is not the same for everybody; Maslow maintains that it is *ideally*, at least along its main lines.

People are variably sensitive and competent, moreover, with regard to requirednesses. Some do not seem to discover moral obligations to which they feel obliged to respond. Others do not understand Shakespeare or Bach. Some do not have any use for rock-and-roll. Others still do not understand the value of perpetual consumption. Freud dealt with patients who indicated to him that the requiredness of pleasure was "all but omnipotent" in the governance of life's activities. A whole culture can place the requiredness of life low on the scale of important goals. Another culture can rate a certain race genetically inferior. Some people have deep feelings for music but only contempt for great numbers of their fellow human beings.

We have to know something about the relevant circumstances to make sense of the way any individual—or, for that matter, any culture—ranks its requirednesses. The law of good gestalt dictates, after all, that a gestalt will be precisely as good, as positively required, as the circumstances allow. People's proficiencies and inclinations co-organize the meanings that encounter them. The language they are brought up with largely predetermines, moreover, the range of the potential lifeworld signifyings available to them. To understand people's behavior, we have to know where they are coming from, we have to know what they consider important, the necessities governing their life. We have to enter into *their* context of significance.

7 Value

Human living would simply collapse
if all value experiences and
corresponding activities were suddenly
to disappear. Is the psychologist
permitted to ignore the most important
parts of his subject matter?

—*Köhler*, 1938, p. vii

A psychology which has no place for
the concepts of meaning and value
cannot be a complete psychology.

—*Koffka*, 1935, p. 19

Definition of Value

The All-Determining Law of Requiredness

Directed (law-governed) tensions, stretches in the direction of an ideal state of affairs, are what make any meaning the meaning it is. The law of requiredness governs the formation of all meanings, in what regards both the internal self-regulation of their constitutive moments and their relations of significance beyond themselves to other meanings, as well as to the lifeworld as a whole. Requiredness determines what becomes figure, what gains "world-entry" as a meaning (a la Heidegger), and what recedes as its ground. The law of requiredness determines what figure-ground reversals will occur. It determines how sensible qualities concretely stretch to signify one another, and thus how they form a meaning in the first place. It determines how a meaning unfolds and grows dimensionally in terms of its destiny, and perhaps how it must improve to fulfill its law of structure. It rules those transformations by which meaning becomes something else again. Requiredness determines how incomplete contexts are resolved—how the right name, for example, finally makes its appearance—and indeed how such contexts are discovered in the first place—how problem situations initially arise. All in all, the law of requiredness formulates the dynamic organization

133

(directed tensions) determinative of the lifeworld as a whole, as well as of the self-showing of its particular meanings. The principle of requiredness, a law of meaning and not of the psyche, governs the lifeworld in its total structuring, the dynamic self-distribution of all gestalts (process) as the meanings (outcome) they immediately are.

This chapter investigates the manner in which the law of good gestalt or requiredness issues in certain preeminent outcomes, namely, values. Although not by name, a discussion of value already was underway in Chapter 6, especially in its latter sections. Many of the examples given there indeed were examples of value. This chapter therefore continues and expands on the earlier one.

Some Illustrations of Internal Requiredness

Examples illustrative of the law-governed dynamics internal to gestalt formation follow. The relations of such dynamics to the topic of value are discussed in the following two subsections.

In the first illustrations of Chapter 6, X's and O's were seen to require each other either as an array of columns or as an array of rows. A factor of similarity was said to be in play.

```
X X X X X X X X X X
O O O O O O O O O O
X X X X X X X X X X
O O O O O O O O O O
X X X X X X X X X X
O O O O O O O O O O
X X X X X X X X X X
O O O O O O O O O O
X X X X X X X X X X

X O X O X O X O X O
X O X O X O X O X O
X O X O X O X O X O
X O X O X O X O X O
X O X O X O X O X O
X O X O X O X O X O
X O X O X O X O X O
X O X O X O X O X O
X O X O X O X O X O
```

Figure 7–1

The lines in Figure 7-1 signify each other as three pairs, in accordance with the factor of proximity. The five angles in Figure 7-2 are seen as a single star and not, at least not in the first instance, as five distinct figures, in accordance especially with the Gestalt factor of closure. The x's that are near one another are seen as pairs: *x x   x x   x x*. But the x's forming a pair sometimes can be too close to one another: *x x   x x   x x   xx*. A figure can be thrown off balance, moreover, by what is recognized, in accordance with the law of good continuation, as a distortion in its unfolding, as in Figure 7-3.

Value as Meaning in its External Requiredness

Values are meanings that have a certain distinctive positive or negative requiredness about them. Some such distinctive positive requirednesses are a beautiful song, a lovely face, a magnificent sunset, a courageous action, someone we love, an absorbing problem, a hammer, the correct answer to a problem, a friend, a good meal, a valid line of reasoning. Some such distinctive negative requirednesses are an approaching hurricane, a

Figure 7–2

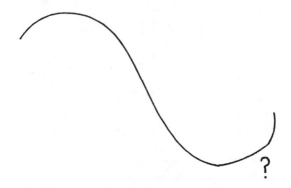

Figure 7–3

garbage-strewn lawn, a marred performance, a cold-blooded murder, a missing or broken tool, a hostile act, a fallacious argument, a job poorly done. Meanings such as these (values) are characterized by their place in the referential totality of the world. The examples of the preceding subsection, by contrast, display the character of being essentially self-contained figures, of being abstract and worldless gestalts attaining their organization solely in view of internal factors (similarity, proximity, good continuation, closure). Examples of the latter sort, not uncommon in the Gestalt literature, are presented as though unencumbered by the involvement that a chair, for example, has in relation to a table and to our breakfast and, beyond that, to the lifeworld as a whole. These segregated figures are seemingly in no need of a place within a broader context of significance to be the unities they are; they are found to make an appearance rather in their mere presence-at-hand in-themselves. These figures, except for the white background that sets them off, and which indeed is no less present-at-hand than they are, seem to possess an essentially self-sufficient internal requiredness that renders them the meanings they are. Values, in sharp contrast to such abstract and worldless figures, never can be considered solely in terms of their internal requiredness. Values, never self-sufficient, rather have about them an excitement that is codetermined in every case by their everyday lifeworld context. What is distinctive and preeminent about values is precisely their status as wholes of meaning required for what they are in their place, things or persons brought close and mattering to an everyday concernful preoccupation, in the fullness of their lifeworld dimensionality. *Value is a whole of meaning that is positively or negatively required in its place within a lifeworld context.* The term *value* specifies in particular, then, what was termed in Chapter 6 meaning's *external requiredness*, the signifying external to a meaning (Chapters 3 and 4), place—in which signifying, to be sure, a meaning's internal signifying (Chapter 5) is in every case necessarily implicated.

The Value of the Present-at-Hand

Value, by the present hermeneutic account, then, is a whole of meaning brought close in the requiredness of its lifeworld place, an internal requiredness within its context of external requiredness. It is in fact as thus brought close, in first mattering to us in the excitement of its requiredness or place as a value, that our others gain "world-entry" (a la Heidegger) as meanings in the first place and that we are "at" them at all. The law of requiredness essentially is a law of value. Only later is it possible to strip the world of external requiredness—of meaning in its place, of value—and look at entities in their sheer presence in-themselves (presence-at-hand). Only later is it possible to become involved with things solely with a view to their sheer valuelessness. The illustrations of Gestalt theory can indeed be *taken* as if they stand alone, can be taken as present-at-hand and without reference to any external lifeworld context, can indeed be taken as utterly valueless, the way units of mass are in Galilean physics, nature as pure spatial extension. These figures can be examined solely in terms of their inner structure, in view of the internal requiredness of their constituents alone. And indeed that is how they were presented, as abstract demonstrations of internal Gestalt dynamics, in sharp contrast with the external requiredness of everyday value. And yet, such apparently worldless figures themselves can be seen to possess external requiredness, in fact to be values. These figures arise precisely as meanings within a broader lifeworld context. They originate only *within* the broader context of Gestalt theory, only *as* relating to and making certain points within that theory, only as *good* demonstrations of such points, and only *for* an observer who has had certain relevant life experiences and who has some interest in them at the moment. They also serve *broader* ends, to expand human understanding and contribute somehow to the improvement of the human lot; science is thoroughly permeated with values such as these. These illustrations, moreover, have a *place* of their own on a lifeworld page, begin here, end there, take up so much space; and they stand *within* a discussion of requiredness that leads up to and takes its further departure from them. These figures, then, no less than a chair, are what they are in their place. They, too, take their origin in the excitement of their external requiredness. They, too, are values. What is taken as present-at-hand, it was pointed out in Chapter 3, is relative, too; relative, for one thing, to its being taken as such ("The Origin of the Present-at-Hand in the Ready-to-Hand"). To first attain merely present-at-hand meaning, as Heidegger has pointed out, one must penetrate beyond the world of everyday concern; one must move beyond value. But one penetrates beyond the lifeworld, one moves beyond value, only on the basis of the lifeworld, only on the basis of value. Value is preeminent reality, preeminent meaning, and not one kind of meaning alongside others. In the final analysis, then, there are no gestalts good or "not good enough" in-themselves, no merely internally good or bad gestalts; the reader may recall that this was the stated reason for the reformulation in Chapter 6 of the law of *good gestalt* as a law of requiredness. All gestalts are implicated in a lived dimensionality as broad as the world itself.

A Gestalt as Value Itself

Value, it has been seen, is meaning in its external requiredness, a whole of meaning positively or negatively required in its place within a context of significance. Value is meaning, suchness, gestalt quality. But, given that law-governed action (gestalt, process) is at one with law-determined meaning (gestalt quality, outcome), given, in other words, that a gestalt is lifeworld meaning in its immediacy, it then becomes evident that *a gestalt is value itself*. A gestalt in the originality of its lived dimensional unfolding (process) is precisely value in its internal and external requiredness (outcome). Value is nothing else than that which has been in process in the circular signifying of lifeworld moments from the first, the outcome that has always been at issue. Law-determined value, what a gestalt is in the fullness of its internal and external context, what the Gestalt process has been about from the first, is intrinsic to a gestalt, *intrinsic value* (see Chapter 6 subsection "Intrinsic Requiredness"). Value in the structural necessity of its process is a matter of what something *can be* as a meaning, of meaning in its originality.

The concrete majesty and power of Niagara Falls is not a "value" we place on top of a founding, three-dimensional ("real") world. This meaning does not arise through a subjective "value judgment," it does not reside inside our "value system"; values are not indifferent things " 'invested' with value" (Heidegger, 1962a, p. 132). Rather than a second thought, a quality extrinsically tacked on, Niagara Falls is the very dimensional tenseness of its ·sensible qualities signifying one another as this required whole of meaning: the thunderous roar and drop of cascading waters, the cool and dampening mist, the immensity of it all. Niagara Falls *is* precisely this, all this excitement. What Niagara Falls is all about is intrinsically this, structural necessity of process with just this suchness of outcome, gestalt in the immediacy of the intrinsic requiredness of its meaning. In being brought close in its lifeworld law, as thus arising in its value as just what it is, Niagara Falls originally happens as itself. Value is the necessity at the origin of the lifeworld, the very law and universal origin of meaning.

The Demand Character of Value

The tensions structurally at play in the origin of lifeworld requiredness constitute a demand made upon someone. Value is *lifeworld demand character,* something "to be accepted"—to be loved, welcomed, appreciated, grateful for, respected—for its positive requiredness; something "to be rejected"—to be loathed, pushed away, regretted, looked down upon—for its negative requiredness. Value is not a meaning that *also* has a gestalt quality of demandingness, added on perhaps. Value rather is a whole of meaning that, in its very coming to formation in its requiredness—in the very experience of its directed tensions—is "to be accepted" or "to be rejected." Originating in its requiredness, intrinsically required value makes certain intrinsic demands on us. A thing of beauty, for example, already is experienced, in its very positive requiredness, as a meaning to be accepted for the meaning it is. Meaning, in its very origin as a positive value, is experienced in the "to be accepted" of its beauty, or goodness or truth or usefulness. Outstanding meanings show themselves from the first as "to be admired," as intrinsically worthy of the admiration we already feel toward them, as admirable. To experience something's positive requiredness, then, is to find ourselves already obliged to it. Loathsome behavior on someone's part, or something's falseness or ugliness or uselessness, on the other hand, presences precisely in its character of "to be rejected." Our original experience of loathsome behavior already is a certain pushing away of it, a certain contemning of it, for the negative requiredness it represents. Loathsome behavior has the negative demand character of "to be contemned," of contemptibility. All in all, then, demand character is inherent in the experience of value for what it first is as a meaning; that is, as a positive or negative lifeworld requiredness. The demand character of value, in Köhler's words, is "the 'ought' or 'requiredness' in it" (1971, p. 367).

The experience of a value is from the first, then, the experience of the "to be accepted" of its "ought to be" (positive requiredness), the experience of the "to be rejected" of its "ought not be" (negative requiredness). "No value attribute seems to deserve its name if it has no such demand character" (ibid.). Psychology, if it is to do justice to its subject matter, Köhler argues, must come to realize that human experience is quintessentially the experience of demands (ibid., p. 193). And yet, at least in the sense in which Köhler uses it, the term *demand* does not appear in the index of today's introductory psychology texts.

The demand character of an original value, one in process in the necessity of its lifeworld requiredness, is something that in every case makes sense to us. We find this character to be *understandable,* in our very experience of it (insight). "We understand it as sensible," Köhler writes, "that we are attracted by objects which have certain characteristics, and that we are disgusted by others" (ibid., p. 369). This is understandable, Köhler asserts on phenomenological grounds, because structurally some things *are* attractive, whereas others *are not.* Value is not adequately considered as the effect of a subjective valuation on our part, this is only a theory atomistic logic needs to round itself out and account for a lifeworld that it found necessary to leave behind. The notion that demand character belongs to the meanings themselves in our very experience of them, that it does not arise on the basis of our subjective valuation, is discussed further later in the section, "The Nonsubjective Character of Value."

Demand Character and Motivation

Values originally in process make sense to us. That they ought to be or ought not be, and hence are "to be accepted" or "to be rejected," is understandable. We find it quite sensible, moreover, that values motivate further behavior in their regard, that our values are, at least much of the time, good enough reasons for our actions in their regard. Rather than being irrationally, mechanically, *pushed* by unconscious or environmental forces, people not uncommonly find themselves rationally *pulled*, invited, by the live tensions at play in their values. "Impulses toward the most important actions," Köhler writes, "may . . . arise in a way which we can thoroughly understand" (1947, p. 204). We have insight, then, not only into the "ought to be" or "ought not be" of original values, into the nonpsychological necessity of their requiredness, and at the same time into our immediate feelings of acceptance or rejection of them, but also into the way values motivate us to engage in further activities in their regard.

Values not only engage a certain initial accepting or rejecting attitude on our part, then, but also insist upon certain follow-up behaviors. "To the contrast between 'ought to be' and 'ought not to be' there corresponds the antithesis of such verbs as point to opposite tendencies in human striving" (Köhler, 1938, p. 57). "The self is virtually always directed toward something or away from it" (Köhler, 1947, p. 176). Positive values are meanings "to be reached," "to be supported," "to be maintained." Negative values are meanings "to be avoided," "to be changed in the positive direction," "to be eliminated" (Köhler, 1971, p. 367). We are more than merely inclined to down the inviting cool drink, to take steps to avoid the imminent danger. The troubling tenseness of negatively required meanings, but also the evenly balanced tenseness of positively required ones, induce us to action, and with good reason, rationally. "People like or dislike things," Köhler writes, "they seek some and avoid others" (1938, p. 57). People want to bring to actuality things they appreciate, would like to eradicate things they find detestable. "Human living would simply collapse if all value experiences and corresponding activities were suddenly to disappear" (ibid., p. vii): people would stop taking trains, reading books, moving from one room to the next. What could be more obvious than that people become involved in some things because of their positive requiredness and withdraw from others because of their negative requiredness (ibid., p. 52)? The law of requiredness governs not only our initial experience of values, then, but our later motivation in their regard as well. Values are the reasons people do things. "Is the psychologist permitted to ignore the most important parts of his subject matter?" (ibid., p. vii).

The Nonsubjective Character of Value

In keeping with phenomenology's notions of intentionality and existential surpassing, value is not something "here" as a subjective modification of the mind, but something "over there"; not over there in-itself, but over there in every case in its place relative to a context of significance. Nonmental lifeworld values can be of various sorts, another being possible like ourselves, for example (Chapter 4 subsection "The Place of Other People"), or a ready-to-hand piece of equipment (Chapter 4 subsection "The Place of Ready-to-Hand Meanings"). In any case, value is something we are "at," something that we are not, nonmental meaning "over there" in the lifeworld. Values are requirednesses in their place, not ideas inside our heads. Phenomenology prefers the primacy of clearly distinctive lifeworld requirednesses over the primacy of clear and distinct modifications of the mind (a la Descartes). In the paragraphs that follow, the argument is made on descriptive grounds, first by Köhler then by Wertheimer, that value is not the result of a valuation on our part, that we do not confer value on things, that value is not some "more" subjectively added on, but rather that the life of value and the demands value makes on us issue from beyond us; in other words, that some things *are* valuable, intrinsically (structurally) valuable, and that some things *are* worthless, intrinsically (structurally) worthless. The special interest of this section lies in the new examples provided, as well as in the strikingly nontraditional manner in which these eminent psychologists present them.

Values do not, Köhler argues, "spring from the self's subjective attitudes" (1971, p. 362), as a result of our subjective strivings and valuations. Values, descriptively, are not the self's doings, but belong rather to things and events as their attributes. "We should therefore falsify our primary observational data if we were to say that the essence of value is valuation. Phenomenologically, value is located in objects and occurrences" (Ibid., p. 364). When a man finds a woman to be particularly attractive, Köhler goes on to say, it is absurd to claim that her female charm is something that male interests come to project onto an actually neutral object. No, Köhler asserts, such charm is not an illusion originating in male striving; it is no component of masculine motivation. It is the other in its quality rather that confronts even a highly interested someone: "value is located in objects and occurrences." We simply do not find it to be the case that value is something we put onto indifferent things. "That face looks mean—and I abhor it. Dignity I hear in those words which I have just heard Mr. X speaking—and I respect him. Her gait is clumsy—and I prefer to look away" (Köhler, 1938, p. 70). Value qualities are found everywhere as actual characteristics of the meanings we encounter. "Qualities belong where we find them," and no theory will ever convince us that they are somewhere else (ibid., p. 72). The time even will come, Köhler remarks, when psychology, as a "principle of method," will no longer allow itself to "interpret black as really white" (1971, p. 363).

Typically, the presently perceived imminence of harm, Köhler similarly points out, is the reason for our fear, and not fear that takes indifferent things and gives them their dangerous appearance. "When suddenly an object looms dangerous and threatening, it is not felt to have that appearance because there is first fear and a tendency to escape in the self" (ibid., p. 365). To the contrary, our fear, along with our desire to escape, is experienced as resulting from the threatening danger itself. Whereas our feelings and motivations at times do distort our meanings, in phobias, for example, more often than not these feelings and motivations, as noted earlier in this chapter, are structurally appropriate to our meanings. The connection between meanings and our feelings and motivations in their regard typically is understandable.

Sometimes, Köhler remarks, what ought to be, the positive value, is an action we feel obliged to perform, in which case a moral pressure weighs upon us from beyond. We find it hard to resist the demand made on us, for example, when someone in need asks for our help. Clearly the requiredness in such a case, rather than issuing from the self, arrives at it (1938, p. 77). Or again, we read until we begin to feel a nagging sense of a task that has to be completed by next week. Where does the pressure initiate, in the self or in the task to be fulfilled? Certainly not in the self, "which, at the moment, feels hunted, driven, compelled by something else" (ibid.). Demands, arising from beyond, target the self.

Köhler insists, moreover, that things can prove to be wrong and yet have nothing at all to do with any wrongness on the self's part. Someone presents an argument in clear violation of the rules of logic. "We feel almost offended by such an obvious mistake" (ibid., p. 86). We are not wrong or make the argument wrong, rather the argument itself is wrong, intrinsically wrong and "to be rejected."

Wertheimer, in a similar vein, writes of the requiredness intrinsic to the structure of situations confronting us (1961, pp. 34–41). Often, he points out, the structure is such that it contains a gap that can be filled in various ways. Sometimes, however, only one completion does justice to the demands of the situation, above and beyond any subjective will or whim on our part. The gap and what can fill it in are meanings with a standing of their own beyond the self. And not only they, but the very stresses and strains (play of tensions) at work in the direction of the situation's appropriate, intrinsically required, completion have a similar standing of their own beyond us. The tensions in evidence represent not our needs, but the structural needs of meaning, the demands it makes on us in what regards the situation's possible resolution. Consider, for example, the situation in which we are confronted with the problem, Seven plus seven equals? "The one completion, fourteen, corresponds to the situation, fits in the gap, is what is structurally demanded in this system in this place, with its function in the whole" (ibid., p. 36). To fill in the gap with fifteen because one "loves" fifteens violates the structure of the situation. No two ways about it, fifteen is wrong here, intrinsically wrong. Fifteen ignores the demands instituted by the law of good gestalt as these presently confront us, the function of the gap in the structure. Fifteen, in the terminology of this book, is a negative requiredness in this place (negative value). "There are requirements, structurally determined" (ibid.). Only one completion does justice to the "structurally determined require-ments" of the situation under consideration. Fifteen is "to be rejected."

Or, consider the example Wertheimer provides of a judge who takes a bribe from the guilty party and convicts an innocent one. "The most important question is . . . the relations within the happening itself, how the action meets the requirements of the situation, the *zueinander* of the two, the relation between the situation and the action. . . . [The judge's] decision is unjust" (ibid., pp. 34–37). The behavior does violence to what the situation's structure requires. The important question does not revolve, then, around a subjective evaluation superimposed on an indifferent object. "If we try to understand such cases . . . in terms of the arbitrary addition of a subjective evaluation to an object, then there is a lack of clarity, something does not jibe" (ibid., p. 34). A positive or negative valuation on someone's part does nothing to change the injustice of the judge's action, nor does the judge's subjective preference for the action make the action itself any the less intrinsically wrong. Value is no arbitrary matter. Though we must sometimes weigh values against one another and choose between them, value is not something we manufacture, not something we add to merely neutral things (see Heidegger, 1962a, pp. 131–133). Some jokes *are* sick, some actions *are* unjust, some rooms *are* messy—that's their manner of presencing, their being. Value does not arise from valuation, either for the Gestalt psychologists or for the existential phenomenologists. Value has a life and place of its own rather, and when original, when arising in the structural necessity of its requiredness, value is precisely what it shows itself to be: intrinsic value (for a discussion of the validity of value, see Chapter 13).

Some Types of Value

Gestalt laws are "concrete structural principles" (Wertheimer's words), laws governing the individuation of meanings, and not abstract rules. It is not "goodness in general," not formal structural goodness alone, that the law of requiredness seeks, not the greatest possible evened-out status, for example (Chapter 6 subsection "Force and Counterforce in the Dynamics of the Good Gestalt"), but the formal excellence *of this meaning*. The balance and simplicity sought by the law of good gestalt is the balance and simplicity of a meaning fulfilled in just those possibilities that are most characteristically its own. What is prior in the realm of value, then, is not any sort of formal absolute, but an individual meaning's structural necessity. Values nevertheless are seen to cluster together in terms of the particularity of their lifeworld place, as use values, for example, or as person, knowledge, or morality values. Such different sorts of value are considered in the following sections. The intention here is to gain some understanding of the range of structural possibilities open to lifeworld meaning, and by no means to codify value. Other sorts of value, moreover, religious and political values, for example, might well have been considered but are not. This chapter concludes with a survey of a number of psychological theories of value.

Use Values

The requiredness of ready-to-hand equipment lies in its usefulness, in its being a *use value* (compare Chapter 3 subsection "Ready-to-Hand Meanings within the World"; Chapter 4 subsection "The Place of Ready-to Hand Meanings"). A positive use value is a means to some goal, an "in-order-to." A negative use value is an obstacle to a goal, something harmful or noticeably deficient in its usefulness as a means to some end. Among positive use values are things that are life-sustaining, practical, nourishing, helpful, efficient, well-made, versatile, or functioning. Among negative use values are things that are useless, impractical, lethal, wasteful, hindering, shoddily made, spoiled, dangerous, broken, out of service, or clumsy.

The practical requiredness of ready-to-hand use values belongs to them, as pointed out in Chapter 3, by reason of their concrete involvement or place, their external requiredness, within the referential totality of the world. "Equipment," Heidegger writes, "is essentially 'something in-order-to' " (1962a, p. 97). In the "in-order-to" is an assignment of one thing to another (ibid.). Positive equipmental quality is precisely what useful things are as things, an intrinsic value. "A being is not what and how it is, for example, a hammer, and then in addition something 'with which to hammer.' Rather, what and how it is as this entity, its *whatness* and *howness,* is constituted by this in-order-to as such, by its functionality" (Heidegger, 1982, pp. 292–293). We no more read instrumentality into the things we use than we read wrongness into fifteen as the answer to the mathematical problem cited earlier. As fifteen *is* the negative requiredness of its incorrectness, so *is* the hammer the positive requiredness of its usefulness. "The possibility of being guided along the blackboard and of being used up is not something that we add to the thing by thought" (Heidegger, 1959, p. 25). Neither the chalk nor the hammer is an aggregate of "sensations with values attached" (Heidegger, 1967, p. 209), "a point of mass in motion in the pure space-time order," only with a special value adhering to it (ibid., p. 51). Both are rather precisely what they are, in the external requiredness of their place.

Person Values

A functioning ready-to-hand use value is a means to someone's further ends. Dasein encounters such useful things alongside other someones who share the world with it, other Daseins who, like itself, are open to events of meaning presencing (Chapter 3, "The World and Other People"; Chapter 4 subsection "The Place of Other People"). As one of our meanings, a fellow human being is another "myself." Other people as such special positively or negatively required meanings are referred to here as *person values*. Other persons become values to us in a variety of ways: as worthy, contemptible, loving, lovable, cheating, friendly, hostile, manipulative, small, aloof, warm, concerned, honest, spiteful, dishonest, helpful, interfering, glib, barbarous, refined, sound, wise, shallow, and so on. Persons as our required others are our friends, our lovers, our enemies, those from whom we have learned something, those who care for us and will hear us out, our parents, our children, those who perform a service for us, those who turn their backs on us.

Person and use values, like morality and knowledge values, are distinguished on the basis of the structural possibilities of meaning open to them in their place, and to us in their regard: a person value as a bodily someone, a use value as a ready-to-hand thing. A person value presences as an end, a final goal (being possible)—an end like ourselves, a center of meaning "for the sake of itself" (for the sake of possibilities of its own, that are also meaning's possibilities of presencing within the world)—and not as a means to some further end, not as an "in-order-to." This is so even when others show themselves as worthy only of contempt. Indeed only a someone, only a being whose being is possible (being possible), can truly merit contempt, can engage in behavior with the intrinsic demand character of contemptibility. We do not hate or love a use value the way we hate or love another Dasein. Ready-to-hand things do not matter, do not get "under our skin," do not grow on us, the way people do. All in all, then, the positive or negative requiredness of another person is in their very being possible itself. Another someone is accepted or rejected precisely as a self, as an end "for the sake of itself," for the someoneness they already are and have to be.

People are not instruments, then, whose goodness, whose balanced and clear fulfillment as a meaning, lies in their being put to use. Rather, the fulfillment of the being possible of other human beings is only in view of the unique possibilities of being-in-the-world that are properly their own. Being motivated, in accordance with the law of good gestalt, to actualize other someones, these special meanings of ours, in the law of their structure (positive person values)—to help them become as fulfilled as possible in their place relative to significance—means respecting and promoting them in their being possible, in their inner structural necessity (cf., for example, Fromm, 1956). This requires an effort on our part, but in the long run so does any value.

People are sometimes made into mere replaceable commodities, to be used for certain ends, like computers, for example. Persons remain ends "for the sake of themselves," however, even when they are treated as means: ends treated as means. Ready-to-hand things, on the other hand, sometimes are converted into final goals. Passions develop towards possessions, for example, which then come to function as ends rather than means. Food can become our reason for living or money accumulated for its own sake. Just as person values remain ends even when turned into means, use values remain means even when turned into ends, means turned into ends. Person values and use values are different in kind.

Knowledge Values

We frequently discover, try to discover, or are actively thwarted in our attempt to discover how matters actually stand with our lifeworld meanings. What we thus find out, or perhaps don't find out (the latter precisely as not found out), are positive or negative lifeworld *knowledge values*. A disturbing gap in our knowledge is an instance of a negative knowledge value, as is "knowledge" found to be incorrect, incomplete, or misleading. The structural filling in of a gap with a problem's fitting resolution, on the other hand, is a primary instance of a positive knowledge value, as is the confirmation by the matter at hand of what had only been supposed to be the case. Although the experience of an original value always involves knowing something, what is special about our intentional directedness to knowledge values is its more or less explicit concern with the lifeworld standing of something. In gaining knowledge, confirming the knowledge we already seem to have, recognizing false "knowledge," knowledge as knowledge is the issue. Knowledge, it may be noted, as that with which we are preoccupied, as a meaning or value, has a nonpsychological character (see Chapter 11 subsection "Feeling and Cognitions").

Wertheimer considered situations troubled by a gap (earlier, this chapter), situations with an incomplete knowledge structure. We occasionally find ourselves, for example, unable to remember someone's name.

Troubling tensions, springing directly from the structure of the defective knowledge situation itself (negative knowledge value), then are found to militate in the direction of filling in of the gap with the right name, the one thing intrinsically required in this context. The context's completion with the appearance of the right name (positive knowledge value) spells an attainment on the part of such tensions of a state of balance and rest. Solutions that are "not good enough," the names that come to us but are wrong, on the other hand, do anything but reduce the troublesomeness of the lifeworld context confronting us.

Certain formulations show themselves to be true (positive knowledge values); others present themselves as clearly false (negative knowledge values). "Vermont is in Connecticut" is a meaning with a negative value character about it, one that wants to be changed into something like "Hartford is in Connecticut." "Albany is the capital of New York state," on the other hand, is a meaning that strikes us as knowledge with a positive quality (positive value). "7 + 7 = 14" is satisfying in the knowledge it affords, whereas "7 + 7 = 15" clearly is not. The following syllogism is structurally disturbed (negative knowledge value): "All humans have heads; monkeys have heads; therefore, monkeys are humans"—the law of good gestalt, when it comes to forming syllogisms, particularizes itself as certain laws of logic. We find that newspaper reports are sometimes accurate (positive knowledge value), sometimes not (negative knowledge value).

A principal source of knowledge, moreover, is the self-giving perceptual lifeworld itself. We come to know how things stand in that world by exploring it for ourselves and discovering, for example, that the post office is (or is not) just down the street from the library, that the willow tree harbors a path that leads up to the top of the hill and a view of the valley and town below.

Other persons, ends "for the sake of themselves," often are taken as positive goals of our lives, as in love or respect. Positive knowledge values at times similarly come to be valued as final goals, the acquisition and expansion of knowledge for its own sake, and not as a mere opportunistic means to some further end. People become absorbed, for example, in scientific problems, such as the attempt to determine the wellsprings of human behavior, or in religious or philosophical questions, such as the problem of evil. Problems in knowledge sometimes become ends in themselves, then, and motivate a lifetime of reflection and inquiry, the knowledge gained in the process not uncommonly bringing with it a great deal of satisfaction. Humans, according to psychologist Abraham Maslow, have a "need for knowledge" (1954, pp. 48–51). Cognitive needs "to know, explore, and understand" are among the highest ones in Maslow's *hierarchy of needs*. All in all, the law of good gestalt presses for truth, the original self-manifestation of things in accordance with their intrinsic structural law,

in the realm of knowledge. "The desire not to be structurally blind
. . . seems strong. . . . There is a tendency to structural clearness,
surveyability, to truth as against petty views" (Wertheimer, 1959, p. 244).

Morality Values

Given the structure of a situation, a certain action may display itself as
the right or wrong thing to do. An action already executed, on the other
hand, may show itself as "to be approved" or "to be condemned." The thing
"to be done" and the deed "to be approved" are positive *morality values*.
The thing "to be avoided" and the deed "to be condemned" are negative
morality values. Actions viewed in terms of their moral rightness or
wrongness sometimes are our own, sometimes those of other people, and
sometimes have merely a hypothetical character. The search for and
discovery of moral requiredness in and through the immediate sense we have
of ourselves and the structure of our situation is *conscience* (see, for
example, Frankl, 1969, pp. 63–67; 1975, pp. 115–119). Conscience, no
irrational superego, is a concretely involved someone engaged in an informed
and ongoing confrontation with the possibilities of moral action; a particular
someone in search of the solution of a moral problem with "a maximum of
stability, clarity, and good arrangement" (Gurwitsch, 1966, pp. 27–28), a
solution with integrity and that represents the "pure embodiment of essence"
(Rausch cited in Arnheim, 1986b, p. 821).

Morality values possess what the Gestalt psychologists called *demand
character* to a preeminent degree. We are submitted as Dasein to the
demands morality values make on us from the first and always. We indeed
may find that offering assistance to someone in dire straits is presently
required of our behavior (positive morality value), that it is simply not
possible to reduce a structural demand such as this to a mechanical
conditioning of our behavior by the environment. As Köhler notes, structural
pressures dynamically target us—occasioning at once a certain attitude of
acceptance or rejection on our part—and they target us *now*. Wertheimer, in
one of his examples, comes right out and says that the judge who sends an
innocent person to jail has done something wrong. The judge's action is
immoral, intrinsically characterized by a negatively required gestalt quality.
The action is structurally wrong, according to Wertheimer, in its inner law:
wrong is what it is. The action itself, when grasped in its originality as a
meaning, is already experienced as "to be condemned." The holocaust is not
immoral extrinsically only in people's minds, but intrinsically wrong as the
nonmental event it was: the holocaust neither was nor is an inner
psychological occurrence. It is a completely inadequate appraisal of the
structure of the act of cold-blooded murder to view it as the mere
rearrangement of molecules in objective space. Following Wertheimer's

lead, and abiding by phenomenological methodology, certain actions, given their context, clearly present themselves as morally right or wrong on their own ground, and by no means in an inner and private realm of "value judgments." Convicting an honest person and the holocaust present themselves as structurally wrong, as negatively required morality values.

Morality values have significant motivational consequences. The moral action demands "to be executed," the immoral action is "to be refrained from." Such further demands on our behavior are implicit in our initial experience of value's demand character, implicit in our initial experience of the intrinsic "to be accepted" or "to be rejected" of a certain course of action. A guilt that is healthy, and not a mere leftover from childhood, is a consequence of moral actions not followed through on or of immoral actions carried through. Guilt, psychologist Gordon Allport remarks, is a "sense of violated value" (1955, p. 73).

It may well be that we cannot get very far in composing a hard and fast list of morality values. Indeed, how could we if a gestalt's emergent possibilities of meaning are themselves critical structural determinants of the rightness or wrongness of actions; if becoming in fact governs the presencing of meaning, as well as the corresponding demands made on our behavior? There can be no definitive list of unvarying morality values, or of any type of value for that matter, because values, rather than existences in-themselves, are concrete actualizations of structural possibilities of significance, various ways in which meanings can unfold in a necessity exacted of them by the law of requiredness. Morality values, the discovery of what is "to be done" or what is "to be avoided," on the one hand, are never merely arbitrary; and yet, on the other, they are not a set of present-at-hand rules. Morality values, like all values, have neither a subjective nor an objective character.

The law of good gestalt governs the formation of all meaning. Morality values are concrete embodiments of the law of good gestalt in the sphere of moral action (see Chapter 6, "Hierarchy of Requirednesses"), the moral face of the law of requiredness, the way use values, for example, are its practical face.

Beauty Values

Meaning presencing in accordance with its law unfolds in the direction of the best gestalt possible under the circumstances. Such a law of good gestalt confronts us in various ways: in the proper or improper instrument, the right or wrong thing to do, the correct or incorrect solution to the problem, the person who turns out to be a friend or an enemy. A meaning's structural law is experienced in an especially pronounced manner when we encounter things that are truly (intrinsically) wonderful, truly beautiful. We marvel at such things, recognizing in them something special, ideal states of affairs. Such meanings presence in the purity and clarity of their positive demand character. Noticeable successes of the law of good gestalt, *beauty values* are clearly "to be accepted" and "to be promoted."

Chapter 6 endorsed Arnheim's assertion that two forces are at work in gestalt formation, one seeking the articulation and enhancement of a meaning in all that is properly characteristic of it as a meaning, the fulfillment of all its structural possibilities, the other seeking the simple, clear, and balanced organization of the meaning thus articulated and enhanced. Arnheim remarks in this connection that the esthetic dimension found in gestalt formation is due to the dynamic interplay of both tendencies (tension enhancement, tension reduction). A meaning's beauty lies in the excellence with which both tendencies are achieved at once in a meaning, in the formal elegance with which a meaning achieves the "inner necessity" (in Wertheimer's words) of a destiny properly its own. A meaning is beautiful when it comes to formation with "relative simplicity" (Arnheim, 1974, pp. 58–60); that is, when something has achieved the simplest, least complicated but also most orderly (clear, well-organized), possible form in which it can successfully come to expression in what is most characteristically its own; when form incarnates meaning with a high degree of success, whatever the meaning's degree of intricacy. The gorgeousness of a rose lies in the especially simple and harmonious manner in which it presences in the truth of itself, that is, as a rose. People, artists and poets among others, work at bringing gestalts to such a simple and balanced state of goodness and beauty, to the purity of their essence (the "pure embodiment of essence" a la Rausch). Regarding works of art especially valued for their beauty, Arnheim remarks, "The very term *Gestalt* indicates in German a sublimated or exalted shape or form" (1986b, p. 821). Arnheim then proceeds to point out that works of art and music were frequently cited in the Gestalt literature as striking examples of gestalts, "not only because they depended so obviously on perfect structural organization but also because they purified perceptual form to obtain the clearest and most incisive expression of the work's meaning" (ibid.).

Beauty is a certain way, then, in which meaning is realized in the intrinsic goodness of its internal and external organization. All "good gestalts," in their balanced fulfillment as meanings, have something beautiful about them. There is, in the final analysis, no special class of beautiful things. The law of good gestalt or requiredness could almost as well be called a law of beauty. In the existential space of the possible, anything at all can be beautiful—if, given its place within significance, it is fulfilled at once in its form (structural organization) and its content (meaning expressed). A meaning is beautiful when it attains its inner law, the necessity of its structure, the elegance of its essence. Good plain food is beautiful when we are famished. A telephone is beautiful when our car breaks down in the middle of the night. In these situations, the food or the telephone represent just what is dimensionally needed: no more, no less. Both meanings are simply right, as right as they can be, in their relative simplicity; they are *sweet*. As meanings they balance the lifeworld situation out perfectly, bringing the tensions intrinsic to its structure to a most satisfying state of rest.

All in all, then, beauty values are meanings that are especially pure and excellent. They are meanings that are outstanding *in the beauty of their goodness*. Beauty is the sheer nonpsychological rightness of an original meaning. A scientific theory can be "Beautiful!" A well-designed can opener can be beautiful, nature can be beautiful, a beautiful piece of apple pie can be placed before us, an elegant solution to a problem is beautiful, a truly moral action is beautiful, certain persons are beautiful persons, tomato plants are beautiful in the food they provide, a movie can be beautifully sad, music can be beautifully harrowing. All such meanings, to name but a few, are intrinsically beautiful for just what they are in their place in their nonpsychological lifeworld context.

Nature can be an instrumental means to certain human ends; providing the food we need for our sustenance, for example. But in its esthetic dimension, nature—the rose, the tree in the meadow, Niagara Falls, a pet cat—becomes an end to stand in awe of for its own sake, in its "endness" (a la Maslow). Nature then no longer serves as a mere means to other ends, but, like person and knowledge values, becomes itself an end. Appreciated in its beauty, nature is exactly itself, the sheer structural rightness of itself, admirably itself.

Arnheim points out that not even what is at rest is without its tensions, without the presence of dynamically active forces; that seeing is the perception of action (compare Chapter 6, "The Tenseness of the Good Gestalt"). A disk within a square "is most stably settled when its center coincides with the center of the square. . . . Wherever the disk is located, it will be affected by the forces of all the hidden structural factors. . . . At the center all the forces balance one another, and therefore the central position makes for rest. . . . 'Dead center' is not dead. No pull in any direction is felt when pulls from all directions balance one another. To the sensitive eye, the balance of such a point is alive with tension" (1974, pp. 12–16). And again, "It turns out that every visual object is an eminently dynamic affair. . . . *Visual perception consists in the experiencing of visual forces*" (ibid., p. 412). Experiences of lifeworld beauty are particularly telling as regards the claim that not only "not good enough" gestalts are charged with dynamic tensions, but good ones as well. The experience of beauty is a moving one, at times even changing people's lives. Its tensions powerfully in harmony, the beautiful is surprisingly alive, its signifying tense and even brimming with goodness, a living presence. The beautiful is anything but a dead *res extensa* to which a value quality of beauty has been extrinsically tacked on. When we are desperately in need of it, we could kiss what would otherwise be just a dumb screwdriver. Nothing, not even a screwdriver just lying there, is without its tensions (dynamic stretchings). Any meaning is an action, "things are relations" (a la Heidegger). Meanings always and already are overleapt in existential space, dynamically stretched to and signifying one another. All in all, then, even what is at rest is in existential motion, forever coming to expression in the directed (law-governed) tensions presently constitutive of it as a meaning.

Beauty values, like the other values considered here, have profound motivational consequences. Beauty can become a final goal "to be cherished," "to be promoted," and "to be instituted" wherever possible in the lifeworld. Esthetic needs for "symmetry, order, and beauty"—like the cognitive needs "to know, explore, and understand"—are among the highest in Maslow's *hierarchy of needs*. Beauty is, Maslow suggests, a necessity of our life.

Psychological Theories of Value

Conventional Psychology and Value

Very little need be added at this point to convey conventional psychology's attitude towards value. The essentials of that view have in fact already been reviewed in chapter 1. Conventional psychology holds that value, as meaning, is a psychological entity, an inner and private, subjective outcome effected by objective events both inside and outside the organism. There is no way, on the basis of such a point of view, that value could possibly be a nonpsychological lifeworld event. Since conventional psychology, true to its objectivistic presupposition, requires the prior exclusion of quality from the "real" world, since no place is preferable to any other in the "real" objective space of meaning, this psychology must end up denying the "real" rightness or wrongness of any meaning whatsoever. Granting beauty and ugliness, good and evil, truth and falsity no place in "reality"—excising them from "reality" in the name of "science"— conventional psychology takes a strong, even ominous, position on value.

Skinner and Value

B.F. Skinner allows that observable events alone are to be taken into consideration in a radical behavioristic account of human behavior, and that observable behavior is strictly determined by observable stimuli. While the reasons for any behavior's initial occurrence are not to be specified, such an occurrence being random in character, by reason of "contingencies of reinforcement" behavior tends to be brought under the domination of environmental events, under "stimulus control."

Skinner thus holds that personal dimensions of lifeworld meaning (value) need not be taken into consideration to understand human behavior. He concerns himself as a consequence not with something's intrinsic meaning to someone, but only with observed behavior and its observed environmental circumstances. "Meaning" for Skinner belongs to the contingencies responsible both for the shape of the behavior and for the control exerted by the stimulus. Thus, if a rat is reinforced with water when it presses a lever in the presence of a flashing light, but with food in the presence of a light that is steady, it can be said that the steady light "means" food and the flashing light "means" water. These are references not to some property of the light, but to the contingencies of which the lights have been parts (Skinner, 1974, p. 91). Varying "meanings" are "aspects of the contingencies which have brought behavior under the control of the current occasion" (ibid., p. 90). Having reduced "meaning" or "value" to the environmental contingencies observed to be governing behavior, Skinner may be said not to have a theory of value at all. It may be worth noting in this connection that Skinner, objecting to the conventional positing of a duplicate world inside the organism, refuses to turn the environment into any sort of inner psychological occurrence (representation). On this point Skinner and phenomenology are in accord.

Underlying Skinner's approach to behavior is the linear model that we have come to associate with objectivistic psychology. A particular behavior *first* occurs randomly under a certain set of circumstances; something *then* follows the behavior; if the behavior in question *later* tends to increase in frequency, it may be said that it was reinforced by the environmental stimulation that followed its emission. By reason of the linear model necessitated by objectivistic ontology, the past alone, of the three dimensions of time, is granted a role in the radical behavioristic account of behavior: objective cause necessarily precedes objective effect in objective space. "Future" behavior merely plays out in the present those contingencies of reinforcement that in the past have brought behavior under stimulus control. "The meaning of a response," Skinner writes, "is to be found in its antecedent history" (ibid). In such a scheme, where circular relationships between behavior and lifeworld events are excluded in advance, it is inconceivable that someone could enter into structural contact with a meaning on the ground of its lifeworld law. Behaviors of love, for example, interest the radical behaviorist as experimenter-defined behaviors varying in frequency with the varying environmental stimulation that immediately follows their occurrence. In no way intrinsically related to the environmental other, such behaviors can hardly be thought of as reaching and releasing the being possible of the loved one. Intrinsic value simply does not enter into the human equation for Skinner the scientist.

Maslow and Being-Values

Maslow's psychology is in pursuit of valid values, values people can reasonably live by. To his hierarchy of biologically based needs (1954, pp. 35–51), for example, corresponds a hierarchy of intrinsically required values, values that are biologically grounded through the very needs they fulfill. The highest need, better "*metaneed,*" in the hierarchy is self-actualization. The highest values, correspondingly, are associated with this metaneed.

Self-actualized individuals, said to be "better cognizers and perceivers" than most (Maslow, 1971, p. 6), are more accurate in their perceptions of reality and as a consequence have had more frequent experiences of *Being-values,* values Maslow considers to have been his principal discovery. Maslow found that people, asked to describe reality (Being) when noninterferingly cognizing it on its own ground and for its own sake, do so in terms of the values of Being. Reality is then said to be true, good, beautiful, whole, alive, unique, perfect, complete, just, simple, rich, effortless, playful, self-sufficient, and meaningful (1968, p. 83). Reality, it is to be noticed, thus is described only as something that is full of value, solely as good and "to be accepted." These Being-values, Maslow asserts, are spiritual values, the highest values in the hierarchy of values (1971, pp. 108–109).

Described attributes of reality, Being-values are gestalt qualities of Being. They are what reality is, facets of its experienced excellence (Maslow, 1968, p. 84; 1971, p. 194). In the experience of the Being-values, what "ought to be" is found already to exist, to be a fact—in fact, to be the most factual thing of all to those who are most adept at cognizing things. In the experience of Being-values, reality is encountered in its *endness,* as a completely worthwhile end, an ideal state of affairs, as just right, a universal positive requiredness. Reality in its totality, it might be said, in accordance with the law of good gestalt, shows itself to its best advantage, and this self-showing turns out to be of a perfection, an "inner necessity," that already belongs to it. In the experience of Being-values, circumstances (observer capability, lifeworld availability) are such as not to impose their usual limitations. Boundaries rather are seen to fall and the whole of reality to show itself to be purely and simply good (1968, pp. 81–82), to be as right and as fulfilled as it possibly can be, to be unadulterated by any negative. Such an experience of the inherent values of reality, Maslow believes, is open in principle to all.

As nonpsychological aspects of reality, Maslow distinguishes Being-values from the psychological attitudes and feelings of the Being-cognizer (1964, p. 94). Among the Being-cognizer's psychological states are awe, love, adoration, worship, humility, approval, sense of mystery, gratitude, fusion with, bliss, and ecstasy. Such participatory feelings are the highest human satisfactions possible. In thus marking the difference between psychological processes, on the one hand, and nonpsychological cognitions (meanings known), on the other, Maslow is at one with phenomenology.

Self-actualizing people tend to live for Being-values, according to Maslow; to make them and not themselves (not pleasure or power, for example) their final goals. They live for truth, for example, or justice or beauty. Self-actualizing people are found to be "working at something which fate has called them to somehow and which they work hard at and which they love, so that the work-joy dichotomy then disappears. One devotes his life to the law, another to justice, another to beauty or truth. All, in one way or another, devote their lives to the search for what I have called the 'being' values" (1971, p. 43). Thus viewed, self-actualization turns out to be anything but the search for some illusory "true inner self." Not out to actualize, and thus strengthen, themselves, self-actualizers are characterized rather by their ability to dedicate themselves to solving problems: "Our subjects are in general strongly focused on problems outside themselves" (1954, p. 159). All in all, self-actualization consists in an ability possessed by some to coactualize or co-organize certain lifeworld meanings: to discover, cherish, embody, and spread Being-values. Psychological actualization of the self thus is seen as rooted in the actualization of the nonpsychological values of Being. The pleasant feelings of satisfaction that go with Being-values, or with any value, are not pursued in events of self-actualization, then, but the values themselves, in accordance with their intrinsic demands. The satisfaction occurs, to be sure, but it occurs precisely *in the meaning*. Not pursuing strength out of a sense of deficiency and weakness, moreover, and nurtured by the values of Being, self-actualizers have deep inner strength.

Acceptance of both the validity of Being-values and the law of good gestalt as presented in Chapter 6 would amount to accepting the paradox that, although reality is already perfect when assessed from an Olympian point of view (Being-values), on a more mundane level reality's perfection is yet to be attained (law of requiredness). Goodness, although ultimate and already the most factual thing of all, would always be "to be fulfilled."

Frankl and Value

Existential psychiatrist Viktor Frankl has challenged Freud's notion that pleasure is the organism's fundamental life goal, its principal value. Rather than a "will to pleasure" (a la Freud) or a "will to power" (a la Adler), Frankl, on phenomenological grounds, argues that a "will to meaning" is the most characteristically human motivation: a search for meaning, not a search for oneself (1969, pp. 50–79). What for Freud is humankind's basic, if not only, "value"—tension-reduction or pleasure—for Frankl is a psychological state, and psychological states in Frankl's view, as in that of Maslow and this book, do not qualify as values. Satisfaction—esthetic feeling, self-actualization, happiness, pleasure—is not legitimately a final goal. Frankl of course knows that people sometimes pursue pleasant inner states for their own sake, but he believes that such a pursuit is a mistake that gets in the way of life's true goals, an inherently self-defeating and ultimately self-destructive mistake. All in all, for Frankl the person who makes pleasure the goal of life is already leading a life that has been pathologized.

Psychological states, rather than valid life goals, transcend to what for Frankl are alone values in the proper sense of the word, nonpsychological meaning. Satisfactions of whatever sort are held to be psychological byproducts that accompany the fulfillment of life's true goals (1975, pp. 84–85); namely, intrinsically required meanings, and especially those connected with love, beauty, and moral action. What human beings are after, according to Frankl, is the actualization of goals beyond themselves, goals inherently worth pursuing, the actualization of as many positive values as possible. As long as it has not been "neurotically distorted," human existence, in Frankl's view, in every case is directed to something that is not itself, "a meaning to fulfill or another human being to encounter lovingly" (ibid., p. 78). Put simply, people "want what they want" (1962, p. 41). They are out for the meanings that bring satisfaction, and not for the satisfaction itself. Meaning, it could be said, is the meaning of life. Happiness, although not our life's goal and not directly attainable through a search for it, follows quite naturally when people find and choose meanings worth living for: people are happy, Frankl says, when there's a reason for happiness (1969, p. 34).

Phenomenological Psychology and Value

Whereas many psychologies reduce value to psychological processes, phenomenological psychology insists, with Frankl, that value is a lifeworld, and not a psychological, occurrence. Although value thus is no subjective opinion, neither does phenomenology find it to be an objective something ready-made and in-itself. Value in every case is in a circular relationship with someone proficient at releasing it. Value is an event of meaning for someone. Value has its place as a meaning, moreover, in some broader context, an instrumentality perhaps within its network of significance or a solution to a larger intellectual or moral problem. Finally, with value as quintessential meaning, it turns out that "the good"—the good gestalt, or the "not good enough" gestalt against the standard of the good gestalt—is at the heart of everyday reality. Factually, *being* and *the good* turn out to be altogether inseparable. The search for goodness is a structural invariant of events of meaning presencing.

8 The Behavior of Insight

The desire not to be structurally blind
. . . seems strong. . . . There is a
tendency to structural clearness,
surveyability, to truth as against petty
views.

—Wertheimer, 1959, p. 244

The attitude of looking for objective
structural requirements of a situation,
feeling its needs, not proceeding
willfully but as the situation demands,
facing the issue freely, going ahead
with confidence and courage—all
these are characteristics of real
behavior, growing or withering in the
experience of life.

—ibid., p. 64

The Turn to Psychological Processes

This investigation's primary concern up to this juncture has been with meaning, with its place in the lifeworld, with its law-governed dynamic self-distribution, with lived dimensional value. A concerted effort has been made in all this to dislodge meaning from the psychological realm, to which conventional philosophy and psychology have resolutely consigned it, and to locate it, along with its dynamics, squarely in the lifeworld. Nevertheless, as has been suggested any number of times, psychological processes necessarily are involved in all events of meaning presencing, and the ultimate intentions of this study indeed are psychological in character. The turn to psychological processes, and more specifically to insight, is made in this chapter. With this shift in emphasis to what is properly the domain of the psychologist, nonpsychological lifeworld meaning, which has required some effort to clarify, by no means shall be left behind. The understanding of behavior at the human level can be only through meaning. The behavior of insight is

157

properly accessed only by way of its intentional directedness to meaning, only as a "here" that, surpassing, is in every case "over there" alongside the world of its concern. "There is no inner man, man is in the world, and only in the world does he know himself" (Merleau-Ponty, 1962, p. xi).

An original meaning is the self-regulating action of its constituent moments (a la Chapter 5), sensible qualities signifying one another in accordance with a necessity set by the law of requiredness (a la Chapter 6). Insight co-organizes this signifying, codetermining even what lifeworld moments make themselves available to form a gestalt in the first place. Insight is a structural understanding of the functional interdependence of moments as an intrinsically required whole of meaning. By playing meaning's game and following meaning's rules, by thus participating in meaning's search for its "inner necessity" (a la Wertheimer), structural understanding sponsors meaning's self-formation on the ground of its proper (structural) necessity. Meaning's original becoming is inexorably interwoven with insight from the first.

The chapter begins with a review of the notion of insight as championed by Köhler. The relations between insight and the law of requiredness then are considered and an attempt made to sketch a consistently descriptive theory of insight. The two chapters that follow this one discuss the behavior of insight's two sides, impact (in Chapter 9) and interpreting (in Chapter 10). Chapter 11 considers insight in terms of affectivity (disposition and feeling). Köhler's psychology is considered once again in Chapter 12, in the light both of conventional psychology and the radically phenomenological orientation to psychological processes undertaken in Chapters 8 through 11.

Köhler on Insight

Considered in turn in this section are Köhler's definition of insight, some examples he provides of this behavior, and the signal importance he attributes to its role in human life.

Definition of Insight

"Insight," Köhler writes, "is insight into relations that emerge when certain parts of a situation are inspected" (1969, pp. 152–153). Such emerging relations are characterized, above all, by the fact that they are found to follow directly from the facts under consideration (Köhler, 1961, p. 6), from the properties of the parts involved. Insight, in other words, is the awareness of directly given relations of functional dependence, directly given interconnections, among the facts of experience (Köhler, 1971, p. 87). In insight is an immediate awareness of "the structure of a situation" (Köhler,

1927, p. 169), of how one meaning stands with regard to another—or perhaps of how a meaning affects the self—an experience of their "understandable relationship" (in Dilthey's words). Insight, all in all, is an immediate awareness *that* something is directly affecting something else, including an awareness of the *how* of this "direct determination," of the manner in which one thing is determining the other. Insight is *felt awareness of direct determination; structural understanding,* for short.

Should we feel a sharp discomfort in our foot, finding at the same time someone standing on it, Köhler points out that it is hardly necessary for us to *infer* the source of our pain (1947, p. 201). The connection instead is given to us directly in the structural understanding of the way the other person's weight is in present relation to our foot, which is to say, the connection is given to us directly in insight. Other of Köhler's examples of insight, as they appear in his various writings, are considered in the following subsection.

The behavior of insight into relations, rather than a mere carry-over from past experience, is a presently occurring event, the moment of grasping something structural in the whole, present structural awareness. "What a radiant smile," Köhler writes, "spreads over the face of a small child who has just grasped the meaning of a game that an adult has started to play with him" (1971, p. 169). Wertheimer similarly remarks, "It is wonderful to observe the beautiful transformation from blindness to seeing the point!" (1959, p. 47). Gestalt psychology, as suggested in Chapter 5, introduces the present dimension of time into psychology.

Examples of Insight

Insight in Problem Solving

Insight in thinking occurs with the emergence of just those relations that bring about the desired solution of a problem. "In the solution of the problem, . . . we suddenly become aware of new relations, but these new relations appear only after we have mentally changed, amplified, or restructured the given material" (Köhler, 1969, p. 153). "Often, the decisive step is what we may call a restructuring of the given material" (ibid., p. 147). Insight is not the mere solving of a problem, which could come about, after all, by chance, but the structural awareness of the problem's solution in the newly emerged relations. Insight is awareness of the manner in which such and such a solution *is* the solution to this problem; of just how, in a reconfiguring of lifeworld moments, meaning has now come to directly determine meaning as the problem's sought after solution. When the problem consists in a gap in our knowledge of a situation's structure, understanding occurs precisely with the attainment of the complete organization (Köhler, 1971, p. 184).

In a problem's insightful solution there is attained, then, a clear understanding of why just these meanings fittingly belong together as a certain overall intrinsically required whole of meaning, why this structural interdependence of these meanings "ought to be" and thus is "to be accepted." Fourteen is the fitting (positively required) resolution to the problem $7 + 7 = ?$ and fifteen clearly is not. On the basis of the direct determination of one another of definite characteristics, certain meanings thus are found to fit or not fit one another in certain contexts. "In logic and also in aesthetics we have many cases in which there is to this extent *insight* into the actual foundations of requiredness" (Köhler, 1938, p. 257), "direct awareness of fitness" (ibid., p. 35). In Köhler's well-known experiments, a chimpanzee attains insight when it grasps that, put end to end, the two available sticks will enable it to obtain the desired food. Solving a problem means the transition to a "clear organization," to the "good gestalt," a changing over in perception to "a definite, stable organization," to one in which lifeworld tensions come to fittingly balance one another out in accordance with the demands of the situation's structure. The adequate handling of a situation requires a proper understanding of its structural requirements: "understanding or not understanding . . . usually shows itself in an ability or inability to coordinate one's actions to the event as its meaning, i.e., its principle of organization, demands." (Köhler, 1971, p. 179).

Making a Direct Comparison

Directly comparing things, two lines, for example, and discovering that "this line is longer than that one," is a further instance of insight. Here as elsewhere, insight is the immediately felt awareness of the directly interdepending characteristics of the related terms, felt awareness of the "how" of their structural interconnection. The relation "*clearly* longer than" is grasped as belonging to the very structural determining of one line by the other (Köhler, 1969, pp. 142–143), to the way the two lines are beyond themselves, in what is properly their own, to one another. Although past experience clearly makes a difference in our ability to manage things, nevertheless frequent associations in the past do not make for structural understanding, but the meanings themselves, the lines themselves in the illustration under consideration, in their present structural relativity to one another.

Understanding a Lecture or a Book

There is more to grasping a lecture or reading a book than the mere passive recording of words or the relating of them to what we already know (Köhler, 1971, pp. 169–170). Rather, meanings have to commune with and express one another as a system of functional significances in accordance with the structural demands established by the unfolding lecture or book itself. A grasping of the structural interconnections among the meanings being expressed, insight, has to occur, and this requires a certain capability and activity on our part.

Insight into Meanings Affecting Us and into Motivation in Their Regard

Many of our attitudes are felt to be adequate responses to the things confronting us (see Chapter 7, "The Demand Character of Value"). Admiration is felt to be directly and sensibly related to the wonderful musical performance, being charmed to be understandably related to a child's smile, enjoyment to the drink's refreshing coolness and taste on a hot afternoon, anger to the fact that one's home has been ransacked, fear to imminent threat, restlessness to the restaurant's stuffy atmosphere, and consternation to an unresolved conflict. In each of these cases cited by Köhler, "a particular fact of psychological causation [is] directly experienced as an understandable relationship" (1947, p. 190). In all these situations, we are affected by a meaning, and in each one we are at once aware of the structural dependencies directly in play and the way in which the self's attitude is being directly determined by the meaning in question. We have an immediate experience of our joy, fear, and so on, but also, and simultaneously, of the reason for our reaction *in the meaning* affecting us. "I experience directly, *hic et nunc,* how these surroundings disturb and confuse me. Such conditions I feel to have this effect necessarily; the causal connection is part of my experience" (ibid., p. 192). No one has to explain to us, for example, that the cool drink is affording us satisfaction at the moment. The reason for our pleasure instead is immediately experienced and understood. The relation between anger or joy and the situation from which it springs is similarly understandable, which is to say that emotions such as these generally "appear adequate with reference to the facts from which they derive" (Köhler, 1971, p. 369). We are quite aware that it is the income tax form, and not the shape of some book on the shelf, that fills us with horror (ibid., p. 432). There is an insightful experience of a functional (structural) relationship not only between meaning and meaning, then, but also "between experienced facts and experienced inner responses" (Köhler, 1947, p. 194).

As for insight into motivation (see Chapter 7 subsection "Demand Character and Motivation"), someone's impulse to do something about an unpleasant situation "follows from the given situation just as directly as does his displeasure. Thus the man has insight both in emotional and motivational causation. . . . Impulses toward the most important actions may . . . arise in a way which we can thoroughly understand" (ibid., p. 204). There is an "understandable relationship" in the realm of motivation, then (we apprehend "that one thing follows from another as its natural consequence"), just as in the strictly intellectual field. It is understandable that attractive meanings pull us in their direction, that unattractive ones push us the other way. A young man does not need "the indirect techniques of induction," Köhler comments, to find out why he is moved to strike up a conversation with an attractive young woman (1971, p. 431). It is indeed Köhler's belief that people generally understand the reasons for their behavior (ibid., p. 400).

Scope and Importance of Insight

Köhler asserts that insight permeates our everyday experience; scarcely a single total field lacks it entirely (1947, p. 200). He insists that awareness of relations of functional dependency is crucial to the way our "mental activities take their course" (1971, p. 432), that in all probability "all problems with which we may be confronted, and also the solutions of such problems, are matters of relations" (1969, p. 143), and that without insight into relations "thinking in any serious sense of the word" simply would be impossible (1971, p. 432).

Having pointed out the importance and scope of insight, Köhler laments, "And yet, among the psychologists only a small minority seems fully to realize that this is one of the most important psychological concepts" (1947, p. 200). He further remarks that sometimes he feels that "the chief dividing line among contemporary psychologists would separate those who acknowledge direct determination . . . from those who acknowledge only 'connections' in the sense of machine theory" (ibid., p. 206). Conventional psychology even today, as pointed out in Chapter 5, has yet to take Gestalt principles of organization with the seriousness they merit.

The Limitations of Köhler's Theory of Insight

Köhler's theory of insight represents a significant theoretical breakthrough to the pervasive role of organizational features in human cognitive and affective life. If reservations now are expressed about Köhler's work, and indeed about Gestalt psychology in general, this should not be taken as belittling his accomplishments or those of the other Gestalt psychologists. Just the contrary! The following objections and proposed revisions are offered as the corrective that Gestalt psychology needs to remain true to the most original of its formulations, and thus for it to attain the fulfillment of its most proper promise. Ideas along the lines of the ones suggested here have been proposed before, most notably by Gurwitsch and Merleau-Ponty, and are taken up once again in a somewhat more systematic manner in Chapter 12.

To come right to the point, the basic shortcoming of Köhler's approach—and with it that of classical Gestalt psychology as a whole—is its objectivism. Köhler holds psychology to the scientific ideal of an objective science of physical processes. Thus, although Köhler, championing the phenomenological clarification of all psychological concepts (Chapter 2, "Phenomenological Psychology"), initiates his treatment of psychological issues descriptively, he invariably concludes it by attempting to explain what he has come to describe by means of objective processes "beyond phenomenology." Psychological organization (law-governed dynamic self-distribution) for Köhler fundamentally is an objective causal process taking place in the cortex by reason of spreading and dynamically interacting electric currents. The essentials of gestalt formation thus are viewed as occurring transphenomenally in the objective brain. In the brain viewed physically, part-processes are envisioned as interdepending in a dynamically self-regulating manner as whole-processes. Köhler considers the law of good gestalt, moreover, as itself a physical law, as the operation of a tendency inherent in physical processes to attain a state of maximal regularity and simplicity. The directed tensions experienced in meaning events thus are reduced to the dynamics of physical tensions in the brain. It is precisely the objective tendency of physical reality to attain a balanced state (tension reduction), Köhler believes, that is in large measure responsible for the truly remarkable cognitive accomplishments of which humans are capable. The phenomenal self, in Köhler's view, has itself, along with all of the self's meanings and indeed the lifeworld as a whole, a seat in the objective realm of the brain. And, any relations the phenomenal self may have with its lifeworld meanings are said to be but reflections of objective relations between the cortical "self" and cortical "meanings." Motivation of the self by this view now is the motivation of the cortical "self" by cortical "meaning." Neither the phenomenal self nor phenomenal meanings *do* anything, then, in Köhler's psychology. For Köhler there is only one kind of activity in the universe, activity as the physicist studies it, physical activity. The physical is the real. This forms Köhler's objectivism.

Our ongoing experience with meanings, in Köhler's view, does not contribute anything at all per se to the formation of meaning. Insightfully gained meanings do no more than reflect more basic cortical activities, and indeed cortical activities conceived objectively; that is, as belonging to a space from which meaning, along with the self, has been denied a determining role in advance. Cortical processes are held to attain the essential organization and reorganization. The self's insight into meaning, as described in the first sections of this chapter, turns out for Köhler to be but a mirroring in consciousness of the direction taken by physical forces structurally at work in the cortex, of transphenomenal formations and transformations. Experience (insight into meaning) and cortical events are said to possess essentially the same structure, functionally interdepending phenomenal facts paralleled by functionally interdepending transphenomenal facts; this is the well-known Gestalt theoretical notion of *isomorphism*. The pertinent physical processes cannot themselves be reflected in experience, but what the physical processes accomplish is reflected in the very understandability of the determinations experienced; because there is no direct access to the physical processes underlying consciousness, Köhler can but infer the character of these processes from their reflected conscious counterparts. Although the more complete cortical context does not come to be mirrored in consciousness, in insight we are said to be given a clear indication of the structural sensibleness of the underlying physical relationships.

Insight *as* felt awareness of "functional relations among psychological facts" does not determine anything of and by itself, then, in Köhler's view. Insight does nothing to accomplish the structural relationships the understanding of which constitutes its very essence. A passive outcome, insight is but the reflection of activities unfolding elsewhere, in another realm of being, in a purely extended space (*res extensa*) where only physical activities prevail.

A Phenomenological Theory of Insight

The deficiencies of Köhler's approach, it is suggested, spring from his objective presuppositions. Science for Köhler is natural science; and thus psychology, to qualify as science, must be *natural-scientific* psychology. Psychology, by this view, is destined to become a branch of physics. A radically consistent phenomenological approach in psychology, by contrast, brackets just such an objectivistic ideal. Phenomenological psychology finds that, Köhler notwithstanding, an activity of insight does indeed make a difference in the meanings we actually grasp: that insight is an invariantly required co-organizer of meaning, that insight has a standing of its own. But phenomenological psychology also finds that meanings have a standing of their own, too, that they accomplish themselves precisely as phenomena, phenomenally, as events of meaning presencing. What is truly original is not meaning's transphenomenal counterpart in objective space, but meaning itself in its structural truth as a lifeworld event. There is for phenomenology, as argued especially in Chapter 2, nothing behind or beneath lifeworld meaning which is more basic than it and to which it would stand as a mere reflection. The functional interdepending in evidence in our everyday experience of things is not "really" the overlapping of spreading electric currents. Rather, a network of meaning forms all around us, beyond the cortex, beyond us altogether in the lived dimensionality of the existential space of possibility. The phenomenal interdepending of lifeworld moments, their signifying one another as meanings (as tulips, smiling faces, books, and subways), is for these moments to first happen as meanings, for them to first happen on any level. Organization indeed is given immediately (Chapter 5): in the lifeworld. All in all, the bodily self is a historically situated center of meaning (a la Merleau-Ponty and Chapter 4, "The Bodily Self"), and meaning is a phenomenal event through and through. The self and its meanings are simply not the upshot of objective processes in the cortex, as Köhler supposes. They could not be and still be what they are.

Insight, Meaning Formation, and Requiredness

Existential phenomenology finds that meanings originate in an internal and external signifying of one another in existential space, on meaning's own level, and not in the causal forces presumed operative in objective space. Insight is the openness of events of meaning presencing, Dasein itself. The "there" of such events, structural understanding plays an essential, rather than merely peripheral, accompanying role in meaning formation. The insightful self, being possible ahead of itself to structural possibilities or demands belonging to lifeworld meaning itself, sponsors meaning, in this way releasing it to its self-showing. Insight is the psychological counterpart to the coming to formation of nonpsychological meaning in its structural originality; that is, in those lawfully prescribed direct determinations that are the essence of any original meaning. The event of grasping self-forming meaning in the structural necessity of its requiredness, insight co-organizes original meaning. The activity of insight is the sponsor of an original signifying, of an action on the track of its intrinsic value.

Requiredness: Meaning's Inner Law

A gestalt is a whole accomplished in the dynamic interdepending of its constitutive moments (Chapter 5). There is a law intrinsic to this process of gestalt formation (Chapter 6), a law of structural goodness, that determines the relativity of a gestalt's moments to one another throughout the history of their dynamic self-distribution. This law of good gestalt formulates a fundamental role of requiredness in what regards meaning both as formative process (gestalt) and as outcome (gestalt quality). Meaning's law, requiredness guides the signifying that constitutes any meaning toward its "inner necessity" (a la Wertheimer) in its place, sometimes successfully and sometimes not. Meaning first becomes a meaning, a potential signifying actualized, in just such a search for an ideal state. Available lifeworld materials first gain "world-entry" precisely as required meanings. Required- ness, at once internal and external, which is to say, value, makes any meaning the meaning it is.

The Excitement of Insight and Meaning's Original Self-Forming

Requiredness, the law of any meaning's structural necessity, guides the formation of meaning in its totality, in both its internal and external signifying. But requiredness, and hence the actualization of available lifeworld potentialities, is only *for someone*. The origin of a meaning on the ground of a necessity properly its own, in the structural necessity of its requiredness, is only in view of the interest phenomenally held by the requiredness for someone. Original meaning or value arises precisely in the fresh and live excitement that its law of requiredness presently spells for a bodily someone (Chapter 6 subsection "Meaning's Origin in the Excitement of Its Requiredness"). Meaning originally unfolds in the event of its intrinsic requiredness for that being whose being it is to exist (that is, to be its openness to events of meaning presencing), for that being whose being it is, in becoming excited by things, to let them show themselves from themselves, for the first time ever, for just what they can be: in the beauty and power of their goodness, the tree in the meadow as the tree in the meadow. Bodily Dasein—the being that can be touched, that can be affected one way or the other, and that thus can let meanings matter structurally in their positive or negative requiredness—affords just the dimensional opening that Gestalt lawfulness needs to function as dimensional meaning's inner structural necessity. Human preoccupation and proficiency *let* meanings *be* in their intrinsic value. Lifeworld meanings form in their rightness or wrongness as meanings from the point of view of a someone who, situated, already has become an interested party.

Original meaning is an action that self-forms on its own phenomenal level, then, in the excitement it holds dimensionally for an able and interested someone. The bodily excitement of insight, this structural incorporation of an exciting other into the self's deepest interiority, is intrinsic to events of original value. The activity of insight is the psychological root of lifeworld meaning formation. Potential signifyings are actualized as intrinsically required meanings through a bodily feeling that reaches and is touched (excited) by the law-governed tensions (excitement) constitutive of any meaning; through a feeling that is coordinated "to the event as its meaning, i.e., its principle of organization, demands" (Köhler, 1971, p. 179). An interested, caring insight coactualizes meaning in the firstness and freshness of its originality, in the necessity of the direct determinations constitutive of its requiredness. Psychological being excited sponsors the nonpsychological excitement of meaning. Insight as felt awareness tuned in and tense with lifeworld tensions (stretchings) in the direction of the good gestalt is behavior that structurally is a match for its meanings, a living of meaning into the truth of its possibilities: structural understanding. Insight, grasping a meaning's law, is midwife to the original emergence of meaning out of its sensible tensions.

All in all, then, insight, vital interest on someone's part, is partner to the formation of meaning in an existential space of possibility. There is no disinterested observer and no "mere" facts. "Understandable relationships" come to formation only for an involved someone, for a bodily self who, existing (and hence not finished the way things are), can come under the sway of a law of requiredness and immediately be affected by the tensions thus set in motion; direct determinations stand revealed only for a bodily "I can" that, feeling itself, is able to feel the excitement inherent in the genesis of original meaning. Insight is involved, excited understanding. An account of insight in terms of objective activities simply has to miss the point. Physical activities do not care and cannot get excited. They thus are incapable of letting lifeworld moments signify one another in the excitement of their requiredness, and thus directly determine one another in their originality, as such moments in fact are found to do. Uninvolved, unfeeling objective processes cannot provide the openness meaning needs to come to a self-showing in its necessity.

Insight and the Originality of Meaning's Requiredness

In the light of these considerations, it is the same thing to say that there is insight and that lifeworld meaning is forming in the originality of its structural law. These, insight and original meaning (meaning in process in the necessity of its requiredness), are the complementary sides of a single whole, one event of truth. Lifeworld part-processes interdepend with a positive or negative quality for an inquiring attitude that, in tune with the law of good gestalt governing them, sponsors the play of tensions (stretches) between them. Insight partakes of the original having it out of meaning's phenomenal tensions, of the struggle of these tensions with their destiny.

Insight is insight into the necessity of a certain lifeworld signifying. The necessity of a meaning's positive or negative requiredness, the excitement inherent in a meaning's direct determinations and thus said here to be at the very origin of a meaning in insight, is in evidence in Köhler's various illustrations of insight as sampled earlier in this chapter. It is precisely the *negative requiredness* of the other's foot on mine (the relation "foot on mine causing discomfort") that structural understanding discovers. It is the *rightfully* longer of the two lines that insight comes to determine. "Line A" *ought* to be the answer to, "Which of these lines is longer?" "Line A" is the *positively required* answer, in the context of the question posed. "Five" *ought* to be the answer to the question, "What can two and three be said to be *fittingly* equivalent to?" The equation $2 + 3 = 5$ is fulfilled in the law of its structure, *positively required* as an equation; that is its origin as the meaning it is. The chimp discovers the two sticks *demanding* one another a certain way as a means to the banana. A cool drink is just *right,* an *intrinsic requiredness* indeed, on a hot afternoon. Salt water, on the other hand, is directly experienced, in the drinking, as *wrong* on such an occasion and is "to be rejected." A *negative requiredness,* the restaurant's stuffy atmosphere is found to be *unpleasant*; it *ought* to be otherwise. Some solutions to problems present themselves as *correct,* in which case there is "direct awareness of *fitness*" (Köhler, 1938, p. 35), whereas others present themselves as *incorrect,* as intrinsically *unfit.* Such and such an action presents itself as *inappropriate* under the circumstances. The points made in the lecture or in the newspaper account directly determine one another as a *coherent* narrative. All in all, then, insight shows itself in all these examples to be a grasping of the manner in which one thing directly and originally determines something else *with a certain direction of requiredness.* Insight is insight into requiredness in its place, into value.

Insight into Value

Insight is immediate contact with reality, with original lifeworld meaning in its place (external requiredness). Insight is insight into value, insight into original value, the origin of meaning for someone in its intrinsic value. Insight is psychological activity; value is nonpsychological meaning. Joined, these two sides of an original meaning event, and they are indeed fully correlative, are the phenomenon of phenomenology itself, the very event of meaning presencing; hence, the title of this book.

Insight into use values is finding our way about in a complex of ready-to-hand things, adjusting ourselves to them—and to the task to be performed—and putting them to use. Insight into morality values is conscience: the discovery and appreciation of the structural law of actions "to be performed." Insight into person values is love and respect for another someone like ourselves. Insight into beauty values is admiration and wonder over the way a meaning has come to balanced structural fulfillment. Insight in problem solving is thinking. Insight is many things, then, a using, a loving, conscience, admiration, respect, a thinking. There are exactly as many possible sorts of psychological insight as there are of nonpsychological value.

Insight into Negative Requiredness

Good, strong gestalts tend to persevere. Challenges arise even to such gestalts, however, and not uncommonly in a gestalt's very search for its necessity (see Chapter 6 subsection "Force and Counterforce in the Dynamics of the Good Gestalt"). Indeed, if there were no negative to upset even strong gestalts—if good gestalts did not run into their own intrinsic limitations, if good gestalts were never besieged by outer intrusions—such gestalts would never have a reason to change, and the lifeworld would be at a standstill. The negative, as a matter of fact and whether we like it or not, plays a central role in our necessarily finite sphere. The negative, on the one hand, may occasion an increase in the richness and complexity of our meanings, for the law of good gestalt, all the while seeking a state of balance, works to integrate new and disturbing elements into existing wholes of meaning. What always had been viewed as only positive in its requiredness, on the other hand, may come to show itself as thoroughly permeated with negativity, which self-showing may have far-reaching consequences. It may be seen, for example, that a social system credited all along as the very will of God in fact inherently is exploitative. It is an event of some moment for people thus to feel and name the exploitation being perpetrated for the injustice it is, for people to first feel its "ought not be," its "to be rejected." If meanings remained only neutral or good, if the status quo never manifested its internal and external structural limitations, problems of all sorts could never arise, much less solutions.

Manifestness of the Law of Requiredness

As seen earlier, the immanent law of meaning's structural requiredness is not behind or beneath meaning but phenomenally of the very essence of meaning. It is exactly this law of meaning that the psychological event of insight helps to bring to lifeworld expression, to self-manifestation. Properly speaking, requiredness is nothing other than meaning itself in its intrinsic impulse to structural originality; nothing other than the law governing the dynamic self-distribution of lifeworld moments as a gestalt, original meaning's most proper gestalt quality (suchness). The law of good gestalt formalizes something that touches every meaning, its manifest search (process) for an ideal state of intrinsic requiredness (outcome).

Insight's Privileged Status

Insight is bodily Dasein's very openness to events of meaning presencing, to the original self-showing of things for what they are structurally on their own ground of significance. Insight is nothing other than "there-being" itself. Although required meanings only happen for someone oriented in their regard, insight in every case nevertheless remains the attaining of that which is not insight, not Dasein, the attaining of nonmental meaning. Insight's prerogative consists in just this, its being a grasping of the structural determinations intrinsic to original meaning, its letting meaning attain a necessity all its own, which is to say, its letting something attain its "can-be" as a meaning. Insight is being possible's openness to a necessity beyond itself, the coactualizing of meanings in accordance with structural demands all their own. It is precisely in the being actualized of original meanings, moreover, that the bodily self's actualization lies and not in the pursuit of its inner fulfillment or happiness (compare Maslow and Frankl). Dasein's self-actualization lies in that to which it has been surrendered from the first.

The Nonoccurrence of Insight into Requiredness

Meanings arise in their nonpsychological originality for psychological behaviors of insight; but insight does not characterize all our experiences or originality all our meanings. Some meanings simply repeat themselves, for example, in their over-familiarity. Not structurally alive in their requiredness at the moment, such merely habitual meanings barely touch us. Merely conventional values, on the other hand, although often very powerful, may be mere illusions, wishes for the return of a lost childhood, without the hint of an "inner necessity" (in Wertheimer's words). Good and strong gestalts, merely habitual and conventional values tend to persevere.

Insight into value may fail to occur, moreover, in any of a number of situations, for any of a variety of psychological and nonpsychological reasons. A major nonpsychological reason is the sheer unavailability of the meaning in question: no matter how hard we look for the Eiffel Tower in New York Harbor, we must go away disappointed. Then again, we do not actualize a great many meanings in their structural necessity for any of a number of psychological reasons. We may know something only by rote, never having taken the pains that would have allowed its necessities to articulate themselves for us on their own ground. We may simply not have any interest in the matter, in all the features, for example, of some new piece of electronic equipment. Given our strong feelings on the topic, the joke may only anger us. Enjoying our society's benefits, we may never come to realize how it exploits certain groups. We may be prejudiced when it comes to certain meanings, blinded to their original requirements. Our emotional state—anger, phobia, panic, confusion, depression—may close us to the meaning's structure, to the future it could have coming to it on the ground of its own possioilities (see in this connection Chapter 11, "Disturbed Disposition"). Our minds made up, we may not want to be bothered with the facts. Not wanting to undergo negative emotions, we may refuse to let something presence in all its terribleness. We simply may be preoccupied and thus unable to give something the attention it requires. We may share in our culture's repression of certain things; of death, for example. We may simply be too tired to tackle a certain meaning.

9   *Insight as Impact*

We ourselves are one sole continued
question, a perpetual enterprise of
taking our bearings on the
constellations of the world, and of
taking the bearings of the things on
our dimensions.

—Merleau-Ponty, 1968, p. 103

I am nothing but an ability to echo
[things], to understand them, to
respond to them.

—Merleau-Ponty, 1964b, p. 94

Insight as Impact and as Interpreting

Insight, the communion (a la Merleau-Ponty) of a bodily someone with law-governed sensible qualities, is *structural understanding of intrinsically required meaning* (original or intrinsic value). Required meaning arises invariably for a historically situated someone who, interested and able, lets lifeworld moments stretch to and signify one another with a particular lived dimensional quality. Thus coactualizing the directed tensions at its origin, being possible *determines* meaning. Insight as such a determining of meaning is *interpreting,* the topic of the next chapter. In the interpretive determination of meaning, the self releases meaning to meaning's own possibilities of significance, in the letting be (determining) of meaning, interpreting grasps (determines) meaning on the ground of its own lifeworld law, for precisely what the meaning is (can be) from itself. But released to itself and a necessity of its own, meaning in turn comes to have a bearing on the self, "to bear on our dimensions" (Merleau-Ponty, 1968, p. 103); to weigh upon and *determine* being possible. The very openness of Dasein, after all, as noted in Chapter 3, lies in its being submitted to such possibilities of presencing as belong to meaning itself, in and from meaning's place within a context of significance. Insight as determined in openness by lifeworld meaning is *impact,* the topic of this chapter. Structurally determined in impact by

171

meaning, insight is a being encountered by meanings in what they hold in store for us. The insight that determines its meanings does not create them, then, but rather also is determined by their original structural integrity. Insight, all in all, at the same time is a determinative making out of meanings, an interpreting, and a determination by them, an impact.

Insight as impact is moved by the direct determinations that, structurally intrinsic to original meaning, render it either positive or negative in its requiredness, a positive or negative intrinsically required or structurally necessary value. Impact is a felt sense of things, a being affected by them. The bodily self, excited by a meaning's tensions, shares in their excitement in any number of ways. The impact that is intellectual satisfaction goes with a problem's solution; that of grief, with loss; joy, with good news; frustration, with a part that does not fit; tranquillity, with a peaceful state of affairs; rapture, with beauty; and so forth. Impact takes on the shape, then, the dimensional particularity, of the meaning currently affecting the self. Like the meaning that determines it, this bodily sense we have of a meaning is either positive or negative in sign, a being stressed when the requiredness confronting us is negative, a being satisfied when the requiredness is positive. Insight as impact is our bodily self determined by and identified with the directed tensions structurally constitutive of emergent meaning.

Insight is both interpreting and impact, both determinative of and determined by meaning in its structural originality. The being determined of insight as impact and the determining of insight as interpreting are not two separate behaviors, but rather two ways of considering the same psychological reality: insight as *impact-interpreting*. Determining (interpreting) meaning, we are determined by (feel the impact of) it: interpreting meaning is feeling the impact of meaning. Determined by (undergoing the impact of) meaning, we determine (interpret) it: feeling the impact of meaning is an interpreting of meaning. Insight is interpreting and impact at once. Insight interpretively releases a meaning's tensions to their everrenewed pursuit of a balanced state of fulfillment. At the same time insight is moved by these very tensions, by the action that any meaning is. We determine meaning, Self → Meaning. Meaning determines us: Self ← Meaning. Rather than two influences going back and forth linearly and externally, first one then the other, bodily self and sensible meaning (the life and destiny of each internal to the life and destiny of the other) determine one another circularly, reciprocally and simultaneously, each influence influencing the other even as it is influenced by the other: Self ↔ Meaning.

Impact as Being Affected by Meaning

"My perception is the impact of the world upon me" (Merleau-Ponty, 1973b, p. 137). The presencing of a lifeworld meaning on the ground of a necessity all its own takes place precisely in the bodily self's coming to be structurally affected by the meaning in the impact of insight. A meaning first happens when, touching someone in the direct determinations at the heart of its requiredness, it comes to count for something, to matter to that someone. What affects in impact are the tensions, moments stretching to one another, that, in the live pursuit of the structural necessity of their internal and external requiredness, of their intrinsic value, are the very self-formation of any original meaning. What affects in the impact of a positive value are tensions achieving the balanced state of fulfillment of "something as something"; what affects in the impact of a negative value are tensions that have failed, but perhaps not given up the struggle, to attain such a state. Insight is the impact of an action (compare Arnheim, "Seeing is the perception of action.").

What originally affects someone in the impact of insight is the intrinsically required meaning itself: the notes themselves as the beautiful melody; the nose, eyes, mouth, cheeks, forehead as the expressive other person; sensible qualities expressing one another as the rose; the words themselves as the story being narrated. In the tenseness of a current lifeworld signifying of one another of their moments, meanings affect us in what *they* are, in the originality of *their* law. To paraphrase the notion of intentionality, in their affecting us in impact, lifeworld meanings are "at" us. In impact things overtake us and achieve a hold on us. Heidegger writes, "To undergo an experience with something—be it a thing, a person, or a god—means that this something befalls us, strikes us, comes over us, overwhelms and transforms us. When we talk of 'undergoing' an experience, we mean specifically that the experience is not one of our own making; to undergo here means that we endure it, suffer it, receive it as it strikes us and submit to it. It is this something itself that comes about, comes to pass, happens" (1971a, p. 57). And again, "To know means: to be able to stand in the truth. Truth is the manifestness of the essent. To know is accordingly the ability to stand in the manifestness of the essent, to endure it" (1959, p. 17). Insight as impact is our bodily life seized by possibilities intrinsic to a meaning's law, structural impact upon us *of an other* in its sensible otherness. "Every bodily state," writes Heidegger, "involves some way in which the things around us and the people with us lay a claim on us or do not do so" (1979, p. 99). Insight is impact of a power beyond us.

Insight as impact is being moved, becoming excited over what is inherently exciting about a meaning, becoming attuned to lifeworld qualities, our bodily dimensions resonating with a meaning's life. The concrete dimensional suchness of a particular sensible quality, its power to touch and "saturate" us, in Merleau-Ponty's words, are due "to the fact that it requires and obtains from [our] gaze, a certain vibration" (1962, p. 451). Impact is a bodily feeling that, feeling itself, assumes the likeness of its lifeworld other, echoes it, takes on those very qualities that in their togetherness form the meaning confronting it, "vibrates" with them. " 'Nature is on the inside,' says Cézanne. Quality, light, color, depth, which are there before us, are there only because they awaken an echo in our body and because the body welcomes them. Things have an internal equivalent in me" (Merleau-Ponty, 1964a, p. 164). Casting our gaze upward, the sky in all its blueness comes to think itself within us (a la Valéry); we become the sky itself "as it begins to exist for itself; [our] consciousness is saturated with this limitless blue" (Merleau-Ponty, 1962, p. 214). Sensible meanings strike a responsive chord in us, then, in the impact of insight. The itself visible and tangible bodily self and the sensible qualities that form the lifeworld share a common bodiliness, one and the same pulsing dimensionality, a single life. The bodily self (no subject) and sensible lifeworld (no subject) are internal to one another, woven the one into the other as a single tapestry, inseparable. Our body is not one more sensible thing among other sensible things but is itself sensitive to things, "reverberating" to all sounds, "vibrating" to all colors (ibid., p. 236), at once sensible and sentient (Merleau-Ponty, 1968, p. 136), a dimensionally stretched sensitivity to things. In the impact of insight an other is felt and, thus felt, is internal to our life. In impact the very bodily sense we have of ourselves—bodily feeling, our deepest interiority, our very self itself (see Chapter 11, "Feeling and the Bodily Self"; also Chapter 4, "The Bodily Self")—takes on the bodily life of the other, mirrors it. The bodily life of the other becomes the fullness of our bodily life, becomes our bodily existence, becomes us. In this sense, we *are* our values, they *are* the substance of our life. Dasein is a bodily feeling, and what Dasein feels is its values. In perception, "assimilating its structure into [our] substance" (1962, p. 132), meaning gets through to us, penetrates to our core. Our body is the very fabric into which all things are woven (ibid., p. 235).

In becoming us, the other certainly does not become a real part of us psychologically, a piece of the mind (conventional psychology). In impact we incarnate the other and reflect *it,* it itself. The other remains other in and through such impact, through the bodily effect it has on us. In fact, precisely by touching us in impact, by stirring up intimations of itself within us, by becoming us, meaning originally becomes other, becomes itself; in touching us in impact, meaning assumes a lifeworld integrity all its own, beyond psychological processes of every sort, and we surpass to it. Given phenomenology's emphatic rejection of an objective space of meaning and human life, the assertion that meaning becomes us certainly may not be taken to mean that the other, in its effects, crosses the physical boundary of the skin and takes up residence inside us in the form of a subjective replica, as textbook psychology actually has it. The felt likeness of itself that the other institutes within us, this bodily form our life takes, simply is not properly conceived as being inside us objectively and subjectively, for what this likeness in fact accomplishes is to place us immediately and directly in touch with the other itself, "over there" in the lifeworld where alone it stands. Mirroring meaning in impact, literally embodying it, we find ourselves existentially beyond ourselves, outside alongside meanings. We indeed are "pervaded by the blue of the sky," the loss of a relative, the child's smile, the dreary weather; nevertheless the blue sky, the lost relative, the smiling child, the dreary weather remain other, remain nonmental lifeworld meanings. The other takes up residence in our life, and nonpsychological meaning is born. With us in its impact on our bodily life, we are "over there" with it. To perceive things, writes Merleau-Ponty, "we need to live them" (ibid., p. 325). Impact, the effective participating of meaning in our life and destiny, by the same token is our participating in the life and destiny of meaning. "There is no coinciding of the seer with the visible. But each borrows from the other, takes from or encroaches upon the other, intersects with the other, is in chiasm with the other. . . . The things touch me as I touch them and touch myself" (Merleau-Ponty, 1968, p. 261). All in all, then, our taking the meaning in, our absorbing it into our bodily substance, is for it to presence in its nonpsychological otherness. "It is when objects. . . have that direct manner of taking hold of me," writes Merleau-Ponty, "that I say they are existing" (1963, p. 211). Moving us in the deepest recesses of our bodily interiority, things gain "world-entry" (a la Heidegger) for what they themselves can be, and we are with them. In the participatory excitement of bodily impact, meaning first arises in the excitement of its otherness.

The outstanding examples of the incorporation of meanings into our life and their becoming precisely themselves in the process are found in the realm of what are commonly called *emotions* (a different terminology will be adopted in Chapter 11, which is devoted to a further examination of the topic of human affectivity). Consider grief, for example. Grief is being moved by a loss of some significance, by the death of a friend, for example. Grief is the painful incorporation of such a loss into our bodily life. Overcome with grief, our bodily self takes on the likeness of the loss, mirrors it in its life. We are not ourselves the loss, but the loss has us firmly in its grips, to the point where we feel ourselves at a loss, lost, deadened. Nonpsychological loss determines psychological grief. It determines us: impact. Such impact is not the forging of a copy of the lifeworld situation, the loss in miniature inside ourselves; to say that is to thoroughly falsify the human experience of loss. We do indeed embody the loss "here" in its impact, in grief, but the loss is "here" only to the extent that this "here" is "over there" alongside the lifeworld where the loss has taken place and where alone it is destined to remain. Distressed by the loss, we participate in it, find ourselves immediately transported "over there" where the other is lost to us, "over there" where we used to hold conversations with our friend. It is the very standing on its own of the loss, its original self-presenting integrity, its irreversible finality (an integrity and a finality that we would wish away if we could, but cannot), that stresses us in the being affected of its impact.

A meaning becomes itself in its impact on our life. The loss becomes a lifeworld loss, a structurally original loss "over there," precisely in its present taking hold of us in the grief we feel. The loss becomes itself—this original meaning, this intrinsically negative value, in the fullness of its lived dimensionality—precisely through its incorporation into our bodily dimensionality, through being reflected "here" feelingly in its impact. Mirrored in us, the loss comes into the open as itself, and we at once are carried away to it "over there." A meaning arises only for an existing someone who comes to be affected by it. No grief, no loss. Deaths and departures there would be, but, occasioning no grief, no losses. People have danced in the street at the announcement of a tyrant's death. What grief? What loss? All in all, then, someone's death is first discovered as a loss precisely in and through its impact on bodily feeling, in and through the impact that is bodily feeling. Grief is the advent of loss, loss and grief are dependent part qualities of a single larger whole with an overall negative sign. A meaning either happens or it does not, which is to say, it either has an impact for what it is or it does not. It may be noted that insight as being determined by meaning, impact, already is described as a determining of meaning. Given that impact and interpreting are the same behavior, impact-interpreting, this anticipation of impact as interpreting is unavoidable.

All in all, insight as impact is Dasein's very dwelling in openness with meanings (see Chapter 3, "Dasein: Openness to the World"; also Chapter 11 and, in particular, its subsection "Positive and Negative Knowing"). Being able to become affected is Dasein's basic opening to itself, and also to the world, its opening to original meaning (intrinsic value). Bodily feeling is the very openness of events of meaning presencing. Meanings self-form in their impact, become meanings, when their requiredness breaks in upon our individual bodily life. A landscape has an impact on us, for example, and gives rise to certain personal feelings. For this reason, because it is our own view of the landscape, Merleau-Ponty points out, we "enjoy possession of the landscape itself" (1962, p. 406): something that will never be understood so long as the world is conceived as objective nature; something that is immediately understood if the world is "the *field* of our experience, and if we are nothing but a view of the world, for in that case it is seen that the most intimate vibration of our psychophysical being already announces the world" (ibid., p. 406). The world is at the core of our individuality.

Impact as the Mattering of Meaning

In the excitement of impact a meaning is brought close in the intrinsic requiredness of its place in existential space. It is this something or someone that interests us at the moment. The self and the nonpsychological other dwell together in one cleared openness, a "here" and an "over there" in the same "there." The other in its impact is what matters at the moment, sometimes happily so, sometimes unhappily. The impact of a meaning is the "mattering" of some "matter," of something of some concern to us. Thus, for example, preparing to do some gardening, we bring the hoe close in its direct determination by the task at hand of breaking up clumps of earth. Signified as just what is needed in its place, the hoe matters to us at the moment in the necessity of its use value, in its utter *fittingness*. Things matter in impact in accordance with the concernful preoccupations of the moment, whether we instigate these preoccupations or they are thrust upon us. The hoe matters because we have the know-how of the situation, because we understand its requirements, because the hoe, the hoe itself, registers as meeting these requirements. Precisely in this way the hoe is grafted onto our life in its impact.

What matters in insight as impact is precisely a meaning brought close in the necessity of its requiredness, and thus a meaning in the process of originally coming to formation as what it can be in its place (outcome). Everyday meanings are positive or negative—always exciting, never indifferent—lifeworld requirednesses, values. The mattering of lifeworld meaning is either a positive or negative determining of our bodily dimensions; psychological processes taking over meaning's positive or negative sign; our life positively or negatively excited at a meaning's coming to determine it in impact. Indeed, what else could it mean for anything to matter except as brought close one way or the other, with a positive or negative sign?

Impact as Difference Structurally Told upon One's Life

Insight as impact, the mattering of an intrinsically exciting value in our being originally affected by it, is the psychological difference self-presenting lifeworld differences make on our lives, nonpsychological differences felt structurally in the positive or negative requiredness of their directed tensions, in the direct determinations at the heart of original lifeworld signifying. "Perception [is] differentiation" (Merleau-Ponty, 1968, p. 197). The things themselves show us how they are constituted vis-a-vis one another, how one thing leads to another, how this tie relates structurally to this jacket, how the solution to the problem lies in these very relations, how this meaning fittingly continues that one. Without such a dimensional telling of differences upon bodily feeling, without structural impact, there would be no lifeworld, no self-presenting reality.

The structural being affected of psychological processes is an invariant of all insight, even when the *feel* of the meaning's impact is not so pronounced as in grief or love. When the bank presents itself as just around the corner from the post office, for example, our understanding is affected by available structural differences and relationships. We feel the impact made by lifeworld meanings presently directly determining one another and coming into their own as a larger self-giving whole of sensible meaning. Insight into relations as the personal impact of these relations is exactly our realizing how this lifeworld meaning structurally continues that one, and in this way how it helps make that one be what it is; exactly our realizing how that lifeworld meaning continues and decides this one. The impact of insight is feeling the internal and external requiredness of dynamically self-distributing lifeworld moments. Insight is letting self-presenting lifeworld meanings be themselves as they have their impact on us in the tenseness of their differences from and relationships to one another, entertaining them in a way that enables them to remain themselves as they come to coconstitute a larger whole of meaning. Insight, in other words, is letting meanings, every last sensible moment, every last whole of meaning, show themselves from themselves, letting their signifying of one another show itself from itself as well. Insight is *letting* lifeworld differences *be* in letting them *touch* us.

We come across a willow tree. Undeniably physiological processes go with the present perceiving of this tree, which are not themselves perceived. But these processes are not legitimately invoked to whisk the meaning away as but the final stage in a causal chain. Meaning discriminated is not a result to be referred for its true essence to "molecules in motion." Perceptual meaning is irreducibly itself. The perceiving of the tree is an event of meaning (phenomenon) that stands on its own in that the tree arises in vision precisely when the tree presents itself as the meaning it is from its place at the foot of the hill. The tree is perceived in the very impact of the direct determinations at play in its various sensible qualities as these harmonize with one another, in its very being discriminated as a lifeworld whole of meaning. The tree stands where it stands in the positive requiredness of its place as a necessary part of the terrain we are engaged in exploring, and we see it precisely when it announces itself in its impact as the self-presenting unity of differences it is. It is in its very being discriminated in the self-giving requiredness of its lifeworld structure, on its own phenomenal level of excitement, on its own level of meaning, that any meaning originally happens. There is simply no way for meaning to be meaning and yet first arise as a subjective reflection inside us of objective cortical processes (Chapter 8, "The Limitations of Köhler's Theory of Insight"). No meaning could possibly come to pass in such a way. The world of formed differences, the organized lifeworld, is not in our heads, but rather given immediately all around us. Meanings are born of events of lifeworld excitement. Manifold possibilities of meaning, manifold potential signifyings (potential gestalts), are presently *given* in abundance in any lifeworld, in any social setting, readily available for an impact on our lives as this or that system of functional significances. Psychology does not need to manufacture connections. It does not have to resort to a warehouse of past memories or learned connections, for example. What psychology does need to do is take seriously the law-governed dynamic self-distribution of lifeworld meanings, which is to say, their self-regulating (internal and external) signifying of one another.

Insight as structural impact has been characterized as the "aha! experience." When things click, when we get it, when it gets us in its impact, we could well say, "Aha!," "Eureka!," "That's it!" For something to impact is for it to hit us. When we really understand a maxim, say, A stitch in time saves nine, we are struck by its wisdom, its truth. Everyone had always said it, and it is not that we did not believe them, but now it strikes us for the first time in the freshness and liveliness of its structural necessity. What was merely an accepted, conventional meaning has been structurally transformed into an originally live one. Taking us by surprise and personally touching us, the maxim attains its law, attains actualization on its own level of meaning.

Impact as the Holding Sway of Meaning

A meaning, structurally integrated into bodily feeling, brings its own weight to bear on us, and it does this in a great variety of ways, in as many ways as there are different values that confront us. The other helps us, gives us comfort, inspires us, encourages us to do better, makes us think, but also gets in our way, thwarts us, forces us to go around it or to otherwise adapt to it, and displaces us. "On the basis of [the ecstatic being-toward-possibilities, the swinging over into possibilities]," Heidegger writes, "Dasein is, in each case, beyond beings, as we say, but it is beyond in such a way that it, first of all, experiences beings in their resistance, against which transcending Dasein is powerless" (1984, p. 215). Original meaning holds sway over our lives in its impact, then, ruling us in the structural integrity of its proper law. An intrinsically required meaning has an impact precisely as itself, with all the self-giving dimensional density of the lifeworld itself. Any meaning, the lifeworld at its place, brings with it the weight of the lifeworld to which we are surrendered from the first.

A book's meaning, self-presenting in the utterances that, signifying one another, form it, may challenge our existing life goals, our prized ideas, our usual ways of going about things. "If the book really teaches me something," Merleau-Ponty writes, "at a certain stage I must be surprised, disoriented" (1973b, p. 142). And again, a literature is "a conquering language which introduces us to unfamiliar perspectives instead of confirming us in our own" (1964c, p. 77). Originally emergent meanings address us in *their* law of requiredness, and do so in unpredictable ways.

Speaking of Heidegger's view, Joseph Kockelmans writes that we are "looked at by beings in their Being; [we are] seized by beings as they open themselves up in their Being" (1970, p. 201).

Meaning, in the positivity or negativity of its impact on our bodily life, then, assumes a power over that life, even as we (interpretively) co-organize it in its very law of requiredness. Meaning insists on having its own way, on following the star of a logic all its own. The novelty of a meaning's thrust sometimes startles us. We find it necessary at times to struggle with meaning in order to get its gist. The joke breaks us up, the artwork bowls us over, the demonstration convinces us. Melodies haunt us. The vision of the future inspires, or perhaps terrifies, us. Memories stalk us. It is the exciting adventures of the hero that excite us—under the sway of their impact, adventure stories make our lives exciting, too. Meanings have a priority and fill our lives. "Perception has me," says Merleau-Ponty, "as has language" (1968, p. 190). Any gestalt is "a perception 'being formed in the things'. . . . The things have us, . . . not we who have the things" (ibid., p. 194).

People are not objectively and subjectively inside themselves, but instead existentially beyond themselves, expressing those meanings of concern to them at the moment. When someone is rapt up in a book, the book's law has taken over and holds sway. In grief the self is totally absorbed in the particularities of the loss, in the loss itself. The painter becomes the bird being painted. We begin to tap our feet with the music; where do we begin, where does the music end? Some people turn us the wrong way. So close indeed are we to meanings, and they to us in their impact, that we disentangle ourselves from them at times only with the greatest difficulty, sometimes not at all, and never in totality. Nothing of us is left untouched by our always and already having been submitted to events of lifeworld meaning. Value, becoming the self in its impact, rules. For existential phenomenology there are no longer subjects and objects, only mirror play.

10   *Insight as Interpreting*

Our life . . . contributes to [the]
making [of the perceived world].

      —Merleau-Ponty, 1964a, p. 25

Facts is precisely what there is not,
only interpretations.

      —Nietzsche, 1967, p. 267

When that which is within-the-world
is itself freed, this entity is freed for
its *own* possibilities.

      —Heidegger, 1962a, p. 184

Insight as the Activity of the Self

In events of insight an objective external reality is not establishing replicas
(representations) in miniature of itself in the brain, cortical models of reality
reflected in turn in the mind as mere causal outcomes (Chapter 8). Insight
into meaning in the originality of its law of requiredness is not something an
objective realm delivers, not the mere passive receiving of something in a
subjective sphere of inner consciousness. Insight is not the weighing upon the
organism of an environment that is ready-made in any sense of the term.
Insight is not the "impact" of objective stimuli. What affect us rather in their
impact are the lifeworld meanings themselves. But even then insight is not
only such impact. Insight is the excitement of impact, to be sure, a being
determined by lifeworld others, but insight also is our life (being possible)
determining lifeworld others, our life determining even how others can affect
us in the first place. Insight, co-organizing the very world that comes to meet
it from the first, is *interpreting* as well as impact. To experience the world's
meanings is to take them up and live them, to go about discovering the
signifying intrinsic to them, and not to assimilate them merely passively
(Merleau-Ponty, 1962, p. 258). Our lives are situated, interested, pursuits
and determinations of the lifeworld in those possibilites of self-manifestation

181

that are properly its own; historically situated enactments of meaning. Not only does meaning, with its law-governed tensions, exercise an activity in events of insight, not only is there an impact on our lives of the structural determinations constitutive of a meaning, of its dynamic self-distribution, but the self is active, too. The self, determining a meaning's directly given structural determinations, interpretively releases meaning to its necessity. Insight is not properly understood unless both impact and interpreting enter into the account. Insight, as noted in Chapter 9, is impact-interpreting. Determined by meaning, insight determines meaning; determining meaning, insight is determined by meaning. Meaning holds sway in each impact within the limits proper to it, but a bodily life, the concrete network of proficiencies and preoccupations as which any someone exists, at once sets the limits within which the other can presence. The sensible dimensions of meaning reach our bodily dimensions as they can, and our bodily dimensions reach the sensible dimensions of meaning as they can. Insight into original value is a reciprocal limiting or conditioning by one another of self and meaning.

The insightful self is invariably active, then, an interpreting with a role of its own to play in the self-actualization of meaning on the ground of its proper necessity. For the landscape to come to an original self-display, the bodily self must come to visually discriminate (actively tell differences with regard to) trees, paths, hills, valleys, meadows, and so on in their significance relative to one another. For a complex piece of music to arise in the originality of its law, it has to be given the attention it requires. To learn something, we must become personally involved in it. To locate the door behind us, we have to reorient our bodily dimensions; we have to turn and look its way. Nonpsychological lifeworld differences indeed are structurally told upon our lives in the impact of insight, but the self's temporal preoccupations at once interpretively tell these nonpsychological differences. Insight is at once a being engaged by meanings holding sway over us and a discriminative making out of these very meanings, an active determining of how one thing leads to another, of how one thing goes with another.

In insight Dasein interpretively expresses possibilities beyond itself in the lifeworld. "All perception," in Merleau-Ponty's words, "all action which presupposes it, and in short every human use of the body is *primordial expression*" (1964c, p. 67). "Expressing what *exists* is an endless task" (1964b, p. 15). Interpreting, we are ahead of ourselves, expressing what meaning has to express in its law, codetermining how what is available in the lifeworld comes to self-expression in the necessity of its requiredness (see the subsection "The Paradox of Interpreting and Impact"). "Our life . . . contributes to [the] making [of the perceived world]" (1964a, p. 25). Interpreting is not a behavior that extraneously synthesizes fragmented sensory impressions internal to the organism, as textbook psychology has it. Bodily interpreting rather sets to work on meanings (signifyings) potentially available in the lived dimensionality of the existential space of significance. When successful, when insightful, interpreting helps these lifeworld others attain possibilities of expression intrinsically their own. Interpreting "processes" a world rich with sensible meaning from the first, not inner sensations.

Interpreting and Situatedness

Being possible comes to meaning events as an already concretely situated being-in-the-world. This concrete situatedness of Dasein will be referred to here as Dasein's *alreadiness* (a la Heidegger). This alreadiness of ours, on the one hand, is all that we always have been: openness to events of meaning presencing, our very Dasein itself. On the other hand, it is all that we have ever been through: sensitivity to whatever meaning and meaning contexts we have become familiar with in the course of our life, precisely to the extent that they continue to weigh upon us and somehow matter, precisely to the extent that we still care about them. Our alreadiness is the way we already are open to the world, the way we already can be affected by and become actively involved in things; in view of its affective dimension Dasein's alreadiness is termed *disposition* in the next chapter. Our alreadiness is by no means behind us, then, something over and done with; that is the *past,* the way things actually happened some time ago. There is no changing the past because, over and done with, it no longer exists. Although there is no such thing as the past, our alreadiness, very much with us, is exactly the way we already are, our bodily capacity to feel things, ourselves as already concretely turned to and dimensionally tuned in to the world, already a match for, already able to enact, its intrinsic possibilities. "Dasein *is* as having been" (in Heidegger's words).

Our alreadiness is the way we have been changed and shaped by experience, by our involvement in things, and, thus conditioned, have been enabled to shape and be shaped by events now occurring, as well as by those yet to come. Our alreadiness is the way our proficiencies and interests have been structured by events, the way we thus have come to be structured. It also is the way our world has come to be structured, for as we are structured and restructured, so, too, is our reality, so, too, is the way we can structure reality. We never put our foot in the same river twice, in part, because intervening events have occasioned a restructuring of our alreadiness. The alreadiness of insight is a particular ability to determine and be determined by meanings, to grasp them, to let them gain entrance into our bodily dimensions, to release them to possibilities they have coming to them dimensionally on the ground of their own law. The alreadiness of insight is an alreadiness of both impact and interpreting, a particular network of capacities for determining things and thus for being determined by them. All in all, then, our alreadiness, ourselves, is our capacity for and inclination to meaning, the way we can interpretively enact them, the way meanings can touch and excite us in their positive or negative impact, the "there" of events of meaning. Dasein *is* how it can determine and at the same time be determined by meaning. Perception, in Merleau-Ponty's words, "takes advantage of work already done" (1962, p. 238).

Interpreting as Enactment Situated in an Ongoing Context

Insight is a concretely situated event. Meanings affect, excite, us in the originality of their intrinsic value because we already somehow are inclined to them. Insight as interpreting is situated determining of lifeworld meaning: of its lifeworld "can-be," at once of the impact of this "can-be" on our lives. Although the subsection after this one concerns itself with the alreadiness of interpreting as shaped across a lifetime, this one considers alreadiness as taking shape currently in an unfolding meaning context. Structural understanding emerges from within our lives as an unfolding temporal complex of activities geared to the lifeworld. Dasein futurally enacts that which it is already capable of enacting, releasing meaning to a present self-showing. The interpretive determining of meaning is a situated enactment. Our life's temporal moments—alreadiness, present, future—are in active communication with one another at any given moment, reciprocally determining one another. "The unity of time's three dimensions," Heidegger writes, "consists in the interplay of each toward each" (1972, p. 15). Although this subsection and the next one concentrate on the alreadiness of interpreting, on interpreting as *situated* enactment, a section after that, "Interpreting as Imagining," turns specifically to interpreting as futural imaginative enactment of meaning, as situated *enactment*.

Our life is in process temporally, and those original meanings that in fact are discriminated, those intrinsic values that affect us in the truth of their impact, depend on our alreadiness as it is currently developing, on what we have been concerned with just now, on how that concern has concretely unfolded up to and including the present moment. The sensible meanings that we reach, that reach us, depend on our present situatedness: on our having attained our present location; on our current interests and intentions; on what we have just witnessed; on where we want to be later; and the like. We are always coming from somewhere, and this "from somewhere of ourselves," as it is concretely structured at the moment, interpretively determines the meanings we encounter. The available lifeworld continues to present itself in its originality in keeping with preoccupations that structurally are a match for it. Whatever insight gained into the layout of the terrain, for example, depends precisely on our having developed and maintained certain interests in its regard. Responding structurally to our given pursuits, to our bodily alreadiness as concretely assumed and lived forward at the moment, the terrain turns its lived dimensionality our way. Insight into the directed tensions constitutive of the terrain is accomplished, on our side, by looking, by a seeing that leads to further looking, by a looking and seeing that brings into play activities of walking, looking around, listening and hearing, wondering, taking a look back, deciding, climbing, getting a foothold here and then there, losing our balance and regaining it, squinting, looking again and pushing forward once more. Original meanings arise through just such activities of a bodily life in historical process. Our turning to look at a tree, our enactment of the tree, itself already is situated, belonging to an alreadiness taken up and furthered in turn. Turning to look, we are geared to possibilities of meaning about to emerge, and we presently see the tree. Given the concrete dimensionality of our present alreadiness and given this available lifeworld potentiality, the tree is what will be insightfully discriminated in its structural law. If, on the other hand, we are in mourning, if we are chasing butterflies, if we are in a hurry, we may barely notice the weeping willow tree just over there or how it directly determines, as well as is directly determined by, all those things that surround it. Insight into the terrain in the law of its necessity as the unity of meadow, tree, path, hill, and valley is not something that happens for someone simply because he or she is in the neighborhood. Room has to be made in existential space rather for the terrain's constituents to signify one another in accordance with their "principle of organization" (in Köhler's words). The development of an exploratory situatedness, an exploratory interest, on someone's part clears a space for the landscape to be brought close and to show itself from itself. Situated in a certain field of meanings, accommodated to their law, our bodily dimensions allow lifeworld moments to stretch to one another and functionally interdepend with a certain positive or negative requiredness, permits the enactment of a certain domain of meanings.

We are situated in our example in a particular way. We are set on exploring the terrain. And as we pursue our investigations, we do not merely gaze at the tree and then at the path, etc., as these make an appearance before us. We are responsible rather for what we actually come across in everyday life, in that what we encounter depends on what we freely turn to, on the alreadiness into which we are entering at the moment. We are responsible for our own situatedness—not for creating it, but for how we take it up and live it into its future. To determine what something rightfully is and how it fits into its context, we must make it out. We see the tree in the requiredness of its place at that very moment when we turn to look its way. What makes something be figure and something else be ground, Merleau-Ponty remarks, is the way we concretely relate to them in our act of looking (1962, p. 278). Certain necessary consequences follow the decisions of the moment; some meanings present themselves to our view, while others withhold themselves.

We look; we see. Listening, we hear. The experienced behaviors of looking, of otherwise orienting ourselves, of behaving in such a way as to ensure the continued existence of the present context, help bring the world we are encountering at the moment to its actual organization. The alreadiness we presently are developing and assuming determines our meanings. It is the self itself that is psychologically engaged—a personal history, an individually dimensionalized life, that turns, that looks and that sees—and not a complex of objective processes essentially on this side of selfhood and meaning. It is the bodily self as presently situated that interprets meaning.

Interpreting as Enactment Situated across a Lifetime

The particular network of competencies that we already are to enact meaning, and thereby to release it to its structural law, is not limited to those capacities of ours developing only now. Rather, our alreadiness embraces all our developed capacities, our total openness as shaped by a lifetime of experience with the lifeworld and its meanings. This total being disposed on our part, everything we are and have been through, this overall interest of ours in things, is the very forward thrust of our lives, the promise of our future. Even though we are unable to recall Van Gogh's various paintings with any great degree of accuracy, Merleau-Ponty points out (ibid., p. 393), they nevertheless have their place in our lives forever, shaping our entire esthetic experience. We carry forward all we have ever been through. "What we have experienced is, and remains, permanently ours" (Ibid.). Our youth remains with us, whatever our age.

Situated Enactment as Capacity of Recognition

All the events of our life have contributed to our present capacities for enacting a certain range of the world's requirednesses. Although these former events were experienced at the time, as past events they now forever are gone. And yet, mediated by an alreadiness that they have had their part in shaping and into which they are now integrated, these former events effectively are in play at the moment, contributing to the impact on our life of an actual lifeworld. The role of these events, along with that of our alreadiness quite in general, nevertheless is a silent, receding one. Our life centers not on ourselves as shaped by what we have been through, not on our capacities for meanings, but on the meanings themselves with which we are preoccupied at any given time. Access to our alreadiness and to the events that have concretely shaped it is precisely through the meanings coactualized by that alreadiness, through our meanings and the felt sense we have of them.

Historically situated in certain definite ways, being-in-the-world is savvy in what regards its world. A match for the referential totality of meanings to which we are submitted from the first, we are already familiar with a great number of particular things, with meadows, trees, paths, hills, and valleys. We depend on our acquired familiarity with such lifeworld meanings for their current enactment as a novel whole of meaning, the terrain we are presently exploring. If we had never before seen, say, a tree, we would undoubtedly become interested in familiarizing ourselves with its composition, in developing an alreadiness able to release it as the functional whole it is. But we have already insightfully discriminated those direct determinations that structurally make a tree a tree, in a past that has long since disappeared. And now, competent in regard to tree-gestalts—in both their internal and external requiredness—we immediately *recognize* this particular tree, even though we have never seen it before in our life, for the meaning it is.

Our former encounters with meanings shape our alreadiness, then, making us competent in their regard. We are a bodily repertoire of cognitive capabilities of a certain lifeworld. Already skilled at certain meanings, we now readily enact them, trees and paths and valleys, in all their familiarity and proceed to concern ourselves with the law intrinsic to the larger gestalt of the moment, with which we are not already familiar and to which familiar sorts of gestalts stand as defining moments. Present discriminative perceiving of a whole of meaning as it self-forms in its original lifeworld requiredness builds upon former expenditures of time and effort. And once we have completed our current explorations, the meadow-tree-path-hill-valley itself will be a recognizably familiar meaning and other "terrains" will hold our interest.

All in all, then, present enactment of the original possibilities meanings have coming to them depends on those lifeworld potentialities already effectively coactualized by activities on our part. The interpretive determination of meaning is a situated enactment of lifeworld possibilities.

Differential Coactualizing of Meanings

At any given moment of our life, we readily can coactualize certain requirednesses but not others. We presently have the interpretive capability to insightfully enact the law of certain unfamiliar wholes of meaning, whereas the law of certain other unfamiliar wholes are presently, and perhaps forever, beyond our reach. We can follow the plot of most movies, but may be completely at a loss when it comes to comprehending an advanced text in economic theory. Unable to grasp the way in which such a treatise's mostly familiar moments directly determine one another as a whole of meaning, we simply are not up to its style, its "can-be." Deficient in the alreadiness that would be a match for it, we are unable to release it to the structural truth of its impact on our bodily dimensions.

The interpretive capacity to codecide the lawful signifying of lifeworld moments by one another, to let them dynamically stretch to one another this way or that, with this determination (quality) or that, is by and large an acquired, learned, capacity. Learning, rather than a mechanical becoming programmed of the organism, is essentially structural in character, the concrete articulation of relations between behavior and its world (see Chapter 14, "The Bodily Self–World System and Learning"). All in all, then, people insightfully enact meanings in different ways, in accordance with the varying interpretive competencies they have become in their lifetime. Thus, where we readily and in all orginality see interesting geological formations, someone else, just as readily and originally, will see whatever it is he or she has become skilled at discriminating when faced with "givens" such as these. Some people know every car on the road, others cannot tell a Corvette from a Chevette. The requiredness of a meaning is an event that either happens or does not. Of two people listening to the performance of a Bach fugue, one hears a masterwork, the other only notes rising and falling. The music unfolds in its intrinsic requiredness, it comes to fulfillment in accordance with its "principle of organization" (a la Köhler), for one listener, for one history, but not for the other. The "same" notes are not the same phenomenally for the two listeners. The notes are differentially told, differentially interpreted, in the two cases, with differential impact. The notes modify (signify) each other in two distinctly different ways: $Ai \leftrightarrow Bi \leftrightarrow Ci \leftrightarrow Di$ and so on, as opposed to $Aii \leftrightarrow Bii \leftrightarrow Cii \leftrightarrow Dii$ and so on; i and ii specify differing gestalt qualities (gestalts) formed by notes A, B, C, and D. The "same" fugue is heard as different by the two listeners, the notes signify one another as two different gestalts, as the musical piece it rightfully can be or as just so many sounds. The whole is not the sum of its parts. The actual way the "same" notes modify each other, the way each sounds as a member of one or the other of the two systems of functional significances, depends on one's background with classical music and one's consequent interpretive skill. One's overall historical situatedness (alreadiness) determines in a general way how, on a first hearing, notes constituting pieces of a certain style come to be interpretively enacted, with or without structural understanding of their law. People are variably competent in what regards different sorts of meanings.

Two different readings of a good poem, by two different people or by one person on two different occasions, can both attain authentic possibilities of the work, both be accommodated to the structural law intrinsic to it, and yet be considerably different. The poem thus shows what it can be in distinct configurings, in terms of varying life-historical conditions. This indeed is what one would expect from a law of good gestalt that dictates that a meaning become every bit as fulfilled as it possibly can. Given the inherent possibility of new manifestations of goodness, and given the right circumstances, it is to be expected that such manifestations will occur. The poem, and classics of all sorts, indeed may come to say things that never occurred to its author. A work, neither the *product of* the author's mind nor having ever occupied a place *in* it, has a life and dynamic of its own that transcend the mere awareness of the author. "As for the history of art works," Merleau-Ponty writes, "if they are great, the sense we give to them later on has issued from them. It is the work itself that has opened the field from which it appears in another light" (1964a, p. 179). Actively interpreting a classic, a sensitive someone almost always can find it has something new to say. Meaning thrives on its ability to change, and Dasein is differentially open to meaning.

Interpreting as Imagining

Structural understanding is the situated self's active taking up and determining of the future meaning has coming to it on the ground of its own law, a situated enactment of meaning. Such understanding liberates possibilities of significance that properly are meaning's own. But, to be a liberating of this sort, understanding has to let meaning be what it dimensionally can be, has to give meaning a "go," has to *venture* meaning. Insightful interpreting is a venturing of the way in which available lifeworld moments *can* signify one another in accordance with their structural law, a psychological venturing of nonpsychological possibilities. Just such an interpretive venturing grants lifeworld moments the freedom of their possibilities, the free space, the room, they need to signify one another on the ground of their own lawfulness. A venturesome interpreting gives meaning its lead, the very opportunity available lifeworld moments need to self-form as an original whole of meaning, as intrinsically required value in its place. Such interpretive venturing or possibilizing of meaning is *imagining*. Insight as interpreting is an imagining of the possibilities inherent in a meaning's law-governed tensions, a venturing that is "over there" with meaning, a participating in the future a meaning has coming to it. "When that which is within-the-world is itself freed, this entity is freed for *its own* possibilities" (Heidegger, 1962a, p. 184). Imagining, our access to the manifold possibilities of meaning, is our access to what is our "first, last, and only world," to "our reality."

With interpreting viewed as an imaginative enterprise, as a venturesome enactment of meaning, the creative dimension of insight comes to the fore. "Perception turns out to be not a mechanical recording of the stimuli imposed by the physical world upon the receptor organs of man and animal," writes Arnheim, "but the eminently active and creative grasping of structure" (1986a, p. x). And yet the creativity of insight by definition is not novelty or invention at any price. As a "grasping of structure," as an accommodating to meaning's "principle of organization" (a la Köhler), creative insight, rather than an exercise in subjective whim, is an openness to the requirements of meaning, to the authentic possibilities meaning itself has coming to it. Insight in its imaginative dimension is a creative engagement with directed lifeworld tensions, an active joining of forces with meaning in its search for balanced self-expression. Insightful imagining, rather than any mere wishing for something, is the very behavioral openness that available lifeworld moments need to originally signify one another on the ground of their own necessity. Meaning is freed to follow a necessity of its own through the creative freedom of insight.

Reviewing the principal results obtained thus far in this chapter, the behavior of interpreting may be said to be a *situated or disposed imagining* of meaning, a situated and venturesome taking up and living forward of meaning into its future, situated enactment of the possibilities of meaning. This behavior's being *situated* is the alreadiness of interpreting discussed earlier in the chapter. Its being an activity of *imagining,* the imaginative enactment of meaning, is interpreting in its futural dimension, a venturesome determining of meaning in the future (possibilities) meaning has structurally coming to it. A futural venturing of meaning with an alreadiness all its own, interpreting is a present releasing of meaning. Insight is the temporal interplay of time's three dimensions (present, future, alreadiness), a unified play consisting "in the interplay of each toward each" (Heidegger, 1972, p. 15). On the one hand, what we are interested in futurally brings a certain alreadiness into play; whereas, on the other, what we already are opens up a certain future for events of meaning presencing. Our future plays into our alreadiness: what we are imagining awakens our capabilities of the world. Our alreadiness plays into our future: we imagine what we are already capable of. Our alreadiness and our future playing into one another both play into and are played into by our present releasing of meaning: situated imagining gives rise to our present releasing of meaning, present releasing redirects our situated imagining. The moments of time interpretively determinative of meaning, circularly related to one another, constitute a *threefold temporal interplay.*

Interpreting ahead of Itself

A descriptively oriented phenomenological psychology, it turns out, finds interpreting to be an imaginative enactment of meaning. Venturing meaning, insight is ahead of itself to those possibilities of signifying that meaning already has coming to it in its originality, possibilities to which we already somehow are attuned. Dasein as ahead of itself imagining the possibilities meaning has coming to it is the future of an event of meaning presencing.

The "future" for conventional psychology, as has been previously noted, is but the playing out of past causal activities in objective space; in such a space an effect can come only *after* its cause. External stimuli, linearly and in conjunction with memories established in the past, engender perceptions or meanings as effects inside the organism; external stimuli and memories, accounting for our perceptions, precede them. Perceptions, functioning as stimuli in turn, "trigger" emotions; perceptions, internal stimuli accounting for our emotions, precede them. *Past* tense is what behavior is all about for conventional psychology, behavior's origin.

For Köhler, as for Gestalt psychology generally, stimuli bombarding the organism do not provide it with isolated sensations. The cortical processes objectively instituted by environmental stimulation rather are viewed as immediately and presently organizing one another. The Gestaltist approach, to account for our actual perceptions, thus stands in no need of a supplementation from memory to round it out. Köhler introduces a *present* dimension into psychology.[1]

Neither conventional psychology nor Köhler envisions the human being as ahead of itself to the referential totality of the world and to the possibilities of meaning resident in such a totality. For neither approach is behavior outside itself futurally, imaginatively enacting, and at once being determined by, meaning's original possibilities of significance. Phenomenological psychology introduces the *future* into psychology and, with that, the coming into its own of meaning, as well as of the self as the openness of events of meaning presencing.

Imagining as Imaging

Imagining is sometimes an imaging, which is to say that interpretive venturing sometimes possibilizes meanings by "picturing" them, always, to be sure, as nonpsychological lifeworld others. But this subset of imaginative behaving is not imagining's fundamental thrust to meaning. We need not "picture" things, even when we are dealing with them in their absence, as when we are searching for our lost glasses. Nor do we have to "picture" things that are perceptually available in the lifeworld but whose grasping nevertheless requires, as do all originally occurring meanings, a venturesome possibilizing. We imaginatively venture, without imaging, the terrain that is all around us. We imagine, without "picturing," the story as it unfolds in the alreadiness, the present, and the future of its narrative. We venture, without mediation, the other person we are with. All in all, what we imagine in the first instance is this perceptual lifeworld of ours (Chapter 4, "The Primacy of Perception"). The basic character of imagining, along with that of the lifeworld to which it is surrendered from the first, is perceptual. The venturing of our lifeworld sometimes takes place in images: as in what Freud calls *illusions* (wish fulfillment), for example, or in anticipating futural aspects of the perceptual lifeworld, but not always. And, when it does, such venturing has itself an ultimately perceptual character.

Actual and Possible Meaning

Imagining, it has been seen, is crucial to insight as structural understanding of original meaning. Meaning stands in need of a creative venturing to arise in the necessity of its requiredness. Merely habitual or conventional meanings, by contrast, involve no current imaginative venturing, at least in the regard of what is essential to their unfolding at the moment. The mode of presencing of such lifeworld meanings—*as* conventional, *as* habitual—might be said to be *actual*. An actual meaning, rather than a meaning whose tensions are being originally ventured at the moment, is one that is merely reenacted, merely repeated. The authentic possibilities of self-revelation of an actual meaning not lying ahead of it, it has nothing structurally fresh and new to say to us. A conventional or habitual meaning is not a *possible* one, not one in the process of arising in the necessity of its requiredness. A possible meaning is a live meaning of the moment, then, one that is presently coming to formation in what it properly can be, for the first time ever, or at least as if for the first time ever. Imagining an original meaning is venturing a possible signifying (possible meaning), giving its "can-be" a try: Venturing ↔ A Possible Signifying. What is available (potential) in the lifeworld is actualized in the structural requirements of its law through a venturing of possibilities. The potential is actualized through the possible. An original meaning always is a matter of structural possibilities. Original meanings are possible meanings; authentically possible meanings, conversely, are original meanings.

The interpretive venturing of possible structures, this taking up and living forward of the alreadiness of our being-in-the-world, is an activity on someone's part. The imaginative venturing crucial to insight is altogether inconceivable as a physical occurrence. The category of the possible is an existential one that cannot be encompassed in objective space. It is not that the body and brain cannot venture meaning (see Chapter 4, "The Bodily Self"), but that the body and brain *conceived objectively* cannot. The body and brain that imaginatively venture original meaning can be only a personal body, a caring bodily self dimensionally enacting lifeworld meanings on the basis of its situation in existential space, some-body, someone. Insight into meaning, as seen in Chapter 8, occurs on its own phenomenal level, that of the self, that of lifeworld meaning.

The Paradox of the Self and Its Meanings

Insight: Active Receptivity

Perceiving the terrain with insight is an event in which lifeworld moments originally come to organization as a network of meanings. The meanings individually, and as they continue one another as the larger whole of meaning, so to speak, are laid out all around us. "Givens," with *their* "principle of organization" (in Köhler's words), these meanings lend themselves to our explorations. The potential whole of meaning such individual "given" meanings are able to form is actualized in its "givenness" only in and through events in which its various constituent meanings are taken up and made out by a bodily someone. Bodily Dasein opens up existential space, making room for and releasing its meanings, as bodily Dasein goes (Chapter 4, "The Bodily Self's Familiarity with Lived Space"). Insight is not the lifting of a veil behind which lie preexisting objects ready-made in-themselves (natural attitude), but a venturesome involvement in things of a historically situated self. "There is no brute world," Merleau-Ponty writes, "only an elaborated world" (1968, p. 48). Active behaviors on the part of an interpreting someone help bring a meaning to its given organization in the lifeworld, which also is its impact on that someone's life. Interpreting is a co-organizing essentially determinative of meaning's very self-givenness. No matter how "given" and "obvious" any lifeworld other is, its lifeworld availability simply has to be interpreted, imaginatively enacted by a properly disposed someone, for its lifeworld requiredness to first arise in its originality. Something has to come to be determined for it to show itself for what it is, for it to determine us on its own ground of requiredness. *Active* behaviors of interpreting must occur for the other to be *received* in the bodily impact of its structural necessity, for it to affect us in its law. Insight is both active and receptive, an *active receptivity*. A situated determining of meaning's possibilities of structural unfolding (the alreadiness of interpreting futurally ahead of itself), insight is a situated being determined by such possibilities (the alreadiness of impact futurally ahead of itself). "At" the terrain (interpreting), the terrain is "at" us (impact). The terrain "becomes what it is" through the singleness of impact-interpreting.

The Paradox of Interpreting and Impact

Modern thought typically has resorted to entities in-themselves, in particular to mutually exclusive subject (mind as private inner realm) and object (nature as pure extension), in accounting for any occurrence whatsoever. Because, descriptively speaking, insight is not an affair of an entity encased in-itself (subject) and related in a linear and external fashion to environmental entities in-themselves (objects), insight is neither cause nor effect, neither producer nor produced, and neither is the lifeworld. Contrary to the prevalent notion that an influence is the linear action of a subject *or* an object, a phenomenological psychology finds insight to be a single behavior at once circularly influenced (impact) and influencing (interpreting), an impact-interpreting. Given insight's circular relations to its world, the self's interpretive determination of that world is by no means seen to deprive it of its otherness, of its power to wield an influence over the self. Just the contrary, for as already noted in this chapter, interpreting, venturing the other, gives the other the very chance it needs to first show itself as itself and thus for its law to bring its weight to bear upon us in its impact. The *activity* of interpreting releases meaning to itself as an original *action* (directed tensions). The paradox of impact and interpreting has to do with the fact that a lifeworld other depends on determinative activities on our part for it to engage us and hold sway over our life as the meaning it can be. The real question, Merleau-Ponty suggests, is how we can be open to meanings that, on the one hand, are beyond our psyche and that, on the other, exist only insofar as we actively take them up and live them (1962, p. 363). All in all, then, the fact that behavior interpretively determines every last one of its meanings in no way detracts from their possible integrity, from their ability to determine behavior on the ground of a necessity all their own (see Chapter 13, "Interpreting, Variability, and Validity"). The latter impact indeed could never occur without the former interpreting, all of which can appear only as nonsense to an understanding still within the bounds of the subject-object dichotomy.

Not only does the way meaning determines us depend on our determining of it, but our determining of meaning likewise depends on the way meaning determines us, on its possibilities of structural unfolding. Not only is insight an active receptivity, it is a *receptive activity* as well. On the one hand, impact is itself only in and through interpreting: interpreting is the very possibility of an impact. But, on the other, interpreting is itself only in and through impact: impact is the very possibility of an interpreting. Impact, the influence of the lifeworld on the self, and interpreting, the influence of the self on the lifeworld, each is what it is only in terms of the other. The full paradox of impact and interpreting thus runs something like this: to determine us for what it can be, a meaning has to be determined by us; for us to originally determine a meaning, the meaning has to determine us. The door determines us in its meaning when we determine it to be an exit; nothing is taken away from the self-presenting door by our determining it. We determine the door as an exit when the door determines us in its meaning; nothing is taken away from our role as openness to events of meaning by the door having a determining influence on us. Meaning and self simply do not stand to one another as subject and object in-themselves. Circularly determinative of one another, they are to one another rather as interwoven strands of a single fabric, interdepending nodes of a single live system (Chapter 14): where the influence of the self on meaning is influenced by meaning in the very influence the self is bringing to bear on meaning; where the influence of meaning on the self is influenced by the self in the very influence meaning is bringing to bear on the self ("circular causality" a la Merleau-Ponty).

Insightful discrimination as interpreting is a life telling lifeworld differences; insightful discrimination as impact is lifeworld differences told upon a life. *We determine meaning;* and in our historically situated determining of meaning, meaning determines us. *Meaning determines us;* and determined by meaning in its lifeworld availability, we determine it. Not only are we determined by the loss the death of our friend comes to signify, not only does the loss give rise to grief on our part, but we play a determining role in the origin of the loss as well: our grief releases the death in its structural necessity as the loss it can be. The death determines us in impact: Self ← Meaning. We determine it interpretively: Self → Meaning. Self and meaning determine one another reciprocally and at once, circularly: Self (grief) ↔ Meaning (loss). The death arises as a lifeworld loss in this circle, and so as does our grief, with a common negative sign. The loss determines our grief; thus determined, our grief determines the loss; thus determined, the loss determines our grief; and so forth. Not action following action, but both actions simultaneously. Determined by meaning, we determine meaning ↔ Determined by us, meaning determines us. Just as behavior is both determined and determining, an impact-interpreting, so, too, is lifeworld meaning, an interpreted self-showing.

Earlier, it was suggested that modern thought tends to suppose that, when something comes about, this something is an effect in-itself that something else in-itself has brought about, as though our reality were a collection of beings affecting one another only externally and linearly by way of production. There is a tendency, moreover, to attribute the whole business of production either to a realm of subjects in-themselves or to a realm of objects in-themselves, as the case may be. Either attribution in psychology amounts to what might be termed an *incomplete relativism*. In the one case, whatever we encounter in the way of world is considered to be simply and totally *relative* to an activity on the part of the self, to an all-determining subjective interpreting. The "world," so to speak, is "our idea"; "beauty is in the eye of the beholder"; "nothing is right or wrong but thinking makes it so"; "everyone's entitled to their opinion"; "anything goes," and "nothing stands." In the other attribution, whatever the self is or does, whatever it feels or thinks or imagines or decides, is said to be accomplished in reality by an all-controlling objective "world" surrounding the organism, to result from the impact of such a "world," and thus to be simply and totally *relative* to such a "world." Each of these relativisms is incomplete because each presupposes a linear determination proceeding in only one direction.

What is proposed here, by way of an alternative, is a completed relativism: circularly determining one another, the self and the lifeworld reciprocally determine one another; a paradox of the self and the lifeworld, a paradox of impact and interpreting. In a completed relativism, the self is relative to the world, determined by it in its impact, and the world is relative to the self, interpretively determined by the self. The self and the world, completing or complementing one another, are relative to one another reciprocally and simultaneously. A thoroughgoing, rather than a onesided, relativity rules. Relativized, the *duality* of the self and the world is no longer the *dualism* of the subject and the object. No longer are ready-made objects envisioned as determining an essentially passive subject; no longer does Self ←World. But no longer does a subject fashion its objects out of its own substance either; no longer does Self → World. Rather, Self ↔ World. In sum, what is wrong with conventional relativisms is not that they are relativisms, not that they allow relativity, but that they are not relative enough.

Insight as Responsible Situatedness

Insight, submitted to the world from the first, is in the service of events of meaning presencing, in the service of being. Insight amounts to a suffering, an active enduring (active receptivity), of the other in its structural possibilities, whether the requiredness of such an other is distressingly negative or satisfyingly positive in its impact. Imagining the other in the freedom of what it originally can have coming to it by way of a future, we are never quite sure what will confront us. We can only give ourselves to it, to the "can-be" at the core of the other. This requires a certain courage on our part, a certain working through of our fears and anxieties. Insight risks being addressed by the "concrete structural principles" (in Wertheimer words) of the lifeworld, risks being put into question by those things it is capable of enacting on the ground of a structural necessity properly their own.

Insight is faithful listening on the part of the whole self, commitment, a trusting in openness. Insight is the total regard the bodily self gives the lifeworld that addresses it, a lifeworld that in its originality sometimes challenges it, sometimes rebukes it. It often would be easier not to listen, "better not to know." Then we would not have to endure the impact of many unpleasant realities; then we would not have to change. Insight risks the essential limits imposed on any self, lives them for better or for worse, in their very unpredictability. Insight is openness, the imaginative openness of a concretely situated bodily life, responsible situatedness. Insight is responsible answering to meaning, a responding that disposes itself to the structural necessity of meaning events. Responsibility is an attitude of opening oneself to intrinsic values, preparing of oneself for their advent, everrenewed process of becoming dimensionally responsive.

11 *Feeling*

All understanding is essentially related
to an affective self-finding which
belongs to understanding itself.

—*Heidegger*, 1982, p. 281

The Temporal Circle of Impact-Interpreting

Temporal aspects of insight—interpreting as alreadiness, as futural imaginative venturing, as releasing of meaning—came to the fore in the last chapter. Nor are such temporal aspects any the less involved in insight as impact; insight has been seen, after all, to be the singleness of impact-interpreting. Time has been of central concern to the phenomenological movement at least since Husserl's 1905 lectures, published as *The Phenomenology of Internal Time-Consciousness* (1964). Moreover, the title of Heidegger's masterwork, pointedly, is *Being and Time* (1962a). Phenomenology locates time at the very core of human life and its preoccupation with events of meaning.

Insight into value is temporal through and through, a temporal undertaking. Futurally, insight is the imaginative venturing (interpreting) of possibilities intrinsic to a meaning's requiredness (impact). As present, insight is the releasing of meaning (interpreting) to its capacity to affect us for what it is from itself (impact). As alreadiness, insight is the situated approach to meaning (interpreting) on the ground of meaning's own availability (impact). Insight as interpretively determinative of meaning temporally is the imaginative (future) releasing of meaning (present) from a perspective (alreadiness). Insight as impact of meaning temporally is the mattering to someone of a meaning (present) in those of its possibilities (future) it already has coming to it (alreadiness). Insight is a situated, imaginative releasing of meaning (interpreting), the mattering of already available lifeworld possibilities of meaning (impact).

Circular relationships have figured prominently at various junctures in the present essay. A gestalt's sensible lifeworld moments, no longer mere sensations, circularly constitute a gestalt (Chapter 5). Our environmental others, no longer mere stimuli, are what they are circularly for a responding organism (Chapter 6); self and meaning circularly determine one another in insight into intrinsic value, insight is the paradox of impact and interpreting (Chapter 10). Time, no longer the mere measure of a linear sequence of events in a space of pure extension, is a circle, too, a threefold circular interplay of present, alreadiness, and future (Chapter 10).

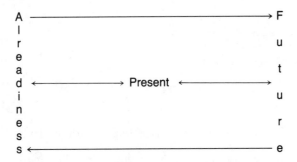

The threefold interplay of time turns out, moreover, to be the circular relationship that embraces the circular relationships constitutive of a gestalt, as well as those between an observer and its observed. A gestalt is the circle of its moments precisely within the circle of impact-interpreting, and the circle of impact-interpreting is itself the temporal circle of a determined and determining self *already ahead* of itself to the *available possibilities* of meaning; the circular unity of an impacted-interpreting self *already futurally releasing* meaning. Insight is a temporal circle, then, in which the alreadiness of impact-interpreting, its future and its present play into and reciprocally determine one another in the determining of one another of self and world.

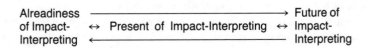

Disposition

Whereas the imaginative venturing of meaning's original possibilities of significance is insight in its *futural* aspect and the mattering of the meaning being released is the *present* of insight, the self as already open to available meaning is the *alreadiness* or situatedness of insight. This alreadiness, as pointed out in Chapter 10, is ourselves in everything we already are, all we have ever been, all we have been through: historically situated bodily self. The term *disposition* is used in the present chapter to indicate Dasein in the aspect of its alreadiness, for the overall way being possible finds itself already attuned at the moment to lifeworld possibilities of significance. Insight in the temporal dimension of its alreadiness, by this terminology, is *disposed* impact-interpreting, disposed being determined and determining. What the term *disposition* readily conveys, and the term *alreadiness* does not, is the affective dimension of Dasein's situatedness in things, bodily Dasein's felt sense of itself as an attuned immersion in the realm of sensible meaning. *Disposition* is meant to convey approximately what Heidegger calls *Befindlichkeit,* the alreadiness of the "affective self-finding" of Dasein. *Mood* is used occasionally in the following as an equivalent term for disposition.

Disposition is Dasein's very openness to things, its original submission to the world, the mode in which Dasein is its own "there." *"Disposition expresses a way of finding that Dasein is in its being as being in each instance its own there, and how it is this there"* (Heidegger, 1985, p. 255). Disposition is Dasein's being already able to be touched by things, its being capable of becoming affected by them in the way it is already open to them. It is precisely the being that is already *disposed* to the world that can become affected (Heidegger, 1962a, p. 396). It is as already fondly disposed toward someone that we are ahead of ourselves distressed by that someone's misfortune. It is in the disposition of vulnerability that we find ourselves becoming afraid. It is as already sensitive to moral issues that we attain a measure of insight in their regard. Disposition is our openness for a determination by things, our being already ready for things to matter to us, and in this way to hold sway over our life (see Chapter 9, where the "being affected" of the self in the impact of insight was first considered). Disposition, our being already submitted in openness to the world and indeed to a certain world, is the possibility of things encountering us. "We must as a general principle leave the primary discovery of the world to 'bare mood' " (ibid., p. 177).

Disposition is the affective alreadiness of impact, then, a disposed impact; the way we already have been shaped in our deepest interiority for a being affected by things. Disposition, of course, equally and at once, is the affective alreadiness of interpreting: a disposed interpreting (compare Chapter 10, "Interpreting and Situatedness"); the way the self already is affectively open to meanings and thus already able to enact, to feelingly venture and release, them; the way the bodily self is already able to determine things and hence to affectively reach them, to be personally in touch with them on their own terms. Being possible, already sensitive to lifeworld possibilities, already feeling something for a meaning, already fond, already vulnerable, already morally attuned, is the ability already to imagine and hence release certain meanings to the destiny of their place. Disposition is the affective alreadiness of impact-interpreting, then, the openness by which the self, already feeling itself, already can feel meanings, can already be touched by (impact) and touch them (interpreting); the alreadiness of an impact-interpreting ahead of itself playing into the future it has coming to it at the moment, being played into at once by that future.

Such openness of disposition makes an individual a someone, an existence with a stake in itself, in how it can touch things and be touched by them in turn, a "who" and not a "what" (see Chapter 3 subsection "Dasein: Existence"). Only such a someone, already affectively open to itself, and with that to world, only a caring someone can bring things close and let them matter in the integrity of lifeworld possibilities intrinsic to their "principle of organization" (a la Köhler). Disposition is the "someoneness" we have always been, the "someoneness" we have always and already had coming to us as what we have to be in the world. Ready-to-hand things are not disposed, not affectively self-finding. "A stone never finds itself but is simply on hand" (Heidegger, 1985, p. 255). A use value, not affectively open to itself as only a someone can be, and thus not open to world, is unable to be touched by things.

It is in Dasein's concrete and lived sense of itself, then, in its being already "toward itself" as a "who" (a la Heidegger), in its disposition, that Dasein is open to world, that it is "toward meanings." Standing open to itself affectively in one mood or another, Dasein at once stands open to world. Disposition is a "basic mode of the being of Dasein," of its being-in-the-world (ibid.); disposition is "a basic existential way in which Dasein is its there" (Heidegger, 1962a, p. 178). Disposition, as "how we are," is the very way we find ourselves already caring about things, a dwelling with things that lets them gain "world-entry" (a la Heidegger) for what they can be. Disposition, Dasein's felt sense of itself as whatever it is already, is its felt sense of just those things it cares about already. Dasein, as disposed, already is implicated in a certain set of possibilities, in a certain world (ibid., p. 183).[1] All in all, then, the attunement of a disposition is the very openness of being-in-the-world itself (ibid., p. 176), the concrete way sensible meanings are woven into Dasein's bodily dimensions and Dasein's bodily dimensions into sensible meanings. "Dasein as concern is essentially a situated being, a being disposed toward the disclosed world" (Heidegger, 1985, p. 257). Being disposed is being always and already in a world.

Disposition, as much the sense of how things stand with us as it is of how we stand with ourselves, is anything but an inner subjective occurrence. Always and already beyond itself to world, Dasein does not come across itself inside itself, but in things (see Chapter 3 subsection "Dasein: Submitted to World").

Feeling is not something that runs its course in our "inner lives." It is rather that basic mode of our Dasein by force of which and in accordance with which we are always already lifted beyond ourselves into being as a whole, which in this or that way matters to us or does not matter to us. Mood is never merely a way of being determined by our inner being for ourselves. It is above all a way of being attuned, and letting ourselves be attuned, in this or that way in mood. Mood is precisely the basic way in which we are *outside* ourselves. But that is the way we are essentially and constantly. (Heidegger, 1979, p. 99)

Disposition is Dasein's current aptitude for things, its ability to imaginatively venture a certain world, to let a certain range of meanings matter. Dasein typically finds itself attuned to the world of the ready-to-hand. Thus disposed, Dasein, setting out to achieve this or that practical goal, finds its way around in a network of use values. A certain shift in mood or *reattunement*, however, spells the breaking open of a different sort of meaning context altogether, with a different range of meanings. The physicist, for example, adopting a disposition appropriate to natural-scientific investigation, and thus deliberately losing the everyday realm of the ready-to-hand, is now confronted by the objective realm of the present-at-hand: "even the coldness of calculation, even the prosaic sobriety of planning are traits of an attunement" (Heidegger, 1956, p. 91). Then again, sharing an evening with someone we love, contemplating our newborn child, or engrossed in a great piece of music or work of fiction, we may find ourselves tuned in or disposed to the values of Being (a la Maslow); what makes a self-actualizing episode different from an ordinary experience is precisely the disposition on the basis of which it proceeds. Dasein, in a single day, can go from a practically disposed preoccupation with the world to an absorbed attunement to nature in its endness (Being-values) to an objective constructing of nature as *res extensa*. Thus attuned, reattuned, and reattuned anew, first one set of possibilities, then another, then yet another present themselves to Dasein, each on the ground of a necessity all its own. Disposition is our openness to things, the power of our imagination to venture worlds, the power of the possible.

Disposition, Feeling, Insight

Disposition is the way we are, the way we already find ourselves; the affective openness to ourselves and to the world that we already are; the felt sense we have of ourselves as already implicated in all those meanings and meaning contexts with which we are familiar. It is all we presently are capable of; the alreadiness of insight. Insight, impact-interpreting, was described earlier in this chapter as a temporal circle, the threefold temporal unity of the self's alreadiness, its present, and its future. The term *feeling* will now be used to specify the totality of this threefold temporal interplay of insight. Feeling thus envisioned is the breadth of being already disposed to available meanings, the depth of imagining the possibilities meaning has coming to it, the immediacy of a present releasing of and being touched by meaning, precisely as these temporal dimensions of the self play into one another at the moment. The reason for introducing yet another term for insight is that the word *feeling* signals the affective character of our involvement in the world with an immediacy that the term *insight,* with its intellectual overtones, does not. The term *feeling* is thus meant to convey the thoroughly affective character of the temporal circle of insight, the way the term *disposition* is meant to convey the thoroughly affective character of Dasein's alreadiness. Feeling is insight, then, viewed as permeated with affectivity, the affective totality of the threefold temporal circle of impact-interpreting.

Feeling is exactly Dasein's total movement toward the world, a disposed imaginative releasing (interpreting) that allows meaning to matter in those possibilities already available to it (impact); a structural being affected (impact) determinative of meaning in its self-giving originality within the world (interpreting). Feeling insight, insight itself, is both an affective suffering of the other, a receiving of it in impact, and an affective movement outward toward it, an interpretive codeciding of it. In the former insight as impact, an already sensitized someone is reached and touched by authentically available possibilities of meaning. In the latter insight as interpreting, an imaginatively venturesome bodily someone manages to dimensionally stretch all the way to dimensionally stretched meaning, to reach all the way to it and personally feel its tensions, the tensions themselves, in the necessity of their lifeworld requiredness. Note that some affective states fail to attain an insightful character and therefore, by the present usage, cannot be called *feelings* (see, later in this chapter, "Disturbed Disposition").

Just as a gestalt's gestalt quality is nothing other than the gestalt itself, the self's quality of feeling is simply the self itself, the very *way* the self lives its openness to itself and to world, the self in its deepest interiority beyond itself, outside, to what is not itself. No more than requiredness or value is an extra tacked on to a neutral perception is feeling an extra added on to the self. Rather than a stimulus-induced subjective state of consciousness, one such state among others (as in conventional psychology), feeling is precisely what the self *is.* As requiredness makes a meaning be a meaning, feeling makes the self be a self. As requiredness is intrinsic to meaning, feeling is intrinsic to the self. *Intrinsic feeling,* the self itself, moreover, is a dependent part quality of a context that also embraces intrinsic value, meaning itself. Both the feeling self and meaning in the necessity of its internal and external requiredness are what they are as part qualities of the larger circle they form at the moment.

The Positive or Negative Direction of Feeling

Feeling, like the requiredness of the meaning it complements, has either a positive or negative sign to it. Feeling insight is either a positively or a negatively qualified self. Intrinsic requiredness (intrinsic value) is meaning itself in its directional rightness or wrongness in its place, an "ought to be" or "ought not be" that commands Dasein's accepting or rejecting attitude. Intrinsic feeling is the self itself with either a positive or a negative affective character, a directed standing open to requiredness in the positive or negative possibilities of its place, an accepting or rejecting movement toward original meaning. Feeling is the positive sense we have of a positively required meaning, our bodily accepting of it; the negative sense we have of a negatively required meaning, our bodily rejecting of it (see Chapter 7, "The Demand Character of Value"). Given over to meaning from the first and always, which is to say, to meaning's directionally determined law of structure, feeling is distressed impact-interpreting in the event of a negative lifeworld requiredness, with its troubling tensions; satisfied impact-interpreting in the event of a positive lifeworld requiredness, with its balanced tensions.

Feeling is the feeling of value. Value is value felt. Feeling and meaning, it has been seen, are interwoven parts of a single event that embraces them both. Each side of this event has its dependent part quality in accordance with its place in the whole. Ultimately, however, the undivided context, this surpassing of anything absolute and in-itself, is what has a direction of rightness or wrongness about it. Rather than one linearly conferring the other's quality upon it, in the manner of producing, the quality of feeling and the quality of lifeworld requiredness, the self itself, meaning itself, circularly beyond themselves to each other from the first, take their origin from one another in the singleness of the quality of the event. What is original is the undivided positive or negative *event* of *feeling value*, the single event of *fearing threat*, of *rapture over beauty, grief over loss, joy over an especially opportune turn of events*. Feeling and value are beyond themselves in their quality to one another, then, interpenetrating and taking their sign from the undivided event they coconstitute at the moment.

The law of good gestalt indeed is a law of meaning, of the direction lifeworld signifying is to take. Meaning in every case is for someone, however, for a feeling someone who coactualizes meaning as the meaning's "principle of organization" requires (a la Köhler), for a someone who is a being surrendered through and through and without remainder to the law of lifeworld meaning. The law of good gestalt, to attain its goals, needs the openness of just such a someone, a feeling someone who can touch and be touched by meaning on its own ground of requiredness, an interested and caring bodily self capable of intimacy with meaning. The law of requiredness needs a bodily someone able to be excited by a meaning's dynamically self-distributing excitement. Whereas requiredness structurally only qualifies the lifeworld side of an event of meaning, the law of requiredness or good gestalt, it turns out, is a law regulating such events in their totality, interwoven bodily self and lifeworld meaning (see Chapter 14, "The Bodily Self–World System and the Law of Good Gestalt"). The law of good gestalt governs meaning, then, but also the feeling self that is given over to meaning from the first and always. A satisfied or distressed self is the psychological side of the operation of the law of good gestalt.

Feeling and the Bodily Self

The body, as pointed out in Chapter 4, is by no means foreign to the self. "Our century has wiped out the dividing line between 'body' and 'mind,' and sees human life as through and through mental and corporeal" (Merleau-Ponty, 1964c, pp. 226–227). That human life is not the dichotomy of subject (inner mind) and object (material body) perhaps is best seen from the vantage point of the topic of the present chapter. Feeling, this quality of the self, on the one hand, has been seen to be what makes the self a self, the very essence of selfhood. Our body, on the other hand, is given immediately to itself in its felt sense of itself, in the way it echoes the things that surround it, in the way it feels both itself and its meanings. Our body is not a mere thing among things, Merleau-Ponty points out, but, sensitive to things, "reverberates" to all sounds, "vibrates" to all colors (1962, p. 236). "Every bodily state," Heidegger writes, "involves some way in which the things around us and the people with us lay a claim on us or do not do so" (1979, p. 99). Our body is a dimensionally stretched sensitivity to things, "the sensible sentient" (Merleau-Ponty, 1968, p. 136). With feeling precisely the self itself, with feeling the very way the body is—the way we are bodily, bodily feeling—there simply is no distinguishing the self from the body. Feeling is the common denominator of a body that is not an object and a self that is not a subject. To be a self is to be a feeling body. To live this bodily life is to be a self, a feeling bodily self (see Chapter 4, "The Bodily Self").

In feeling, the body already permeates the self. Remarking on this bodily character of the feeling self, Heidegger writes, "Feeling, as feeling oneself to be, is precisely the way we are corporeally. Bodily being does not mean that the soul is burdened by a hulk we call the body. In feeling oneself to be, the body is already contained in advance in that self, in such a way that the body in its bodily states permeates the self. We do not 'have' a body in the way we carry a knife in a sheath. . . . We do not 'have' a body; rather, we 'are' bodily. Feeling, as feeling oneself to be, belongs to the essence of such Being" (1979, pp. 98–99). The self is a bodily feeling. *The self is a body.*

But if the body can be said to permeate the self, the self with equal justice can be said to permeate the body. The body always and already is a feeling body. One is a bodily self, but also a personal body. One's body is, as Merleau-Ponty asserts, "a knowing-body" (1962, p. 408), "a body made to explore the world" (1973b, p. 123), "the vehicle of our being in the world" (ibid., p. 129). The body, the body itself, has the quality of selfhood. *The body is a self.*

The usual natural-scientific account of the body, as found in conventional psychology, for example, as no more than a composite objective thing with a specific location in objective space, overlooks the essential character of the human body as a dimensionally stretched someone feeling its world, overlooks the body as permeated with selfhood from the first. This usual misinterpretation, moving as it does within the body-mind split, has yet to grasp the body as a personal body that, surpassing itself, embodies the world, internalizes it, in feeling; the view has yet to come to terms with the body as a dimensional becoming excited by that rightness or wrongness of things by which they become the meanings they are. "Most of what we know from the natural sciences about the body and the way it embodies," Heidegger comments, "are specifications based on the established misinterpretation of the body as a mere natural body. . . . Every feeling is an embodiment attuned in this or that way, a mood that embodies in this or that way" (1979, pp. 99–100).

The self is a body. The body is a self. The bodily self is nothing other than the totality of our life: the bodily feeling (embodiment) of all we have ever been through and already are; the self as dimensional openness feelingly venturing and releasing lifeworld meaning, the self being touched in turn by meaning's available possibilities: temporal circle of impact-interpreting, being determined-determining.

In bodily feeling we feel ourselves, which feeling of self at once determines how things appear to us. Bodily feeling is our affective unity with things, our oneness with things in the structural necessity of their requiredness, bodily insight. The feeling of grief embodies loss; the feeling of fear, threat; that of joy, a felicitous turn of events; that of "getting it," the solution of a problem; and so on. Feeling ourselves in each case is the embodying of positive or negative value, the internalization of values into our deepest interiority. Feeling ourselves bodily is an imaginative venturing of values for what they are on the ground of their own law. Just as bodily Dasein is destined to be immersed in a referential network of meanings from the first, meanings are destined from the first to be incorporated into the life of bodily Dasein. Meanings are taken up and lived bodily or they are not meanings.

All in all, the notion of a feeling self embodying the world—of a bodily self, of a personal body—moves the discussion of human behavior and its meanings beyond the categories of subject and object altogether. Discussing rapture over beauty, Heidegger remarks, "Rapture is feeling, an embodying attunement, . . . attunement woven into embodiment. . . . We may not take [rapture as a state of feeling] as something at hand 'in' the body and 'in' the psyche. Rather, we must take it as a mode of the embodying, attuned stance toward beings as a whole" (ibid., p. 105). The feeling of rapture is no subjective state in Heidegger's view. But then neither does beauty have an objective character: "Beauty is not something on hand like an object of sheer representation. As an attuning, it thoroughly determines the state of man. Beauty breaks through the confinement of the 'object' placed at a distance, standing on its own, and brings it into essential and original correlation to the 'subject.' Beauty is no longer objective, no longer an object. The esthetic state is neither subjective nor objective" (ibid., p. 123).

Feeling No Inner Psychic State

Emotions, in the view of conventional psychology, are *inner reactions*. Stimuli, both internal (thoughts and memories) and external (environmental events), give rise to emotions or feelings by "triggering" them. Emotions or feelings, charges inside the organism as it were, thus come to accompany the stimuli that set them off. In textbook phraseology, "As memory and expectation develop, emotions can be triggered by thought as well as by a wider range of stimuli" (Zimbardo, 1988, p. 407), [2] "The stimuli that trigger our emotional responses aren't always external; they can be inside us in the form of images and memories" (Smith, Sarason, and Sarason, 1986, p. 309), "Our emotions are triggered by a wide range of events and thoughts. When David saw the technician prepare to take his blood, he felt a surge of fear" (Rubin and McNeil, 1987, p. 264), "Emotions such as joy, fear, disgust, and anger are evoked by stimuli that have the power to reinforce or punish our behavior" (Carlson, 1984, p. 523), "We define *emotion* as a response to a stimulus" (Pettijohn, 1989, p. 232). Emotion thus is considered to be a psychic state inside the organism, an in-itself at the ready for a linear being set off by a "triggering" in-itself (stimulus). Instead of the circle of feeling ahead of itself thinking or remembering or perceiving this or that meaning, what is proposed is the linear chain of, *first,* inner or outer stimulus, *then,* emotion or feeling.

A relatively sophisticated view of human emotional life commonly represented in introductory psychology texts is that of Plutchik, who maintains that emotion (our internal affective constitution) is inborn. One textbook describes Plutchik's theory this way, "There are eight basic inborn emotions, made up of four pairs of opposites: joy and sadness, fear and anger, surprise and anticipation, and acceptance and disgust. All other emotions are assumed to be variations, derivatives, or *blends* of these basic eight. For example, love is a combination of joy and acceptance; awe of fear and surprise" (Zimbardo, 1988, p. 406). Another frequently cited theory, that of Izard (cf., e.g., Kagan and Segal, 1988, pp. 314–315), lists ten, rather than eight, basic emotions: anger, contempt, disgust, distress, fear, guilt, interest-excitement, joy, shame, surprise. As in Plutchik's theory, in Izard's two or more of these emotions can blend with one another to form a new emotional expression. It is clear that the structure of existence as a self affectively open to itself, and thus to the world and its events of meaning presencing, does not figure in portraits of human affective life such as these. In accordance with an objectivistic ontology that is apparently beyond all question, affectivity instead is reified. Emotions are treated as innate, present-at-hand stuff, eight or ten kinds of stuff that, mixed with one another, yield the full range of human affective responses. Rather than taken "in conjunction with the basic movement of Dasein itself" to the world, human affectivity thus is classified in a "table of emotions or feelings" (Heidegger, 1985, p. 256). Instead of concepts clarified on the basis of the possibilities of actual human life, we are provided with a list. Forgetful of that which is disclosed through Dasein's affective attunement to things, all we are left with is isolated feelings that we can, in Heidegger's words, "analyze and contrast with other feelings in the well-known assortment of psychological stock-types" (1949, p. 354). "'Feelings' and 'emotions' . . . treated as a class of lived experiences remain unclarified in their primary structure of being as long as one does not take up the task of exposing the basic constitution of Dasein" (Heidegger, 1985, p. 256).

What truly exists in the present view are not present-at-hand "feelings" inside us, but various possible ways in which being possible can originally enact lifeworld possibility. Bodily feelings, like their complementary lifeworld values, are possibilities of existential space, not things inside us. Any feeling, and its interwoven meaning, is the actualization of basic disposed possibilities of existence.

Feeling and Knowing

As the very thrust of being possible to the world, as being possible itself, feeling does not merely accompany the "real understanding" gained by other mental faculties; by thinking, for example. The temporal-affective unity of feeling is itself structural understanding (insight) rather. To know is to feel; to feel is to know. Feeling, the innermost submission of the self to original events of meaning, is itself cognitive of reality.

Positive and Negative Knowing

Precisely through being positively or negatively affected by a meaning does it come to be originally disclosed in its positive or negative lifeworld character, does it first enter into the structural necessity of its requiredness (compare earlier, "The Positive or Negative Direction of Feeling"). A negatively required meaning is a structurally troubled meaning, one whose tensions have failed to attain harmony in just those features that ought to characterize them. Such a meaning, it is felt, "*ought not be.*" The meaning is wrong somehow—immoral, false, ugly, useless, loathsome—and "to be rejected." We know such a meaning to be wrong precisely in our troubled bodily feeling of it, in our being bothered by the negative structural tensions plaguing it, those direct determinations constitutive of the meaning's wrongness. We know positive requiredness, on the other hand, through the bodily satisfaction we take in the harmonious and fulfilled way lifeworld tensions articulate themselves as a whole of meaning, through the satisfaction we take in a meaning's "*ought to be,*" by our being positively affected by the "to be accepted" of its moral goodness, its beauty, its usefulness, its grace, and so forth. Negative requiredness forms in its negativity only for a sponsoring bodily feeling that is itself negative in character (being bothered or distressed). Positive requiredness forms, in the law of its meaning, precisely for a sponsoring bodily feeling that is positive in character (being satisfied or pleased). Meaning arises precisely in the positive or negative excitement of its requiredness. Feeling, this bodily excitement, knows, and meaning forms. Feeling is a bodily knowing, a bodily insight, that is party to what it knows, an interpreting bodily self undergoing meaning's impact. That being possible is positively or negatively affected by positive or negative meanings, and that meanings achieve their self-display in the process, is due to Dasein's always and already being submitted in its innermost substance to the world and its lawfulness, due to Dasein's standing open to meanings in the structural necessity of their requiredness from the first.

For meaning to originally matter in the necessity of its positive or negative requiredness is for meaning to first become itself; that is, for meaning to be interpretively released to possibilities that are properly its own. Had we not the psychological capacity to structurally feel meanings in the requiredness of their tensions, to know them, nothing would ever come to be discriminated in its intrinsic requiredness (value) in the first place, which is the same as saying that nothing would ever show itself in its reality, its "inner necessity" (a la Wertheimer). Without a someone to feelingly disclose something in its beauty, nothing would be beautiful. Without a positive or negative feeling, nothing would ever display itself as either good or evil; the difference could never have broken open in the first place. Without feeling, no problems would ever be discovered, much less solved. Without feelings of indignation, exploitation would never be shown up for the injustice it is. Without feeling, there would be no losses, but also no gains; no one worthy of love or contempt; nothing worth living for; no arts; no sciences; no valid meanings at all. Feeling, as pointed out earlier, is knowing, original cognizing: feeling insight. Feeling is the sensitivity necessary for the structural originality of meaning. Gestalts develop, meanings are emergent, in their being felt. "What is phenomenologically decisive in the phenomenon of feeling is that it directly uncovers and makes accessible that which is felt and it does this not, to be sure, in the manner of intuition but in the sense of a direct having-of-oneself" (Heidegger, 1982, p. 133).

Venturing its meanings by feeling them, the self risks itself. Imaginatively enacting an original lifeworld signifying, one is never quite sure what will emerge. Some venturings, in the venturing itself, coactualize meanings that are negative in their structural law. The self that feelingly ventures such meanings also participates in their negativity. In fact, precisely in suffering them, in suffering from them—in the discomfort that their troubling tensions, their restless protest of their present state, represent for our life—does the negative requiredness first come to stand revealed on its own ground. Feeling, and feeling alone, lets meanings matter in their intrinsic negativity, or positivity, as the case may be.

Feeling and Cognitions

Although feelings are psychological states, and indeed the very self itself, the things that feeling insight knows, its cognitions, are not. Cognitions are not, as Cartesian philosophy and conventional psychology have supposed, subjective modifications of the mind (see Chapter 2, "Phenomenology's Theory of Intentionality"). Rather than inner replicas, cognitions are nonpsychological lifeworld meanings. The relation of feeling to its cognitions is that of a self beyond itself to its lifeworld. The *knowing* that is feeling insight is the psychological counterpart to cognitions as original lifeworld values, things *known* on the ground of their structural law. The knowing that is feeling is conscience in the discovery of morality values; thinking, in problem solving; comprehending, in making connections new to us; skillful handling, in the releasing of use values to their place; awe and admiration, in coming to appreciate meanings in the beauty of their goodness; regard and love, in disclosing the someoneness of other persons.

Feeling insight is primordial access to meaning in meaning's original self-forming; that is, in the necessity of its requiredness. Feeling is not properly characterized, then, as just one more compartment inside the organism, and cognition another. Neither feeling nor cognition is a subjective faculty or stage inside us (see "Feeling No Inner Psychic State"): cognition, because it is not in us, it is not us, at all; and feeling, because feeling is essentially beyond itself to lifeworld cognitions. Affects are not bursts of excitement secondarily attached to cognitions (perceptions, thoughts, memories), linearly "triggered" by them, because cognitions are not pure forms without an inherent excitement of their own. Cognitions, everyday meanings, do not need to be extrinsically furnished with excitement because they arise precisely in the excitement of their lifeworld requiredness. Affective character needs no more to subjectively accrue to neutral perceptions (and other sorts of cognitions) than subjective perceptual character does to formless sensations. Feeling—psychological openness, the self as already proficient in certain ways in what regards its world, the self as already ahead of itself imaginatively venturing the internal and external requiredness of meaning—is involved in the self-formation of all cognitions, sometimes with more, sometimes with less, intensity.

An Illustration of Feeling: Fear

Heidegger points out that the usual interpretation of fear bases its account on the evil approaching from the surrounding world, and hence on things; fear by this account is the expectation of the oncoming evil (1962a, p. 392). Köhler reflects just such a "commonsense interpretation" of fear when he writes that fear, along with the desire to escape, is experienced as *springing from* the threatening danger (1971, p. 365). Existential thought rejects just such an interpretation, the notion that a threatening object linearly and externally "triggers" fear on our part. Even though everyone "knows" it to (natural attitude), fear does not stand to threat as effect to cause. An in-itself of fear does not come *after* an in-itself of threat. The feeling of fear rather already is ahead of itself, venturing lifeworld possibilities, releasing something as the threat it can be.

A meaning can be threatening to Dasein only because Dasein, already disposed to it, already is open to it. Disposition, ahead of itself, outlines in advance how we can reach things at any given moment, which also is how they can touch us. Dasein can become threatened, a meaning can become involved in a lifeworld context as threatening, because, preoccupied with things from the first, Dasein already has the felt sense of vulnerability, of being thus open to the possibility that harm can come to it. "The threatening thing comes upon a concern which, along with what it has at its direct disposal, is insufficient to cope with the threatening thing" (Heidegger, 1985, p. 287). Fearing, rather than dominated by a threat that linearly sets it off, which is to say, rather than being causally instigated ("triggered") by an antecedent in-itself, already futurally is ahead of itself, imaginatively venturing a meaning in its inherent capacity for inflicting harm.

Fear does not result subjectively, then, in the existential interpretation, from the mere drawing near of a present-at-hand stimulus. Fearing is not the "impact" of an objectively given threat, but the circle of an interpreting self already ahead of itself and releasing the fearsome to the negative impact on our lives of its fearsomeness. "Fearing is," in Heidegger's words, "precisely the mode of being in which something threatening is uniquely disclosed and can be encountered. . . . I see and can only see the threat in its genuine character and can only have the threatening thing as such from the primary access to it in fearing" (1985, pp. 286–287). In fearing, properly understood, that which threatens is "freed and allowed to matter" (Heidegger, 1962a, p. 180). Fearing, as a "slumbering possibility" of disposed being-in-the-world, already has provided just the opening that the fearsome needs to draw close (ibid.). Already ahead of itself venturing possibilities of meaning to which it is sensitive, fearing is our "primary access" to threat. Fearing, and fearing alone, is original knowing of threat; without it, no threat gains "world-entry" (a la Heidegger).

As duly noted, there is no catalog of present-at-hand feelings, or of corresponding present-at-hand values. Feelings rather are various possibilities of our existence in the world; values are lifeworld possibilities complementary to these possibilities of existence. There is no prior group of feelings, only being-in-the-world unfolding according to its character.

Disturbed Disposition

Disposition or mood is affective openness to ourselves and to things as we already are. Sometimes, and in some regards, our bodily disposition is disturbed: rather than standing open to the authentic possibilities of meaning, it in fact stands in the way of the unfolding of a meaning in the originality of its law, in the way, too, of the self's fulfillment. Some forms of disturbed disposition were alluded to in Chapter 8 ("The Nonoccurrence of Insight"). Many more are given in the chapters of "abnormal psychology" textbooks. In the disturbed mood of phobia, for example, instead of finding ourselves flexibly open to what might realistically do us harm, and indeed to what might not, we discover ourselves irrationally "threatened" by things that in fact portend no significant harm to us at the moment. Phobia has its reasons, to be sure, but these reasons, rather than being ahead of our lives, lie behind them, mechanically and linearly governing present reactions, robbing both meaning and ourselves of a future. Phobia is a disturbance of our temporal openness to things, an inability to imaginatively sponsor the possibilities meaning has coming to it in accordance with meaning's own "principle of organization" (a la Köhler). Our bodily alreadiness having lost the freedom of its future, our future having reciprocally lost its power to bring into play an alreadiness open to and capable of a certain range of lifeworld meanings, phobia amounts to the loss of the freedom of the threefold temporal interplay (temporal circle) of impact-interpreting.

This interplay, our very affective openness to world (a la Heidegger), similarly is curtailed in the disturbed mood of depression. Depression is no more the openness of the feeling of sadness than phobia is the openness of the feeling of fear; conceptual differentiations such as are being made here between depression and sadness and between phobia and fear are possible only phenomenologically (see Chapter 3 subsection "The Clarification of Psychological Concepts"). Depression, like phobia, is not ahead of itself imagining the possibilities meaning lawfully can have coming to it on its own ground. Depression is a being "down," but not over an original status of lifeworld meaning. Depression is not interpretively reaching, not personally undergoing the impact of, a lifeworld meaning in the structural necessity of its requiredness. Going to pieces over a minor loss has its reasons, as does the terror of phobia, but these reasons are not legitimate lifeworld possibilities of the moment.

When one's situatedness in things (disposition) is disturbed, one's behavior irrationally under the control of incomprehensible forces and without a future of its own, we may with some justice speak of *unconsciously* motivated behavior. Caution is in order here, however, for our bodily disposition always, and indeed in what is its essential, is a *relation* to significance. Disposition, never inside us the way conventional thought presupposes it to be, precisely is the way we are beyond ourselves to the world. If disposition is linked with unconscious motivation, then, in no way is there a question of "the unconscious" as an inner compartment of the organism, underneath, say, the compartment of consciousness. What is unconscious about unconscious motivation rather is the way behavior is irrationally and incomprehensibly driven in its manner of involvement in lifeworld meaning contexts. It would be more precise to speak of an unconscious relation to meanings, an unconscious drivenness in their regard, than of "the unconscious." The term *unconscious* indicates a compulsive affective involvement in meaning, a state of possession of sorts (a la Jung), a preoccupation with the world that lacks the imagination for the world's authentic possibilities of meaning.

What is *not conscious* in all this is not one's meanings. Meanings continue to presence for one, phenomenally, even when one is "open" to them unconsciously, even when their presencing is distorted by behavioral compulsion. The phenomena of phenomenology are events of meaning, not fully present events of consciousness. What is not conscious, what is unconscious, are the reasons for such behavior, for what one has become affectively, for what one now already is. What is not conscious, and indeed altogether absent, is the sensibleness of the event, its understandability. When the platform for one's relations to the world is unconscious, one literally no longer knows what one is doing. Unconscious behavior is behavior that, driven, does not make conscious sense, behavior that does not relate in freedom to the necessity of a meaning's requiredness, behavior originating, so to speak, behind one's back. Unconsciously motivated relations to the world stand in the starkest contrast, then, to relations of feeling insight to the world, where one has felt *structural understanding,* on the one hand, of the *understandable relationship* that prevails between one's meanings, and, on the other, of one's feelings and motivation in regard to these meanings. This lack of understanding, this unconsciousness, this antirationality, on one's part lies precisely in the compulsive manner in which one's behavior is under the domination of the past, lies precisely in behavior's lost freedom. This unconscious counterpart to insight is falling prey to meaning, falling under its spell. No longer actively sponsoring meaning in the originality of its law, the self lacks insight into its motivation. No longer in tune with a meaning's direct determinations, the self is unaware of what it is doing. Blind mechanisms now are in charge—an it, the *Id*—not the self.

12 The Fulfillment of Gestalt Psychology

[Gestalt psychology] has never broken
with naturalism. But by this very fact
it betrays its own descriptions.

—*Merleau-Ponty*, 1962, p. 47

The Promise of a Nonobjectivistic Gestalt Psychology

Gestalt psychology is one of the two traditions brought to bear on one another in this inquiry into "insight into value," the other, of course, being existential phenomenology. This study, in portraying feeling insight into meaning as an essentially phenomenal event, as the impact-interpreting of an original lifeworld signifying, nevertheless departs significantly from classical Gestalt theory. In the final analysis, Köhler, the champion of insight in psychology, proposes that insight is essentially the result of ahistorical, and indeed prepersonal, objective brain processes (Chapter 8, "The Limitations of Köhler's Theory of Insight"). The moment Köhler's psychology moves "beyond phenomenology," its character as an objectivism manifests itself. In keeping with its ultimately phenomenological orientation, this investigation finds that a gestalt's moments ultimately meet and change each other in the lifeworld, in their place within a context of significance, in an existential space of possibility, rather than in an objective space of the cortex. Gestalt psychology, to be sure, has taken a landmark step beyond the mechanism of conventional psychology (see later). Freed from its objectivistic premises and true to its own basic discoveries as a descriptive theory of organization (Chapter 5 through 8), and thus brought to its proper fulfillment, Gestalt psychology has within itself the ability to radically renew scientific psychology. This chapter expands the book's presentation of Gestalt theory and its promise in the context of a review of the other two psychological approaches to meaning and meaning-oriented behavior that have figured prominently throughout this study; namely, conventional psychology and phenomenological psychology. Such an approach necessarily entails a certain amount of repetition, which seems justified in view of the direct comparisons and conclusions allowed.

215

Review of the Conventional Approach to Perception

The conventional, pre-Gestalt and preexistential, approach to cognitive processes opens its account of basic psychological processes with a discussion of stimuli and stimuli-induced sensations. By this account (Chapter 1), atomistic stimuli, which will be symbolized here by $S1$ and $S2$, affect the organism's sense organs, giving rise to equally atomistic ("raw" or unprocessed) sensations, symbolized here by si and sii. The conventional account considers what we naively take to be a tree in the meadow in reality to be something objective, a source of physical energies (stimuli) that bombard the objective organism. Stimuli, radiating out from various parts of the "tree," objectively effect transformations inside the organism, "objectively on this side of the skin boundary." These transformations (sensations) are viewed as impressions of the external physical world inside the organism. It bears repeating that, at this juncture in the conventional account, there is not yet what we take to be a lifeworld, not yet the everyday meaning tree, only disconnected stimuli in physical space, on the one hand, and disconnected sensations inside the physical organism, on the other. How, then, does the organism come to have a tree at all by this account? The brain is said to convert the sensations of the moment, typically with the help of objectively encoded and stored memories, into the subjective perception of the "tree." The brain synthesizes otherwise fragmented sensations, adding meaning (form) to them, represented later by a plus sign ($+$). By reason of an extraneous intervention on the part of the objective cortex, then, disjointed sensations are said to be converted into a perception. This position is the traditionally modern one of "sensation and perception." Conventional psychology regards perception as the brain's "interpretation" of sensations as a "meaning" ("tree"). All the while, the meaning is presumed to be and remain objectively, but also subjectively, *inside* the organism. Because, in all this, we are in contact with only our own internal mental states (the theory of ideas, a la Gurwitsch), there is no warrant for any claim that in fact there is a tree, a lifeworld meaning, "over there" in the meadow in the first place. "Tree" is merely the end product in our mind of a causal chain that begins with the physical environment and involves several physical way stations inside the organism, where the incoming information is processed. Stimuli are admitted access to the organism, information is processed, and the message is passed on. Even to this day, then, introductory psychology texts presuppose that the "tree" does not stand in the meadow, that it is something "more" instead, a form that the brain generated in memory some time ago, we are never told how, and that the organ now retrieves and bestows on presently existing sensations. And likewise for all our perceptions. Physical transformations of energy occurring in accordance with certain objective causal laws are considered to be "true reality," and "meaning" to be but a subjective outcome inside subjective consciousness. The "tree," along with the lifeworld as a whole, by the conventional account, is an epiphenomenon, a mere inner outcome of founding objective events.

This process, as conventionally presupposed, may be represented as in Figure 12-1. The experience of the "tree" (perception) arises through a synthesizing (+) of sensations *si* and *sii* (and any number of other sensations), themselves instigated by stimuli *S1* and *S2* (and any number of other stimuli). Because the brain typically is viewed as working this "organizing" on the basis of the past, as this past has attained a present-at-hand standing within us in the form of objectively stored memory, meaning is viewed essentially as an affair of the past. How the brain will bring the sensations to an interconnection with one another—that is, how they will be brought to meaning, how meaning will be brought to them—is predetermined by our former experiences with things. The "tree," by such an account, does not belong to our present bodily existence in the world, but instead results from the past history of the organism. The past thus is viewed as ruling the organism's perception, on the one hand, through the presently existing (present-at-hand) effects of antecedent environmental stimuli and, on the other, through the presently existing effects (present-at-hand memories) of former experiences.

Gestalt Psychology's Approach to Cognition

Köhler's Rejection of Mechanism

Köhler was particularly disturbed by the arbitrariness with which conventional approaches to behavior made human perception into an outcome originating in former occurrences instead of present stucturations. He was troubled in particular by the manner in which the conventional theory had the past institute constraints inside the organism that serve to mechanically channel the fragmented sensations of the moment into the particularly limited and rigid forms of *what was.*

Köhler rejects the mechanistic view that action in the brain by and large is determined by rigid constraints established by learning, preferring instead an account in terms of the "dynamic self-distribution of cortical processes,"

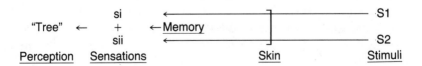

Figure 12–1

in terms of presently interacting and self-regulating cortical events. "At the time, we had been shocked," he says, "by the thesis that all psychological facts (not only those in perception) consist of unrelated inert atoms and that almost the only factors which combine these atoms and thus introduce action are associations formed under the influence of mere contiguity" (1961, p. 4). Köhler directly challenges the notion that whatever order there is among mental events is to be explained "in terms of either inherited machine arrangements or secondarily acquired constraints" (1947, p. 67). Köhler, along with Gestalt psychology in its entirety, rejects the notion of sensation altogether, of the element upon which learning confers "organization" (form). There is nothing sensory for Gestalt psychology that is not always and already organized (Chapter 5), no sensory atoms or sensations to begin with. This is a rejection of the *constancy hypothesis*; that is, of the view that there is a one-to-one relationship between stimuli and sensations, that a given sensation depends exclusively on a given stimulus (see, e.g., Gurwitsch, 1966, pp. 4–5). Gestalt theory, Gurwitsch remarks, does not allow of any elementary raw material in need of organization (ibid., p. 30). "Raw" sensations in need of being admitted into perception do not exist.

Dynamic Self-Distribution

Order is not accomplished in Köhler's view, then, by an extraneous synthetic intervention carried out upon unformed sensory materials. There are no such materials, there are no sensations, and hence no such intervention is needed. Perceptual facts (meanings) always and already are organized (Chapter 5). Such sensory order is possible because of the "dynamic self-distribution of cortical processes" (Köhler). The mutual interaction of parts and the effects of such interaction Köhler calls "the dynamics of the system" (1969, p. 75). Whereas the conventionally presupposed "machine theory excludes any dynamic interrelations among the parts of a field" (Köhler, 1947, p. 68), Gestalt theory excludes just such an exclusion. "A system which is not a machine can be called free only inasmuch as it is free from constraints; in their absence, it merely becomes free to follow the principles inherent in its dynamics alone" (Köhler, 1969, p. 78). And Köhler is quick to point out that free dynamics in physical systems typically yields order rather than the conventionally expected chaos (compare Chapter 6, "The Law of Good Gestalt"). Orderly events are rendered possible by "tendencies in dynamics" (ibid.). If the planets follow an orderly course without being on some sort of runners (Köhler, 1947, pp. 76–77), why cannot the brain achieve a comparable order without constraints? "The order of facts in a visual field is to a high degree the outcome of [a dynamic] self-distribution of processes" (ibid., p. 78); "dynamic distributions are functional wholes" (ibid., p. 80).

Köhler insists that a presently experienced gestalt is the outcome of present, self-governing interactions among the processes involved, of a present "dynamic self-distribution of cortical processes." The past, in its effects, does not mechanically regulate present perception. Central rather to the formation of perceptual wholes is the dynamic interaction of the very parts that constitute the whole in question (in the proper medium, of course, which for Köhler is the brain). What prevails is "regulation" in the "absence of any regulating devices" (Köhler, 1938, p. 232).

A theory of perception must be a *field* theory. By this we mean that the neural functions and processes with which the perceptual facts are associated in each case are located in a continuous medium; and that the events in one part of this medium influence the events in other regions in a way that depends directly on the properties of both in their relation to each other. This is the conception with which all physicists work. The field theory of perception applies this simple scheme to the brain-correlates of perceptual facts. (Köhler, 1965, pp. 61–62)

All in all, then, Köhler contrasts "the basic forces and processes of nature as free to follow their inherent, dynamic, causally determined directions, and the same forces and directions almost or entirely compelled to take courses prescribed by constraints" (1969, p. 81). Köhler holds that dynamic interaction in the brain permits our actual physical environment to be reflected inside the organism with a fair degree of accuracy, first physically in the brain, but also phenomenally in experience, in accordance with the "hypothesis of psychophysical isomorphism," the belief already mentioned that "psychological facts and the underlying events in the brain resemble each other in all their structural characteristics" (ibid., p. 66).

A whole as perceived and its physical correlate in the cortex thus are viewed by Köhler as structurally (functionally) equivalent, isomorphic, to one another. Cortical organization is mirrored in consciousness. But the cortical organization said to be mirrored phenomenally itself accurately reflects the objective constitution of physical objects in the external world. There thus is a structural equivalence between the physical object outside and its cortical representation, and between that representation and the phenomenal appearance of the object in consciousness. Environmental object and phenomenal meaning can be said to be structurally equivalent, through the mediation of cortical organization. "The fact which mediates between the physical and the perceptual structure is now found to be *cortical* organization, which, as a rule, resembles both" (Köhler, 1938, p. 170). The image of a "physical elephant" before us in physical space is projected upon our retina, and circumscribed cortical processes become "immediately segregated as a particular macroscopic unit" (ibid.). One thing appears phenomenally in our visual field: the perceived elephant. The images of the various parts of the elephant, Köhler argues, are projected in an orderly manner on the retina: the distribution of the legs, head, trunk, and so forth on the retinal image are similar to the orderly distribution that would be projected on film if we were taking a picture of the environmental elephant. Both the impulses from the retina as they make their way to the cortex and the resultant cortical processes, moreover, "are no less well distributed than is stimulation on the retina" (ibid., p. 109). What reaches the cortex, then, faithfully reflects the distribution of the retinal image; which in turn reflects, with a fair degree of fidelity, the actual physical elephant in our environment. The cortical processes interdepend from the first, according to Köhler, there is an immediate "dynamic self-distribution of cortical processes," and units (wholes) immediately are segregated in cortical space. Reaching the cortex are not "raw" sensations, which would then need unification. Although stimulation on the retina is a mosaic of disconnected impressions (faithful nevertheless to the external elephant), according to Köhler, segregated units immediately are formed in the brain, by reason of the dynamic self-regulation that prevails there and that, in structural fidelity, restores the distribution of the external physical elephant: legs here, trunk there, and so on. There indeed are no objects (no gestalts) on the retina, only a "retinal mosaic." However, there are objects, with structure, in the external world, and there is a physically segregated unit in the cortex, and a corresponding phenomenally segregated unit, a gestalt, in consciousness. Undergoing immediate organization upon its very arrival, what reaches the cortex (and, isomorphically, consciousness) always and already is organized. The elephant of perception and that of physics, even in terms of pointer-readings, are structurally in close agreement; both have a trunk and a tail, four legs, two tusks, and so on (ibid., p. 132). The physical river is between its physical banks, moreover, just the way the perceived river is between its perceived banks. And there is a physical hole just where the ring has a perceived hole. "The similarity between physical and perceptual structure approaches an agreement in form. . . . Up to this point isomorphism is almost complete" (ibid., pp. 134–135). All in all, then, sensory organization, and unit formation in particular, tends to agree with the status of entities in the physical world, through the mediation of cortical organization. Corresponding to three physical people on the physical street are three units in our cortex and three people in visual space (ibid., p. 170). The physical people, the units in the cortex, and the people we see are all isomorphic to one another.

Köhler's account cites free dynamics rather than machine arrangements, then, as rendering brain processes, and the corresponding experiences, a fairly accurate portrait of what actually is before us in the physical environment. All resort to an extraneous intervention undertaken upon "raw" sensory data thereby is rendered superfluous. Instead, an account is given in terms of the present dialogue of the effects of *S1* and *S2* (and of any number of stimuli). Such effects, no longer sensory fragments, and hence no longer properly symbolized as sensations (*si* and *sii*) are here symbolized as cortical representations (*cri* and *crii*). Köhler's position may be represented as in Figure 12-2. The terms *cri* and *crii* are to be thought of as representing the differential impact of the physical environment on the brain. The term *cri* is the cortical outcome of *S1*, *crii* of *S2*. The arrows between *cri* and *crii* indicate that these are in reciprocal interaction with one another from the first. Internal cortical effects of stimuli *S1* and *S2*, *cri* and *crii* interdepend and self-organize in their very arising, in such a way that they never are not in touch with and changing one other; they never do not interact. Deriving their concrete character from one another, they are "characteristics in relation." The terms *cri* and *crii* thus are not merely the respective effects of *S1* and *S2*; they are not "raw" sensations. Rather, each is determined *from the first* by the other for the cortical process the other is. What is reflected in experience—leaves, branches, trunk—likewise is organized from the first. "We must have the courage to abandon the basic view from which it becomes necessary to treat field organization as a secondary, derived phenomenon" (Köhler, 1971, p. 176). Figure 12-2, of course, is an immense oversimplification; a leaf, for example, is itself a segregated unit, its perception necessarily involving any number of interacting *cr*'s.

Insight

What happens in insight, according to Köhler, is the following. Not only are the units that have come to be segregated in various cortical regions represented in consciousness, but so, too, at least up to a point, is the manner in which these cortical units are in present physical contact and determining one another's properties. Insight ("felt awareness of direct determination," Chapter 8) is, in other words, the reflection in awareness of direct determinations currently in process between interdepending cortical processes, the conscious reflection of the way one cortical region presently is in direct contact with another cortical region and doing something to it. What is

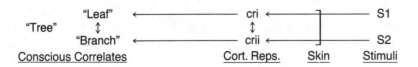

Figure 12–2

being reflected consciously, then, in accordance with the principle of psychophysical isomorphism, is something of the very manner in which physical processes in the cortex presently are in contact with and directly affecting one another. Our insight into the fact that the glass of beer brings satisfaction on a hot afternoon thus is a reflection of the following cortical situation: The cortical "self" (region of the cortex at the base of the phenomenal self) is in interaction with the cortical "glass of beer" (region of the cortex at the base of the phenomenal glass of beer), in such a way that the cortical tension in the cortical "self" (cortical correlate of the phenomenal thirst) is directly affected, removed, by the cortical "glass of beer" (cortical correlate of the phenomenal drinking of the beer). The structural dynamics of the interrelating occurring in the cortex, the way in which this interrelating in fact is taking place, is represented phenomenally in the felt awareness that indeed the beer is the direct source of the pleasure being felt. This phenomenal reflection of what in the final analysis is cortical dynamics—the cortical requiredness of the cortical "beer" by way of relation to the cortical "self," the direct determination of the cortical "self" by the cortical "rightness" of the cortical "beer"—is insight for Köhler.

The Objectivism of Gestalt Psychology

Phenomenological psychology has much to learn from the important descriptions of cognitive processes with which Köhler and the other Gestalt psychologists have furnished us. But, as already noted in Chapter 8, preferring an ultimate presupposition of objectivism, the Gestalt theorists found themselves unable to remain true to their descriptions to the very end. "Meaning" for Köhler is seen to arise as the terminal phase of a physical process, precisely as for conventional psychology. This section is a further reflection on Köhler's objectivism.

Psychology as Physics

Human life for Köhler belongs to the same nature studied by physicists (1938, p. 295), being in fact "a stupendous amplification of physics and chemistry" (1969, pp. 86–87). All human functions are said to be governed by the same laws that govern everything else in nature (ibid., p. 86). What goes on in the brain, therefore, is something natural science already must know something about (Köhler, 1971, pp. 76–77). And Köhler points out that, in a sense, beginning in the 1920s, Gestalt psychology became a kind of application of field physics to psychology and brain physiology (ibid., p. 115). Köhler's most fundamental intention indeed was nothing other than to make psychology into a branch of physics and chemistry, thus realizing the typically modern dream of a universal Galilean science. Köhler could well be taken as the ideal of the psychologist as natural scientist.

The human brain, for which physics must ultimately provide us with an understanding, is thought to underlie experience and hence both meaning and the phenomenal self. This objectivistic presupposition is central to Köhler's attempt to make psychology into physics. The brain is said to "underlie" and to "determine" experience; experience is said to be "based" and to "depend on" the physical brain. Köhler assumes that the order found in experience depends "upon physiological events in the brain" (1947, p. 38), "as a specific case of isomorphism" (1969, p. 91); that the formation of units is "the effect of dynamic interaction throughout the field in the physiological process" (1971, p. 51); and that all relations of which we are aware in visual space rest on functional relationships arising within self-distributing cortical processes (1947, p. 126). Whereas an observed environmental object is "a remote effect of a corresponding physical object" (Köhler, 1938, p. 93), it equally is "the result of certain organic processes" inside the organism (Köhler, 1947, p. 20). The space of the "dynamic self-distribution of cortical processes," cortical space, is an objective space of three-dimensional extension, an objective space of meaning.

Insight and the Self

As for insight into meaning, as suggested in Chapter 8 and just alluded to again, what is essential to it is said to occur outside the mental field altogether, as an accomplishment of the objective brain. Only the results of the underlying organizing process enter consciousness, which results (phenomenal insight) make their appearance ready-made on the mental scene. Insight into meaning is an event of the objective space of meaning, which is to say that meaning is not an event of meaning, not a phenomenal event, in what is its essential. Meaning is said to originate on a level other than its own, to be produced by a realm defined in advance as the very exclusion of meaning.

Köhler views the self, as also pointed out, as itself a reflection of a certain segment of objective brain processes. "Particular processes in the brain . . . underlie our experience of the self in its various states" (ibid., p. 201). When the self reacts phenomenally to the qualities of an object, Köhler assumes that cortical processes underlying the self are being affected by cortical process underlying the determining object (compare the example of the glass of beer); that processes underlying the object are physically represented in the very physical location where processes underlying the self are occurring, the former processes inducing changes in the latter ones (ibid., pp. 201–203). If the heat in the room makes us uncomfortable, for example, the essentials of this event are viewed as occurring in the brain between correlates of the self and correlates of the heat. "The process which underlies the feeling of discomfort is . . . the . . . direct effect of the heat as represented in the brain" (ibid., p. 209). The tendency to move away from the heat similarly is viewed as a physical event occurring essentially in the objective brain: "the behavior of vectors in motivational situations is the same as the behavior of forces in nature" (Köhler, 1961, p. 13).

The Law of Good Gestalt

The law of good gestalt for Köhler, along with perception and cognition in general, is an affair of brain dynamics, a psychological rather than a lifeworld law. Forces in physics are said to act in the direction of more regular and even configurations (1938, p. 266). Confronted with the illustration provided in Chapter 7 (Figure 7–3), for example, a "correctionist tendency" tends to arise. The disturbing part ought to be rounder, it ought to bend further downward (ibid., pp. 264–265). There is a tendency toward greater balance, as in Figure 12–3. The perceived direction in which improvement is to be gained coincides, in Köhler's view, with the direction of the stress in the underlying cortical substratum; the perceived requiredness has a physical correlate in the brain, which "correlate is the tension which the neural substratum of the situation contains" (ibid., pp. 267–268). The law of good gestalt thus finally is understood as the physically lawful way in which the present-at-hand objective brain works. Concerned with present-at-hand cortical processes alone, Köhler comes to consider the "good gestalt" itself, along with its immediately given ground, as in Figure 12–3, as simply present-at-hand; he comes to make the law of good gestalt a law of ready-made figures standing in-themselves against their ready-made ground, the reflection in consciousness of ready-made cortical processes. Köhler thus loses sight of the broader external requiredness that makes any meaning the meaning it is.

It may be further noted that Köhler, concerning himself solely with the

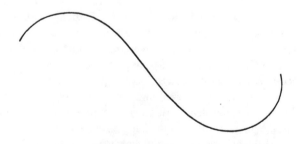

Figure 12–3

lawful tendency of meaning (more properly, the lawful tendency of meaning's neural substratum) to be as simple and regular as possible ("tension reduction"; see Chapter 6 subsection "Force and Counterforce in the Dynamics of the Good Gestalt"), neglects to consider meaning's equally lawful countertendency to become as fulfilled as a meaning as it possibly can ("tension enhancement"). It would seem impossible, moreover, to account for such a countertendency, governing as it does the unfolding of meaning precisely on its own terms, within the bounds of meaningless physical processes.

Gestalt Psychology and Time

The existential space of meaning has a special time of its own. Gestalt psychology, by contrast, explains time in terms of the objective space that it, along with Galilean science and Cartesian philosophy in general, projects as the final ground of all events of sensible meaning. This account views the time we presently experience (that is, events as they are presently unfolding) as the phenomenal reflection of the "time it takes" for the cortical processes being reflected in consciousness to run their course in the objective space of extension (*res extensa*); for example, a reflection of the "time it takes" for excitations emanating in one cortical region to make their passage across cortical space and establish contact with processes occurring in another region somewhere else in the cortex. Thus, if a table is tapped twice, at the moment when the second tap is occurring, the first tap exists only as a physical trace in the brain. The now-occurring second tap has a location of its own in the cortex, as does the trace of the first tap. For us to hear a pair of taps, there must be "dynamic intercourse" between the two cortical regions, perhaps by reason of "a leap of electrical potential between the two areas" (Koffka, 1935, p. 441). A field of forces must exist between the two cortical regions. Forces extending from the present tap to the trace of the first are what make the first tap also be in consciousness. Phenomenal time is the representation in consciousness of the physical course of these underlying processes, the representation of one region making contact with another region through its effects in the three-dimensional space of the cortex. It "takes time" for an objective cortical process with a certain objective location to make contact with another such objective process with a different objective location. The former objective process (the first tap, through its trace) necessarily happens *before* the latter one (the currently occurring tap, through its cortical representative); the latter, *after* the former. Time, rather than the circular interplay of time's three dimensions, thus is made into a linear causal sequencing in the realm of pure spatial extension; time, rather than the circular temporality of possibility, becomes the linear temporality of the in-itself. "It was one of the features of our hypothesis," Koffka remarks, "that it spatialized time in the brain" (ibid., p. 452).

Critique of the Objectivism of Gestalt Psychology

All in all, then, classical Gestalt psychology in general, and Köhler in particular, have adhered to the objectivist position according to which meaning and the self are completely determined by the physical forces presumably underlying them in objective space. Psychology, by this view, is destined to become an application of physics to human behavior. Gurwitsch, describing such a position, remarks,

> Starting from the perceptual world, we elaborate, by way of construction and inference, the scientifically true and valid universe of physics. In the course of this elaboration, physical systems progressively are substituted for perceptual things. Accordingly, a special physical system, the organism conceived by physiology, is substituted for the body as given in immediate experience. The task of psychology is then to conceive of organismic processes in such a way that the appearance of the entire perceptual world, including the body, will be explained as resulting from those processes. Köhler's formulation may well serve as an illustration of the orientation of psychological problems with regard to physical science. (1964, p. 169)

The Gestalt psychologists, in the words of Merleau-Ponty, "preferred to affirm—by a pure act of faith—that the totality of phenomena belonged to the universe of physics and merely to refer to a more advanced form of physics and physiology to make us understand how, in the last analysis, the most complex forms have their foundations in the most simple" (1964b, p. 85). Not even the self, it has been seen, escapes being turned into a mere causal outcome. "Ultimately the real world is the physical world as science conceives it, and it engenders our consciousness itself" (Merleau-Ponty, 1964a, p. 23).

Attempting to base psychology on the action of physical forces as studied in physics, and thus to fulfill the ideal of a Galilean science of psychology, Köhler takes objective processes, an objective space of pure extension, as ultimate reality. Cortical regions are held to be "at" other cortical regions. Processes located in various parts of the cortex are said to interact and become "characteristics in relation" through the operation of force fields, through electric currents that spread with great speed across considerable distances in the brain (Köhler, 1969, p. 96). The cortical correlate of the self is objectively located somewhere in the cortex—

everything physical is located in one objective somewhere rather than in another objective somewhere—as are the cortical correlates of all our meanings, other people included, and as are the very direct determinations (between meanings or between meaning and the self) of which insight is the felt awareness. The objective correlates of the self and of the self's meanings interact, as do the correlates of the moments that form our meanings. These correlates interact objectively, in an objective space of pure extension, by reason of physical forces that proceed from and surround them (objective electric currents). Through such force fields, objective correlates of experience "reach" and have effects on one another. These correlates all the while retain their localized cortical existence, where they constitute the region of the cortical "self," for example, or the region of one or the other cortical "meaning." Cortical regions enter into communication with one another, in their proper characteristics, by reason of the objective force field that each correlate generates in the continuous medium of the brain. Meaning, arising on a level other than its own, thus comes to be defined by meaninglessness, by a realm of electric currents devoid of meaning. Sense proceeds from non-sense. Nor does Köhler, any more than conventional psychology, offer an account of such a truly mysterious procession of meaning from non-meaning.

Locus a in the brain and Locus b (each a specific process instigated by specific stimulation of the organism, each with a "circumscribed local existence," a la Köhler), by reason of electric currents that spread out from them, both are objectively beyond themselves in the continuum of the brain. Locus a is beyond itself, in its effects, to b: $a \rightarrow b$; and locus b is beyond itself, in its effects, to a: $a \leftarrow b$. Loci a and b interact in objective space by reason of the reciprocal linearity of their locally spreading objective effects.

A process a cannot determine what happens to a distant process b (and vice versa) unless the presence of a is somehow represented at the locus of b (and vice versa). . . . If in a certain sense the correlate of a percept may be said to have a circumscribed local existence we shall none the less postulate that as a dynamic agent it extends into the surrounding tissue, and that by this extension its presence is represented beyond its circumscribed locus. . . . This halo or field of the percept process may be responsible for any influence which the process exerts upon other percept processes. (Köhler, 1965, pp. 70–72)

All in all, the local processes, the medium in which they interact (the brain), and the very forces by which they interact (electric currents) are all conceived as objective occurrences in a realm of pure extension. The objectively extended brain represents for Köhler the ultimate sponsor and locus of gestalts. Itself objective, the brain sponsors the organization of objective processes. Although in all this a "dynamic self-distribution of cortical processes" indeed is proclaimed, no existential surpassing is anywhere in evidence. The dynamic self-distribution of sensible lifeworld moments signifying one another in the final analysis is brought down to the dynamic self-distribution of cortical events overlapping in objective space: the effects of a cortical process a overlapping, through its force field, with cortical process b, the effects of cortical process b overlapping with cortical process a. There is no bodily self beyond itself to events of meaning unfolding in accordance with meaning's own law of lifeworld requiredness. Requiredness in fact is viewed as an objective relationship of interacting cortical processes, of one cortical region with certain objective characteristics objectively extending to and "requiring" another region, with objective characteristics of its own. There is no room in such a scheme for a lifeworld moment to surpass to and change another lifeworld moment, no free space for lifeworld moments thus in communication with one another to give birth to a whole of meaning on the ground of a phenomenal integrity all its own. In this scheme, meaning is treated as but an upshot of localized present-at-hand processes, without existential beyondness to a broader context of significance. Meaning has lost its possibilities, and there is no being possible.

The Atomism of Gestalt Psychology

Köhler rejects a certain version of atomism, that of independent sensory elements (sensations) in need of an extraneous synthesis. But, when all is said and done, whereas Köhler's *descriptions* indeed are holistic, his *explanations* are no less atomistic than the atomism of the elementarism he rejects. Anything defined as objective is an atom, for the simple reason that anything defined as objective has the character of being absolute and in-itself, with a "circumscribed local existence," which is precisely the definition of an atom. Interacting cortical processes, coinciding exactly with what they are in objective space, are as essentially atomistic as any sensation ever could be. It is just that cortical processes are atoms that exert a reciprocal influence on one another, their effects objectively radiating out far beyond themselves via force fields. Rather than the static and still-to-be-organized atoms of conventional psychology, dubbed "inert atoms" by Köhler, cortical processes as conceived by Köhler are dynamically self-distributing atoms, atoms contacting one another in objective space and immediately, without the mediation of any "more," causally influencing one another.

Any single constituent region of the cortex, atomistically in-itself, for Köhler is what it is and where it is locally; any influence such an objective region brings to bear on another such region is what it is and where it is locally; and a force field is constituted by radiating energies, through electric currents that, spreading locally, are what they are and where they are locally. The cortex viewed objectively is a collection of atoms, of local regions in-themselves, of local forces in-themselves, of local force fields interacting locally; it is a collection of atoms that always are somewhere in objective space rather than somewhere else, which location in the space-time continuum always is specifiable in principle. The local objective atoms that constitute the cortex viewed as a physical system have their local effects linearly; local influence, the only way nature conceived as objective *res extensa* works, can be exercised only in an end-to-end fashion. Any cortical region or entity can have an influence on any other region only by generating effects that emanate from it in a line, a single line or a great number of lines at once; one region or entity is able to immediately influence only a locally contiguous region or entity. Objective effects thus are passed along in the cortex locally and externally, by linear, "end-to-end causality" (Merleau-Ponty, 1968, p. 232), first this, then that; now here, now there; objective forces making their way through, measure by measure, influence by influence, with no intervening interval skipped, to whatever it is that comes to be affected along the line. In such a manner alone do essentially atomized objective forces spread. When cortical processes *a* and *b* are said to influence one another simultaneously, the reciprocal influencing in process only is a linear one atomistically passed along, all the local in-themselves (atoms) in between being influenced in turn: *a* and *b* are to one another only locally. The atomism that prevails in Köhler's Gestalt psychology is one in which a number of linearly unfolding local cortical processes come to locally have a variety of effects on one another. Dynamically self-distributing atoms affect one another only linearly, in a reciprocal linearity.

By thus abiding by the objective in-itself, by adopting atomism, albeit a more sophisticated version of it than the one dominant in conventional psychology, Köhler and the other Gestalt psychologists have sabotaged their landmark discovery of the gestalt. Gestalt psychology simply has been unable to see that atomism is only a particular case of what Merleau-Ponty calls the more general "prejudice of determinate being"; that is, they are unable to see that the objectivistic belief in things as ready-made and in-themselves of itself already is a form of atomism. Owing to just this "prejudice," Gestalt psychology loses sight of the best of its descriptions when it comes to establishing its theoretical framework (Merleau-Ponty, 1962, p. 50n). The Gestalt psychologists made the descriptive discovery that a gestalt is the immediately organized dialogue of its moments, which is to say that a gestalt is meaning from the first. Although the promise of its fulfillment lies precisely here, in this truly momentous finding, Gestalt psychology shied away from it, preferring to believe that what they had discovered (namely, the immediacy of the phenomenal conversation of a gestalt's moments) in fact was but the reflection of underlying objective events. The Gestalt psychologists thus, for philosophical reasons, found themselves unable to remain true to their descriptions, found it necessary to explain (away) their discovery. "The return to description and the appeal to phenomena as a legitimate source of psychological phenomena," writes Merleau-Ponty, "precludes in principle treating the *gestalt* as a lesser or derivative reality and allowing the linear processes and the isolatable sequences to retain the privilege granted them by scientism. But [the Gestalt psychologists] shrank before these consequences" (1964b, p. 85).

And the fact of the matter is, as suggested in various places, that Köhler cannot give an objective explanation—no objectivism can—for the expressive power gestalts possess, for gestalts as Köhler himself describes them, for the actuality of meaning. Nor can objectivism account for new meanings, for unpredictably emergent meanings, for the attempt on the part of meanings to become more themselves, or for the becoming in which we find ourselves grounded alongside our meanings and which could never be a mere outcome of present-at-hand processes. The physical "in one another" of overlapping cortical processes proposed by Köhler can never be the "in one another" of sensible moments signifying each other as lifeworld wholes of meaning. Cortical regions locally and linearly extending, in a space of extension, never can make sense of lifeworld meanings dimensionally stretched to and qualifying one another. Present-at-hand cortical processes viewed as in mere causal contact with one another should not be represented as a and b circularly signifying one another ($a \leftrightarrow b$) but as the two essentially independent linear processes they are:

$$a \rightarrow b$$

$$a \leftarrow b.$$

Linearly related cortical regions a and b are not *really* beyond themselves to one another, only their objective aftereffects, in the course of time. Cortical processes in mere linear contact with one another never could yield meaning, where the influence of moment A on moment B is translocally influenced by moment B in the very influence moment A is bringing to bear on it, and vice versa: circularly. Lifeworld moments A and B internally refer to one another across existentially possible space, and not across objectively continuous space: Moment $A \leftrightarrow$ Moment B.

An objective realm can never explain meaning; can never show the origin of lived dimensional meaning in its requiredness; its coming to expression in the necessity of a requiredness that never could be that of objective cortical processes objectively "requiring" one another. Because of his objectivism, Köhler has to miss this most crucial of all points. There is no relationship of signifying, and hence no circularity of expression—no circularity, no expression at all—in objective space, nor could there be. Neurons and electric currents taken objectively cannot come to expression, cannot circularly express one another. This requires a form of communication they simply do not possess. All in all, then, the objective *explanations* Köhler gives, meanings (gestalts) emanating from *res extensa,* betray his phenomenological *descriptions,* meanings (gestalts) as the essentially phenomenal conversation of their moments. Meaning, surpassing itself, surpasses every objective (atomistic) account (see "The Existential Phenomenological Alternative").

Köhler and the Theory of Ideas

By making meaning a mere reflection of an all-determining realm of objective processes, by objectivizing meaning, Köhler also subjectivizes it, making it into an event taking place in an inner and private sphere of the subjective, exactly the way conventional psychology does. It is absurd indeed to give meaning a place of honor, any sort of primacy, in a realm of objective processes, which realm is the very prior exclusion of meaning. Hence, in accordance with the logic internal to the subject-object dichotomy, and in spite of the deep respect Köhler and the other Gestalt psychologists displayed toward meanings of all sorts, and in particular toward logical, esthetic, and moral meaning, meaning can be only subjective. Like any objectivism, Gestalt psychology simply has to be a subjectivism in its account of meaning. Meaning is the brain's inner creation. Nor does the theory of isomorphism do anything to mitigate this situation, for meaning is of an order altogether different from the physical order of which it is said to be the reflection. Physical structure, being one of reciprocally interacting atoms, and phenomenal structure, being one of lifeworld moments circularly referring to and signifying one another, have nothing in common. The latter could not be the reflection of the former.

Meaning, then, for Köhler, sensible quality, rather than being self-giving in the lifeworld, is a subjective outcome occurring inside the organism. Köhler thus is seen to affirm, with the whole of the modern tradition, that the only things to which we have direct and immediate access are our own internal mental states. Köhler is a proponent of the theory of ideas (a la Gurwitsch), and necessarily so. The mind has direct access only to private and subjective aftereffects of cortical activities and not to the "real" external "world," a "world" that "really" is a realm of electrons, atoms, molecules, wavelengths, reflecting surfaces, and the like. Meaning has the status of an internal idea for Köhler, a private affair. Two people looking at the same object are said not to be seeing the same object, because each is only in touch, subjectively inside himself or herself, with the end product of a complex chain of objective events. The object of their "observation is the result of certain organic processes, only the beginning of which is determined by the physical [object] itself" (Köhler, 1947, p. 20). The observed object (meaning) is "only the final result of such processes" occurring in the organism (ibid.).

By taking things as he knows them from the surrounding lifeworld and locating them inside a subjective sphere of consciousness, by "making perceptions out of things perceived" (Merleau-Ponty, 1962, p. 5), Köhler is committing what he himself calls the *"experience error"* (1947, p. 95; see also p. 106). Köhler makes the basic, yet widespread, error of locating everyday meanings in consciousness, of turning things perceived in the lifeworld into inner outcomes, mere representations. Köhler, with psychology in general, presumes upon what he already knows from the surrounding lifeworld, upon matters that indeed can be known only from that world. Meaning, smuggled in from a domain other than that of inner consciousness, is made to constitute that very inner domain.

According to Köhler's theory, we are in touch with physical reality (the physical elephant, for example) mediately. A mosaic of stimuli (that is, elements without organization, raw elements) triggers a mosaic of reactions on the retina, a retinal mosaic. Further processes essentially independent of one another then are instituted, until eventually processes are activated in the cortex, where there occurs a "dynamic self-distribution of cortical processes," which cortical processes, consisting of independent local atoms in linear contact with one another, are no less atomistic than the entire process that has preceded it. The result in consciousness of the latter immediately occurring organizing is a perception, a meaning. We do not, cannot, see the "real" (external, physical) elephant, as noted, for perception is only a final subjective result generated by a long chain of objective processes, beginning with the objective elephant itself. The traffic in the chain moves linearly in only one direction: from the physical elephant to the physical organism, to inner experience. The phenomenal lifeworld is "our idea."

The Existential Phenomenological Alternative

The alternative to objectivism, be it the objectivism of conventional psychology or Köhler's, is to take the threefold temporal interplay of impact-interpreting, insight as already ahead of itself releasing meaning to possibilities of significance of its own, with the seriousness it deserves, on its own level of phenomenal occurrence. As already amply noted (see, for example, "A Phenomenological Theory of Insight" in Chapter 8; subsection "Positive and Negative Knowing" in Chapter 11), meaning comes to original formation in its structural necessity only in events of feeling insight, only in an upsurge of excitement. No more than the insightful self is meaning the reflection of objective brain processes. What happens on the phenomenal level as insight into value is an accomplishing: a reciprocal determining, meaning doing something, the bodily self doing something. Self and meaning each has a standing of its own on its own level of occurrence. Bodily self and meaning, dependent part qualities of an event of meaning presencing, simply are themselves and not to be reduced to transphenomenal occurrences behind or beneath them. Note that saying that insight into value unfolds on the phenomenal level is not to say that such an event is an event *of consciousness*, but that insight takes place on meaning's own level. A phenomenon, it has been pointed out a number of times, is an event of meaning rather than an event of consciousness, an event of presence and absence rather than an event of sheer presence, which is precisely why a descriptively oriented phenomenological psychology must be a hermeneutic discipline (see Chapter 2 subsection "Phenomenological Interpreting"). A consistently phenomenological psychology could never say, for example, that insight into meaning occurs "in consciousness," because for this psychology there simply is no such inner realm.

Meanings, affecting someone in their impact, come to be precisely in the excitement their requiredness holds for someone. But impact, as seen, is anything but reactive, anything but being influenced by a ready-made stimulus. Impact, becoming affected, belongs rather to the temporal circle of impact-interpreting, to Dasein's thoroughly active affective openness to meaning. A feeling bodily self, preoccupied with meaning from the first, is ahead of itself temporally, venturing meaning in being touched by it, being touched by meaning in venturing it in the lifeworld. Köhler, as pointed out in Chapter 7 ("The Nonsubjective Character of Value"), quite correctly from a phenomenological point of view, rejects the position that subjective valuation confers their threatening character on objects. He replaces subjective valuation, however, with the mere drawing near to the self of an imminent objective threat, with an object that is threatening in-itself. The threat, no longer subjectively imposed on a neutral something but now given objective status, is viewed as preceding the subjective state of fear and as "triggering" it. Fear, by this account, is not an impact-interpreting ahead of itself disclosing lifeworld possibilities, is not itself a discovering of threat (see Chapter 11, "An Illustration of Feeling: Fear"). Köhler's self does not surpass to the lifeworld; it does not, under the guidance of a law of good gestalt that belongs to the lifeworld rather than to the physical system of the cortex, futurally enact available possibilities of meaning. Köhler makes active cortical correlates underlie both the self and the world, as well as their linear interactions. Cortical field forces organize the world and determine the self's standing in relation to it, "interpret" the incoming world and furnish the self with perceptual meanings. The organism, according to this view, is not existentially outside itself to the world, is not carried away to the world in that "upswing into possibility" that characterizes bodily being-in-the-world.

The insightful bodily self, by the present existential phenomenological account, then, is an essential co-organizer of lifeworld gestalts. It is incorrect, by this view, to represent the influences in play in perception as having a linear character:

Self ← Physical Brain ← External Physical World

A lifeworld other affecting us does not objectively enter us at all; it does not cross the boundary of the skin and deposit a replica of itself inside us. Impact-interpreting already is ahead of itself rather, "at" the tree in the meadow itself. The tree's branches and leaves are not cortical representations (*cr*'s) inside the organism. Leaves grow on branches, branches spread out from the tree's trunk, and the tree is in the meadow. All in all, then, moments enter into one another's life as a whole of meaning only in an existential space of meaning, where they signify one another for that being constituted in its being as openness to significance.

Organization Occurs in the Lifeworld

The interdepending of a gestalt's moments, and of gestalts with one another, which for Köhler is at root an affair of objective electric currents in the brain, for phenomenology is lifeworld meanings signifying one another on their own nonpsychological ground. Organization occurs in the lifeworld (see Chapter 6, "Dynamics: Within the World"). Such organization, in sharp contrast to dynamic self-distribution as conceived by Köhler, is truly nonatomistic in character. Prevailing in the lifeworld, as between the self and the lifeworld and among the dimensions of time, is a circular rather than linear causality; translocalness rather than localness; internal rather than external relations. Circularly relating to one another, lifeworld moments signify and determine one another as a whole of meaning; circularly relating to one another, lifeworld wholes of meaning signify one another as a context of meanings, and ultimately as the final context of the world itself. The translocalness of meaning means that all of the intervening in-themselves standing between meanings always and already have been overleapt in existential space, along with the interdepending beings themselves (moments, gestalts), and the very self itself. Merely local space, where entity linearly influences contiguous entity, is surpassed in existential space. Atomism in its most proper sense is never having gotten far enough to first understand the referential totality of the world. Circularly signifying one another in a space where divisions already have been transcended, lifeworld moments are in internal communication with one another, translocally signifying and changing one another. All in all, then, existential space represents a serious alternative to the atomism that necessarily characterizes an objective space of meaning.

The shortcomings of Köhler's position thus are to be overcome by a consideration of the manner in which moments signify each other as wholes of meaning in an existential space of possibility, by a consideration of the way in which meaning originates in the dynamically self-regulating necessity of its internal and external requiredness, in all the concrete richness of its lived dimensional suchness. Internally related to such lifeworld signifying, to be sure, is the psychological impact-interpreting of insight (see earlier), the excitement of a bodily someone already ahead of himself or herself to the exciting requiredness of meaning. It is in view of meaning as a lifeworld accomplishment for someone, in view of the complementary notions of an affectively open impact-interpreting and of a law-governed lifeworld signifying, that Gestalt psychology can attain the fulfillment its descriptive origins hold in promise. Figure 12–4 diagrams the phenomenological position on perception. Inner representations of the outer world, as represented by either si and sii (conventional psychology) or cri and $crii$ (Köhler), are no longer pertinent in the present account. Therefore, letter a is meant to convey the self as interwoven with one lifeworld something, A, and b to convey another such involvement, with B. Both a and b are ahead of themselves to the lifeworld. The interpreting self is a determining factor in what is discriminated in its impact: $a \rightarrow A$, $b \rightarrow B$. Meaning in turn decides the interpreting self on the ground of a requiredness all its own: $a \leftarrow A$, $b \leftarrow B$. Things decide our life; our life decides things. Hence, a mutual directedness between self and meaning: $a \leftrightarrow A$, or aA; $b \leftrightarrow B$, or bB. Experiences aA and bB, moreover, decide one another. Thus a proper, though greatly oversimplified, representation of perception might be the one in Figure 12–4.

The self and the moments of a lifeworld meaning are what interact and not physical energies in-themselves (a la Köhler). Phenomenology descriptively locates insight into value in the essential free play between the self, always alongside other selves, and available lifeworld meaning, in its

$$a \leftrightarrow A$$
$$\updownarrow$$
$$b \leftrightarrow B$$

Figure 12–4

external as well as internal requiredness. Lifeworld moments signifying one another for a life are what come to be interpreted, are what have an impact on a life. The self-presenting meanings themselves, in this account, replace stimuli, sense data, and the replicas of things in the objective brain and subjective mind. Organization takes place in the lifeworld among the self-presenting tree, path, hill, and valley, as well as among the moments that constitute each of them. These stand where they stand, interacting there as the structurally grasped terrain, and not in the cortex. "What we 'first' hear," Heidegger writes, "is . . . the creaking wagon, the motorcycle. We hear the column on the march, the north wind, the woodpecker tapping, the fire crackling. . . . Dasein, as essentially understanding, is proximally alongside what is understood" (1962a, p. 207).

A Review of the Three Positions

Representing the three positions with regard to the status of our perceptions is figure 12–5. One thus sees that, whereas the first two accounts (and indeed any objectivistic account) have the tree standing in our head as an idea, the existential account has it standing where it stands in the meadow. In the first two accounts, the "world" is inside the organism—it in truth is no world—whereas in the phenomenological account the world is the surrounding lifeworld itself. By the first two accounts, there is a clear-cut

1. Conventional Approach

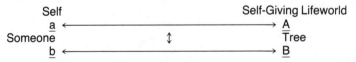

2. Köhler's Approach

3. Existential Phenomenological Alternative

Figure 12–5

boundary between the objective organism and its objective "environment," whereas by the third account no physical boundary is in evidence at all, no objective inside as opposed to an objective outside. The essential difference between the first two accounts and the third one is the kind of space invoked in the various theoretical accounts: physical and objective or existential. Projecting a three-dimensional objective space of equally appearing intervals, one discovers in the skin and other sense organs a clear line of demarcation between a locally circumscribed organism and its "environment." Presupposing an existential space of possibility, by contrast, one discovers a temporal transacting between self and world in the open expanse of the "there," a thoroughgoing interpenetration of self and its meanings.

13 The Variability and Validity of Meaning

The contact between the observer and
the observed enters into the definition
of the "real."

—*Merleau-Ponty*, 1968, p. 16

The Decidability and Variability of Meaning

A lifeworld gestalt, its organization immediate and without extraneous intervention, is decided all at once as this meaning or that. A gestalt may undergo progressive transformations, and even reversals, but it presents itself in any of its self-giving manifestations in one definite manner, as one discrete signifying of one another of its constituent members. Citing experimental results, Gurwitsch points out that, even though stimuli are continuously modified, there does not occur the continuous varying of the corresponding phenomena. The transformations of the phenomena rather are found to take place "by sudden jumps from one Gestalt to another," which implies that there are no gestalts intermediate to the ones in fact realized (1966, p. 45). A specific phenomenon simply does not correspond to every geometrical stimulus: "Instead, the phenomena develop in a discontinuous way" (ibid.). Such discontinuity, which is not what would be predicted by the constancy hypothesis, where "the differences between sensory data strictly follow those between the corresponding stimuli," "recalls some conceptions in quantum theory" (ibid.). Lifeworld organization, Gurwitsch remarks, proceeds by reason of *pregnance;* that is, in terms of any meaning's attaining the best form it can under the circumstances (law of good gestalt). The organization of our meanings— meaning formed, meaning transformed—is a matter of the dynamics of Gestalt lawfulness, then, and not something achieved through an external mechanical coupling of the fragmented inner effects of a ready-made geometry of environmental stimuli. Lifeworld moments (sensible qualities) converse with one another in existential space and, by reason of law-governed tensions, discontinuously jump into definite form as this meaning or that. Meaning, its moments attaining one or another dynamic self-distribution, is something that comes to be decided. Meaning is an action, an event.

239

That self-organizing lifeworld moments leap into one determinate status or another is evidenced, for example, in reversible figures. In Figure 13-1 one sees the goblet or the faces (Rubin, 1921), the young woman or the old one (Boring, 1930), the cube (Necker Cube) with this or that side facing us. Viewing any one of these illustrations we indeed may find the two possible configurations (potential signifyings) alternating back and forth between one another. We may find a similar alternation to occur between two contemplated courses of action, or between the two possible meanings of the phrase, "Love means nothing to a tennis player," or between the two different figures (one composed of narrow propellers, the other of broad ones) in the illustration of Chapter 5 (Figure 5-1). Lifeworld moments, nevertheless, in their very being understood, are decided all at once, discontinuously, as one gestalt or the other, *as something* (meaning). Any alternation that may be seen to take place between gestalts does so in a sudden jump from one organization (figure) to another.

That meaning forms and transforms discontinuously is not a quirk of the preceding illustrations. The coming to organization of any gestalt whatsoever involves a deciding leap into determinate lifeworld status. For phenomenology, there is no one "real" objective world, with a variety of subjective meanings superimposed on top of it. "Real reality" simply is not ready-made and determinately in-itself, the same for anyone who, possessed of the proper method, can pierce the veil of the varying subjective appearances with which it comes to be disguised (a la Gurwitsch). With a gestalt immediately the organization of its constituents, reality is meaning from the first rather, and meaning is many things. The realm of meaning—the lifeworld, "our first, last, and only world," *our reality*—is an

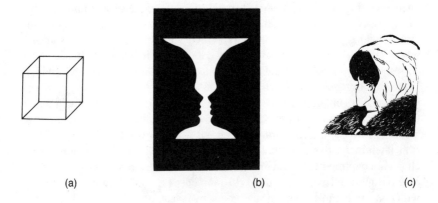

(a)   (b)   (c)

Figure 13–1
**(a) Necker Cube, (b) The Goblet-Faces Figure (After Rubin), (c) The
Young-Old Woman Figure (After Boring)**

essentially variable one. Reality is plural, irreducibly and irrevocably so. Saying that moments can be decided in one definite way is saying that they can be decided in quite different ways. The fact that lifeworld moments decide one another in a discontinuous leap into determinate status ensures a variability in meaning.

The examples cited thus far in this chapter essentially have been ones in which the "same" moments self-form in more than one way. Although such examples indeed are instructive, it is not infrequently the case that the moments that constitute our meanings themselves vary from gestalt to gestalt. Perception is a selective deciding of an available lifeworld that is incredibly rich in its possibilities of expression. In and through a disposed activity of imagining, available moments come to be decided one particular way, as one particular meaning. Other particular gestalts always are possible, however, in any environment. Different people, in the "same" locale, always can perceive something else, in its necessity. A tree sacred to one group as the very residence of The Divine is mere firewood to another. All in all, then, reality, in all its versions, is a decided reality, a variable one.

The Variability of Meaning and Its Validity

The Validity of Meaning

Reversible figures display a variable organization. The "same" moments are decided first as one gestalt and then as another. A variable deciding of meaning is in evidence. Available lifeworld moments are imaginatively ventured and, thus ventured, leap into determinate status. On the one hand, the lifeworld's unyielding pursuit of an ideal of requiredness ensures a variability in meaning formation, ensures that meanings already formed will undergo transformation. This holds not only for reversible figures but for meaning quite in general. On the other, the lawful manner in which the lifeworld unfolds holds out to meaning the prospect of progressing to a truth all its own. Meaning formation is never an arbitrary matter, this was the point of Chapter 6. The way a meaning's moments determine one another shows a necessity rather, a law-determined urgency. To be sure, there is a certain freedom with which we imaginatively interpret lifeworld meanings, but there is a certain necessity about the way meanings come to bind us in their impact, about the way meanings are "to be accepted" and "to be rejected" in their very origin as meanings. A certain freedom is inherent in how we approach things, but a certain necessity in the way things respond to us on their own ground.

Requiredness, once again, is the very origin of meaning, its structural law. Insight, for its part, is structural understanding of the direct determinations in play in a meaning's requiredness. To say that a meaning's requiredness is structurally attained is to say that something is structurally what it shows itself to be; that the demands actualized indeed are those of the meaning in question and not the result, for example, of a disturbed disposition (Chapter 11); and that the requiredness at the origin of meaning holds up to scrutiny. A meaning's being "structurally what it shows itself to be" is referred to here as a meaning's *validity*. A valid meaning is one that intrinsically, structurally, *is* required, a meaning whose "ought to be" or "ought not be" *is* structurally as it presents itself as being. A valid meaning is a meaning that represents the actualization of demands latent in the very structure of the lifeworld itself, be these demands practical, moral, logical, or whatever. A valid meaning is one actualized in accordance with the requirements of "its principle of organization" (in Köhler's words).

An original meaning, as seen in Chapter 6, is a live meaning, one on the cutting edge of our lives, one whose structural necessity is in process at the moment. An original meaning is an intrinsically required one, meaning in the intrinsic requiredness of its process. But, as also seen, a meaning that is intrinsically required by reason of the originality of its process is equally intrinsically required as an outcome, which is to say, as the meaning it shows itself to be. Intrinsic requiredness of outcome, after all, is what has been in process structurally all along. Intrinsically required process issues in an intrinsically required outcome. Such a requiredness of outcome is precisely what is being called a *valid meaning*: a meaning that is as it shows itself as being in its place; a meaning that is intrinsically the requiredness we take it to be; a meaning that is presencing, either positively or negatively, in accordance with its "can-be." Thus, with the originality of a meaning referring to a meaning in the intrinsic requiredness of its process, the validity of a meaning refers to a *meaning in the intrinsic requiredness of its outcome* (Chapter 6 subsection, "Intrinsic Requiredness"). Outcome being precisely what has been in process from the first, a meaning is valid to the very extent that it is the outcome of an original process of meaning. Meanings that formerly presenced in their originality, moreover, may continue to present themselves in their validity, even when not currently underway in the originality of their process. A hoe retains the validity of the "can-be" it has attained as a hoe, its intrinsic requiredness of outcome, even when, in our routine use of it, we are thinking of something else altogether. Two and two still are four even when the originality of the equation is not currently in process. One can discuss the character of what Maslow calls *Being-values* without undergoing a current experience of them. Should questions of validity arise, however, in the final analysis only an original experience of the meaning in question can address them.

Meaning: Variable and Valid

Although it is claimed here that original meanings validly bind us for the structural outcomes they are on the ground of their necessity, likewise it is claimed that lifeworld moments, dynamically signifying one another in freedom, variably decide one another as this whole of meaning or that. But can meaning be both variably decided and valid? Phenomenology's response is that it is precisely *because* lifeworld moments can freely signify one another, and be variably decided in the process, that meanings are able, in accordance with the law of requiredness that prods them on, to self-form in their originality, and thus to attain the status of valid outcomes. Free to variably signify one another, lifeworld moments are free to seek the ideal of their structural necessity; free, then, to achieve an intrinsic state of original positive or negative requiredness; and free, that is, to be just what they show themselves to be. Only in a process in which meaning is able to variably pursue the necessity of its requiredness can valid outcomes arise. Variability permits a meaning to be original in process and valid in outcome. Meaning truly can have its own possibilities coming to it, indeed can miss out on these possibilities by failing to achieve positive fulfillment, only if its possibilities can be imaginatively ventured in freedom, only if it can arise this way or that, only if it is variable. All in all, then, variability in meaning is a necessary, but by no means sufficient, condition for the validity of meaning. To fulfill itself, meaning needs the freedom to pursue its necessity.

Intrinsic requiredness of outcome, validity, is variable, and necessarily so. In the same locale where someone readily and quite correctly sees a path beginning, someone else will readily discriminate types of rocks or patterns of vegetation. One person sees a beautiful sunset, another ponders the molecular patterns involved. In our culture we readily recognize three kinds of snow; in another twenty kinds are validly discriminated. She sees books, he sees scrap paper. This someone sees a solid surface, that someone knows what is there is mostly empty space. One person hears a divine masterpiece, a second person merely notes rising and falling, and a third contemplates the wonderful mathematical properties involved. We have insight into the immense diversity of the wholes forming the lifeworld, they perceive the profound unity and harmony of all things. One someone sees just a leaf, someone else sees a beautifully intricate pattern, someone else again sees a cure for a certain ailment, other someones discriminate it as tea, as an ornament, as just the right thing to cover up one's nakedness. In all these examples of variable requiredness, who is legitimately in touch with reality? Which of the requirednesses come to manifestation are valid? If someone sees a goblet and someone else sees two faces, who is in touch with the meaning's "principle of organization"? If we first see a goblet and then two faces, when did we get it right? Is it not in fact that meaning is decided *with insight* in both cases; that in each of the two experiences the meaning has a weight of its own that is structurally required in terms of the law of good gestalt? Is it not correct to say that there are two self-giving "principles of organization" here? The leaf is accurately taken as just a leaf, as beautiful, as medicine, as tea, as ornamentation, and so on. No meaning has it *in-itself* to be valid, which means that many meanings can be precisely what they show themselves to be: plural validity in the realm of meaning. We may be mistaken about lifeworld gestalts. We may wrongly take the leaf to be poisonous, for example, or mistakenly take a plastic leaf for a real one. Notwithstanding the very real possibility of error, variability in the realm of meanings does not undermine the possibility of their validity. On the contrary, this variability is essential to the law of good gestalt and is the very bursting open of plurality in the realm of truth.

Signifying as a Condition for Variability and Validity

The variability of meaning, issuing in multiple validities, is essential to the operation of the law of requiredness. What defines a gestalt (Chapter 5) is not an extraneous unification that an objective brain imposes on raw material: a gestalt is "not more than the sum of its parts." What characterizes the unity of a gestalt rather is the very relationship to one another of its constituent moments. This relationship is simply the conversation in which available lifeworld members signify, and thus express, one another in the fullness of their lived dimensionality. What defines a gestalt is the emptiness, the nothing, the signifying, between the members forming it, the emptiness that allows available moments to dialogue with one another in their possibilities of a shared future. Moments make each other be in their reciprocal signifying of one another in the open expanse of the "there." Moments A and B define each other because they are in communication with one another in an existentially open space: $A \leftrightarrow B$. But, because a gestalt is nothing but the relating of A and B in the lifeworld, where and as they are, A and B can signify or express one another in more than one way, can form more than one gestalt. A and B can become $Ai \leftrightarrow Bi$ or, then again, $Aii \leftrightarrow Bii$. A and B signify each other in the two cases in two different ways. Two different signifyings are taking place, two different meanings are in process. Or, as is frequently the case, A enters now into relation with B to form a certain gestalt, and now with other lifeworld moments, C or D, to form that one. All in all, then, because there is not something (some thing) slipped in between lifeworld moments, some constraint (warehoused form) imported from memory, a gestalt can come to formation at the moment for what *it* can be as a meaning. The very freedom lifeworld moments have to signify one another a particular way, and thus to self-form with originality as such and such a valid meaning, is their freedom to signify one another in some other original way, as some other valid meaning.

If A and B (or C or D) could not variably modify each other on their own ground for what they *can be* when signifying one another as a certain whole of meaning, then their unity could never validly present itself in its requiredness. Meaning would be locked into connections already established: already established by heredity (instinct), by the environment (stimulus control), by the fatalities of an insistent past (repetition compulsion). Without a dynamic self-distribution of lifeworld moments, meaning would be fixed and without internal and external possibilities of its own. Because the space it holds to is essentially the objective space of determinate things in-themselves, the space-time continuum, conventional psychology finds itself bound to fill in every square millimeter of space. Abhorring a vacuum, it bridges every last gap with something, with hyphens, objectively stored memories, extraneous interventions, and so on. But if everything in fact were decided in advance by reason of rigid connections already in place, then meaning could never come to formation from itself in accordance with a law of requiredness all its own: now, as it now can be. Because of the nothing (emptiness, opening, interaction, signifying) between moments of the lifeworld, these are freed to be themselves even as they change one another and come to form this or that intrinsically required whole of meaning. Signifying one another, lifeworld moments are able to enter into original communication with each other. Whereas an objectively unbridgeable gap in objective space spells the breakdown of causal influence, the very absence of such a bridge in existential space, its always and already having been surpassed, allows moments to signify one another in freedom. The very absence of objective linkages forms the point of departure for an existential account of meaning. If interventions of the brain or mind (associations, judgments) were what really and truly conferred unity on our lifeworld others, then these others would have no standing of their own. They would be merely psychological, *our* doing. But, with no-thing constituting the "between" of its moments, a gestalt can come into its own, can be and remain itself, as and where it stands in the lifeworld. Whereas conventional psychology is always introducing objective subjectivizing interventions to round out its reduced image of human life, existential phenomenology, with the lifeworld ever firmly in view, is decidedly antisubjectivistic in attitude.

The differential deciding of lifeworld meanings is all-pervasive in the lifeworld. Precisely because of the "upsurge into possibility," precisely because there is an opening (the nothing of signifying) between lifeworld moments, such moments can meet variably and thus perhaps originally on the ground of their own law. Signifying spells variable interacting of lifeworld moments; and variable interacting, the possibility of original and hence valid meanings.

Interpreting, Variability, and Validity

Moments come to formation in a signifying that allows them the opportunity to self-form differentially as one whole of meaning or another. Such variable deciding of meaning, it has been pointed out, is prerequisite to the originality of process of a meaning and, hence, to a meaning being what it shows itself to be; that is, to the validity of its outcome. The signifying at the heart of original meaning formation, moreover, is a functional interdepending (structure) released by a disposed imaginative venturing on someone's part (Chapter 10). An interpreting someone makes it possible for directed lifeworld tensions to freely express themselves and thus for lifeworld moments to decide one another on the ground of their own possibility. All in all, then, the disposed imagining of insight is just what a meaning needs to first become itself, to first show itself as itself. Insight as interpreting gives meaning just the chance it needs to originally pursue the necessity, which is at once the freedom, of its future, and thus to have an impact on someone in the validity of its outcome.

Interpreting and the Variability of Meaning

Meaning becomes itself, the best way it can, precisely upon observation. Meaning comes to its defined organization (form, gestalt) when it is interpretively determined in its impact by a temporally disposed self, a bodily self already ahead of itself. Observation interpretively ventures the signifying of one another of lifeworld moments, with their law-governed tensions, and some one particular meaning leaps into definite form. Environmental things are not ready-made and in-themselves, not stimuli that, linearly affecting an essentially passive self, give rise to inner copies of themselves. Everyday lifeworld things are decided anew rather in events in which the observer plays a determining, though certainly not all-determining, role. "The contact between the observer and the observed enters into the definition of the 'real' " (Merleau-Ponty, 1968, p. 16). The following illustration, it was pointed out in Chapter 7, can be made out, without much difficulty, as an array of rows or of columns, as three pairs of columns or as four rectangles:

```
X  X  X  X  X  X
O  O  O  O  O  O
X  X  X  X  X  X
O  O  O  O  O  O
X  X  X  X  X  X
O  O  O  O  O  O
```

It also was pointed out there that the "given" pattern cannot be called a stimulus, for the simple reason that one's very manner of approaching the material as it is available codetermines how it in fact presents itself to us, how it leaps into determinate status in perception. The observer co-organizes the gestalt that in fact arises. We perceive what we already are ready to perceive, on the basis of our established competencies and currently adopted attitude (disposition, the way something already can have an impact on an imaginative venturing ahead of itself to the world). The "same" recording of our favorite piece of music is differently decided on various occasions, in accordance with our prevailing mood. Decided one way, moments can be decided another way. Meaning is variably decided, in accordance with the given sensitivity of a participant observer.

Interpreting is the possibility, then, of variable meaning. Looking here, we see this. Looking there, we see that. An imaginative venturing of possibilities determines how potentially available lifeworld moments decide each other this, that, or the other way with this, that, or the other requiredness. Interpreting, in conjunction with the law of good gestalt, codecides how available lifeworld moments decide each other as perceived gestalts; codetermines the manner in which meaning leaps into concrete status at the moment. Concretely situated interpreting, although not creating its meanings, indeed is an active ministering to the world. Essentially partnered to the impact on their own ground of variably required gestalts, then, is variably disposed interpreting.

Interpreting and the Validity of Meaning

It might be objected, from within the subject-object dichotomy, that a perspectival characterization of the essence of insight, as disposed imaginative venturing, disqualifies insight as the grasping of valid structural relations. The objection does not hold, however (see Chapter 10 subsection "The Paradox of Interpreting and Impact"). In our everyday discrimination of the lifeworld, limit is a condition of understanding (see later, this section). What is crucial for a proper structural understanding of meaning, however, is that our presupposing be appropriate to the matter at hand, that our imaginative enacting of meaning proceed on the basis of a disposition adequate to the law (the structural demands) of whatever is to be encountered. Our manner of conceiving that which we are interpreting, Heidegger points out, "can be drawn from the entity itself," or we "can force the entity into concepts to which it is opposed in its manner of Being" (1962a, p. 191); our presupposing of meaning ought to proceed from what is to be understood and never from "fancies and popular conceptions" (ibid., p. 195). And again, "The task is to being Dasein itself into the kind of understanding which pertains to its being at the time so that it can have access as understanding to the matter to be understood" (1985, p. 259).

The way not to understand an available work of fiction, for example, the way not to actualize its potential validity, is to presuppose it as a historical account of actual events. We can misinterpret meaning, miss its point. Not every viewpoint has equal rights.

As already noted, precisely through turning and looking are we able to see the tree as the tree it is, which is to say, as the tree it can be. Only when we appropriately situate ourselves in a meaning's regard, only when we are able to bring off a venturing that is adequate to it, only then is a meaning able to presence in its validity. We simply have no way of knowing what something is other than by approaching it from a perspective. We have to look at things to become acquainted with them, Merleau-Ponty points out, and we have to do so "from a certain point of view, from a certain distance and in a certain *direction*" (1962, p. 429). A thing has a front and a back, which is to say, it is a real thing, only for a someone who can confront it from one side or another, "so that it is through [our] upsurge into the world" that the thing has a front or a back (ibid., p. 430). For the Taj Mahal to validly manifest itself to us in all that it can be as a meaning, we have to situate ourselves by voyaging to India and taking whatever other measures are necessary to gain the right perspective on it. Attainment of the proper limits is precisely what any meaning needs for it to be originally enacted in possibilities truly its own. To be properly determined by a meaning (impact), to be legitimately in touch with it, requires that we properly determine it (interpreting), which is one expression of the paradox of interpreting and impact. An adequate alreadiness is needed for the valid presencing of anything whatsoever. Arnheim writes,

> The gestalt studies made it clear that more often than not the situations we face have their own characteristics, which demand that we perceive them appropriately. Looking at the world proved to require an interplay between properties supplied by the object and the nature of the observing subject. This objective element in experience justifies attempts to distinguish between adequate and inadequate conceptions of reality. Further, all adequate conceptions could be expected to contain a common core of truth. (1974, p. 6)

Some perspectives simply are better attuned to particular meanings, and hence better able to sponsor their self-showing, than others. Given the meaning, given indeed the meaning's total context, some disposed imaginative venturing is superior to other disposed imaginative venturing. All and all, then, limit and structural understanding are complementary in our knowledge, not antithetical. For something to originally determine us in the validity of its impact, it has to be appropriately determined from a perspective, and indeed from a multiplicity of perspectives. It is only ever within the variable limits of one disposition or another that insight interpretively sponsors the valid impact of a meaning. Being conditioned (limited) is our very openness to lifeworld possibility. Perspective frees meaning by giving it the leeway it needs to presence as itself.

What presents itself in its structural validity in the lifeworld is there in part, then, because it is in the process of being grasped by a history that takes the time to interpret it and, so to speak, to cogive it. A book becomes what it structurally can be, for example, only when someone engages in reading it. An appropriate reading permits the book to validly speak, to say what it has to say. Interpretively expressed by someone, the work expresses itself.

Lifeworld interpreting, moreover, geared to the structural law of good gestalt guiding a meaning's self-formation, is not an exercise in arbitrariness. An interpreting true to itself, which is to say true to the matter at hand and its structural principles, is no mere opinion. What we interpret is not subjectively inside ourselves, and anything does not go—not in real life. Interpreting responsibly entered into is an attempt on the part of a responsive bodily someone rather to release meaning to a self-showing on the ground of its own law, to release it to its intrinsic requiredness. The demands of meaning guide a supple interpreting down certain structurally necessary lifeworld paths. To interpret is to strive to disclose nonmental lifeworld meaning, to provide it with just the opening it needs. It is precisely to this end that interpreting unavoidably takes a stance. If the stance is adequate (and the meaning available), the truth of the whole of meaning being pursued is enabled to have an impact on someone's life. In sum, insight is itself only as interpreting; and interpreting, when successful, is insight into meaning in the validity of its structural determinations.

We have actively interpreted our whole lifeworld, co-organized it in its entirety alongside other Daseins, and this world continues to unfold, in part, through our doing. The lifeworld terrain being originally explored depends on the efforts we make toward it. We contribute most fundamentally to the face the world turns our way. Reality, the lifeworld, essentially is relative to our life. Nevertheless our behaviors come to coactualize a validly self-presenting layout of the lifeworld itself. And anyone who has the capabilities and the inclination, who, approximating our situation, "gets into our shoes," will attain the insight into the terrain we have. "The thing imposes itself . . . as real for any subject who is standing where I am" (Merleau-Ponty, 1964a, p. 17). The terrain makes the same structural demands on anybody who ventures it on the ground of an alreadiness adequate to it. It has the same potential validity for everybody.

Interpreting and Truth

Saying that insight is interpreting is one way of saying that truth is a historical event, the situated structural understanding of variably valid meaning. Truth occurs within historical limits. "Since we are all hemmed in by history," Merleau-Ponty writes, "it is up to us to understand that whatever truth we may have is to be gotten not in spite of but through our historical inherence" (1964c, p. 109). Without a point of view, one sees too much, one sees everything at once, which is to say that one sees nothing in particular. This typically is what happens when we come across a complex and unfamiliar arrangement of lifeworld moments, a flea market, for example. To gain structural understanding in such situations, we have to turn our back, often literally, on a great number of things and limit our attention to some narrower meaning context. Making a start somewhere, we have to adopt a specific perspective.

Criteria for Judging Meaning's Validity

This chapter has defined a valid meaning as one that is structurally the requiredness it purports to be, intrinsically required outcome, a meaning or value (outcome) presencing in accordance with its laws of requiredness, in accordance with its lawful "can-be." But the thorny question then arises as to how we are to know whether a particular meaning is valid. Because meanings do not exist in an absolute manner in-themselves, rather being decided in all their relativity in finite events of meaning presencing, a hermeneutic science hardly is free at this juncture to smuggle in standards for judging meaning from some realm beyond the ever changing lifeworld. Phenomenology has no resources at its disposal for evaluating meaning other than the phenomena themselves. The following preliminary criteria for gauging the validity of meanings, both positive and negative, consequently are derived from ways in which people find themselves already engaged in evaluating meanings in everyday life.

The Criterion Of Meaning Itself

The principal criterion for judging meaning's validity is meaning itself. Validity, after all, is a meaning being structurally the requiredness it shows itself to be, lawfulness of outcome. What indeed could offer better instruction about such a state of affairs than the meaning under consideration? Meanings teach us about themselves. A certain potential signifying can be actualized in approximately the same manner on any number of occasions and for any number of people on the same occasion. Meaning does not subsist in-itself through the passage of time; but, as potential, as a potential signifying, its law can be stirred to life time and again. An original experience with meaning, an experience of meaning in process in the necessity of its requiredness, ultimately is the true test of any meaning's validity. Although gauging the originality of meaning itself is no easy matter, when a meaning strikes us as original on a number of occasions, when it strikes others the same way, we tend to become confirmed in our belief in its validity. Thus, rereading a historical account some years later, we may find it just as sound and exciting as ever. The validity of the account in this way gains support. A work of art may be similarly confirmed, turning out to be as evocative and beautiful this time as it was on other occasions. An argument may prove specious time and again, whenever we hear it made. A fellow worker, encountered day after day over a number of years, may prove to be the nice (or unpleasant) person we initially took her for. The testimony some meanings offer about their present and former validity holds up remarkably well in the course of time. Further encounters with a meaning, on the other hand, may reverse our first impressions, impressions assumed at the time to be quite valid. The person we took to be so very helpful may turn out in fact to be only after our money; the expert, to be a fraud; the caring parent, a sadist; the restaurant, a laundromat; the mugger, a tree branch; or the salesperson, a mannequin. The presumed validity of certain prejudices sometimes collapses before our very eyes, moreover, in a firsthand encounter with the matter itself.

Further experience with meanings sometimes supports, sometimes adjusts and corrects and improves, and sometimes cancels former experiences of their validity. Meaning, showing its true colors, gives us feedback on the truth of its requiredness, or on the lack thereof. Lifeworld signifying is an education. People constantly are using the present criterion of meaning itself in their ongoing transactions with lifeworld things. Meaning's validity, its being intrinsically the positive or negative requiredness it presents itself as, is crucial for our survival, as well as for a great many other things in our life. We always are testing reality: testing the ice to see if it will hold our weight; testing the milk to see if it is sour; testing the switch to see if it is in working order. The test of meaning itself, for good reasons, has itself stood the test of time.

The Criterion of Best Perspective

Any meaning best comes to fulfillment in its structural law when actualized on the basis of the best perspective possible. The adequacy of one's approach to things thus is a measure of the intrinsic requiredness of outcome of a meaning. Seeing things in person generally is better, for example, for assessing the validity of meanings than merely hearing about them from someone else. One particular way of approaching meaning, moreover (getting a closer look, for example, or perhaps moving back a little), usually turns out to be better for judging a meaning's legitimacy than another. A certain alreadiness, the openness of one disposition, generally is better than another when it comes to a meaning's validity. Testing the intrinsic requiredness of our solution to an intellectual or moral problem, its validity as a solution, moreover, may require gaining a second or third perspective on it.

Our attunement of the moment sometimes provides a clue as to a meaning's status. Moods such as panic, frustration, depression, fear, rage, and heightened suggestibility may well serve to blind us to the structural requirements of a meaning (see Chapter 11, "Disturbed Disposition"). A relatively calm and relaxed disposition, on the other hand, contributes to the rational consideration of a variety of problems and their solutions.

The criterion of best perspective in the final analysis tends to coincide with that of meaning itself, for the meaning alone (its requirements) dictates the best possible approach to it. Meaning itself determines that a certain alreadiness in its regard is, or is not, appropriate to the law governing its signifying. Meaning forevermore is our best guide, indeed our final guide, to itself. Self-showing meaning is itself the measure of the best perspective on it.

The Criterion of Consequences for Life

A further criterion for judging the lawfulness of outcome of a meaning is how the meaning comes to affect our life, the feedback we get (our personal success, our personal failure) from taking up a certain meaning and living it forward into its future, meaning's consequences for life. We tend to judge a positively required meaning valid when it furthers our undertaken tasks, when it generally promotes our being possible. Validity, by this criterion, is judged by the ascertainable difference a meaning makes in our life; for example, by how it leads to new insights.

The long-range satisfaction we take in our meanings is far from the immediacy of merely "feeling good." Such satisfaction, if it is deep and broad, necessarily involves suffering valid meanings that have a negative character, as well as executing valid meanings that, although positive, cost us in various ways. Happiness is a by-product of a certain style of living with meaning, of a certain overall disposition or sensitivity to the lifeworld, of cultivating the balanced and responsive openness to the world that is being possible's lot, and not our life's goal (Chapter 7 subsection "Frankl and Value").

The Criterion of Other People

Insight into meaning in its validity, at one level or another, always is a communal occurrence. We are in the world together, coperceiving meanings and jointly assessing their legitimacy. Two people see the city's sights together, correcting and furthering one another's impressions of it

(Merleau-Ponty). People share their insights about the lifeworld status of things, confirm each other's beliefs, and spread their misgivings to one another. Inquirers of all sorts (scientists and philosophers, for example), in pursuit of the valid "can-be" of a certain range of meanings, are constantly questioning their own findings and those of others. Public debates rage on such issues as the morality of abortion. People are constantly giving meanings to one another and testing their validity in a social give-and-take that is neither infallible nor accomplished once and for all.

Individuals, confronted with questions about a meaning's validity, not infrequently seek advice from those who are especially sensitive and capable in what regards the meaning in question. Struggling with a moral dilemma, people consult those who have had some experience in the matter, those who have thought long and hard on the issue. People read books, on gardening, for example, to see what they are doing wrong. Others show us how meanings work and correct us in our use of them. People tell us when and in what way we are missing a meaning's point, and we tell them.

Balancing of Validities

A valid meaning is one that is structurally required, just the way it shows itself to be. Not infrequently, however, valid requirednesses compete with one another for our attention and implementation. Instances of conflicting positive requirednesses are getting some needed rest or exerting oneself and going shopping for food, eating a sundae or sticking to a diet, reading a book or finishing homework, going to a concert or visiting an ill friend, making a donation to a good cause or buying a compact disc, buying this compact disc or that one, having the roast beef or the fish, working out or repairing the fence, taking up law or joining the Peace Corps. We find ourselves in situations such as these weighing one requiredness against another.

At times, the balancing of requirednesses is nothing short of a moral demand. What is to be achieved in such cases is a higher-order meaning, a higher-order field of requirednesses in which the various individual requirednesses come to bear on one another in an as balanced (clear, regular, simple) and fulfilled a manner as possible. What is needed, in other words, is a higher-order intrinsic requiredness that takes all the relevant factors into account, a higher-order meaning that reveals to us what is to be made of the various alternative meanings with which we are confronted; a higher-order meaning, that is, that reveals to us what it is that we are to do. Such a balanced weighing of requiredness against requiredness—in what is most characteristic of each and in their relation to one another—is sponsored by higher-order insight. Such higher-order insight, higher-order conscience (compare Chapter 7 subsection "Morality Values"), is a, if not *the,* paramount task of our lives. One's integrity as a person lies not in an inner sphere of a subject, but in just such a balancing of nonpsychological requirednesses, the actualization of a broad spectrum of intrinsic values. One's deepest interiority is to be found outside, in a certain manner of surpassing to meanings.

Variability and Validity in Objective and Existential Space

All locations are indifferent to one another in an objective space of meaning, none is superior to or indeed in any way qualitatively different from any other. There in fact are no qualities at all in space projected objectively, no meanings of any sort. It is a presupposition of objective thought rather that "meanings" exist only as an inner realm of subjective outcomes, effects of a "real" world of physical energy exchanges. The requiredness of our everyday meanings, in the view of conventional psychology, is a matter of mere subjective opinion, of inner "value judgments." Any inquiry into the validity of meaning (value) within such a frame of reference, therefore, is nonsense. By defining meaning in advance as *not* the way it seems to be—"*What we see, hear, and otherwise sense is not what is really there in the outside world*" (Kalat, 1986, p. 86)—conventional psychology precludes any possible validity of meaning. The only validity objectivism allows is the ultimately objective nature of all things and, if one is consistent, even that becomes suspect.

Phenomenological psychology takes requiredness and its validity at their face value from the first, which is not to say that it raises no critical questions about the validity of meaning (see "Criteria for Judging Meaning's Validity"). Asserting that meanings can, but need not, be valid is claiming that nonpsychological meanings can be what they seem to be, where and just as they stand in the lifeworld, and indeed that such valid meanings are precisely what, in the first instance, constitute our "first, last, and only world," reality itself. Valid values are just what they originally show themselves to be in their place relative to significance, no more, no less. Phenomenological psychology finds that required meanings can have an impact on our lives with a legitimacy of their own, then, in existential space. Meaning can matter for what it is, for the "ought to be" or "ought not be" that is its essential. What allows meanings to be themselves, to weigh on us in their own law, to be valid, is the existential "upsurge into possibility" (Heidegger). Dasein as the "there" of meaning events is the occasion for things to show themselves for what they are on their own ground, from themselves.

14 The Self-Others-World System

Our task will be, moreover, to
rediscover phenomena, the layer of
living experience through which other
people and things are first given to us,
the system "Self-others-things" as it
comes into being.

—*Merleau-Ponty*, 1962, p. 57

Psychology beyond the Subject-Object Split

Dasein's affective openness to world, the self-presentation of lifeworld meanings to bodily Dasein—such is original reality in the view of existential phenomenology and not the division of things into subjects and objects. What is decisive, Heidegger remarks, is to avoid splitting the phenomenon into two sorts of present-at-hand things in the first place, to steer clear of dividing the singleness of the event of meaning presencing, on the one hand, into a "thinking and representing" subject, and, on the other, into objects existing in-themselves, outside of any impact they might have on someone's life (1984, p. 130). Openness to world is a unitary, though indeed differentiated, phenomenon, not the joining up of a self-sufficient subject with already existing objects. "Objective" and "subjective," Merleau-Ponty writes, are "two orders hastily constructed within a total experience" (1968, p. 20). Phenomenology's task, Merleau-Ponty asserts, is to revive this total experience. As moments of the "total experience" that embraces them both, as Heidegger puts it, the self is "no longer subjective, no longer a subject," and meaning "no longer objective, no longer an object" (1979, p. 123).

The question of how the body is to be understood, beyond the subject-object dichotomy, in terms of the self already has been addressed in this study, in particular in Chapters 4 ("The Bodily Self") and 11 ("Feeling and the Bodily Self"). It has been noted that the human body is nothing other than our very openness to things, being possible itself. The body is a self, a personal, feeling body. But the reverse is asserted with equal justice. The self is a bodily insertion in things, through and through the sensitivity of a body that, sharing a common bodiliness with sensible things, resonates with them. Permeated with bodily states, the self *is* bodily (ibid., pp. 98–99). The self is a body. All in all, one is a personal body, a bodily self. The relationship between body and mind (self) is no more a relationship between an object and a subject than is that between world and self: neither the relationship of an object-body producing the mind (subject), nor that of the mind (subject) controlling the body as an extraneous instrument (object). In Merleau-Ponty's words, "Our century has wiped out the dividing line between 'body' and 'mind,' and sees human life as through and through mental and corporeal" (1964c, pp. 226–227).

Lifeworld others, in the impact-interpreting of insight, affectively are incorporated, literally embodied, into our life (impact), imaginatively determined (interpreted) as our life's personal meanings. The bodily self and the world are not objectively outside one another, but, forming a single interwovenness, live in, and off, one another (see Chapter 10 subsection "The Paradox of Interpreting and Impact"). Body and meaning interpenetrate in the openness of Dasein's surpassing to world in a way that no objective forces ever could. The term *system* is used here for this interpenetration, this circular relativity, of the bodily self and the world, for the interpenetration, moreover, of any number of bodily selves implicated at once in one another's lives and in the world: the bodily self–other selves–world system. The notions of gestalt and system formally are the same. Both are structures (a la Köhler), the functional interdepending, in law-governed free dynamics, of their constituents; of feeling bodily selves and lifeworld in the case of system, of lifeworld moments in the case of gestalt. Existential phenomenology calls not for subjectivizing the real, that would merely be a maneuver *within* the metaphysics of subject and object, but for a more basic "revision of our ontology" (Merleau-Ponty), for the replacement of the metaphysics of subject and object with the self-distributing structural dynamics of system. The term *system* represents a move, then, beyond the dichotomy of a subject standing over against its objects, including the object that is its body. Rather than the relations of linear, "end-to-end causality" (Merleau-Ponty, 1968, p. 232) that prevail in objective space, the term *system* is meant to indicate the relations of significance that prevail between the bodily self and its meanings in existential space, to signal, in the fullness of its dimensional concreteness, all that the phrase being-in-the-world implies.

In terms of system relations, the bodily self and a network of meanings are engaged in intercourse with one another. Perception, in Merleau-Ponty's words, is a "communion, . . . a coition, so to speak, of our body with things" (1962, p. 320). The bodily self, an acting, perceiving body (ibid., p. 106), interprets its world, giving it form, being formed by it in turn. It is the bodily self that, taking its cue from things and responding to them in intimacy, looks and sees, listens and hears; that, in answer to things, is a living question directed at the lifeworld. Moving one's body means aiming at things through it, responding to their call, waiting for their answer (ibid., p. 139). One dimensionally echoes the very things that, thus aimed at, make their response to us, "reverberating" to all sounds, "vibrating" to all colors (ibid., p. 236). All in all, the bodily self and the world, reciprocally determining one another, stand to one another in circular system relations. Merleau-Ponty points beyond the subject-object split back to such "a unity before segregation," to the "*antecedent* unity" of "me-world, world and its parts, parts of my body" (1968, p. 261). "Our task," he says, "will be . . . to rediscover . . . the system 'Self-others-things' as it comes into being" (1962, p. 57). In what follows, the system of the bodily self and the world first is considered and then the system of the bodily self, other selves, and the world. Two basic areas within psychology, learning and remembering, next briefly are examined in terms of system relations. Final considerations are left to the event character of system.

The Bodily Self–World System

The body and the world, "in a functional interdependence similar to that which prevails, for example, between the dependent areas of the visual field" (Köhler, 1971, p. 61), interweave to form a single structure. Things are woven into our body; our body, into things. "Our own body is in the world," writes Merleau-Ponty, "as the heart is in the organism . . . and with it forms a system" (1962, p. 203).

Feeling insight (impact-interpreting) and intrinsic requiredness (value) together are embedded in the single larger context of a bodily self–world system. Positive interest and positive meaning, desirous organism and desired banana, for example, in the classic experiments of Köhler (1927) with chimpanzees, are in mutual dependence on one another and not arbitrarily so. In the words of Merleau-Ponty, "The 'milieu' and the 'aptitude' [are] like two poles of behavior and participate in the same structure" (1963, p. 161). And again, the thing and the act of looking, "two 'moments' in an organization which embraces them both," enclose one another (1962, p. 278). And finally, the self and the world are in a "quasi-organic relation" with one another (1964a, p. 12). Desirous attitude does not exist in-itself, then, but rather, in Köhler's words, is "a stress *between man* (or animal) *and the field* or some part of it, determined by the relative conditions of both sides in this *total situation*" (1971, p. 60). Or, as Köhler states in another context, "We *are* aware of definite and very concretely organized dynamic contexts. There are not separately: a self, an interest and many things in the field, but, surrounded by many other items, a-self-interested-in-one definite thing" (1938, p. 67). The whole question of the relation between the organism and its environment stands in need of being posed anew, in Wertheimer's opinion, in view of the Gestalt theoretical notion of the organism as a part of a larger field: "The stimulus-sensation connection must be replaced by a connection between alteration in the field conditions, the vital situation, and the total reaction of the organism by a change in its attitude, striving, and feeling" (1967b, p. 6).

The bodily self, as already suggested, is by no means a stranger to the things among which it is dimensionally situated. As Merleau-Ponty states, "My body is made of the same flesh as the world (it is a perceived)" (1968, p. 248). The body is the very world itself bending back over itself and looking at itself, the world become self. "We perceive the things themselves, . . . We are the world that thinks itself . . . . The world is at the heart of our flesh. . . . There is a ramification of my body and a ramification of the world and a correspondence between its inside and my outside, between my inside and its outside" (ibid., p. 136n). The world is wholly interior to the bodily self, and we are wholly outside with the world, with its bodiliness, which is our bodiliness. Our body is a self "caught up in things. . . . Things are an annex or prolongation of [our body]; they are encrusted into its flesh, they are part of its full definition; the world is made of the same stuff as the body" (Merleau-Ponty, 1964a, p. 163). It is in the same thrust to the world by which we perceive the lived dimensions of our own bodies that we perceive those of other bodies. The bodily self and its world do not form a system secondarily, then, but are an original unity in the lived dimensionality of existential space, a single "flesh." The body and its sensible others are "in" one another from the first, the way a gestalt's moments are.

Structural Analysis of Behavior

Both behavior and meaning are what they are as emergent moments, dependent part qualities, of an event of the body-world system. As such moments, each is to be understood structurally in terms of prevailing system relations. A human-scientific psychology sets out to account for the lawfulness of behavior, then, through an analysis of the bodily self–world system in process at the time of the behavior in question, through a *structural (functional) analysis* of the body-world system in the fullness of its temporal circularity. A hermeneutic science of psychology has as its task just such a deciphering of system relations; both healthy and psychopathological functioning are matters of such relations. The body-world system is the smallest unit to be mastered for an understanding of behavior at the human level. A descriptive psychology, like any psychology, necessarily concentrates on only one side of the total behavior-meaning structure. Such a psychology is concerned with disclosing the bodily side of the body-world system, the side of the interpreting bodily self under the impact of its world. But, the overall system always has to be kept in mind for a truly scientific understanding of human behavior. A human-scientific psychology thus chooses to be imbued with the full relativity that essentially characterizes behavior, to be a thoroughgoing "relativity theory" of human behavior.

The Bodily Self–Other Selves–World System

Writing of Dasein's relations to other people, Heidegger remarks, "The Dasein is, as such, essentially open for the co-existence of other Daseins" (1982, p. 296). Human beings are determined from the first and always by *being with* other human beings. This *being with* others is our shared preoccupation with world (see Chapter 3, "The World and Other People"). We meet up with other people in their *being-in-the-world,* preoccupied with the same ready-to-hand meanings we are. "Being-with-others means . . . being-with-in-the-world" (ibid., p. 278). The world always is a world shared with other people (Heidegger, 1962a, p. 155). " 'Thou' means 'you who are with me in a world' " (Heidegger, 1982, p. 298).

For Heidegger, then, we surpass to the world with other people, we are beyond ourselves and alongside things together. All traditional psychologies agree, by contrast, that, as Merleau-Ponty puts it, the psyche "is *what is given to only one person,*" that the psyche of the other is "radically inaccessible" to us, and that, as a consequence, we can know what is on someone else's mind (a person's thoughts, perceptions, and feelings) only indirectly, through inferences based on external signs (1964a, pp. 114–115). According to this conventional point of view, we only guess at the psyche of another, secondarily reconstituting its inner workings. But, counters Gurwitsch, "from the other's words . . . we *immediately* and openly witness [the other's] joy, see it *directly* in his face. In daily life the idea never arises that we do not have in perception what itself occurs in our fellow human being" (1979, p. 3). Merleau-Ponty similarly remarks that it is not that we "see anger or a threatening attitude as a psychic fact hidden behind the gesture," but that we see anger in it; the gesture, rather than making us think of anger, *is* anger itself (1962, p. 184). Or, as Köhler writes, "If I refer to the calmness of a man before me, I refer to a fact which I perceive" (1947, p. 143). On descriptive grounds, then, in perception we are intentionally "at" other people themselves, immediately and directly. The "mental states" of other bodily selves, in other words, are written all over their behavior. Other people simply are not tucked away inside their skin, any more than we are. The mind is not a sort of inner stage (a la David Hume) on which privately owned sensations play out their assigned parts. Rather, "consciousness," in Merleau-Ponty's words, is "turned primarily toward the world, turned toward things; it is above all a relation to the world" (1964a, pp. 116–117). To be a self is always and already to be outside, to be intentionally stretched all the way to the world and its values. To be a self is to express things bodily, visibly. Other selves are "at" their world from the first, then, as are we; and we are, from the first, "at" other people thus engaged in a world that is common to us all. When we look at the items displayed in a store window, for example, it is the things themselves we are aiming at and that we see. Our friend, aiming at us, as well as at these same items, perceives our aiming itself, our interest is sensibly visible in our acts and in the things being looked at. But we, directing ourselves also toward our friend, perceive our friend's visible aiming at the very things at which we are aiming; we perceive our friend's interest in these same things. The two of us perceive, moreover, our aiming at one another in our joint aiming at the items on display. We are two visibly sensible bodily selves, two unities of sensible qualities, perceiving one another's visible preoccupation with sensible lifeworld meaning. "The other who is to be perceived," writes Merleau-Ponty, "is himself not a 'psyche' closed in on upon himself but rather a conduct, a system of behavior that aims at the world" (ibid., p. 118). Through the world common to us both, then, we know another self, not from reading the individual's mind. Through the music we share the musical feelings of those around us; through the landscape we catch sight of its impact on others.

Our world and that of our friend are variants of "one common world." Our friend's eyes and our eyes, aiming at and falling upon one and the same thing, work in harmony. If there is a synergy among the various parts of one body as it aims at a certain lifeworld meaning, Merleau-Ponty contends, why not a synergy between two different organisms (1968, p. 142)? The same way that the members of one someone's body form a single system, our body and the body of another person form one single whole, "two sides of one and the same phenomenon" (1962, p. 354). "He and I are like organs of one single intercorporeality" (Merleau-Ponty, 1964c, p. 168). Bodily selves harmonize as a single system, then, as a single bodily life. Our behaviors and those of our friend converge in the lifeworld, synergistically. We aim at meanings together, co-organizing them as the very meanings they are on the ground of their lifeworld law. Our town is precisely the one we live in together. The book is the one everyone is talking about. The sofa is the one we are both sitting on. The house is the same one anyone can see who passes its way. The landscape we see and the landscape our friend sees interweave, our actions and the actions of our friend fitting together exactly. We find in the landscape we are viewing the landscape our friend is also viewing, "I recognize in my green his green" (1968, p. 142). Lifeworld meanings are comeanings, coperceptions. Various perspectives—ours and yours at the moment, ours and yours earlier, ours and yours later—open on the same potential signifying (potential meaning), a perspectivally, hence multiply, given signifying constituted for the two of us by the same field of law-governed tensions. Our acts and perceptions intersect with your acts and perceptions, in the thing. The other person appears as "the completion of the system" (Merleau-Ponty, 1962, p. 352). "Our perspective views . . . slip into each other and are brought together finally in the thing" (ibid., p. 353). Our friend, we know, is making something, too, of what we are only now making something. The same landscape, with laws that transcend all psychological processes, is being coactualized through a multiplicity of psychological behaviors of insight presently converging on the single landscape. There, in the landscape, our behaviors and yours meet. There is *"one and the same perceptual world"* for us all, Gurwitsch asserts, the one world we all experience, though from many individual points of view (1966, p. 431). Perceptual presentations of the one world belong to "one total system," *our world*. We form with other someones a single self-others-world structure.

The Bodily Self–World System and Learning

The conclusion was reached earlier that the only proper understanding of behavior at the human level is a structural one, that the self-world system is to be brought to bear on our understanding of psychological processes quite in general. In this section and the next, two fundamental behaviors, behaviors holding a central place in conventional psychology, learning and remembering, are considered in terms of system relations. Chapter 2 specified the clarification of psychological concepts as a major, if not the major, task of phenomenological psychology. Steps have been taken toward executing this task in the book's various descriptions of Gestalt organization and lawfulness, insight, feeling, disposition, unconscious processes, perception, impact, interpreting, imagining, value, and motivation. The following attempts to clarify learning and remembering are in essential continuity with these earlier efforts and meant to round out the "exploration of the premises of a phenomenological psychology" undertaken in these pages.

Learning is the institution of a capability or competence on the part of being possible in its relations of system to the lifeworld. In accordance with such an existential definition, learning is not the mechanical shaping by the environment of an essentially passive alreadiness or disposition; learning is not the programming of the organism, not the laying down inside it of an objective grid of associative forces. Learning indeed is the shaping of our lives, but what thus is shaped is ourselves as embodied openness to the lifeworld, ourselves as already affectively disposed to things. Learning is not impersonal or prepersonal in character, but eminently personal. It is the bodily self's very stance in things, its stance toward them, that is reformed (formed and transformed) through learning. Learning is an enabling of behavior and also of the meanings coordinated to behavior.

Learning is our bodily self's becoming more or less permanently open to the lifeworld in a new way, our body's becoming capable of coactualizing a meaning context, of whatever sort, formerly beyond our reach, a restructuring of our life in what regards such a context. Learning from experience, according to Gestalt theory, is acquiring ways of perceiving things and acting in their regard. "For the gestaltists," writes Merleau-Ponty, "the accumulation of experience merely makes possible a restructuring which will re-establish the equilibrium between the living being and the milieu at another level" (1964b, p. 84n). "The influence of previous experience upon present perception," Gurwitsch remarks, "must be accounted for in terms of reorganization and reconstruction" (1964, p. 265). And again, the past remains effective to the extent it has given rise to certain permanent "structures and forms of organization" (1966, p. 388). Rather than being ruled by the weight of the past, then, learning is a matter of our becoming personally attuned to different structural possibilities of meaning, of becoming disposed to a new future and, with that, to a different present. Learning is structural attunement to things, reattunement. Learning, all in all, is a restructuring of that bodily disposition by reason of which we already are ahead of ourselves in familiarity to the world. Become disposed in some new way to meaning, bodily being possible is now able to enact, and be taken up in, new system relations.

Learning, given this, is not something that takes place inside the organism, after stimuli have worked their effects. Learning rather belongs to the self-world system, to the bodily self's surpassing in affective openness to the lifeworld. Learning spells new possibilities for the functional interdepending of bodily Dasein and its meanings. Rather than taking place inside us, then, learning is *between* us and the world. Learning is system differentiated, a new articulation of system relations. Learning, no objective modification of the organism, takes place precisely in the context of our being always and already submitted to a network of meanings beyond us.

Illustrations and Further Definition of Learning

First gaining familiarity with something in all its complexity, a symphony, for example, the organization that initially confronts us often is massive and without differentiation. But, as we become better acquainted with the music, something begins to happen to it and to us. *It* changes, undergoing reorganization in its law-governed sensible qualities. What was only potential on our first hearing, the symphony's structural law, its "can-be," now becomes actual for us. It is not that we are subjectively adding qualities—beauty, expressive power, melodic line—to a neutral perception. Rather, we are in the process of becoming capable of the music on the ground of its own law; we are becoming capable of letting it structure itself in accordance with its proper necessity. The music is changing; we are changing. Learning is taking place. The music and we change together, within the dynamics of system relations. The music itself undergoes transformation in its entirety as we develop new bodily competencies in its regard. The symphony's constituents come to be reconfigured, to be reformed, where they stand, nonpsychological meaning in the lifeworld. The fate of lifeworld meaning depends on how we are changed by experience, on the interpretive skills we develop, or fail to develop, for releasing meaning to its law. "Experience," Gurwitsch has written, "modifies the psychophysical organism by setting up conditions which permit certain typical transformations of Gestalten" (1966, p. 44).

Faced with the challenge of finding our way around in a city new to us, we have to come to terms with its structure (its functional interdependencies, the way its constituent parts directly determine one another as a given network of requirednesses) and that is what we find ourselves doing from the first. We figure out how the streets run, how they are named and numbered; we attain structural understanding of the city's landmarks and neighborhoods, its cultural and commercial institutions, its parks and restaurants; we try out and master its transportation system; and so forth. We learn how things stand with all of these, and indeed how they connect, articulate, with one another to form the concrete dimensionality that is the city itself. As we thus become an alreadiness or disposition instructed and capable in its regard, the city becomes a differentiated structure for us. We and the city become structurally interwoven, a single system, parts of one another. The bodily self and the city come to form a single space of concrete sensible givens, which shrinks sometimes to the size of our living room, expands sometimes to embrace the city's vast stretches. We competently make our way through the city's spaces, opening them up time and again as we go. We learn the city by becoming capable of it. We do not develop explicit and detailed cognitive maps of the city; whatever maps we do have are in no case internal to us, being sketches instead of the nonmental lifeworld complex that the city is. Our sketches of the city interconnect only informally rather, without any great exactness or precision. What we develop, learn, is a feel for the city, for the city itself, a feel inscribed in the very fibers of our body. We have come to embody the city in learning, and with that to feelingly project it for the unity it is. As we make our way through it, we recognize certain sites, and these familiar sites stir up anticipations of what we will find around the corner; learning has given us just such a capability for anticipating the lifeworld itself. We rehearse symbolic codes that represent the city's layout, its sequencing, "Now, let's see, if we turn right here and walk three blocks, we will reach the post office," or "Route 183 runs into 268, and 268 takes us to the bridge." Such verbal coding is extremely important for the efficient learning, and retaining, of things (a la Bandura). The city is a living being, and our relating to it in familiarity is structural through and through, a personal matter of system relations.

Learning and the Formation of Habitual Meanings

True learning, system relations becoming articulated through insight into originally unfolding meaning, is adapting to the structure of the matter at hand, developing a competency that lets the meaning (the piece of music, the town, the terrain) structure itself in accordance with the structural necessities of its law. "To learn," says Heidegger, "means to make everything we do answer to whatever essentials address themselves to us at the given moment" (1968, p. 8). Becoming an accomplished cabinetmaker, for example, means making oneself "answer and respond above all to the different kinds of wood and to the shapes slumbering within wood" (ibid., p. 14). Learning with insight, one feels one's way into the direct determinations that constitute the other's "can-be." One develops skills, a bodily sensitivity or responsiveness, that answer to it. The apprentice cabinetmaker undergoes an attunement of hand and eye to what the wood requires to be brought to a state of balanced fulfillment as this or that piece of furniture.

Habit, with learning in general, is a reorganization of system relations. "For a habit to become completely automatic after a period of conditioning," Gurwitsch remarks, citing the work of Guillaume, "a complete reworking or reorganization of perception is required" (1974, p. 176). Once restructured, the meanings being dealt with (let us say, the cabinetmaker's wood and tools) become phenomenally and psychologically different from what they were before the development of the habit. The very situation, in Heidegger's example, the workshop, in which the habit is to be executed comes to be transformed, to be concretely structured in terms of the task to be accomplished. The workshop now presents itself in terms of the wood to be shaped. The workshop's fittings no longer appear as curiosities but as functions serving certain ends. The apprentice comes to adapt to the situation's structure, then, to the functional complex of the workshop as a network of relations. The more the apprentice becomes familiar with and a match for the workshop's given structure, the more his dealings with his materials and the tools of his trade become a stable and automatic habit, and the more the felt sense of his bodily handling of things (kinesthetic sensitivity) takes the place of his perceptions of them (ibid., p. 177). His meanings thus become absorbed into his body, in view of the task at hand. Our body understands, and a habit has been formed, "when it has absorbed a new meaning" (Merleau-Ponty, 1962, p. 146). Lifeworld structure and a bodily someone have come to be woven into one another in new ways. System relations have been restructured through learning.

Learning and the Formation of Functional Characters

Learning, it has been seen, is the development by a bodily someone of new system relations to one or another context of meaning. Our world is changed through learning, things take on new meaning. When we now perceive a pen, for example, this thing is immediately grasped as something to write with, something to be handled a certain way, something to be used in conjunction with writing paper. This thing, in other words, has come to be endowed with *functional character,* the functional character of a pen, a character that now permanently belongs to it. A gestalt with functional character is one that has been transformed in such a way that its instrumentality presently is thoroughly assimilated to it. Sensible qualities have been reorganized so as now to be directly *perceived* (Gurwitsch, 1964, p. 101), for example, *as* a pen (something to write with), or *as* a knife (something to cut with), or *as* a steak (hearty food to eat), or *as* a mailbox (something to put letters into), or *as* a raincoat (something to protect us from bad weather), or *as* a chair (something to sit on). A meaning with functional character now simply is experienced as what it is good for. The thing has become its use, even outside of the context in which it might be used; a hammer in a store window, for example. This transformation of one meaning into another, of something into a use value, serves the purposes of everyday life quite well. All in all, a use value arises in its functional character in a new articulation of meaning in existential space, in a perceptual resignifying of one another of lifeworld moments, their rearticulation. "Long ago," Köhler writes, "a red circle in such a place became imbued with the meaning 'stop' . . . just as a green circle is now imbued with the meaning . . . 'go ahead'. . . . When we see this cross + between numbers, it now tells us directly that this is a matter of addition; it now simply looks it" (1969, pp. 139–140). We do not see something with functional character first as a mere neutral something, only then to bestow on it its meaning as a pen or a stoplight. The pen's very arising at the moment is as the meaning it is. It is perceived from the first in its intrinsic lifeworld requiredness as the use it has become.

All sorts of things now immediately confront us in their proper functional weight in the lifeworld. Learning occurred some time ago in their regard. The self, embodying these things as the meanings they then became, took on an alreadiness or disposition capable of competently enacting them time and again. Phenomenology insists that the origin of the pen as a pen, of functional characters, amounts to a restructuring at once of ourselves and of the pen, of our openness ("there") in what regards this ready-to-hand meaning. We became a certain cognitive (knowing) capacity to co-organize a certain lifeworld signifying, to immediately sponsor the pen in its significance as a pen. The short stick was transformed at the time, in our very perceiving of it, and became something to write with. A capacity was born for releasing the law of certain available lifeworld moments as the instrument they can be. Learning for phenomenology is just such a process of reorganization of self-world relations of system. Our future perception forever transformed, the meaning will never be the same again, nor will we. When perceived again, in Gurwitsch's words, the thing appears "reorganized and reconstructed, exhibiting functional characters" (1964, p. 101). Certain empirically acquired forms of organization thus become integral to our perception.

Learning is a structural system transformation, then, and not the accumulation of psychological structures existing in-themselves and layered, so to speak, one on top of the other in the objective space of the brain, in a spatial order mimicking the temporal order of the original events. "The growth of the mind" is to be understood as "reorganization, reconstruction, and transformation of experience itself" (ibid., p. 103). Attaining a certain stage of development means that forms of organization belonging to and experienced at earlier stages have been surpassed by those forms currently operative. Former stages of the body-world system, in other words, now simply are gone. Whatever existed before the arising of a certain functional character, the use value's predecessor in the domain of meaning, now has been reorganized out of existence altogether; for this predecessor to make its return would require the reinstitution of just that organization (articulation of system) that originally supported its presencing. The different stages that use values went through historically to become the meanings they now are do not subsist, then, in-themselves within the psyche or brain—within the unconscious or, for that matter, within any other psychological holding area, such as a warehouse of perceptual forms—as various levels of sense. In accordance with Gestalt theory, there are no such founding layers, no strata of forms superimposed one on top of the other inside us. It may be noted that, whereas other sorts of values (persons, esthetic qualities, etc.) may not be said to possess functional character, they, too, have their transformation history. They, too, became the values they now represent at some time in a history of system relations; compare the earlier discussions of first becoming acquainted with a symphony or a city. "In our theory," writes Koffka, "the effect of experience is not that of adding new elements to old ones, but of changing a prior organization" (1935, p. 393). Reality is process—organization and reorganization, context of meaning succeeding context of meaning.

The Bodily Self–World System and Remembering

Remembering is a possibility of the self in relation to lifeworld possibilities, a matter of the bodily self–world system rather than of a physical in-itself (objectively encoded memory) making its occasional appearance before the lights of consciousness. What we remember is nothing psychological, having its place, its context, instead in the lifeworld. Remembering, moreover, is inseparable from the relatively permanent transformations of the body-world system that occur in learning. Such transformations of our alreadiness or disposition render us capable of coming back to lifeworld meaning contexts and of being mindful of them.

Forgetting

We come back to and take up possibilities already belonging to our relations of system to the world in any number of ways. Forgetting is separating ourselves from some capacity of ours to enact a certain meaning context. Forgetting demands above all, as Heidegger remarks, that it pay no mind to the fact that it is forgetting, that it forgets itself. "The ecstasis of forgetting something has the character of disengagement from one's most peculiar having-been-ness [alreadiness], and indeed in such a way that the disengaging from closes off that from which it disengages" (1982, p. 290). Forgetting is closing ourselves off from something that we have been, from something that we have been through, from something that we are. The commonsense belief that forgetting is nothing at all presupposes just such a closing off.

Recalling

The remembering called *recalling* is coming back to former body-world events through an imaged reliving of them. Recalling is the possibility of bringing such events close again, for the events they were, which is not to say with any great degree of precision or accuracy, in the open expanse of existential space. Though image is indeed the mode in which recalling proceeds, this form of remembering aims not at the image but at the imaged, the nonpsychological meaning with which our life has become personally involved at the moment.

Recognition

The remembering called *recognition* is a coming back in alreadiness to things in their familiarity, things in whose regard we already are somehow skilled, particular meanings or kinds of meanings that have had a place in the history of our body-world system (see Chapter 10 subsection "Situated Enactment as Capacity of Recognition"). Recognition is a form of remembering constantly taking place in body-world transactions. We recognize even a tree we have never seen before, as a tree. We are always coming back in recognition to possibilities that have been. All experience is in this sense remembering.

Retaining

The remembering called *retaining* is coming back and holding on to moments of an ongoing context that have passed. Retaining preserves such moments of a context in and for the "living present" (in Husserl's words). Retaining thus allows what has passed to remain and effectively signify and be signified by other moments only now being released, as well as to signify and be signified by, however indefinitely, moments still to come. Retaining thus plays an important role in permitting lifeworld moments to stretch to one another "across" time; it plays its part in permitting moments that have been, moments that now are, moments that are now only anticipated to functionally interdepend *at the moment* for the meanings they are, to currently circularly signify one another, backwards and forwards, every which way at once. Meaning is an action (directed tensions) *over time at the moment,* and the felt sense of retaining, allowing moments that have been to remain presently active, makes an essential contribution to meaning formation.

Retained moments (*retentions* in Husserl's terminology), including sides of a presently available meaning now out of view, presence at the moment precisely as moments that were, and not as something present. Holding itself back in favor of what is currently presencing as present, the retained presences precisely as absent, a particular retained moment enters in its very absence into connection with a meaning's other moments to form a single system of functional significances. The former events of a soap opera, for example, to the extent we have been following the story line, now presence effectively (as retained) for the meanings they were. They connect with events only now occurring, as well as with events currently anticipated, effectively changing the way such present and future events presence at the moment. Such former events, moreover, themselves take on new significance in the process, coming to be retroactively changed, at the moment, by developing present and future events. Anticipated moments (Husserl calls these *protentions*) presence, for their part, as something looked forward to at the moment; presence, like their retained counterparts, in their essential absence. Note that, because the terms *phenomenon* and *phenomenal* denote the presencing of meaning and not happenings in consciousness, retained and anticipated meanings, not conscious in the usual sense of the word, nevertheless have a phenomenal character.[1]

Any instant of an unfolding event of meaning belongs to the threefold interplay that constitutes existential time: the anticipating of a meaning's future moments (protentions) on the basis of moments already retained (retentions), as well as of those presently presencing; the retaining, by reason of the future anticipated for a meaning, as well as of its present moments, of certain moments that have passed; and the releasing of a meaning's present moments by reason of the meanings presently retained and anticipated. The interplay of time is the dialogue at the moment of lifeworld moments that already have been, that presently are, and that are futurally on their way, the circular flow of meaning in all three temporal directions at once. Meaning is an action, "loaded with tension" (in Arnheim's words), stretched (tense) at the moment over the three dimensions of time. Feeling insight is the perception of such an action. At any junction (jointing or articulation) of a meaning's unfolding, we are in touch with its present, with its anticipated future, and with what it already is, as these stretch to one another at the moment. At each instant, at each deciding of the whole, the whole is transformed, refigured in its totality as a meaning, a whole of meaning forever renewed, forever new. The threefold interaction of retained, anticipated, and present moments is a manifestation in the concrete of the threefold temporal interplay that is being possible already ahead of itself imaginatively releasing meaning to its possibilities, being possible being determined by such possibilities in turn. Being possible in the alreadiness of its capabilities of already available meaning is a retaining. Being possible as an imagining of possibilities meaning has coming to it in the lifeworld is an anticipating. Being possible encountering a meaning's present moments is a releasing of meaning.

Remembering and the Lifeworld

The various forms of remembering and forgetting are events of existential rather than objective space. They are personal matters, relations of system to the world to which we have been submitted from the first, and not prepersonal exchanges between objective brain processes. The inability to remember, for example, is not a failure to get through to some memory objectively stored in-itself, but a failure, a refusal perhaps (compare repression), to assume that disposition as would permit the venturing of a certain context of meaning. Forgetting, recalling, retaining, and recognition are all transactions on our part with nonmental lifeworld meaning. It is our wallet itself that we have misplaced; it is our friend herself that we recognize; it is the beginning of the movie itself that we are now retaining; it is the sailboat trip itself that is being recalled; it is the painful incident itself that we refuse to grant a place in our lives. In all these events we are alongside meanings in their lifeworld place. It is the meanings themselves that we remember and forget, then, and not memories; meanings are imaged in recall, and not images. When we recall the loss of something of some significance to us, it is the loss itself that has come to life once again in its impact. The loss itself is what is paying us a visit and weighing us down, the loss itself that we are coming back to and not some objective or subjective in-itself.

The Bodily Self–World System and the Law of Good Gestalt

As argued earlier (Chapter 6, "Dynamics: Within the World"), the law of good gestalt is not a psychological law but a law of lifeworld meaning. The dynamics of meaning formation by this account is anything but intrapsychic, anything but an activity of an objective cortex or of a merely subjective mind. Gestalt dynamics, law-governed dynamic self-distribution, belonging to lifeworld meaning itself, is to be understood in terms of the world's significance.

The law of requiredness thus governs meaning in its significance. But meaning is a system event, and the system is the structural transacting of bodily selves and their world. System relations ensure that the law of good gestalt reaches and touches the deepest interiority of that being whose being it is to be submitted to lifeworld meaning from the first. The law of good gestalt governs the life of bodily being possible in its entirety, every last one of its activities. Requiredness or value, what meaning intrinsically is as both process and outcome, arises in every case as something of interest to a bodily someone. Without this involvement of a positively or negatively affected and knowing self, no gestalt could unfold in the direction of its perfection. Although the sunset is as beautiful as it could be, its beauty nonetheless arises only for someone who is affectively "there" for it. The event of beauty, such an excitement, is *between* the self and the sunset, in structural system relations. "Good" and "bad" are the ways *someone* takes—gives (insight as interpreting), receives (insight as impact)—meaning. Goodness, the law of any meaning, is only for someone, for someone who can feel it. Feeling travels the path to the good gestalt alongside meaning. Meaning and feeling, the world and the self, are interwoven as a single structure, the body-world system, a single event with a common sign determined by the law of good gestalt. The structural necessity of any meaning is an event of system, of a feeling-value system.

Governing meaning, and thereby that being who is submitted to meaning from the first, the law of good gestalt determines all relations of system between bodily selves and their world. This law captures the principle guiding the unfolding of the bodily self–world system in its totality, the essential ground of its movement, its ultimate motivation. Where meaning ought to be or ought not be, there feeling is also. A single law binds a community of bodily selves and a network of requirednesses together. Requiredness, meaning's law, meaning's completion, in perhaps as yet unsuspected ways, is what existence (being-in-the-world) is all about.

A phenomenological psychology does not give up on the strict lawfulness of behavior, on its nonarbitrary and not merely statistical, its necessary, character. However, such a psychology locates the lawfulness of insight (and insight-related behaviors) not in mechanical constraints set in place by heredity or learning (but see also Chapter 11, "Disturbed Disposition"), but in the lawfulness governing the formation and transformation of lifeworld meaning. Behavior is lawful, and also free (emergent), by reason of its place in system relations. Meaning, at once necessary (law of good gestalt) and free (dynamic self-distribution; possibility, variability), governs the behavior of insight; law-governed meaning is precisely what behavior has been out to determine from the first. All in all, the behavior of insight's lawfulness consists in its being in accordance with the law of good gestalt governing meaning. Such a lawfulness, as always for phenomenology *within* experience and not *beyond* it, pulls behavior rather than pushes it. A psychology that does not see its way clear to take the lawfulness in question here into account puts itself in the position of giving, at best, a partial account of behavior's lawful character.

The Event of the Bodily Self–World System

Meaning emerges in a dynamic process co-organized by three general factors (compare Chapter 6 subsection "Gestalt Lawfulness"):

1. A self, alongside other selves to be sure, capable of embodying, and thus of living forward, a particular meaning context;

2. Available lifeworld moments, in their place relative to a context of significance to be sure;

3. The law-governed dynamic self-distribution of lifeworld moments.

These factors interact in system relations to yield an orderly event of meaning presencing that is neither the imposition of order by a subject nor the discovery of an order lying ready-made in an object. There is a reaching for order on the part of meaning rather, a search for good order everywhere in the lifeworld. In this ordering, whose center, rather than being locally fixed in any one somewhere of the body-world system, thoroughly pervades circular system relations, subject and object always and already have been decentered. The self and meaning exist only as they interpenetrate as a bodily self–world system under the governance of a law of requiredness; only as they interweave as psychological, excited bodily self and nonpsychological, exciting lifeworld meaning. The self and meaning, their system, are an *event*: the action of an interpreting bodily self submitted to the action of lifeworld moment tense with and signifying lifeworld moment, these two actions jointly unfolding as a single action in accordance with law-governed free dynamics. The self and meaning first arise in their interpenetration as a system. Original meaning and the insightful self are jointly decided this way or that. The self is affected as this feeling or that. One moment directly determines another this way or that; moments signify one another as one intrinsically required whole of meaning or another. Meaning and the self are emergent. They come about, meaning in its requiredness (in the excitement it holds for human behavior) and the self in its freedom (as "human freedom" entertaining a self-forming and transforming meaning, as human freedom being formed or transformed in the process). Meaning and the self *become*. The observing bodily self, within its context of a community of bodily Daseins, and the value observed and lived, within its context of the world, circularly determining one another at the moment, thus come to coconstitute the paradox of a meaning event. Behind the thus decided event, phenomenology maintains, is nothing else.

Value, lifeworld meaning, is an event that originally happens in its coming to formation for someone. Values emerge. Developmentally, people tend first to simply ascribe values to their environing world (natural attitude). Realizing that other individuals and other cultures have different values, however, people tend to develop a questioning, even skeptical, attitude toward the whole realm of value. At this point people sometimes decide that values are merely subjective opinions, "value judgments," in an inner sphere of mind, that values are but a vehicle for self-assertion and personal growth. An existential phenomenology finds a way beyond the alternatives of value in-itself and "merely subjective" value: value as a system event under the governance of the law of good gestalt, with essential determinations by both the bodily self and the lifeworld.

First, value was thought to be ready-made in a sphere in-itself; then, it was thought to be merely subjective; here, it is thought to be an event of system. But here, it is also thought to be (possibly) both original in process and valid in outcome, an intrinsic requiredness. An intrinsic requiredness *and* an event? Yes. Having a beginning, a duration, and an end, and perhaps a new beginning (transformation)—being an event—is precisely what allows something to pursue the necessity of its requiredness and thus be original. Having limits is what allows something to be what it is. A limit is not where something merely stops, it is where something begins (Heidegger, 1971b, p. 154). The limit that is the world, made possible by the threefold temporal interplay, is what makes it possible for something to take its place within a context of significance and thus first be itself. Something is what it is in its place, and its place is its limit. Ahead of itself to world, Dasein lets something be temporally particular, in this way allowing it to seek its necessity in its place. Only in its place can there be a question of something's necessity; only as a temporally situated signifying is something able to become and, thus undergoing progressive self-transformations, not excluding troubling interludes and setbacks, to fulfill its law. That we are ahead determining meaning from a limited perspective, interpreting, it has been seen (Chapter 13 subsection "Interpreting and the Validity of Meaning"), rather than impeding validity, is its prerequisite. Value's essentially transitory character, then, is not the contradiction of its originality (and at the same time of its validity) but the point from which it takes its departure. It is in their happening, as tension-charged actions, that values *are*; in their being nailed down that they die.

Value is a paradox (compare Chapter 10 subsection "The Paradox of Interpreting and Impact"). Value first becomes itself, nonmental lifeworld meaning, when someone interpretively reaches all the way to it, ventures it, and is touched by it in turn. The way beyond modern subjectivism requires the retaining of the element of truth in it; namely, that value is no in-itself, that an interested someone plays a part rather in the emergence of any value, in its first becoming itself. But the fundamental insight of phenomenology—that value, belonging to the lifeworld, is beyond all psychological processes—nevertheless also must come to take its deserved place alongside the recognition of the element of truth in subjective approaches to value. Both the lifeworld and the psychological sides of the event of value need to be affirmed, along with the relations of system that bind them together as one. The full paradox of value includes the role value plays in determining its very determination by someone as the value it is. Value and insight into value circularly determine one another; value and insight reciprocally determine their influence on one another. Value is *between* bodily self and lifeworld, standing where it stands, at once expressing itself and being expressed by being possible.

Notes

Chapter 1

1. The final reason why it is impossible for us to have contact, direct or otherwise, with a surrounding objective reality lies in the fact that such "reality" is itself but a qualitative idea, the "world" as mathematically constructed by Galilean science, the "world" in formula. We cannot have contact with such objective "reality" because it does not surround us at all.

Chapter 2

1. Psychology textbooks never provide the basis on which they define and distinguish between various behaviors such as these, even while devoting entire chapters to them. The only possible basis can be a phenomenological one. Because conventional psychology never explicitly engages in phenomenological work, however, the definitions and distinctions it provides can be only informal ones that have never been thought through at their source.

Chapter 6

1. Present objections are leveled not at the notion that meaning is bestowed on the fragmented aftereffects of environmental stimulation (Chapter 5), but at the presumption that organization itself is a property of environmental stimuli, that the world surrounding the organism consists of self-giving "patterns of stimuli."

2. From the present Gestalt theoretical position, the phrase *pattern of stimuli* represents a contradiction in terms, in that a lifeworld pattern is a dimensional whole of meaning that mere fragmented physical energies could never constitute. Stimuli and patterns are of entirely different orders.

3. The standard textbook account of Gestalt psychology's law of similarity (or proximity) runs something like this: people (more exactly, their brains) tend to group "stimulus elements" together (more exactly, to group the sensory aftereffects of environmental stimulation together) that are physically alike (or close together). Upon closer inspection, this account actually turns out to belong to conventional psychology's reworking of Gestalt theory in terms of "sensation and perception" (Chapter 5, "A Gestalt is Not More Than the Sum of its Parts"), in terms of perception as the subjective forging into groups (perception, meanings) of fragmented "stimulus elements" (sensations). Gestalt psychology, this book has emphasized,

locates organization, along with the laws that govern it, not in any secondary interpretation worked on elements, but in the materials themselves. Conventional psychology, not holding to—or apparently even understanding—the dynamic self-distribution of available materials proposed by the Gestalt psychologists, finds itself unable to accept—or, more exactly, to properly understand—the Gestalt laws governing that self-distribution. Gestalt laws, in the eyes of conventional psychology, rather than the constants governing the dynamic self-distribution of nonsubjective materials, amount to the regular ways in which the organism tends to subjectively bestow organization on fragmented "stimulus elements"; amount to the subjective or psychological grouping of objectively given atoms. Gestalt lawfulness as originally understood by the Gestalt theorists having been subjectivized along such lines, it comes as no surprise that introductory psychology texts fail to locate the law of similarity (or proximity) within the context of a broader law of good gestalt, within the context of the necessity inherent in the nonsubjective materials themselves to self-form the best they can, as the best gestalt they can manage to constitute on their own ground of meaning. But conventional psychology in this way finds itself unable to specify *why* moments that are similar to (or close to) one another cluster together in the first place—why do people (their brains) bring this about?

Chapter 10

1. Because Köhler remains an objectivist, it can be argued that the past is in effect for him, no less than for conventional psychology, the only true dimension of time. Although learning and memory are not invoked to explain the essentials of meaning, only a present dynamic self-distribution of processes, for Köhler every event nevertheless occurs only *after* other events that bring it about. It just so happens that some of these "afters" locally overlap in the brain, being in this way in present causal contact with one another. Specifically overlapping, in what concerns meaning, are a first cortical process, induced by a certain environmental stimulus, and the linearly spreading effects of a second cortical process, induced by a certain other environmental stimulus. The second cortical process in this way is "at" the first; and the first, reciprocally, by reason of its spreading objective effects, "at" the second.

Chapter 11

1. What psychology calls *drives* or *motives* are by the present account the bodily self's disposed proclivities to enact certain values in the fullness of their lived dimensional excitement. Drives or motives, always and already outside, are not inner states, but relations to significance, inclinations to a certain lifeworld.

2. When psychology textbooks assert that stimuli "trigger" emotions, they evidence a lack of conceptual consistency and clarity, for the word *stimuli* is no longer used to denote physical energies utterly devoid of organization, as was the case when "sensation and perception" was at issue, but meaningful patterns. Köhler insists, it will be recalled, that meaningful patterns are outcomes of perceptual organization and as a consequence should never be called *stimuli*.

Chapter 14

1. The felt sense of the retained is an instance of the common life experience in which a meaning is phenomenally known, is "on our mind," but is not in conscious awareness. Other instances of things we *know* but are not consciously *aware of* are the name "on the tip of our tongue," an emerging connection between things (including the solution to a problem that's "at our doorstep"), the next logical turn in a developing line of thought, someone else's presence in the house, and something we do not want to face up to (perhaps, because of the pain involved; perhaps, because of the course of action required). We have at any given time, moreover, a sense of the overall course our life has taken—everything we have been through, all that we are—without its being in conscious image. Meanings phenomenally known but not in conscious awareness are a matter of disposition: our being disposed to the story as it has unfolded; our failure to become open in such a way as to sponsor the sought after name (a more relaxed disposition is often witness to the name's appearance); our being creatively disposed to emergent lifeworld connections and lines of thought; the sense we already have of someone else in the house; our refusal of certain life experiences. It is precisely as known that phenomenal meanings such as these make a difference in our life.

References

Allport, G. 1955. *Becoming*. New Haven: Yale University Press.

Arnheim, R. 1961. "Gestalten—Yesterday and Today." In *Documents of Gestalt Psychology*, ed. M. Henle, pp. 90–96. Berkeley: University of California Press.

———.1974. *Art and Visual Perception*. Berkeley: University of California Press.

———.1986a. *New Essays on the Psychology of Art*. Berkeley: University of California Press.

———.1986b. "The Two Faces of Gestalt Psychology." *American Psychologist, 41*, 820–824.

Atkinson, R. L., R. C. Atkinson, E. E. Smith, and E. R. Hilgard. 1987. *Introduction to Psychology*. New York: Harcourt, Brace, Jovanovich.

Benjamin, L. T., J. R. Hopkins, and J. R. Nation. 1987. *Psychology*. New York: Macmillan Publishing Company.

Bootzin, R. R., G. H. Bower, R. B. Zajonc, and E. Hall. 1986. *Psychology Today: An Introduction*. New York: Random House.

Boring, E. G. 1930. "A New Ambiguous Figure." *American Journal of Psychology, 42*, 444–445.

Carlson, N. R. 1984. *Psychology: The Science of Behavior*. Boston: Allyn and Bacon.

Coon, D. 1985. *Essentials of Psychology: Exploration and Application*. St. Paul, Minn.: West Publishing Company.

Crider, A. B., G. R. Goethals, R. D. Kavanaugh, and P. R. Solomon. 1989. *Psychology*. Boston: Scott, Foresman and Company.

Darley, J. M., S. Glucksberg, and R. A. Kinchla. 1988. *Psychology*. Englewood Cliffs, N. J.: Prentice-Hall.

Descartes, R. 1969. *The Essential Descartes*, ed. M. D. Wilson. New York: New American Library.

Dworetsky, J. P. 1985. *Psychology*. St. Paul, Minn.: West Publishing Company.

279

Frankl, V. E. 1959. *Man's Search for Meaning*, trans. I. Lasch. New York: Washington Square Press.

———.1962. *The Doctor and the Soul*, trans. R. Winston and C. Winston. New York: Alfred A. Knopf.

———. 1967. *Psychotherapy and Existentialism*. New York: Simon and Schuster.

———. 1969. *The Will to Meaning*. New York: World Publishing Company.

———. 1975. *The Unconscious God*. New York: Simon and Schuster.

Freud. S. 1949. *An Outline of Psychoanalysis*, trans. J. Strachey. New York: W. W. Norton and Company.

Fromm, E. 1956. *The Art of Loving*. New York: Harper and Row.

Gerow, J. R. 1989. *Psychology: An Introduction*. Boston: Scott, Foresman and Company.

Gurwitsch, A. 1964. *The Field of Consciousness*. Pittsburgh: Duquesne University Press.

———. 1965. "The Phenomenology of Perception: Perceptual Implications." In *An Invitation to Phenomenology,* ed. J. M. Edie, pp. 17–29. Chicago: Quadrangle Books.

———. 1966. *Studies in Phenomenology and Psychology*. Evanston, Ill.: Northwestern University Press.

———. 1970. "Towards a Theory of Intentionality." *Philosophy and Phenomenological Research*, *30*, 354–367.

———. 1974. *Phenomenology and the Theory of Science*, ed. L. Embree. Evanston, Ill.: Northwestern University Press.

———. 1979. *Human Encounters in the Social World*, trans. A. Métraux, ed. F. Kersten. Pittsburgh: Duquesne University Press.

Hassett, J., and K. M. White. 1989. *Psychology in Perspective*. New York: Harper and Row.

Heidegger, M. 1949. *Existence and Being*. Chicago: Henry Regnery Company.

———. 1956. *What Is Philosophy?* trans. J. T. Wilde and W. Kluback. New Haven, Conn.: The New College and University Press.

———. 1959. *Introduction to Metaphysics,* trans. R. Manheim. Garden City, N.Y.: Doubleday and Company.

———. 1962a. *Being and Time*, trans. J. Macquarrie and E. Robinson. New York: Harper and Row.

———. 1962b. *Kant and the Problem of Metaphysics*, trans. J. S. Churchill. Bloomington: Indiana University Press.

———. 1967. *What Is a Thing?* trans. W. B. Barton, Jr. and V. Deutsch. Chicago: Henry Regnery Company.

———. 1968. *What Is Called Thinking?* trans. J. Glenn Gray. New York: Harper and Row.

———. 1971a. *On the Way to Language,* trans. P. D. Hertz. New York: Harper and Row.

———. 1971b. *Poetry, Language, Thought,* trans. A. Hofstadter. New York: Harper and Row.

———. 1972. *On Time and Being,* trans. J. Stambaugh. New York: Harper and Row.

———. 1977. *The Question Concerning Technology and Other Essays,* trans. W. Lovitt. New York: Harper and Row.

———. 1979. *Nietzsche. Vol. 1: The Will to Power as Art,* trans. D. F. Krell. New York: Harper and Row.

———. 1982. *The Basic Problems of Phenomenology,* trans. A. Hofstadter. Bloomington: Indiana University Press.

———. 1984. *The Metaphysical Foundations of Logic,* trans. M. Heim. Bloomington: Indiana University Press.

———. 1985. *History of the Concept of Time,* trans. T. Kisiel. Bloomington: Indiana University Press.

Husserl, E. 1964. *The Phenomenology of Internal Time-Consciousness,* trans. J. S. Churchill, ed. M. Heidegger. Bloomington: Indiana University Press.

———. 1970. *The Crisis of European Sciences and Transcendental Phenomenology,* trans. D. Carr. Evanston, Ill.: Northwestern University Press.

Kagan, J., and J. Segal. 1988. *Psychology: An Introduction.* New York: Harcourt, Brace, Jovanovich.

Kalat, J. W. 1986. *Introduction to Psychology.* Belmont, Calif.: Wadsworth Publishing Company.

Kockelmans, J. J. 1970. "The Era of the World-as-Picture." In *Phenomenology and the Natural Sciences,* ed. J. J. Kockelmans and T. J. Kisiel. Evanston, Ill.: Northwestern University Press.

Koffka, K. 1935. *Principles of Gestalt Psychology.* New York: Harcourt, Brace and World.

Köhler, W. 1927. *The Mentality of Apes.* New York: Random House.

———. 1938. *The Place of Value in a World of Facts.* New York: New American Library.

———. 1947. *Gestalt Psychology.* New York: New American Library.

_____. 1961. "Gestalt Psychology Today." In *Documents of Gestalt Psychology*, ed. M. Henle, pp. 1–18. Berkeley: University of California Press.

_____. 1965. *Dynamics in Psychology*. New York: Washington Square Press.

_____. 1967. "Some Gestalt Problems." In *A Source Book of Gestalt Psychology*, ed. W. D. Ellis, pp. 55–70. New York: Humanities Press.

_____. 1969. *The Task of Gestalt Psychology*. Princeton, N. J.: Princeton University Press.

_____. 1971. *The Selected Papers of Wolfgang Köhler*, ed. M. Henle. New York: Liveright.

Krebs, D., and R. Blackman. 1988. *Psychology: A First Encounter*. New York: Harcourt, Brace, Jovanovich.

Lahey, B. B. 1989. *Psychology: An Introduction*. Dubuque: Wm. C. Brown Publishers.

Landy, F. J. 1987. *Psychology: The Science of People*. Englewood Cliffs, N.J.: Prentice-Hall.

Lefton, L. A. 1985. *Psychology*. Boston: Allyn and Bacon.

Lefton, L. A., and L. Valvatne. 1988. *Mastering Psychology*. Boston: Allyn and Bacon.

Lindzey, G., R. F. Thompson, and B. Spring. 1988. *Psychology*. New York: Worth Publishers.

Maslow, A. H. 1954. *Motivation and Personality*. New York: Harper and Row.

_____. 1964. *Religions, Values, and Peak-Experiences*. New York: Viking Press.

_____. 1966. *The Psychology of Science*. Chicago: Henry Regnery Company.

_____. 1968. *Toward a Psychology of Being*. New York: D. Van Nostrand Company.

_____. 1971. *The Farther Reaches of Human Nature*. New York: Viking Press.

McGee, M. G., and D. W. Wilson. 1984. *Psychology: Science and Application*. St. Paul, Minn.: West Publishing Company.

McMahon, F. B., and J. W. McMahon. 1986. *Psychology: The Hybrid Science*. Homewood, Ill.: Dorsey Press.

Merleau-Ponty, M. 1962. *Phenomenology of Perception*, trans. C. Smith. London: Routledge and Kegan Paul.

_____. 1963. *The Structure of Behavior*, trans. A. L. Fisher. Boston: Beacon Press.

_____. 1964a. *The Primacy of Perception*, ed. J. M. Edie. Evanston, Ill.: Northwestern University Press.

———. 1964b. *Sense and Non-Sense*, trans. H. L. and P. A. Dreyfus. Evanston, Ill.: Northwestern University Press.

———. 1964c. *Signs*, trans. R. C. McCleary. Evanston, Ill.: Northwestern University Press.

———. 1968. *The Visible and the Invisible*, trans. A. Lingis, ed. C. Lefort. Evanston, Ill.: Northwestern University Press.

———. 1973a. *Consciousness and the Acquisition of Language*, trans. H. J. Silverman. Evanston, Ill.: Northwestern University Press.

———. 1973b. *The Prose of the World*, trans. J. O'Neill, ed. C. Lefort. Evanston, Ill.: Northwestern University Press.

Myers, D. G. 1989. *Psychology*. New York: Worth Publishers.

Neisser, U. 1976. *Cognition and Reality*. San Francisco: W. H. Freeman and Company.

Nietzsche, F. 1967. *The Will to Power*, trans. W. Kaufman and R. J. Hollingdale, ed. W. Kaufman. New York: Random House.

Ornstein, R. 1985. *Psychology: The Study of Human Experience*. New York: Harcourt, Brace, Jovanovich.

Pettijohn, T. F. 1989. *Psychology: A Concise Introduction*. Guilford, Conn.: Dushkin Publishing Group.

Price, R. H., M. Glickstein, D. L. Horton, S. J. Sherman, and R. H. Fazio. 1987. *Principles of Psychology*. Boston: Scott, Foresman and Company.

Richardson, W. J. 1974. *Heidegger: Through Phenomenology to Thought*. The Hague: Martinus Nijhof.

Ricoeur, P. 1967. *Husserl: An Analysis of His Phenomenology*, trans. E. G. Ballard and L. E. Embree. Evanston, Ill.: Northwestern University Press.

Roediger, H. L., J. P. Rushton, E. D. Capaldi, and S. C. Paris. 1987. *Psychology*. Boston: Little, Brown and Company.

Rubin, E. 1921. *Visuell Wahrgenommene Figuren: Studien in Psychologischer Analyse*. Copenhagen: Gyldendalske Boghandel.

Rubin, Z., and E. B. McNeil. 1987. *Psychology: Being Human*. New York: Harper and Row.

Santrock, J. W. 1986. *Psychology: The Science of Mind and Behavior*. Dubuque: Wm. C. Brown Publishers.

Scarr, S., and J. Vander Zanden. 1984. *Understanding Psychology*. New York: Random House.

Skinner, B. F. 1974. *About Behaviorism*. New York: Alfred A. Knopf.

Smith, R. E., I. G. Sarason, and B. R. Sarason. 1986. *Psychology: The Frontiers of Behavior*. New York: Harper and Row.

Spear, P. D., S. D. Penrod, and T. B. Baker. 1988. *Psychology: Perspectives on Behavior*. New York: John Wiley and Sons.

Vogel, J. L. 1986. *Thinking about Psychology*. Chicago: Nelson-Hall.

Wallace, P. M., J. H. Goldstein, and P. Nathan. 1987. *Introduction to Psychology*. Dubuque: Wm. C. Brown Publishers.

Wertheimer, M. 1959. *Productive Thinking,* ed. M. Wertheimer. New York: Harper and Brothers.

──────. 1961. "Some Problems in the Theory of Ethics." In *Documents of Gestalt Psychology*, ed. M. Henle, pp. 29–41. Berkeley: University of California Press.

──────. 1967a. "The General Theoretical Situation." In *A Source Book of Gestalt Psychology*, ed. W. D. Ellis, pp. 12–16. New York: Humanities Press.

──────. 1967b. "Gestalt Theory." In *A Source Book of Gestalt Psychology,* ed. W. D. Ellis, pp. 1–11. New York: Humanities Press.

──────. 1967c. "Laws of Organization in Perceptual Forms." In *A Source Book of Gestalt Psychology,* ed. W. D. Ellis, pp. 71–88. New York: Humanities Press.

Worchel, S., and W. Shebilske. 1986. *Psychology: Principles and Applications*. Englewood Cliffs, N. J.: Prentice-Hall.

Wortman, C. B., E. F. Loftus, and M. E. Marshall. 1988. *Psychology*. New York: Alfred A. Knopf.

Wulf, F. 1967. "Tendencies in Figural Variation." In *A Source Book of Gestalt Psychology,* ed. W. D. Ellis, pp. 136–148. New York: Humanities Press.

Zimbardo, P. G. 1988. *Psychology and Life*. Boston: Scott, Foresman and Company.

Index

psychology and, 49, 276n.1 (Chapter 11); unconscious, 212–13. *See also* Demand character of value, the

Natural attitude, the, 27, 29, 193; the alienation of, 31; and the notion of stimuli, 112, 210; and value, 272. *See also* Phenomenological reduction
Natural-scientific psychology. *See* Conventional psychology: the objectivism of
Nature, 45, 151. *See also* Objective, the outer realm of the
Necessity: inner, 114; interpreting and, 241, 249; of a meaning's search for an ideal state, 114, 123–125, 272
Necker Cube, the, 240
Negative requiredness, 118–120, 121, 122; feeling and, 207–208; insight and, 168–169, 172; value as, 135–136, 139
Neisser, Ulric, 41
"Not good enough" gestalt, the, 114–115, 129, 151. *See also* Negative requiredness

Objective, the, 11
Objective, the outer realm of the, 6, 7–11, 164. *See also* Present-at-hand, the
Objective space of meaning, the, 12, 13, 18, 21, 152; existential space and, 62, 63–64, 71, 75–76, 77–78, 237; Gestalt psychology and, 223, 225; as having the status of an idea, 71, 275n.1 (Chapter 1); phenomenology as taking exception to, 24. *See also* objectivism
Objectivism, 13; conventional psychology as, 13–17, 23–24, 30, 33–34, 49, 59, 75–76, 77–78; Gestalt psychology as, 162–165, 215, 222–225, 226, 229–230; phenomenological psychology's rejection of, 21, 25–26, 38, 49. *See also* Objective space of meaning, the

Objectivistic psychology. *See* Objectivism:conventional psychology as; Objectivism: Gestalt psychology as
Order, perception's tendency toward, 106, 218, 271
Organization; cortical, 163, 219–220, 222, 223, 228; Gestalt psychology as a theory of, 81–82, 90, 91, 103; learning as a matter of, 261–266; as lifeworld process, 234–236, 239–241; the problem of, 107–113, 218; remembering as a matter of, 266–267; variability and, 102–103
Original meaning. *See* Meaning: as original requiredness
Ornstein, Robert, 4, 15
Other people: the direct perception of, 51, 259–260; as person values, 145–146; the place of, 76; and shared experience of the world, 49–51; 259–261; and the validity of meaning, 252–253. *See also* Synergy: between people; System of the self, other selves, and the world, the

Paradox of impact and interpreting, the, 193–196, 247–250, 272, 273
Past, the, 183
Past experience: alreadiness and, 183–189, 197–198, 211, 213, 248, 251–252; conventional psychology and the role of, 98–99, 191–192, 216, 217; Gestalt psychology and the role of, 159, 160, 263, 266, 276n.1 (Chapter 10); Merleau-Ponty and, 184, 186, 262; Skinner and the role of, 153. *See also* Disposition; Learning; Mechanism; Remembering
Perception: the creative character of, 189–190; as equivalent term for meaning, 2; field theory of, 219; and figure-ground relationship, 85; the givenness of, 26; interpreting and the validity of, 246–250; the perspectival character of, 32, 69, 248–249; the primacy of, 36, 61–63, 191; role of